Birds of Costa Rica

Foreword by ALEXANDER F. SKUTCH

Birds
of Costa Rica

A FIELD GUIDE

CARROL L. HENDERSON
with photographs by the author

Illustrations by STEVE ADAMS

UNIVERSITY OF TEXAS PRESS, *Austin*

The University of Texas Press wishes to acknowledge the generous financial support by the following foundations, individuals, and businesses that helped to underwrite the costs of producing the original *Field Guide to the Wildlife of Costa Rica*:

The Dellwood Wildlife Foundation of Dellwood, Minnesota, in memory of wildlife conservationist and founder of the Dellwood Wildlife Foundation, Ramon D. (Ray) Whitney. Ray Whitney was instrumental in helping restore trumpeter swans to Minnesota, and he shared a love and appreciation for the diversity and abundance of wildlife in Costa Rica.

The Costa Rica–Minnesota Foundation of St. Paul, Minnesota, in support of cultural and natural resource initiatives fostering greater understanding, educational programs, and habitat protection for Costa Rica's wildlife.

The late Honorary Consul to Costa Rica from Minnesota and former CEO of the H. B. Fuller Company, Tony Andersen, who was a tireless promoter for cooperative projects of benefit to Costa Rica's culture and environment.

Karen Johnson, President of Preferred Adventures Ltd. of St. Paul, Minnesota, a business that specializes in ecotourism and natural history adventures for worldwide travelers. She has been especially active in promoting wildlife tourism in Costa Rica and other countries of Latin America.

Michael Kaye, President of Costa Rica Expeditions, San José, Costa Rica. Costa Rica Expeditions owns and manages Monteverde Lodge, Tortuga Lodge, and Corcovado Lodge Tent Camp. This company has set high standards for protecting sensitive tropical habitats while accommodating the needs of nature tourism and adventure travelers in Costa Rica.

Dan Conaway, President of Elegant Adventures, Atlanta, Georgia. Elegant Adventures specializes in quality, customized tours to Latin American destinations, including Costa Rica. This company has served international travelers since its founding in 1986.

Library of Congress Cataloging-in-Publication Data

Henderson, Carrol L.
   Birds of Costa Rica : a field guide / Carrol L. Henderson ; photographs by Carrol L. Henderson ; illustrations by Steve Adams ; foreword by Alexander F. Skutch.
      p.   cm. — (The Corrie Herring Hooks series ; no. 64)
   Includes bibliographical references and index.
   ISBN 978-0-292-71965-1 (pbk. : alk. paper)
   1. Birds—Costa Rica—Identification. I. Title.
   QL687.C8H46 2010
   598.097286—dc22   2009024605

pg. i: Scarlet Macaw, head and shoulders
pg. ii: Calling Chestnut-mandibled Toucan
Facing pg.: Backlit canal in Tortuguero National Park

To my wife, Ethelle,
and son and daughter-in-law, Craig and Reem,
with whom I share my love of Costa Rica,
and grandson Mazen Nathaniel,
and to
Drs. George Knaphus, James H. Jenkins, and Daniel H. Janzen,
my mentors.

CONTENTS

FOREWORD

To the dweller in a northern land eager to know the rich birdlife of tropical America, I recommend Costa Rica. Readily accessible from the United States, Canada, or Europe, this small Central American republic supports an abundant representation of the great, exclusively New World families—tyrant flycatchers, hummingbirds, antbirds, ovenbirds (spinetails), and woodcreepers—all poorly represented or absent north of Mexico.

Dr. Alexander F. Skutch, left, welcomes a visitor, Dr. Walter Breckenridge, to his home, Los Cusingos, in 1995.

Among the most exciting Neotropical specialties are toucans, jacamars, puffbirds, and guans. With them are more familiar cosmopolitan families, including finches, sparrows, thrushes, swallows, swifts, woodpeckers, cuckoos, and others. Less strange to a visitor from the north are wintering migrants: wood warblers, vireos, orioles, and flycatchers. They are really Neotropical birds returning to their ancestral homes to escape winter's snow and ice. There are also a few migrants from the south, such as the Swallow-tailed Kite, Yellow-green Vireo, and pesky Piratic Flycatcher.

Amid the rainforested Caribbean lowlands, the birder will find the richest representation of the great South American bird families, including species like the White-fronted Nunbird, Keel-billed Toucan, Lattice-tailed Trogon, and Dusky-faced Tanager.

Costa Rica's southern Pacific lowlands support a unique avifauna that it shares with western Panama. Here live such fascinating birds as the Fiery-billed Aracari, Turquoise Cotinga, Golden-naped Woodpecker, and Riverside Wren. In sharp contrast to the southern half of Costa Rica's Pacific side, the northern half has a prolonged severe dry season. Many birds range along the arid western side of Middle America from Mexico to central Costa Rica. Notable among them are the White-throated Magpie-Jay, Long-tailed Manakin, Turquoise-browed Motmot, and Banded Wren.

Isolated by the lowlands of the Isthmus of Panama and the Costa Rica–Nicaragua border, high mountains support endemic birds, including the Scintillant Hummingbird, Timberline Wren, Flame-throated Warbler, Volcano Junco, and the southern race of the Resplendent Quetzal.

All this great diversity of birds is found in a country the size of West Virginia. Good roads and comfortable lodges make them readily accessible to tourists, who nearly everywhere find helpful Costa Ricans who speak English. For an introduction to the rich Neotropical avifauna, Costa Rica offers many advantages.

By their abundance, visibility, beautiful plumage, melodious songs, and endearing ways, especially as they faithfully attend their young in carefully constructed nests, birds rightfully claim much of the attention of almost everyone attracted to nature. But if we permitted them to absorb all our attention, we would miss much of nature's beauty and interest. Indeed, birds often direct our attention to flowering plants, lovely butterflies, other insects, mammals, reptiles, amphibians, and more obscure creatures that we might otherwise fail to notice. In this book, you will find accurate accounts of a liberal selection of a richly endowed tropical country's vast diversity of organisms. This field guide should interest not only visitors from other countries but also many who live in Costa Rica.

ALEXANDER F. SKUTCH
JULY 11, 2000

PREFACE

I grew up as a farm boy near Zearing in central Iowa, and most of my early travels were within twenty-five miles of our family farm. I had quite a provincial view of life and no concept of ecosystems, biological diversity, or tropical rainforests. I just knew that I loved wildlife. I had no idea that Costa Rica, a small country thousands of miles away in Central America, would later play such a dramatic role in shaping the direction of my personal and professional life.

An early and enthusiastic interest in nature led me to major in zoology and minor in botany at Iowa State University. After completing my bachelor's degree at ISU in 1968, I enrolled in graduate school at the University of Georgia, where I studied ecology, forest and wildlife management, journalism, and public relations. During my search for a thesis topic, Dr. James H. Jenkins directed me to an Organization for Tropical Studies (OTS) course in Costa Rica.

When I began my two-month OTS course in tropical grasslands agriculture in February of 1969, I had no idea it would be such a life-changing experience. Every day was an adventure! I tried to absorb all that I could about the land, the people, and the wildlife of Costa Rica. I quickly learned that this is not a country you can visit just once. By March I had already applied for another OTS course and was subsequently accepted. In June 1969, I drove from Georgia to Costa Rica with Dr. Jenkins for an OTS course in tropical ecology.

The author with an oropendola nest during an OTS course in Costa Rica, 1969.

The OTS faculty, recruited from educational institutions throughout North and Central America, included some of the most notable tropical biologists in the world. They inspired me with their knowledge and enthusiasm about tropical ecosystems. By the end of the tropical ecology course, I had fallen in love with the country, with its people, and with Ethelle González Alvarez, a student at the University of Costa Rica. I returned to Costa Rica a third time in 1969. Ethelle and I were married in December of that year and have now been married forty years. We have a son, Craig, who shares our love and enthusiasm for his Tico heritage, along with his wife, Reem, and their son, Mazen.

After returning to the University of Georgia, I wrote my master's thesis, "Fish and Wildlife Resources of Costa Rica, with Notes on Human Influences." The 340-page thesis analyzed human influences that were having significant positive or negative impacts on Costa Rica's wildlife. I included recommendations for changes in the game laws that would improve management of the country's wildlife.

During the forty years since my first visit to Costa Rica, I have returned thirty-three times. Since 1987, our visits to the country have included leading wildlife tours. Ethelle and I have led twenty-five birding and wildlife tours to Costa Rica since 1987 in coordination with Preferred Adventures Ltd. of St. Paul. We continue to see new species on every visit—and every day is still an adventure!

Each year thousands of first-time tourists are still experiencing that same sense of wonder about the country's rainforests and wildlife that I did in 1969. This book is written to share my enthusiasm and knowledge about the country's birdlife with those tourists and with Costa Ricans who share our love of nature. It is written to answer questions about identification, distribution, natural history, and the incredible ecological adaptations of many bird species. It also provides the opportunity to recognize the people and conservation programs that have made Costa Rica a world leader in preserving its tropical forest and wildlife resources.

Birder enjoying Costa Rica's rainforest.

ACKNOWLEDGMENTS

Writing this book has been a real labor of love. It represents the culmination of forty years of personal and professional relationships in Costa Rica. Special appreciation goes to my wife, Ethelle, and my son, Craig, who have traveled with me from Minnesota to Costa Rica many times and helped with everything from wildlife observations to editing and preparing the manuscript. In 1985, Karen Johnson, the owner of Preferred Adventures Ltd. in St. Paul, Minnesota, convinced us to lead a birding trip to Costa Rica. We led our first trip in 1987. It was the beginning of a wonderful annual tradition that has enabled us to meet many special people in our tour groups as well as Costa Rican tourism outfitters, guides, and ecolodge staffs. Sarah Strommen, formerly of Preferred Adventures Ltd., has helped with Costa Rica trip arrangements and with reviewing the manuscript of the first edition.

Michael Kaye, the owner of Costa Rica Expeditions, has been very supportive of this project and has coordinated our travel there. He facilitated travel to visit several sites for photography purposes, including Monteverde Lodge and Poás Volcano Lodge. Carlos Gómez Nieto is the extraordinary guide who has led all but one of our Costa Rican birding trips. Carlos is the premier birder in Costa Rica. He reviewed the original manuscript, and his wife, Vicky, also accompanied us on several photography outings. Manuel Salas and Marco Antonio "Niño" Morales

have been the drivers for our trips and have been invaluable in spotting birds and in providing us with safe and memorable travel experiences. Birding guide Jay VanderGaast, formerly of Rancho Naturalista, and noted ornithologist Dr. Noble Proctor provided comprehensive reviews of the original manuscript.

Other people have helped greatly with facilitating our travels, birding trips, and the collection of information and photos. They include Lisa, Kathy, and John Erb at Rancho Naturalista; Don Efraín Chacón, Rolando Chacón, and the rest of the Chacón family; Amos Bien of Rara Avis; Gail Hewson-Hull; Luis Diego Gómez; the late Dr. Alexander Skutch and Pamela Skutch at Los Cusingos; and the late Werner and Lily Hagnauer, who originally owned La Pacífica. The owners and management of La Pacífica, Cabinas Eclipse, Poás Volcano Lodge, and La Paz Waterfall Gardens provided accommodations while we collected wildlife observations and took photos.

Biologists and scientists provided expertise on species identification and life history data, including Dr. Daniel H. Janzen, Dr. Graciela Candelas, Dr. Alexander Skutch, Brian Kubicki, Dr. Frank T. Hovore, Jorge Corrales of the Instituto Nacional de Biodiversidad (INBIO), and Dr. Jay M. Savage. Other persons who have helped us with wildlife observations, outings, and photography include Dennis Janik and

Henry Kantrowitz at Zoo Ave, Lic. Jorge González Fallas, Lydia González de Alvarez, Lic. Daniel González Alvarez, Roberto Espinoza, Luis Diego Cruz, and Zoíla Cruz. Jim Lewis and Joan Galli provided the original information on the wildlife of Caño Negro National Wildlife Refuge. Additional editing was provided by Pam Perry, Sarah Strommen, and Margaret Dexter. June Rogier and her late husband Ed deserve special appreciation for providing invaluable references on birdlife, including accounts from *The Birds of North America* and the *Handbook of the Birds of the World.*

Two photos in this book portray mounted bird specimens, a Great Potoo and a displaying Montezuma Oropendola. The Milwaukee Public Museum kindly provided the opportunity to photograph these birds, which were mounted by Greg Septon. One photo in this book was not taken by the author; it shows Dr. Dan Janzen teaching in 1967 and was provided by the Organization for Tropical Studies.

Special thanks and appreciation go to Nancy Warrington for her excellent job of editing the manuscript for the original *Field Guide to the Wildlife of Costa Rica,* and to Lorraine Atherton for her fine work on this new volume.

And finally, special appreciation goes to all the Costa Rican travelers who have accompanied us on our birding trips and provided us with the companionship, sharp eyes, and friendships that have enriched our lives.

Birds of Costa Rica

The name "Costa Rica" means "Rich Coast."

INTRODUCTION

Costa Rica! The name generates a sense of excitement and anticipation among international travelers. Among European explorers, the first recorded visitor was Christopher Columbus in 1502. On his fourth trip to the New World, Columbus landed where the port city of Limón is now located. The natives he encountered wore golden disks around their necks. He called this new place "Costa Rica," meaning "Rich Coast," because he thought the gold came from there. The gold had actually come from other countries and had been obtained as a trade item from native traders along the coast.

Spanish treasure seekers eventually discovered their error and went elsewhere in their quest for gold. The irony is that Christopher Columbus actually picked the perfect name for this country. The wealth overlooked by the Spaniards is the rich biological diversity that includes more than 505,000 species of plants and wildlife. That species richness is an incredible natural resource that sustains one of the most successful nature tourism industries in the Western Hemisphere. It also provides the basis for a newly evolving biodiversity industry of "chemical prospecting" among plants and creatures, in search of new foods and medicines for humans.

For such a small country, Costa Rica gets much well-deserved international attention and has become one of the most popular tourist destinations in the Americas. The lure is not "sun and sand" experiences at big hotels on the country's beaches; it is unspoiled nature in far-flung nooks and crannies of wildlands that are accessible at rustic and locally owned nature lodges throughout the country.

It is now possible to immerse yourself in the biological wealth of tropical forests during a vacation in Costa Rica. During a two-week visit you may see more than three hundred to four hundred species of birds, mammals, reptiles, amphibians, butterflies, moths, and other invertebrates. Some vacations are planned for rest and relaxation, but who can do that in such a diverse country where there is so much nature to see and experience? In Costa Rica, every day is an adventure, and the marvelous diversity and abundance of wildlife create an enthusiasm for nature that many people have not experienced since childhood.

The ease with which it is possible to travel to Costa Rica and enjoy wildlife in such a pristine setting makes a visitor think

Every day is an adventure in Costa Rica.

it has always been that way. It has not. The appealing travel and tourism conditions are the product of nearly five decades of social, educational, and cultural developments.

There was a time when Costa Rican wildlife was persecuted at every opportunity. Virtually every creature weighing over a pound was shot for its value as meat or for its hide. Wildlife was killed year-round from the time of settlement through the 1960s. Instead of acquiring souvenirs like T-shirts and postcards in those days, Costa Rican visitors in the 1960s found vendors selling boa constrictor hides, caiman-skin briefcases, stuffed caimans, skins of spotted cats, and sea turtle eggs.

HISTORICAL PERSPECTIVE

To appreciate the abundance of today's wildlife populations, it is necessary to understand the revolution in wildlife conservation and habitat preservation that has occurred since the 1960s. Dozens of dedicated biologists, politicians, and private citizens have contributed to Costa Rica's world leadership in tropical forest conservation, wildlife protection, and nature tourism over the past fifty-plus years. This process occurred in five phases: (1) Research, (2) Education, (3) Preservation, (4) Conservation, and (5) Nature Tourism.

Research

One of the earliest advances for Costa Rica's legacy of conservation was the development of research data on Costa Rica's plants and wildlife. Without such basic knowledge, there can be little appreciation, respect, or protection for wild species. In 1941, Dr. Alexander Skutch homesteaded property in the San Isidro del General valley along the Río Peña Blanca. After

settling there with his wife, Pamela, Dr. Skutch studied Costa Rica's birds for more than sixty years and continued to observe them and record their life history in his prolific writings until his passing in 2004.

In 1954, another biologist, Dr. Archie Carr, started epic research. Dr. Carr, from the University of Florida, began a lifelong commitment to the protection and management of the green turtle at Tortuguero. That effort continues to this day, thanks to the efforts of his son, Dr. David Carr, and the work of the Caribbean Conservation Corporation, which was created in 1959.

Another significant development for Costa Rica's legacy of leadership in tropical research was the creation of the Tropical Science Center. It was founded in 1962 by Drs. Leslie R. Holdridge, Joseph A. Tosi, and Robert J. Hunter. These three scientists promoted research on tropical ecosystems, land use, and sustainable development. Dr. Gary Hartshorn later joined the staff to add more expertise in the development of tropical forest management strategies. The Tropical Science Center was instrumental in establishing La Selva Biological Field Station and the Monteverde Cloud Forest Reserve and in preserving Los Cusingos, the forest reserve formerly owned by Dr. Alexander Skutch. That reserve is now managed by the Tropical Science Center.

Another research catalyst for subsequent conservation and land protection was the creation of the Organization for Tropical Studies (OTS) in 1964. The OTS is a consortium of fifty-five universities and educational institutions throughout the Americas. The OTS operates three tropical research field stations—located at La Selva, Palo Verde, and San Vito. Tropical biologists from throughout the world come to these field stations to pursue pioneering studies on taxonomy, ecology, and conservation of tropical ecosystems.

For many decades, people had believed it was necessary to eliminate tropical forests in the name of progress. They were determined to create croplands, pastures, and monocultures of exotic trees for the benefit of society. Tropical biologists of the OTS changed the way people viewed tropical forests and helped society realize the infinitely greater ecological, climatic, and economic benefits that can accrue from preserving and managing tropical forests as sustainable resources.

Education

In 1963 the National Science Foundation supported the Advanced Science Seminar in Tropical Biology, which was subsequently adapted by OTS. The OTS initiated a second part of its legacy with field courses in tropical ecology, forestry, agriculture, and land use for undergraduate and graduate students from throughout the Americas. Since its founding, the OTS has conducted more than 200 field courses for at least 3,600 students. For many of these students, including the author, the courses were life-changing experiences. The faculty who taught these courses were some of the most prominent ecologists in the world,

Dr. Dan Janzen teaching an OTS course in 1967. Photo provided courtesy of the Organization for Tropical Studies.

including, among others, Drs. Dan Janzen, Mildred Mathias, Carl Rettenmeyer, Frank Barnwell, Rafael Lucas Rodríguez Caballero, Gordon Orions, Roy McDiarmid, Larry Wolf, and Rex Daubenmire.

Another significant source of tropical education and research has been the Tropical Agricultural Center for Research and Education (Centro Agronómico Tropical de Investigación y Enseñanza; CATIE). This center was created in 1942 at Turrialba and was originally known as the Interamerican Institute of Agricultural Science (Instituto Interamericano de Ciencias Agrícolas; IICA). Graduate students come from all over Latin America to study agriculture, forestry, and wildlife management there.

Preservation

By the 1960s, about 50 percent of Costa Rica's forests had been cut, and the clearing continued. It became apparent that national programs for protection of the remaining forests and wildlife would be necessary if they were to be preserved into the next century.

The first wildlife conservation law was decreed on July 20, 1961, and was updated with bylaws on June 7, 1965. These laws and regulations provided for the creation and enforcement of game laws, the establishment of wildlife refuges, the prohibition of commercial sale of wildlife products, the issuance of hunting and fishing licenses, the establishment of fines for violations, and the creation of restrictions on the export and import of wildlife. Complete protection was given to tapirs, manatees, White-tailed Deer does accompanied by fawns, and Resplendent Quetzals. The laws, however, were not enforced.

In 1968, a Costa Rican graduate student, Mario Boza, was inspired by a visit to the

Great Smoky Mountains National Park. In 1969 a Forestry Protection Law allowed national parks to be established, and Mario Boza was designated as the only employee of the new National Parks of Costa Rica. He wrote a master plan for the newly designated Poás Volcano National Park as his master's thesis subject.

In 1970, wildlife laws were still being ignored by poachers, and wildlife continued to disappear. President "Don Pepe" Figueres visited Dr. Archie Carr and graduate student David Ehrenfeld to see the green turtle nesting beaches at Tortuguero. He was considering a proposal to protect the area as a national park. The following account was later written by Dr. David Ehrenfeld (1989):

It was Don Pepe's first visit to the legendary Tortuguero—we had been watching a green turtle nest, also a first for him. El Presidente, a short, Napoleonic man with boundless energy, was enjoying himself enormously. Both he and Archie were truly charismatic people, and they liked and respected one another. The rest of us went along quietly, enjoying

Logging in Costa Rica, 1969.

the show. As we walked up the beach towards the boca, where the Río Tortuguero meets the sea, Don Pepe questioned Dr. Carr about the green turtles and their need for conservation. How important was it to make Tortuguero a sanctuary? Just then, a flashlight picked out a strange sight up ahead.

A turtle was on the beach, near the waterline, trailing something. And behind her was a line of eggs which, for some reason, she was depositing on the bare, unprotected sand. We hurried to see what the problem was.

When we got close, it was all too apparent. The entire undershell of the turtle had been cut away by poachers who were after calipee, or cartilage, to dry and sell to the European turtle soup manufacturers. Not interested in the meat or eggs, they had evidently then flipped her back on her belly for sport, to see where she would crawl. What she was trailing was her intestines. The poachers had probably been frightened away by our lights only minutes before.

Dr. Carr, who knew sea turtles better than any human being on earth and who had devoted much of his life to their protection, said nothing. He looked at Don Pepe, and so did I. It was a moment of revelation. Don Pepe was very, very angry, trembling with rage. This was his country, his place. He had risked his life for it fighting in the Cerro de la Muerte. The turtles were part of this place, even part of its name: Tortuguero; . . . She was home, laying her eggs for the last time.

Don Pepe realized that the ancient turtles, as well as the Costa Rican people, needed a safe place to live and raise their young. The poaching had to end. He declared

Rainbow over the Monteverde Cloud Forest Reserve.

Tortuguero National Park by executive decree in 1970. The tragic poaching incident with the nesting green turtle was probably the pivotal incident that catalyzed the national parks movement in Costa Rica. Mario Boza served under President Figueres as the director of national parks from 1970 to 1974. By the end of 1974, the service had grown to an organization of 100 employees with an annual budget of $600,000. A total of 2.5 percent of the country was designated as national parks and reserves.

Private preservation efforts also began in the 1970s. Scientists George and Harriet Powell and Monteverde resident Wilford Guindon created the 810-acre Monteverde Cloud Forest Reserve. They brought in the Tropical Science Center to own and manage the preserve, which now totals 27,428 acres. The Monteverde Conservation League was subsequently formed to help manage and carry out conservation projects and land acquisition.

In 1984, Dr. Dan Janzen brought more international recognition to Costa Rica when he received the Crafoord Prize in Coevolutionary Ecology from the Swedish Royal Academy of Sciences. This is the ecologist's equivalent of the Nobel Prize. Dr. Janzen received the prize for his pioneering research on entomology and ecology of tropical dry forests. This focused attention on the need for preserving tropical dry forests in the Guanacaste Conservation Area (http://www.acguanacaste.ac.cr).

Oscar Arias was elected president in 1986. He created the Ministry of Energy, Mining, and Natural Resources (MIRENEM) by merging the national land management departments to make them more efficient in managing the nation's natural resources. That agency is now referred to as the Ministry of Environment and Energy (Ministerio del Ambiente y Energía; MINAE).

Since then, Costa Rica's national system of parks and reserves has continued

Dr. Dan Janzen, winner of the Crafoord Prize in 1984.

to grow and mature. It now consists of 161 protected areas, including twenty-five national parks. Those areas total 3,221,635 acres—almost 26 percent of the country's land area. More information on the national park system can be found at www.costarica-nationalparks.com.

Conservation

As the national park system grew and encompassed more life zones, it became clear to ecological visionaries like Dr. Dan Janzen and Dr. Rodrigo Gámez Lobo that they had an opportunity to take another bold step that would place them in a world-leadership role for conservation of biological diversity and creation of economic benefits to society from that biological diversity. They created the National Institute of Biodiversity (Instituto Nacional de Biodiversidad; INBIO). Dr. Gámez Lobo became the first director of INBIO and continues his leadership as president of INBIO. The ambitious goal of this institute was to collect, identify, and catalog all of the living species in Costa Rica. Estimated at 505,000 species, this figure includes 882 birds, 236 mammals, 228 reptiles, 178 amphibians, 360,000 insects, and 10,000 plants. This represents about

5 percent of the world's species. So far, about 90,000 of those species have been described, and INBIO's collections include 3.5 million specimens.

Following the creation of INBIO, MIRENEM developed a national system of "conservation areas" in 1990. This is referred to as SINAC (Sistema Nacional de Areas de Conservación). Eleven conservation areas were established. Personnel in the fields of wildlife, forestry, parks, and agriculture teamed up to manage the national parks and wildlands in each conservation area. Their goal is the conservation of Costa Rica's biodiversity for nondestructive use by Costa Ricans and the world populace. This national scale of ecosystem-based management predated efforts in more "developed" countries by years.

Nature Tourism

Beginning in the mid-1980s, and concurrent with the conservation phase, the value of Costa Rica's national parks (NPs), national wildlife refuges (NWRs), and biological reserves (BRs) was reaffirmed in another way: as a resource for nature tourism. Nature tourism is motivated by the desire to experience unspoiled nature: to see, enjoy, experience, or photograph scenery, natural communities, wildlife, and native plants. The first rule of nature tourism is that wildlife is worth more alive—in the wild—than dead. It has become a great incentive to protect wildlife from poachers and to conserve the forests as habitat for the wildlife.

Nature tourism provided new employment opportunities for Costa Ricans as travel agency personnel, outfitters, nature lodge owners and staff, drivers, and naturalist guides. The best naturalist guides can identify birds, mammals, reptiles,

Birding guide Carlos Gómez Nieto.

amphibians, flowers, butterflies, and trees. These dedicated guides share an infectious enthusiasm for the country as they help visitors experience hundreds of species during a visit. Guides like Carlos Gómez Nieto have seen more than 730 of the country's bird species and can identify most of them by sight and sound.

Rainforests—especially the international loss of rainforests—received a great deal of publicity in the 1980s. Costa Rica's national parks provided an opportunity to attract tourists to experience the mystique and beauty of those forests. Improved road systems and small airstrips throughout the country provided access to those parks and private reserves in the rainforests. Enterprising outfitters recognized the opportunity to establish locally owned and managed nature tourism lodges to cater to this new breed of international tourists.

One of the best-known pioneers in nature-based tourism is Michael Kaye. Originally from New York, he was a white-water rafting outfitter in the Grand Canyon before he founded Costa Rica Expeditions in 1985. In Costa Rica he provides tourists with the opportunity for adventure tourism, including white-water rafting and wildlife viewing. Kaye built three lodges—Tortuga, Monteverde, and Corcovado—and he provided ecologically based innovations and adaptations at these facilities that minimized their impact on the environment and sensitized visitors to the importance and vulnerability of the forests where these lodges were located. Kaye believes that tourists respond to world-class facilities and services that are provided by local ownership and management of smaller, dispersed lodging facilities. Costa Rica's tourism forte is that it is one of the best rainforest destinations in the Americas because it is safe and easily accessible; the attraction is not the beaches where huge hotels are owned by corporations from other countries.

There are now dozens of other locally owned nature-based lodges throughout the country. John Aspinall founded Costa Rica Sun Tours and built the Arenal Observatory Lodge. His brother Peter founded Tiskita Jungle Lodge. Don Perry initiated the Rainforest Aerial Tram facility. John and Kathleen Erb founded Rancho Naturalista and Tárcol Lodge. John and Karen Lewis founded Lapa Ríos. Other local nature lodges are Selva Verde, El Gavilán, Hacienda Solimar, La Ensenada, Villa Lapas, Rancho Casa Grande, Rara Avis, Rainbow Adventures, Río Sierpe Lodge, Savegre Mountain Lodge, Drake Bay Wilderness Resort, El Pizote Lodge, Luna Lodge, and Laguna

Ctenosaur sharing the beach with tourists, Tamarindo.

del Lagarto. OTS research facilities like La Selva and San Vito also provide accommodations for nature tourists.

International connections also benefited Costa Rica's nature tourism. In 1989, Preferred Adventures Ltd. was founded by Karen Johnson in St. Paul, Minnesota, with special emphasis on Costa Rican tourism. Through the efforts of Karen Johnson and the late Tony Andersen, Chairman of the Board and former CEO of the H. B. Fuller Company and Honorary Consul to Costa Rica from Minnesota, these connections resulted in the creation of the Costa Rica–Minnesota Foundation, which has promoted cultural, medical, and conservation projects in Costa Rica for many years.

As nature tourism lodges proliferated after the mid-1980s, the number of tourists arriving in Costa Rica grew steadily. In 1988, about 330,000 tourists came, and over the next eleven years the number increased to 1,027,000 people per year. During the same period, the annual number of foreign visitors entering national parks increased from about 125,000 to 269,000. From 1988 to 1998 the number of tour operators increased from 58 to 180.

Nature tourism has turned heads throughout Costa Rica and Latin America because of the amount of income it has generated. In 1991, tourism contributed $330 million to the Costa Rican national economy. By 1999 that figure had increased to $940 million and exceeded the amount generated by exports of coffee ($408 million) and bananas ($566 million)! In addition, nature tourism created 140,000 jobs. The best thing about nature tourism is that when it is practiced ethically and in balance with the environment, it is a sustainable use of natural resources. Costa Ricans realize that a significant part of the economic health and prosperity of their country is tied to the health and prosperity of their national parks, forests, and wildlife and to the future of the country's macaws, quetzals, tepescuintles, jaguars, and green turtles. Don Pepe Figueres was right. If you make the world a safe place for green turtles and other wildlife, it becomes a better place for people, too.

GEOGRAPHY

Costa Rica, a Central American country between Panama and Nicaragua, is shown in Figure 1. Considering its relatively small size, 19,653 square miles, Costa Rica has an exceptionally high diversity of plant and wildlife species. This is explained in part by the fascinating geological history of the region.

The geological history that led to the creation of Costa Rica goes back about 200 million years to the Triassic Period, when

Figure 1. Location of Costa Rica in Central America.

Highway map of Costa Rica. Source: U.S. State Department.

much of the earth's landmass was composed of a supercontinent called Pangaea.
The supercontinent began to separate
through continental drift, portrayed in
Figure 2, which is the process by which
the earth's landmasses essentially float on
the molten core of the earth, drift among
the oceans, and occasionally separate or
merge. Pangaea eventually separated into
two supercontinents. The northern supercontinent, called Laurasia, later became
North America, Asia, and Europe. The
southern portion, called Gondwanaland,
drifted apart and later became South
America, Africa, southern Asia, and
Australia.

About 130 million years ago the western portion of Gondwanaland began to
separate into South America and Africa.
Concurrently, the North American landmass drifted westward from the European
landmass. Both North America and South

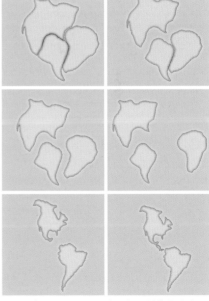

Figure 2. Stages in the process of continental drift that led to
the creation of Costa Rica.

Topographical relief map of Costa Rica.

and rose above sea level to create the land bridge that now connects North and South America. That bridge became southern Nicaragua, Costa Rica, and the central and western portions of Panama.

BIOGEOGRAPHY

Biogeography is the relationship between the geography of a region and the long-term distribution and dispersal patterns of its plants and wildlife. The geological history of Costa Rica, Nicaragua, and Panama created a situation in which they became a land bridge between two continents. Plants and wildlife have been dispersing across that bridge for the last three million years; as a result, Costa Rica became a biological mixing bowl of species from both continents. Those dispersal patterns are shown in Figure 3.

America drifted westward, but they were still separate. By the Pliocene Period, about three to four million years ago, North America and South America were aligned from north to south, but a gap in the ocean floor between the two continents existed where southern Nicaragua, Costa Rica, and Panama are today.

About three million years ago an undersea plate of the earth's crust, called a tectonic plate, began moving north and eastward in the Pacific Ocean into the area between North and South America. This particular tectonic plate, the Cocos Plate, pushed onto the Caribbean Plate

Temperate-climate plants that have dispersed southward from North America include alders (*Alnus*), oaks (*Quercus*), walnuts (*Juglans*), magnolias (*Magnolia*), blueberries (*Vaccinium*), Indian paintbrush (*Castilleja*), and mistletoe (*Gaiadendron*). Most dispersal appears to have occurred

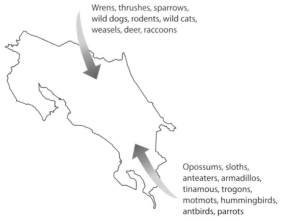

Wrens, thrushes, sparrows, wild dogs, rodents, wild cats, weasels, deer, raccoons

Opossums, sloths, anteaters, armadillos, tinamous, trogons, motmots, hummingbirds, antbirds, parrots

Figure 3. Costa Rica became a land bridge that facilitated the dispersal of wildlife from both North and South America.

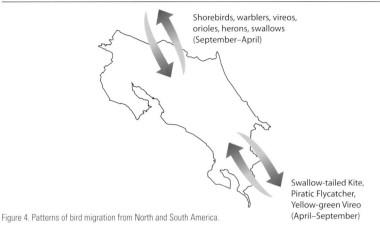

Shorebirds, warblers, vireos, orioles, herons, swallows (September–April)

Swallow-tailed Kite, Piratic Flycatcher, Yellow-green Vireo (April–September)

Figure 4. Patterns of bird migration from North and South America.

during cooler glacial periods. As the climate became warmer, these northern-origin plants became biologically stranded on the mountains, where the climate was cooler.

Wildlife dispersing from North America across the land bridge included coyotes, tapirs, deer, jaguars, squirrels, and bears. Birds that dispersed from North America to Central and South America included wrens, thrushes, sparrows, woodpeckers, and common dippers.

Plants that dispersed from South America toward the north included tree ferns, cycads, heliconias, bromeliads, orchids, poor-man's umbrella (*Gunnera*), *Puja*, and *Espeletia*. Wildlife that dispersed northward from South America through Costa Rica are opossums, armadillos, porcupines, sloths, monkeys, anteaters, agoutis, and tepescuintles. Some species expanded through Central America and Mexico to the United States. Birds that dispersed from South America to Costa Rica and beyond include tinamous, hummingbirds, motmots, trogons, spinetails, flowerpiercers, antbirds, parrots, and woodcreepers.

Migratory Birds

NORTHERN HEMISPHERE MIGRANTS

Among Costa Rica's 882 bird species, about 180 are migratory. Most migrate from North America to winter in Latin America between September and April. Many people consider that the real home of these migrants is in the north and that the birds fly south as if they were going on vacation each winter. They are sometimes referred to by travelers from the United States as "our birds." Patterns of migration from the north and south are shown in Figure 4.

The story behind the migratory traditions and the origins of these migrants is both intriguing and surprising. Migratory birds are believed to have originated in the tropics. In tropical forests, insects are present in a great diversity of species, but the numbers of any one species are low. They can be very difficult for birds to find in adequate quantities to feed young. That is why the parents of many tropical bird species have young from previous broods that help feed their young. In northern temperate forests, the species diversity of insects is lower, but the seasonal abundance of each species can be great—as occurs in outbreaks

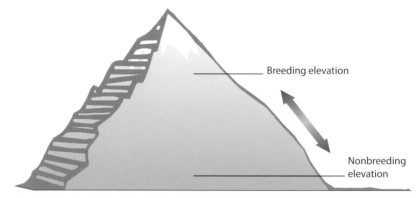

Figure 5. Some tropical insects and birds, like the Three-wattled Bellbird, carry out elevational migrations between breeding seasons and nonbreeding seasons.

of tent caterpillars. This is referred to as a "protein pulse" as it relates to bird food provided by insects. Such a bountiful supply of insects provides ideal conditions for parent birds to reproduce and adequately feed their young. The annual pattern of seasonal migration was likely tied to the passing of glacial periods, when mild northern summers and the increasing presence and abundance of northern insects benefited birds that migrated north to nest.

Considering that most migrants leave their breeding grounds in September and return north in April, they spend twice as much time in Costa Rica each year as in their breeding range in the north. Northern migrants include ducks, warblers, vireos, tanagers, shorebirds, herons, hawks, falcons, and orioles.

SOUTHERN HEMISPHERE MIGRANTS

As most northern migrants are leaving for North America in March and April, a few birds are migrating from South America to Costa Rica to stay from April through September. The Swallow-tailed Kite, Piratic Flycatcher, Blue-and-white Swallow, and Yellow-green Vireo are migrants from South America.

ELEVATIONAL MIGRANTS

North American migrants carry out migration by changes in latitude. Some permanent residents in Costa Rica, like the Three-wattled Bellbird, migrate each year along an elevational gradient from breeding areas in middle- and high-elevation "temperate" forests during the rainy season (April through December) to lower-elevation "tropical" forests during the dry season (January through March), as illustrated in Figure 5. The Silver-throated Tanager, the Scarlet-thighed Dacnis, and many Costa Rican moths carry out elevational migrations.

FLY-OVER MIGRANTS

Some birds migrate between wintering areas in South America and summering locations in the United States and Canada. They pass through Costa Rica but do not winter there in significant numbers. They are primarily observed during spring migratory periods from March through May and fall migratory periods from July through October. These fly-over migrants include Purple Martins, Barn Swallows, Dickcissels, Bobolinks, Scarlet Tanagers, Eastern Kingbirds, Cerulean Warblers,

Swainson's Hawks, Swainson's Thrushes, Blackpoll Warblers, and many shorebirds.

In addition to fly-over migrants, there are many birds, such as Broad-winged Hawks, Peregrine Falcons, Ospreys, and shorebirds, that winter in Costa Rica as well as Panama and countries of South America.

MIGRANTS/NONMIGRANTS

Some birds (and the Monarch Butterfly) in Costa Rica are nonmigratory residents that also occur in the United States and Canada. The Hairy Woodpecker, Eastern Meadowlark, House Wren, Red-winged Blackbird, dipper, and several wading birds are nonmigratory permanent residents in Costa Rica that are also found in northern latitudes. Birds that nest in Costa Rica and are also present as migrants during the wintering period from October through April are the White-winged Dove, Red-tailed Hawk, Turkey Vulture, Common Nighthawk, Cattle Egret, Great Egret, Green Heron, Tricolored and Little Blue Herons, Yellow-crowned Night-Heron, and Streaked Flycatcher.

ENDEMIC SPECIES

An endemic species is one found in one country or region and nowhere else in the world. Costa Rica has three zones of endemism, in which unique species and subspecies are found. These zones occur because geographic barriers created by mountains, arid zones, or oceans have created genetic isolation from other populations of a species until they finally evolved into separate species through natural selection.

Endemic Wildlife of the Highlands

The mountain ranges and volcanoes of

Costa Rica and western Panama include about 160 species of birds out of the 882 species present in the country. The concept of endemic species is often applied to species in a single country, but the Talamanca Mountains are contiguous with those of western Panama. For the purposes of this book, it is considered a single endemic zone. Many birds have evolved into distinctive species or subspecies because they were reproductively isolated from the same species or similar species in the mountains of Guatemala and southern Mexico and from birds in the mountains of eastern Panama and Colombia. This highland endemic zone is portrayed in Figure 6.

An impressive forty-seven birds are endemic to the mountains and foothills of Costa Rica and western Panama. They include the Black Guan, Black-breasted Wood-Quail, Buff-fronted Quail-Dove, Sulphur-winged Parakeet, Red-fronted Parrotlet, Dusky Nightjar, Costa Rican Pygmy-Owl, White-crested Coquette, Coppery-headed and White-tailed

Figure 6. Highland zone of endemic species in Costa Rica and western Panama.

Emeralds, Gray-tailed and White-bellied Mountain-gems, Magenta-throated Wood-star, and Black-bellied, Fiery-throated, Scintillant, and Volcano Hummingbirds.

Other endemics include the Lattice-tailed and Orange-bellied Trogons, Prong-billed Barbet, Ruddy Treerunner, Streak-breasted Treehunter, Silvery-fronted Tapaculo, Dark and Ochraceous Pewees, Black-capped and Golden-bellied Fly-catchers, Silvery-throated Jay, Timberline Wren, Sooty Thrush, Black-faced Solitaire, and Black-billed Nightingale-Thrush.

Additional endemic birds are the Long-tailed Silky-Flycatcher, Yellow-winged Vireo, Collared Redstart, Black-cheeked and Flame-throated Warblers, Zeledonia (Wrenthrush), Golden-browed Chloro-phonia, Spangle-cheeked Tanager, Sooty-capped Bush-Tanager, Black-thighed Grosbeak, Slaty Flowerpiercer, Volcano Junco, and Large-footed, Peg-billed, and Yellow-thighed Finches.

Two species are found only in Costa Rica's mountains—the Coppery-headed Emerald and the Poás Mountain Squirrel (*Syntheosciurus poasensis*).

Many birds, like the Resplendent Quetzal, Magnificent Hummingbird, and Band-tailed Pigeon, are separate subspecies from those found farther north. There are more than fifty subspecies of birds in the Costa Rica–western Panama highlands that are different from subspecies in the mountains of Mexico and Guatemala or in eastern Panama and the Andes of north-ern South America.

Examples of subspecies unique to this highland region are the Sulphur-winged Parakeet, Silvery-throated Jay, and Black-and-yellow Silky-Flycatcher. Over geologic time, some of these birds can be expected to continue to differentiate from other subspecies and be designated as new species.

Endemic Species of the Southern Pacific Lowlands

Costa Rica's mountain ranges serve as a giant barrier that separates moist and wet lowland rainforest birds and other spe-cies that originally dispersed from South America to both the Caribbean lowlands and the southern Pacific lowlands. The mountains have caused reproductive

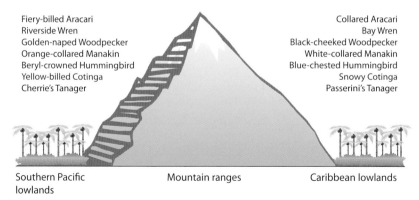

Fiery-billed Aracari		Collared Aracari
Riverside Wren		Bay Wren
Golden-naped Woodpecker		Black-cheeked Woodpecker
Orange-collared Manakin		White-collared Manakin
Beryl-crowned Hummingbird		Blue-chested Hummingbird
Yellow-billed Cotinga		Snowy Cotinga
Cherrie's Tanager		Passerini's Tanager

Southern Pacific lowlands   Mountain ranges   Caribbean lowlands

Figure 7. Closely related pairs of allopatric species of the Caribbean and Pacific lowlands that share a common ancestor but are now separated by Costa Rica's mountains.

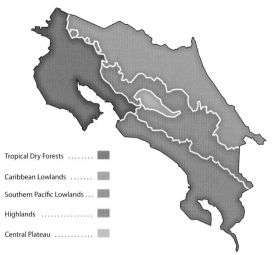

Tropical Dry Forests ....
Caribbean Lowlands ....
Southern Pacific Lowlands ...
Highlands ....
Central Plateau ....

Figure 8. Five biological zones of Costa Rica. In addition, the country's entire coastline, beaches, and mangrove lagoons make up a sixth zone of biological importance.

isolation between populations of species that occurred in both areas. Over geologic time, the species diverged into separate species. This has contributed to a second zone of endemic species in Costa Rica, the southern Pacific lowlands. There are several interesting pairs of species that have a common ancestor but have been separated from each other by the mountains between the Caribbean lowlands and the southern Pacific lowlands, as shown in Figure 7. Since the range of one species does not overlap the range of the other species in the pair, these are referred to as allopatric species.

This divergence of two species from a common ancestor is a continuing process, as evidenced by the recent decision by taxonomists to split the Scarlet-rumped Tanager into two species, Cherrie's Tanager in the Pacific lowlands and Passerini's Tanager in the Caribbean lowlands. The males are identical, but the females are distinctive. Other birds designated as endemic subspecies include the Masked Yellowthroat (Chiriquí race) and the

Variable Seedeater (Pacific race). One day they may eventually become different enough from the Caribbean subspecies to be designated as new species.

Additional endemic species of the southern Pacific lowlands that do not have a corresponding closely related species in the Caribbean lowlands include Baird's Trogon, Black-cheeked Ant-Tanager, Granular Poison Dart Frog, Mangrove Hummingbird, and Red-backed Squirrel Monkey.

Endemic Species of Cocos Island

A third zone of endemism is Cocos Island. This island is 600 miles out in the Pacific, and three endemic birds have evolved there: Cocos Finch, Cocos Cuckoo, and Cocos Flycatcher. Cocos Island is an extension of the Galápagos Island archipelago but it is owned by Costa Rica. There are thirteen finches on the Galápagos Islands commonly referred to as Darwin's finches. The Cocos Finch is actually the fourteenth Darwin's finch.

Tropical dry forest in Guanacaste.

MAJOR BIOLOGICAL ZONES

The most detailed and traditional classification of the habitats in Costa Rica includes twelve "life zones," as described by the late Dr. Leslie Holdridge of the Tropical Science Center. Those life zones are based on average annual precipitation, average annual temperature, and evapotranspiration potential. Evapotranspiration potential involves the relative amount of humidity or aridity of a region.

For tourism planning purposes, that classification system has been simplified in this book from twelve to six biological zones. These zones, the first five of which are shown in Figure 8, coincide with the distribution of many Costa Rican wildlife species and are designed for trip planning by wildlife tourists. The sixth zone consists of the entire coastline of both the Pacific and the Caribbean coasts. A good trip itinerary should include at least three biological zones in addition to the Central Plateau.

Tropical Dry Forest

The tropical dry forest in northwestern Costa Rica is a lowland region that generally coincides with the boundaries of Guanacaste Province. It extends eastward to the Cordillera of Guanacaste and Tilarán, southeast to Carara NP, and north to the Nicaragua border. This zone extends from sea level to approximately 2,000 feet in elevation.

This region is characterized by a pronounced dry season from December through March. The deciduous trees include many plants that lose their leaves during the dry season and flower during that leafless period. Common trees are bullhorn acacia (*Acacia*), *Tabebuia*, strangler fig (*Ficus*), *Guazuma*, kapok (*Ceiba*), *Bombacopsis*, buttercup tree (*Cochlospermum vitifolium*), *Anacardium*, and the national tree of Costa Rica, the Guanacaste tree (*Enterolobium cyclocarpum*). The tallest trees approach 100 feet in height. Rainfall ranges from 40 to 80 inches per year.

Epiphytes are not a major component of the dry forest canopy, as they are in the moist and wet forests. However, some trees are thickly covered with vines like monkey vine (*Bauhinia*) and *Combretum*. The ease with which this forest can be burned and cleared for agricultural pur-poses has made the tropical dry forest the most endangered habitat in the country.

An important habitat within the dry forest consists of the riparian forests along the rivers, also called gallery forests. They maintain more persistent foliage during the dry season.

Wetlands, estuaries, islands, and back-waters of this region's rivers are also a major habitat for wetland wildlife. Especially important are lands along the Río Temp-isque, its tributaries, and the wetlands of Palo Verde NP. Birds found predominantly in the forests and wetlands of Guanacaste are the Wood Stork, Jabiru, Blue-winged Teal, Black-bellied Whistling-Duck, Rose-ate Spoonbill, Muscovy Duck, Snail Kite, Crested Caracara, White-bellied Chacha-laca, Double-striped Thick-knee, White-winged Dove, Inca Dove, Orange-fronted Parakeet, White-fronted Parrot, Black-headed Trogon, White-lored Gnatcatcher, and Yellow-naped Parrot. Other dry-forest birds are the Pacific Screech-Owl, Cin-namon Hummingbird, Crested Bobwhite, Turquoise-browed Motmot, Ivory-billed Woodcreeper, Long-tailed Manakin, White-throated Magpie-Jay, Rufous-naped Wren, Scrub Euphonia, and Stripe-headed Sparrow. The Crested Caracara, Wood Stork, and Muscovy Duck are found in lower numbers in the Caribbean lowlands.

Important examples of tropical dry forest habitat are preserved in Guanacaste Province; Santa Rosa, Las Baulas, and Palo Verde NPs; and Lomas Barbudal BR. The northeastern limit of this zone appears to be at Los Inocentes Ranch. If one travels east from that ranch, the flora and fauna are typical of the Caribbean lowlands, but if one travels west, the flora and fauna are typical of the Guanacaste dry forest. Some species of the dry forest,

including migrant Scissor-tailed Fly-catchers and Mourning Doves, as well as Double-striped Thick-Knees and White-tailed Kites, now appear to be extending their ranges east to the agricultural lands of Los Chiles south of Lake Nicaragua. The southeastern limit of this region is at Carara NP, which has a combination of wildlife characteristic of both the dry for-est and the southern Pacific lowlands.

Southern Pacific Lowlands

The southern Pacific lowlands include the moist and wet forested region from Carara NP through the General Valley, Osa Pen-insula, and Golfo Dulce lowlands to the Panama border and inland to the premon-tane forest zone at San Vito.

The moist and wet forests of this region receive 80 to 200 inches of rainfall per year, with a more pronounced dry season from December through March than occurs in the Caribbean lowlands. These forests have fewer epiphytes than are found in Caribbean lowland forests. The tallest trees exceed 150 feet in height.

Among tree species are the kapok (*Cei-ba*), *Anacardium,* strangler fig (*Ficus*), wild

Southern Pacific lowland forest, Manuel Antonio National Park.

almond (*Terminalia*), purpleheart (*Pelto-gyne purpurea*), *Carapa,* buttercup tree (*Cochlospermum vitifolium*), *Virola,* balsa (*Ochroma*), milk tree (*Brosimum*), *Raphia,* garlic tree (*Caryocar costaricense*), and *Hura.* Understory plants include species like bullhorn acacia (*Acacia*), walking palm (*Socratea*), *Bactris,* and *Heliconia.* Most trees maintain their foliage throughout the year.

Much of this region has been converted to pastureland and plantations of pineapple, coconut, and African oil palm. Among the most significant reserves remaining in natural habitat are Carara, Manuel Antonio, and Corcovado NPs. Corcovado NP is one of the finest examples of lowland wet forest in Central America, and it has excellent populations of wildlife species that are rare in other regions—Scarlet Macaws, Jaguars, tapirs, and White-lipped Peccaries.

Additional private reserves include one near San Isidro del General at Los Cusingos, the former home of Dr. Alexander and Pamela Skutch. It is now managed by the Tropical Science Center. The Wilson Botanical Garden at San Vito is an excellent example of premontane wet forest and is owned and operated by the Organization for Tropical Studies.

The southern Pacific lowland area is of biological interest because it is the northernmost range limit for some South American species, examples of which are the Smooth-billed Ani, Masked Yellow-throat, Thick-billed Euphonia, and Streaked Saltator. Some birds are dispersing farther into Costa Rica. The Yellow-headed Caracara has recently been seen in southern portions of Guanacaste and in the Pacific lowlands approaching Monteverde. The Pearl Kite, Southern Lapwing, and Crested Oropendola are new arrivals and have dispersed from Panama to this region since 1999.

Premontane (middle-elevation) sites like the Wilson Botanical Garden at San Vito are included in this biological region because many of the species typical of this region are found up to about 4,000 feet along the western slopes of the Talamanca Mountains. Premontane forests, like those preserved at the Wilson Botanical Garden, are the second most endangered life zone in Costa Rica, after tropical dry forests.

Central Plateau overlooking San José and suburbs.

Central Plateau (Central Valley)

The Central Plateau contains the human population center of Costa Rica. The capital, San José, and adjoining suburbs are located in this relatively flat plateau at an elevation of approximately 3,900 feet. It is bordered on the north and east by major volcanoes of the Central Cordillera: Barva, Irazú, Poás, and Turrialba. To the south is the northern end of the Talamanca Mountains.

Caribbean lowland wet forest, Tortuguero National Park.

Rainfall ranges from 40 to 80 inches per year, and the original life zone in this area was premontane moist forest, but that forest has been largely cleared. The climate of the region, about 68 degrees Fahrenheit year-round, made it ideal for human settlement, and the rich volcanic soils made it an excellent region for growing coffee and sugarcane. The region is also important for production of fruits, vegetables, and horticultural export products like ferns and flowers.

Although premontane moist forests of the Central Plateau are largely gone, extensive plantings of shrubs, flowers, and fruiting and flowering trees throughout the San José area have made it ideal for adaptable wildlife species. Shade coffee plantations are preferred habitats for songbirds, including Neotropical migrants. Living fence posts of *Erythrina* and *Tabebuia* are excellent sources of nectar for birds and butterflies. Private gardens abound with butterflies and Rufous-tailed Hummingbirds. Remaining natural places, like the grounds of the Parque Bolívar Zoo in San José, host many wild, free-living butterflies and songbirds.

Among wildlife commonly encountered in backyards, woodlots, and open spaces of the Central Plateau and San José are the Clay-colored Thrush, Rufous-tailed Hummingbird, Blue-crowned Motmot,

Tennessee Warbler, Blue-gray and Summer Tanagers, White-tailed Kite, Cattle Egret, Turkey and Black Vultures, Rufous-collared Sparrow, Great-tailed Grackle, Broad-winged Hawk, Red-billed Pigeon, Crimson-fronted Parakeet, Groove-billed Ani, Ferruginous Pygmy-Owl, Common Pauraque, Hoffmann's Woodpecker, Tropical Kingbird, Social Flycatcher, Great Kiskadee, Gray-breasted Martin, Blue-and-white Swallow, Brown Jay, House Wren, Baltimore Oriole, and Variegated Squirrel.

Caribbean Lowlands

The Caribbean lowlands include moist and wet lowland forests from the Caribbean coast westward to the foothills of Costa Rica's mountains. The Caribbean lowland fauna extends from Los Inocentes Ranch southeastward to Cahuita and the Panama border. For the purposes of this book, the region extends from sea level to the upper limit of the tropical zone at about 2,000 feet elevation. The premontane forest, at least up to about 3,200 feet, also contains many lowland species. This region receives 80 to 200 inches of rainfall annually.

The trees grow to a height of over 150 feet. This is an evergreen forest that receives precipitation throughout the year and does not have a pronounced dry season like the moist and wet forests of the southern Pacific lowlands. Trees include coconut palms (*Cocos*), raffia palms (*Raphia*), Carapa, *Pentaclethra,* kapok (*Ceiba*), swamp almond (*Dipteryx panamensis*), *Alchornea,* walking palm (*Socratea*), and *Pterocarpus.* Tree branches have many epiphytes, such as bromeliads, philodendrons, and orchids. The complexity of the forest canopy contributes to a high diversity of plant and animal species in the treetops. Plants of the understory and forest edge include passionflower (*Passiflora*), *Hamelia, Heliconia,* palms, *Costus,* and *Canna.*

Crater of Poás volcano.

Much of this region has been cleared and settled for production of cattle and bananas. Remaining forest reserves include Tortuguero and Cahuita NPs, Gandoca-Manzanillo NWR, Hitoy-Cerere BR, lower elevations of La Amistad and Braulio Carrillo NPs, and Caño Negro NWR. Tortuguero NP is one of the most extensive reserves and one of the best remaining examples of rainforest in Central America. Canals at Tortuguero and open water of the Río Frío and at Caño Negro provide excellent opportunities for viewing wildlife from boats. The grounds of Rara Avis also provide an excellent protected reserve at the upper elevational limit of this biological zone. La Selva Biological Field Station, owned and managed by the OTS, has an exceptional boardwalk and trail system that allows easy viewing of rainforests.

Talamanca Mountains, Cerro de la Muerte.

Lower levels of Braulio Carrillo NP offer excellent examples of moist and wet lowland forest.

The Caribbean lowlands are significant as an excellent example of tropical habitat that supports classic rainforest species in all their complex diversity, beauty, and abundance: Great Green Macaws, Chestnut-mandibled and Keel-billed Toucans, trogons, jacamars, manakins, antbirds, parrots, tinamous, spinetails, Collared Peccaries, tapirs, howler monkeys, spider monkeys, white-faced monkeys, Two- and Three-toed Sloths, bats, morpho and owl butterflies, Strawberry Poison Dart Frogs, and Red-eyed Tree Frogs.

Highlands

The highland biological zone comprises Costa Rica's four mountain ranges. This zone includes lower montane, montane, and subalpine elevations generally above 4,200 to 4,500 feet in elevation.

Five volcanoes near the Nicaragua border form the Cordillera of Guanacaste: Orosi, Rincón de la Vieja, Santa María, Miravalles, and Tenorio.

The second group of mountains is the Cordillera of Tilarán. It includes the still-active Arenal volcano, which exploded in 1968, and mountains that are part of the Monteverde cloud forest.

Third is the Central Cordillera, which includes three large volcanoes that encircle the Central Plateau—Poás, Irazú, and Barva—and Volcano Turrialba southeast of Barva. Poás is active, and Irazú last erupted in 1963. Volcano Turrialba showed some activity in 2008, but there have been no eruptions.

The fourth highland region is composed of the great chain of mountains from Cartago to the Panama border. They are the Talamanca Mountains and Cerro de la Muerte, which are of tectonic origin rather than volcanic. Included is Cerro Chirripó, the highest point in Costa Rica at 15,526 feet. These mountains were formed when the Cocos Tectonic Plate pushed up from beneath the ocean onto the Caribbean Tectonic Plate about three to four million years ago. Much of this mountain range is protected as Tapantí

NP (11,650 acres), Chirripó NP (123,921 acres), and La Amistad Costa Rica–Panama International Park (479,199 acres).

SPECIES DIVERSITY

Species diversity decreases with increasing elevation. Out of Costa Rica's 882 species of birds, about 130 species can be expected above 6,000 feet. About 105 species can be expected above 7,000 feet, about 85 can be found above 8,000 feet, and about 70 bird species can be expected above 9,000 feet.

HUMBOLDT'S LAW

The South American explorer Alexander von Humboldt recognized an interesting relationship in tropical countries with high mountains. As one travels up a mountain, the average annual temperature decreases by 1 degree Fahrenheit for each increase of 300 feet in elevation. As one travels northward from the equator, the mean annual temperature decreases by 1 degree Fahrenheit for each sixty-seven

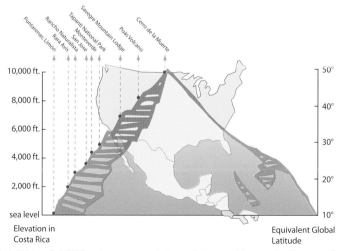

Figure 9. Humboldt's Law: Each 300 feet of ascent on a tropical mountain is comparable to traveling sixty-seven miles north in latitude in terms of changes in average annual temperature.

miles of change in latitude. So an increase of 300 feet elevation on a mountain in the tropics is broadly comparable to traveling sixty-seven miles north. This relationship is portrayed in Figure 9 and is referred to as Humboldt's Law.

Some interesting changes in plant and animal life become apparent in travel up a mountain in the tropics that biologically resemble northward travel in latitude. The relationship of latitude and elevation becomes apparent at higher elevations because there are many temperate-origin plants and birds in the highlands. For example, the avifauna present at 8,000 feet elevation on Costa Rica's mountains includes a higher proportion of temperate-origin thrushes, finches, juncos, and sparrows than found in the tropical lowlands.

Many plants of higher elevations in Costa Rica are in the same genera as plants found in the northern United States and Canada, including alders (*Alnus*), oaks (*Quercus*), blueberries (*Vaccinium*), blackberries (*Rubus*), bayberries (*Myrica*), dogwoods (*Cornus*), bearberry (*Arctostaphylos*), Indian paintbrush (*Castilleja*), and boneset (*Eupatorium*). Of course, in temperate areas there is a great deal more variation above and below the annual average temperature than in tropical areas, where there is little variation throughout the year.

ELEVATIONAL ZONES

To understand the role that elevation plays in plant and animal distribution, it is useful to understand the main categories by which biologists classify elevations and how those zones relate to the highlands. These elevational zones are shown in Figure 10 and described below.

TROPICAL LOWLANDS: The tropical lowland zone ranges from sea level to about 2,300 feet on the Pacific slope and 2,000 feet on the Caribbean slope. The lowland zone includes dry forests like those in Guanacaste as well as moist and wet forests of the southern Pacific and Caribbean lowlands.

PREMONTANE ZONE: This zone is called the "foothills" or "subtropical" zone and is also referred to as the "middle-elevation" zone. Some birds and other animals are found only in the foothills. Examples are Speckled and Silver-throated Tanagers. This zone ranges from about 2,300 feet to 4,900 feet on the Pacific slope and 2,000 feet to 4,600 feet on the Caribbean slope. It could also be called the coffee zone because it is the zone in which the conditions are ideal for coffee production—and for human settlement.

LOWER MONTANE ZONE: The lower montane zone is part of the highlands. It includes the region from 4,900 feet to 8,900 feet on

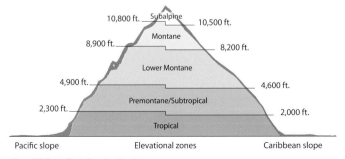

Figure 10. Costa Rica's five elevational zones.

Montane wet forest, Cerro de la Muerte.

Cloud forest vegetation, Monteverde.

the Pacific slope and 4,600 feet to 8,200 feet on the Caribbean slope. One special habitat that occurs within this zone, and in upper levels of the premontane zone, is cloud forest. The cloud forest occurs roughly from 4,500 to 5,500 feet. A cloud forest, like that at Monteverde, is characterized by fog, mist, and high humidity as well as high precipitation—about 120 to 160 inches per year.

Subalpine rainforest paramo.

Orchids, bromeliads, philodendrons, and dozens of other epiphytes grow in lush profusion among the branches of cloud forest trees. The Resplendent Quetzal is a well-known bird of the cloud forest as well as lower montane and montane forests.

MONTANE ZONE: The montane zone ranges from 8,500 feet to 10,800 feet on the Pacific slope and from 8,200 feet to 10,500 feet on the Caribbean slope. Among plants of the lower montane and montane zones are many of northern temperate origins: oak (*Quercus*), blueberry (*Vaccinium*), bearberry (*Arctostaphylos*), bamboo (*Chus-*

quea), alder (*Alnus*), bayberry (*Myrica*), magnolia (*Magnolia*), butterfly bush (*Buddleja*), elm (*Ulmus*), mistletoe (*Gaia-dendron*), boneset (*Eupatorium*), dogwood (*Cornus*), Indian paintbrush (*Castilleja*), and members of the blueberry family (Ericaceae) like *Satyria, Cavendishia,* and *Psammisia*. Other conspicuous plants are *Oreopanax, Senecio, Miconia, Clusia, Bomarea,* giant thistle (*Cirsium*), *Monochaetum,* wild avocado (*Persea*), poor-man's umbrella (*Gunnera*), and tree ferns.

Río Tárcoles estuary.

SUBALPINE PARAMO: Above the montane zone is the area above the treeline called the paramo. It has short, stunted, shrubby vegetation, including bamboo (*Chusquea*), many composites (like *Senecio*), and plants of South American origin from the Andes: a terrestrial bromeliad called *Puya dasylirioides* and a yellow-flowered composite with fuzzy white leaves called lamb's ears (*Espeletia*).

Coastal Beaches, Islands, and Mangrove Lagoons

The sixth biological zone, not portrayed on the map of biological regions (Fig. 8), includes all Pacific and Caribbean coastlines that extend from Nicaragua to Panama. This shoreline habitat consists of the beaches to the high-tide line and adjacent forests, offshore islands, rocky tidepools exposed at low tide, coral reefs, and mangrove lagoons. Among the more notable

islands are Caño Island and Cocos Island. The only coral reef is at Cahuita NP.

Coastal beaches and river estuaries are extremely important as habitat for migratory shorebirds, many of which—such as the Willet, Whimbrel, Wandering Tattler, and Ruddy Turnstone—winter along Costa Rica's beaches. Peregrine Falcons also winter along the coasts and prey on the shorebirds. American Oystercatchers nest along the shorelines above the high-tide line. Lesser Nighthawks nest along

Mangrove lagoon at Quepos.

Pacific beaches. Brown Boobies, Magnificent Frigatebirds, and Brown Pelicans nest on offshore islands and feed in shallow water near shore. Costa Rica's beaches are extremely important as nesting sites for Green Turtles on the Caribbean coast and for Ridley Turtles and Leatherback Turtles on the Pacific coast.

Other important coastal habitats that are critically endangered by foreign beachfront developers and pollution are those of the mangrove lagoons and mangrove forests. These are important nurseries for fish and wildlife. Significant mangrove lagoons exist at Tamarindo, Playas del Coco, Gulf of Nicoya, Parrita, Golfito, Chomes, Boca Barranca, Quepos, and the 54,362-acre Mangrove Forest Reserve of the Ríos Térraba and Sierpe. They provide exceptional wildlife-watching opportunities during guided boat tours.

WILDLIFE OVERVIEW AND SPECIES COVERAGE

The fauna of Costa Rica includes thousands of birds, mammals, reptiles, amphibians, butterflies, moths, and other invertebrates. This diversity can be both overwhelming and inspiring to a nature enthusiast. Even the casual tourist is drawn to the tropical beauty and appeal of monkeys, motmots, and morphos.

Since the publication of the first *Field Guide to the Wildlife of Costa Rica,* in 2002, there has been a huge increase in interest in this kind of reference book that goes beyond basic bird identification. It was also realized that the first edition, although too large for easy use in the field, still left out many species of interest to the Costa Rican natural history enthusiast. For that reason, this revision of the book has been split into three volumes.

The first edition of the *Field Guide to the Wildlife of Costa Rica* included 186 birds. Volume I of this revision includes 310 birds. The birds selected for this volume represent 77 percent of all the bird species we have sighted since 1987, out of the total of 25,938 bird sightings. In other words, this volume includes most of the species that are likely to be encountered by a tourist during a trip to Costa Rica, especially the most common and conspicuous species. Species are selected based on abundance, unique ecological relationships, conspicuousness, and special interest as a rare, endemic, or endangered species. Except for very common species, most of the birds described in the accounts are residents rather than migrants. Special efforts have been made to include gee-whiz facts about life history that make learning fun. Reproductive details have been included for some species that have interesting or unusual reproductive strategies.

Species Accounts

Each species account is preceded by the common name, scientific name, Costa Rican name, number of sightings, migratory or resident status, body length, weight, geographic range, and elevational range. The number of sightings includes a summary of how many trips out of twenty-three Henderson tours a bird has been encountered on, and the cumulative number of times that the species was recorded during those twenty-three trips. For example, "19/23 trips; 111 sightings" for the Brown Pelican indicates that the Brown Pelican was encountered on nineteen out of twenty-three trips and recorded 111 times.

The highest number of sightings recorded for any species was 384, for the

Turkey Vulture. A "sighting" is a record of one or multiple individuals of a species encountered on a walk, boat trip, or drive during a single outing. Among less common species that were included are owls and antbirds that are the subject of keen interest by nature enthusiasts, even though chances of seeing them are low.

The accounts are also accompanied by distribution maps indicating the sites where each species was found on our various trips. During our birding tours to Costa Rica, we have visited seventy-six sites. The location of these sites is shown in Appendix B, along with details for each site and contact information for the lodges at each site. Both elevations and global positioning system (GPS) readings of latitude and longitude were taken so these observations could be used to compile the distribution maps. The pattern of dots within the biological zones portrays the general distribution of a species, but there are obviously many areas we have not visited where these species also occur. There is a seasonal bias to these sightings, as most were recorded in January and February.

The amount of life-history information available for Costa Rica's birds varies greatly among species. Some have been well studied and others are still largely unknown. A large amount of scientific literature has been reviewed and represents the best information available. Much information was obtained from Dr. Dan Janzen's monumental work *Costa Rican Natural History* (1983); the *Handbook of the Birds of the World,* Volumes 1–10 (1992), by Josep del Hoyo, Andrew Elliott, and Jordi Sargatal; and from species accounts in *The Birds of North America* (1992–2006) edited by Alan Poole and Frank Gill, *A Guide to the Birds of Costa Rica* (1989) by Gary Stiles and Alexander Skutch, and *The Birds of*

Costa Rica (2007) by Richard Garrigues and Robert Dean. All literature used is included in the bibliography following the bird species accounts.

Volume II includes species accounts for more than 100 species of mammals, amphibians, reptiles, butterflies, moths, and other selected invertebrates. Volume III includes 116 accounts of mammals, amphibians, and reptiles. More than 100 new species accounts have been added in these volumes, beyond the coverage provided in *Field Guide to the Wildlife of Costa Rica.* Even with more than 200 species in Volumes II and III, it should be understood that this is only a sampler of the wonderful diversity of Costa Rica's wildlife. The species chosen are among the most conspicuous and interesting to tourists based on my experience in leading tours in Costa Rica since 1987. Some of these are the larger, more colorful species like morpho butterflies, some are memorable mammals like monkeys and sloths, and some are intriguing species like silkmoths, army ants, and poison dart frogs that have fascinating life histories.

Photography

Photos by the author have been used to illustrate all bird accounts in Volume I and, except where otherwise indicated, in Volumes II and III. These photos represent the best available from a personal collection of more than 60,000 Costa Rican and Latin American nature and wildlife images. Over 91 percent of the bird images were photographed in the wild, primarily in Costa Rica. Some have been photographed in the wild in other countries of Latin America, but they are the same species or subspecies that occur in Costa Rica. Other photos were taken in captive settings either in Latin America or in the United States. Some photos have been enhanced through the use of Adobe Photoshop to highlight identification marks and remove distracting background features.

It is felt that the postures, behavior, and natural colors provided by these photos provide the best reference for nature enthusiasts, because paintings usually fail to capture the stunning iridescence of many tropical birds and butterflies. Also, paintings frequently fail to convey correct color, proportions, and postures of the creatures involved because they are often painted from dead or faded museum specimens.

All photos taken since 2005 were taken with a Canon 20D digital camera. Before 2005, Pentax 35-millimeter cameras (K-1000, SF-10, SF-1N, and PZ-1) were used. Lenses included a Tamron 200–500 mm telephoto lens, Pentax 100–300 mm telephoto lens, and Sigma 400 mm APO telephoto lens (sometimes with a 1.4\X Sigma teleconverter). Most close-up photos of hummingbirds were taken with a Pentax PZ-1, Tamron 90 mm macro lens, and a 1.7\X Pentax teleconverter. Flash units included a Canon 580EX Speedlite, Pentax AF400FTZ for telephoto flash (used with a Lepp Project-A-Flash), and Pentax AF240FT for macro photography. Fuji 100 Sensia I and Sensia II film was used for the 35 mm slides, and digital photos have been used since 2005.

BIBLIOGRAPHY

Acuña, Vilma Obando. 2002. *Biodiversidad en Costa Rica*. San José, Costa Rica: Editorial INBIO. 81 pp.

Beletsky, Les. 1998. *Costa Rica: The Ecotravellers' Wildlife Guide*. San Diego, Calif.: Academic Press. 426 pp.

Boza, Mario A. 1987. *Costa Rica National Parks*. San José, Costa Rica: Fundación Neotrópica. 112 pp.

———. 1988. *Costa Rica National Parks*. San José, Costa Rica: Fundación Neotrópica. 272 pp.

Cahn, Robert. 1984. An Interview with Alvaro Ugalde. *The Nature Conservancy News* 34(1): 8–15.

Carr, Archie, and David Carr. 1983. A Tiny Country Does Things Right. *International Wildlife* 13(5): 18–25.

Chalker, Mary W. 2007. *Exploring Costa Rica 2008/9*. San José, Costa Rica: The Tico Times. 464 pp.

Cornelius, Stephen E. 1986. *The Sea Turtles of Santa Rosa National Park*. San José, Costa Rica: Fundación de Parques Nacionales. 64 pp.

Ehrenfeld, David. 1989. Places. *Orion Nature Quarterly* 8(3): 5–7.

Franke, Joseph. 1997. *Costa Rica's National Parks and Preserves: A Visitor's Guide*. Seattle: The Mountaineers. 223 pp.

Gómez, Luis Diego, and Jay M. Savage. 1983. Searchers on That Rich Coast: Costa Rican Field Biology, 1400–1980. In *Costa Rican Natural History*, ed. Daniel H. Janzen, 1–11. Chicago: Univ. of Chicago Press. 816 pp.

Henderson, Carrol L. 1969. Fish and Wildlife Resources of Costa Rica, with Notes on Human Influences. Master's thesis, Univ. of Georgia, Athens. 340 pp.

Holdridge, Leslie R. 1967. *Life Zone Ecology*. San José, Costa Rica: Tropical Science Center. 206 pp.

INICEM. 1998. Costa Rica: Datos e Indicadores Básicos. Costa Rica at a Glance. Miami: INICEM Group. Booklet. 42 pp.

Janzen, Daniel H. 1990. Costa Rica's New National System of Conserved Wildlands. Mimeographed report. 15 pp.

———. 1991. How to Save Tropical Biodiversity: The National Biodiversity Institute of Costa Rica. *American Entomologist* 36(3): 159–171.

Kohl, Jon. 1993. No Reserve Is an Island. *Wildlife Conservation* 96(5): 74–75.

Lewin, Roger. 1988. Costa Rican Biodiversity. *Science* 242: 1637.

Lewis, Thomas A. 1989. Daniel Janzen's Dry

Idea. *International Wildlife* 19(1): 30–36.

Market Data. 1993. Costa Rica: Datos e Indicadores Básicos. Costa Rica at a Glance. San José, Costa Rica. 36 pp.

McPhaul, John. 1988. Peace, Nature: C. R. Aims. *The Tico Times* 32(950): 1, 21.

Meza Ocampo, Tobías A. 1988. *Areas Silvestres de Costa Rica*. San Pedro, Costa Rica: Alma Mater. 112 pp.

Murillo, Katiana. 1999. Ten Years Committed to Biodiversity. *Friends in Costa Rica* 3: 23–25.

Pariser, Harry S. 1998. *Adventure Guide to Costa Rica*. 3rd ed. Edison, N.J.: Hunter. 546 pp.

Pistorius, Robin, and Jeroen van Wijk. 1993. Biodiversity Prospecting: Commercializing Genetic Resources for Export. *Biotechnology and Development Monitor* 15: 12–15.

Pratt, Christine. 1999. Tourism Pioneer Wins Award, Hosts Concorde. *The Tico Times* 43(1507): 4.

Rich, Pat V., and T. H. Rich. 1983. The Central American Dispersal Route: Biotic History and Paleogeography. In *Costa Rican Natural History*, ed. Daniel H. Janzen, 12–34. Chicago: Univ. of Chicago Press. 816 pp.

Sandlund, Odd Terje. 1991. Costa Rica's INBIO: Towards Sustainable Use of Natural

Biodiversity. Norsk Institutt for Naturforskning. Notat 007. Trondheim, Norway. Report. 25 pp.

Sekerak, Aaron D. 1996. *A Travel and Site Guide to Birds of Costa Rica*. Edmonton, Alberta: Lone Pine. 256 pp.

Skutch, Alexander F. 1971. *A Naturalist in Costa Rica*. Gainesville: University of Florida Press. 378 pp.

———. 1984. Your Birds in Costa Rica. Santa Monica, Calif.: Ibis. Brochure. 8 pp.

Sun, Marjorie. 1988. Costa Rica's Campaign for Conservation. *Science* 239: 1366–1369.

Tangley, Laura. 1990. Cataloging Costa Rica's Diversity. *BioScience* 40(9): 633–636.

Ugalde, Alvaro F., and María Luisa Alfaro. 1992. Financiamiento de la Conservación en los Parques Nacionales y Reservas Biológicas de Costa Rica. Speech presented at the IV Congreso Mundial de Parques Nacionales, Caracas, Venezuela, February. Mimeographed copy. 16 pp.

Zúñiga Vega, Alejandra. 1991. Archivo de riqueza natural. La Nación, Section B, Viva, February 4.

———. 1991. Estudios de los manglares. La Nación, Section B, Viva, February 4.

BIRD SPECIES ACCOUNTS

Among the memorable experiences of exploring Costa Rica are encounters with birds that possess a kaleidoscope of stunning colors and a repertoire of the most beautiful, and sometimes bizarre, natural sounds and behaviors in the world. This small country, only one-fourth the size of Minnesota, has 882 species of birds! In comparison, about 850 species of birds are known for all of North America north of Mexico. Costa Rica's diversity includes 78 different bird families. For most visitors, many of these bird families are new and provide colorful lasting memories—trogons, motmots, macaws, potoos, toucans, jacamars, woodcreepers, antbirds, becards, cotingas, and manakins.

Some people enjoy making a list of the birds they see, or they enjoy photographing, recording, or sketching wildlife. It is easy to be overwhelmed by the abundance of birds. Newcomers should remember to take time to enjoy the birds and absorb the essence of the tropical forests. One of the best observation techniques is to hire a naturalist guide. Bring your binoculars. It is also productive to sit or stand for extended periods at places that attract wildlife—near a pool or drinking site, a fruiting or flowering tree, or bird feeders—and let the wildlife come to you.

Many people place too much emphasis on trying to see the birds. Listen to the forest. Many birds can be identified by listening for their songs and subsequently locating the birds. You can prepare for a trip to Costa Rica by purchasing one or both of the following CDs before you go: *A Sampler of Costa Rican Bird Songs* (184 species from all regions of Costa Rica) and *Voices of Costa Rican Birds: Caribbean Slope* (220 species from middle and lowland elevations of eastern Costa Rica) by David Ross. These are available from Buteo Books at www.buteobooks.com. There is also a new software program called Costa Rica BirdJam for the Apple iPod that formats and organizes the bird songs of the two-CD set *Voices of Costa Rican Birds: Caribbean Slope*. The current version (about $20) is for Windows users and a Mac version will be available soon. For further information, contact www.birdjam.com (1-800-403-5524).

The species accounts included here represent about 35 percent of the country's birdlife, but they are based on about 78 percent of all the bird sightings recorded on twenty-three birding trips to Costa Rica between 1987 and 2008. It should be understood that this book is not a typical identification field guide that includes all of the country's birds. This is a reference guide that includes more life history and ecological information than is typically included in a field guide. It is a book to read and study before a trip to Costa Rica. It is a book to enjoy after a day afield in Costa Rica, and it is a book to help preserve and relish your Costa Rican memories once you have returned home.

Most field guides use drawings or

paintings to illustrate the birds. This book uses color photos that primarily represent wild birds photographed in the field in Costa Rica. The bird postures and plumages shown, and the supplemental photos of nests, behavior, and immature plumages, are intended to provide accurate portrayals of the birdlife that are not possible with paintings of museum specimens. Instead of broad generic distribution maps, this book identifies specific locations where birds have been seen on our birding tours in order to improve the reader's chances of encountering birds with very limited habitats. The species accounts include many of the most common, conspicuous species and some of the more unusual and unique species that birders are keenly interested in. Although some Neotropical migrants are included, there is a bias toward selection of species that are permanent residents. Reproductive details are included for species that exhibit polyandry, lek behavior, fledgling care by young from previous broods, or use of unusual nesting sites. For general reproductive details, the reader is referred to Stiles and Skutch (1989).

Included in the following accounts are references to the total number of sightings recorded on twenty-five Henderson birding trips. A sighting includes one or more individuals of a species encountered on a walk, drive, or outing on trips that typically involve three outings per day. Based on these data, the dozen most commonly sighted birds in Costa Rica are listed in Table 1. You can benefit from reviewing the identification features of these common birds before making your first visit to the country. All of these birds are included in the species accounts.

Table 1. The twelve birds most commonly sighted in Costa Rica during January and February 1987–2008.

1. Turkey Vulture	8. Great-tailed Grackle
2. Black Vulture	9. Baltimore Oriole
3. Tropical Kingbird	10. Rufous-tailed
4. Cattle Egret	Hummingbird
5. Blue-gray Tanager	11. Rufous-collared
6. Clay-colored Thrush	Sparrow
7. Great Kiskadee	12. Chestnut-sided Warbler

For other birds, their apparent abundance could be grouped by the cumulative number of sightings as follows: 1 to 20 sightings = uncommon; 21 to 100 sightings = common; 101 to 200 sightings = abundant; and 201 to 384 sightings = very abundant. The Turkey Vulture was sighted more than any other bird during our twenty-three trips: 384 times.

GREAT TINAMOU

The well-camouflaged Great Tinamou is one of the most characteristic but seldom seen birds of the rainforest. Its presence is regularly detected, however, by its beautiful, flutelike call—three paired tremulous notes—most often heard at sunset. Dr. Alexander Skutch, Costa Rica's premier ornithologist, wrote of the tinamou's song: "All the beauty of the tropical forest, all its mystery . . . find expression in these exquisite notes." Tinamous, closely related to rheas and ostriches, are represented by five species in Costa Rica: Great, Highland, Little, Slaty-breasted, and Thicket. Tinamous evolved from a primitive family that dates back 10 million years. They even have unique reptilian qualities, including similar blood proteins.

Great Tinamou adult

Tinamus major

Costa Rican names: *Gongolona; tinamú grande; gallina de monte; perdiz.*

18/23 trips; 71 sightings.

Status: Permanent resident.

Length: 15.7–18.0 inches.

Weight: 1 pound 8 ounces–2 pounds 11 ounces (700–1,142 grams).

Range: Southern Mexico to central Brazil.

Elevational range: Sea level to 5,600 feet.

The Great Tinamou, about the size of a chicken, lives a solitary life on the forest floor. Individuals move slowly through the undergrowth, eating fruits, seeds, frogs, small lizards, spiders, worms, and other insects. A Great Tinamou may accompany army ants to catch insects flushed by the ants.

When mating season arrives in December, the female lays three to five bright blue eggs with a glossy porcelain-like finish in a shallow depression on the ground—usually by the base of a tree or log. The male incubates the eggs for nineteen to twenty days and cares for the young for another twenty days before seeking out another female so it can mate again and renest. Meanwhile, the female has sought out other males, and they raise families as well. A female may keep as many as four males busy raising chicks during the nesting season, which extends to August. This reproductive behavior is called polyandry.

On the Caribbean slope, Great Tinamous may be heard at Tortuguero NP, La Selva, Rara Avis, Sueño Azul, and Rancho Naturalista. Listen for them early in the morning and late in the afternoon. On the Pacific slope they occur at Carara NP, Wilson Botanical Garden, Corcovado NP, Las Esquinas, La Cusinga, and Tiskita. The best place to see Great Tinamous in Costa Rica is at La Selva, where they can be observed at close range along trails in the Arboretum, along Sendero Tres Ríos, on the river trail to the successional plots, and also at La Cusinga Lodge and Carara NP.

Great Tinamou nest and eggs

Little Tinamou adult

LITTLE TINAMOU

The Little Tinamou is the most common tinamou in Costa Rica, but it is seldom seen because it inhabits the ground cover of heavy second-growth thickets near forest openings and plantation edges. The distinctive call of the Little Tinamou is, however, one of the more distinctive and memorable tropical sounds—an ethereal series of up to about eight tremulous whistled ascending notes that are most often heard at sunset. Dr. Alexander Skutch wrote of its call: "The Little Tinamou . . . notes are so full, so pure, so charged with feeling that as music they often seem to rank higher than the more complex performances of all but a few of the most gifted of the true songbirds. . . . To rest amid tangled growth while daylight fades, hearing the tinamous' sweet sweet voices sound back and forth from the lush verdure, is a deeply moving experience."

Crypturellus soui
Costa Rican name: *Tinamú chico.*
19/23 trips; 60 sightings.
Status: Permanent resident.
Length: 9 inches.
Weight: 8.8 ounces (250 grams).
Range: Southern Mexico to southeastern Brazil.
Elevational range: Sea level to 5,000 feet.

This tinamou occurs in wet to moist lowlands up to middle elevations in the Caribbean and southern Pacific lowlands and in the southern portions of the Nicoya Peninsula. A small grayish bird about the size of a dove, it can be distinguished from other tinamous by its yellowish legs. It typically walks among thick tangled vegetation in search of grasshoppers, ants, termites, caterpillars, seeds, tubers, and berries.

Like other tinamous, the Little Tinamou has a reproductive strategy called polyandry. Nesting throughout the year, the female lays two glossy lavender to wine-colored eggs on the ground under a bush or at the base of a tree. The male incubates the eggs for nineteen days and continues to care for the young after they hatch.

On the Caribbean slope, the Little Tinamou may be heard, and sometimes seen, at Selva Verde Lodge, Rancho Naturalista, Caño Negro Lodge and NWR, and in the Cahuita vicinity. On the Pacific slope it can be encountered at Manuel Antonia NP, Tiskita, Wilson Botanical Garden, Rancho Casa Grande, Cristal Ballena, Oro Verde BR, and La Ensenada Lodge.

THICKET TINAMOU

The Thicket Tinamou, one of five tinamous in Costa Rica, is found in the dry forests and gallery forests of Guanacaste east to Rincón de la Vieja NP. This large tinamou is more distinctively marked than the country's other tinamous. Its body is ruddy brown, which gives rise to its former common name "Rufescent Tinamou." The wings are heavily barred with white. This barring is absent on the other tinamous.

Thicket Tinamou adult

The call of this tinamou is a ventriloquial monotone whistle described as "hoooo." Most tinamous are associated with rainforest habitats, but this tinamou lives on the ground amid the thick, thorny, shrubby undergrowth of Guanacaste's dry forests. In the dry season it is more frequently encountered in the gallery forests along rivers and marshes. A quiet observer may be able to hear one or more of these birds walking and scratching among the leaf litter like little chickens as they look for fallen fruits, seeds, butterflies, moths, beetles, termites, and ants.

Like other tinamous, the male incubates two to seven glossy, porcelain-like eggs in a shallow scrape on the ground, which usually abuts the base of a tree. The eggs may be laid by more than one female and range in color from bronzy purple to purplish pink. The precocious chicks hatch after sixteen days and are cared for by the male for about twenty days, after which they are able to survive on their own.

Look and listen for this tinamou in protected forest areas in Guanacaste, such as the preserves of Santa Rosa, Palo Verde, Rincón de la Vieja, and Lomas Barbudal.

Crypturellus cinnamomeus
Costa Rican name: *Tinamú canelo.*
2/23 trips; 2 sightings.
Status: Permanent resident.
Length: 9.8–11.8 inches.
Weight: 15 ounces–1 pound 1 ounce (440–480 grams).
Range: Northeastern Mexico to northwestern Costa Rica.
Elevational range: Sea level to 3,300 feet.

BLACK-BELLIED WHISTLING-DUCK

Dendrocygna autumnalis
Costa Rican names: *Piche; pijije común.*
18/23 trips; 37 sightings.
Status: Permanent resident and northern migrant.
Length: 16.9–20.9 inches.
Weight: 1 pound 6.9 ounces– 1 pound 15.9 ounces (650–1,020 grams).
Range: Southern Texas to northern Argentina.
Elevational range: Sea level to 4,000 feet.

The Black-bellied Whistling-Duck is the most abundant of three whistling-ducks in Costa Rica. Others are the Fulvous and White-faced Whistling-Ducks. These birds form an interesting genus different from other ducks: drakes and hens are identical, and the drakes help incubate the eggs and care for the young. This vocal duck is well known for its squealing call that sounds like "peechee" or "peechichichi," giving it the local name *piche*.

Like the Wood Duck in North America, this duck nests in tree cavities, so it adapts well to nest boxes. The Black-bellied Whistling-Duck feeds on sprouting rice in upland fields, grass, seeds of moist-soil plants like smartweed, insects, snails, and other invertebrates. Feeding takes place in daytime or at night.

Nesting occurs from May through October. A hen lays twelve to sixteen eggs in tree cavities, nest boxes, or on the ground. The drake and hen mate for life, and the male assists with incubation and brood rearing.

The wetlands at Palo Verde NP, Mata Redonda, La Ensenada Lodge, and Caño Negro NWR are good places to see this duck. Scan the flocks closely to see if any Fulvous or White-faced Whistling-Ducks are present. Other places where it can be observed are wetlands near La Pacífica, Sueño Azul, and Hacienda Solimar; Río Bebedero; small ponds throughout Guanacaste; the Río Frío region; and wetlands of Carara NP. A few are reported nesting near Cartago and in the Reventazón Valley in the Central Plateau.

Black-bellied Whistling-Duck pair

MUSCOVY DUCK

The Muscovy Duck is often perceived as a huge, tame farm duck across much of North and South America. In Costa Rica, it is possible to see and appreciate this duck as a wary, wild, fast-flying waterfowl species. It lives along wooded wetlands, streams, and swamps, and nests in large hollow trees. The male, more than twice as large as the female, has black plumage with green iridescent highlights and a fleshy face characterized by red and black warty caruncles. It can raise a prominent crest on top of its head when confronting other males. In flight, the shoulder areas on the upper surface of the wings show large white patches.

Muscovy Duck adult male

The best habitat for this duck is in the Guanacaste region along forested streams and rivers. It is also found in mangrove lagoons and wooded swamps. The Muscovy feeds on roots, seeds, leaves, and stems of aquatic plants like water lily and mangrove and on rice and corn. Animal foods include small fish, frogs, tadpoles, crabs, small lizards, spiders, termites, and crayfish.

The best places to observe the Muscovy Duck include marshes at Palo Verde NP, Caño Negro NWR, and Estero Madrigal at Hacienda Solimar. It can also be seen along the Río Tárcoles, in Carara NP, and rarely at Tortuguero NP.

Cairina moschata
Costa Rican names: *Pato real; pato perulero.*
8/23 trips; 14 sightings.
Status: Permanent resident.
Length: 26.0–33.1 inches.
Weight: 2 pounds 6.8 ounces– 8 pounds 13.0 ounces (1,100– 4,000 grams).
Range: Southern Texas to northern Uruguay.
Elevational range: Sea level to 1,000 feet.

BLUE-WINGED TEAL

Anas discors
Costa Rican names: *Cerceta
aliazul; zarceta.*
13/23 trips; 22 sightings.
Status: Northern migrant.
Length: 13.8–16.1 inches.
Weight: 9.4–14.4 ounces (266–410
grams).
Range: Alaska to Peru.
Elevational range: Sea level to
4,000 feet.

The Blue-winged Teal is the most abundant duck in Costa Rica during the wintering season, from September through April. This small North American prairie wetland duck migrates farther than most other waterfowl and demonstrates how important it is for conservationists to preserve both summer and winter habitats for migratory birds. Wetland drainage for crop production has greatly reduced habitat for Blue-winged Teal in the prairie wetlands of the north and in tropical wetlands of the Guanacaste region. Identification marks include pale blue patches on the shoulders and white crescents on the blue-gray face of the drakes.

This duck eats seeds, roots, and leaves of aquatic and moist-soil grasses, sedges, algae, pondweed, duckweed, smartweed, and rice in paddies. Some insects and small crustaceans are also eaten.

Habitats for Blue-winged Teal include Río Tempisque basin marshes like those at Palo Verde NP, La Ensenada Lodge, Hacienda Solimar, and Caño Negro NWR. This duck may be encountered at Las Concavas Marsh near Cartago and in wetlands near the San Vito airport. Scan flocks of Blue-winged Teal closely to look for Cinnamon Teal in winter plumage.

Blue-winged Teal pair

GRAY-HEADED CHACHALACA

The chachalaca is an uncommon but noisy chicken-sized bird of lowland and middle-elevation forests in the Caribbean and Pacific regions of Costa Rica. There are two species in the country: the White-bellied Chachalaca (formerly Plain Chachalaca) in the dry forests of Guanacaste and the Gray-headed Chachalaca throughout the remaining wetter portions of the country. In Costa Rica, a person who talks too much is referred to as a *chachalaca*. The Gray-headed Chachalaca is less vocal than other chachalacas. Its calls include parrotlike squawks, squeaks, clucks, and peeping tones. The primary wing feathers are chestnut on this species but gray on the White-bellied Chachalaca.

Gray-headed Chachalaca adult

Ortalis cinereiceps
Costa Rican names: *Chachalaca cabecigrís; chacalaca.*
15/23 trips; 60 sightings.
Status: Permanent resident.
Length: 18.1–22.8 inches.
Weight: 1 pound 1.3 ounces–1 pound 3.0 ounces (490–540 grams).
Range: Eastern Honduras to northwestern Colombia.
Elevational range: Sea level to 3,600 feet.

The preferred habitat is along brushy edges of forests, plantations, and second-growth forests where there is an abundance of fruits like guava (*Psidium guajava*), pokeweed (*Phytolacca*), *Miconia,* and *Cecropia.* This bird lives in flocks of six to twelve individuals. They follow each other through the trees in search of fruit by hopping, flapping, and gliding in an unsynchronized follow-the-leader procession.

The chachalaca nests from January to July and is one of the only gallinaceous birds that feeds its precocial young for an extended period after hatching. It passes fruits to the chicks instead of allowing them to peck for their own food.

Because this bird has been heavily hunted, it is seldom seen. It may be found, however, in protected areas such as La Selva Biological Field Station, Carara NP, Los Cusingos, Rancho Casa Grande, La Cusinga Lodge, Lost Iguana Resort and Spa, and on the grounds of Talari Mountain Lodge. The best place to see Gray-headed Chachalacas at close range is at Rancho Naturalista, where they visit the feeders in the courtyard.

CRESTED GUAN

Crested Guan adult

Penelope purpurascens
Costa Rican names: *Pava crestada; pava.*
15/23 trips; 47 sightings.
Status: Permanent resident.
Length: 28.3–35.8 inches.
Weight: 3 pounds 9.1 ounces–5 pounds 5.6 ounces (1,620–2,430 grams).
Range: Southern Mexico to western Ecuador and northern Venezuela.
Elevational range: Sea level to 6,000 feet.

The Crested Guan is a large, brown, turkeylike bird most frequently seen peering down from the treetops as it searches for fruits and leaves that make up its diet. As its name implies, this bird has a feathered crest that is frequently raised as it relates to nearby guans or to potential danger. A conspicuous red dewlap hangs from the throat. The call is an extended series of loud, high-pitched toots that may continue at one pitch, increase to a higher tooting note, and then drop again.

A bird of primary and mixed lowland and middle-elevation habitats, the Crested Guan occurs in dry, moist, and wet forests of the Caribbean and Pacific slopes. Guans walk along high horizontal branches as single birds or in small groups of up to six individuals. They silently leap from one branch to another or flap and glide through the treetops. Where foliage conceals the birds, their presence is sometimes revealed by debris falling from the branches. Among fruits eaten are figs, berries, *Cecropia, Spondias, Guatteria,* and wild papayas. The Crested Guan eats the fruits of wild nutmeg (*Virola surinamensis*) and disperses the plant by later regurgitating the seeds.

The best place to look for the Crested Guan is in national parks and in forests where they are protected from hunting, such as Tortuguero, Braulio Carrillo, Palo Verde, Carara, and Corcovado NPs, and at La Selva, El Gavilán, Lost Iguana Resort and Spa, Sueño Azul, Hotel Borinquen Mountain Resort, Rancho Naturalista, Wilson Botanical Garden, Villa Caletas, and the Río Pavo Trail at the Sirena Biological Station in Corcovado NP.

BLACK GUAN

The Black Guan, a turkey-sized bird of the cloud forest and mountains, is endemic to the highlands of Costa Rica and western Panama. It is black with a blue face, red eyes, and red legs. Its habitat includes unbroken forest and disturbed forest with scattered openings and second growth. This bird may be seen moving through the forest canopy as individual birds, in pairs, or in small groups. When in flight, the narrow, sharp-pointed primary feathers make a loud crackling sound. Although usually silent, the Black Guan can make low, deep-toned groaning sounds, grunts, and piping calls. They can also make a loud rattling sound with their wings.

The seeds of many forest fruits are dispersed in the droppings of this guan, so the bird is important for the propagation of tropical trees. Among fruits eaten by the Black Guan are wild avocado (*Persea*), *Urera, Ardisia revoluta,* holly (*Ilex*), *Guarea, Beilschmiedia, Guettarda, Chamaedorea, Citharexylum,* and *Cecropia.*

This big black bird may be seen gliding from one tree to another or perched in the middle to upper canopy of montane forests and cloud forests, including those at the Monteverde Cloud Forest Reserve, Tapantí NP, Talamanca Mountains, San Gerardo de Dota Valley, and in Cerro de la Muerte along the Pan American Highway at kilometers 66, 80, 86, and 96. The best place to see the Black Guan is at Bosque de Paz, where it comes to the bird feeders in the courtyard.

Chamaepetes unicolor
Costa Rican name: *Pava negra.*
16/23 trips; 30 sightings.
Status: Permanent resident.
Length: 24.4–27.2 inches.
Weight: 2 pounds 8 ounces (1,135 grams).
Range: Endemic to highlands of Costa Rica and western Panama.
Elevational range: 3,000–8,200 feet.

Black Guan adult

Great Curassow adult male

Crax rubra

Costa Rican names: *Pavón grande;*
pavón; granadera.

12/23 trips; 18 sightings.

Status: Permanent resident.

Length: 30.7–36.2 inches.

Weight: 6 pounds 13.3 ounces–10
pounds 9.2 ounces (3,100–4,800
grams).

Range: Southern Mexico to
western Ecuador.

Elevational range: Sea level to
4,000 feet.

GREAT CURASSOW

Like the Jaguar and White-lipped Peccary, the Great
Curassow is an indicator of undisturbed tropical forests. It
is eagerly hunted by settlers as roads are built into primary
forests. Unlike chachalacas and guans, which spend most
of their time in treetops, the Great Curassow forages primarily on the ground. The turkeylike male is black, with
a prominent crest of curled feathers, a white belly, and a
conspicuous yellow, knobby cere. The chestnut-colored
hen has a black-and-white head and crest and a barred tail.
These birds are usually encountered as individuals, pairs,
or groups of up to six. The Great Curassow has an interesting repertoire of vocalizations that includes a high-pitched
"peet" that sounds like a small bird; a deep, resonant hum-
ming sound; a high-pitched descending whistle; and an
alarm call that sounds like the yipping of a little dog.

The Great Curassow forages like a turkey, searching
for seeds and fruits that have fallen to the ground, including *Spondias, Chione,* and *Casimira,* and some insects. It
occurs in protected, extensive dry forests of Guanacaste
and lowland and middle elevations of moist and wet primary forests of the Caribbean and southern Pacific slopes.
This bird can exist in secondary forests but generally
disappears in such areas because of overhunting. Curassow eggs are among the largest of all rainforest bird eggs,
almost 3.5 inches long. Curassow pairs are monogamous
and nest from March through May. The Great Curassow is
very long-lived. Individuals may live and reproduce to the
age of twenty-three years.

Tourists may occasionally see a Great Curassow along
the canals of Tortuguero NP, in La Selva, and at the woodland waterhole at Palo Verde NP. Other sites include Las
Esquinas Rainforest Lodge and Rincón de la Vieja NP (Los
Pailos Trail). The best location to encounter a Great Curassow is in Corcovado
NP at the Sirena
Biological Station.
They may also be seen
along the forest trail
leading from Corco-
vado Lodge Tent
Camp to Río Madrigal
in Corcovado NP.

Great Curassow egg with fang punctures
from large snake

Great Curassow adult female

BROWN BOOBY

The Brown Booby is the most common member of this family that can be seen offshore from Costa Rica's Caribbean and Pacific beaches. A goose-sized bird with a brown body, white belly, and large, pointed bill, it is often in the company of Brown Pelicans and Magnificent Frigatebirds.

This booby feeds singly or in small groups by plunge-diving for flying fishes, anchovies, and squids in coastal areas near shore. It can be seen perched on the riggings of offshore fishing boats and on small rocky islands where nesting occurs. This includes islets along the Pacific coast, especially south from Puntarenas to the Panama border. The largest colony is at Isla Cabo Blanco. On the Caribbean coast, the Brown Booby breeds on rocky islets near Isla Uvita near Limón. Although two eggs are laid, only one young typically survives. Incubation requires 43 days, the young spend 85 to 105 days at the nest, and postfledging care continues for another 190 days. The young mature at two to three years of age.

The Brown Booby may be sighted at sea from the beaches at Tortuguero NP, Limón, and in the Cahuita area. On the Pacific coast it can be seen offshore near Manuel Antonio NP, Punta Uvita, La Cusinga, and rocky islets along the western beaches of Corcovado NP, like the ones near Río Llorona and Sirena Biological Station, and in the vicinity of Caño Island BR.

Brown Booby adult

Sula leucogaster
Costa Rican names: *Piquero moreno; monjita.*
12/23 trips; 21 sightings.
Status: Permanent resident.
Length: 25.2–29.1 inches.
Weight: 1 pound 10 ounces–3 pounds 6 ounces (724–1,550 grams).
Range: Widespread in the world's oceans.
Elevational range: Sea level.

Brown Booby immature

PELICAN FAMILY *(Pelecanidae)*

BROWN PELICAN

Pelecanus occidentalis
Costa Rican names: *Pelícano pardo; buchón; pelicano; alcatraz.*
19/23 trips; 111 sightings.
Status: Permanent resident.
Length: 41.3–59.8 inches.
Weight: 6 pounds 10 ounces–7 pounds 11 ounces (3,008–3,490 grams).
Range: Pacific coast from Washington to Peru, and the Caribbean coast from Florida to Venezuela.
Elevational range: Sea level.

The Brown Pelican is the largest waterbird in Costa Rica. The adult is dark grayish brown with whitish highlights over the back. The head and neck are white. Immature birds are brownish. Pelicans fly with grace and elegance as they skim the wave tips in follow-the-leader formations. Also impressive when diving for fish, a pelican will fly no more than ten to thirty feet above the water, bank sharply, and plunge downward. As it strikes the water, the wings fold backward to decrease water resistance as the bird thrusts its open bill over a fish. Pelicans may live up to thirty-one years.

On the Caribbean coast, Brown Pelicans are regularly seen in the vicinity of Cahuita NP, Limón, and along the coast at Tortuguero NP. There are at least four breeding colonies of Brown Pelicans on islands along the Pacific coast, including the largest on Isla Guayabo. Along the Pacific coast, they can be seen from nearly any beach.

Brown Pelican adult

Brown Pelican in flight

NEOTROPIC CORMORANT *(Olivaceous Cormorant)*

The Neotropic Cormorant is a black fish-eating waterbird closely related to pelicans. The only cormorant in Costa Rica, it is the size of a large duck and is often seen sitting on trees, posts, or rocks with the wings outspread in a choir-director pose. In sunlight, the black plumage shows bluish-purple highlights. The long, pointed bill has a downturned hook at the tip, and the legs are positioned far back on the body to provide greater propulsion when pursuing fish. Cormorants are found in coastal saltwater areas, freshwater marshes, rivers, and brackish ponds. Their presence lends a prehistoric touch to wetlands, because fossil evidence for cormorants dates back about 30 million years. Although this bird is generally seen in Costa Rica's lower elevations, it occurs at elevations over 15,000 feet on Andean lakes of South America.

Neotropic Cormorant adult

Phalacrocorax brasilianus (formerly Phalacrocorax olivaceus)

Costa Rican names: *Cormorán neotropical; pato chancho; pato de agua.*

21/23 trips; 83 sightings.

Status: Permanent resident.

Length: 22.8–28.7 inches.

Weight: 4.0 pounds (1,814 grams).

Range: Southwestern United States to southern South America.

Elevational range: Sea level to 2,000 feet.

Cormorants usually fish individually but sometimes form a line and flail the water with their wings to drive fish into shallow water. Then they dive to catch the fish that are, usually, three to four inches long. Cormorants also eat frogs, crustaceans, tadpoles, shrimp, and aquatic insects. They can plunge-dive like Brown Pelicans. While swimming, cormorants sit low in the water with a slightly upturned bill and a posture similar to that of an Anhinga. When perched, both species sit in an upright posture. The neck of a cormorant, however, is shorter and thicker than the snakelike neck of the Anhinga, and the body of the Anhinga is more slender.

In Caribbean lowlands, cormorants may be seen along the beaches and canals of Tortuguero NP and south to Cahuita NP. Cormorants may also be seen along the Río Sarapiquí near La Selva and along the Río Frío. On the Pacific coast, they occur along beaches from the Nicaragua border south to Panama. They also inhabit freshwater marshes of the Guanacaste region like those at Palo Verde NP and Caño Negro NWR.

ANHINGA FAMILY *(Anhingidae)*

ANHINGA

Anhinga anhinga
Costa Rican names: *Pato aguja;*
  aninga.
20/23 trips; 89 sightings.
Status: Permanent resident.
Length: 31.9–35.8 inches.
Weight: 3.0 pounds (1,350 grams).
Range: Florida to northern
  Argentina.
Elevational range: Sea level to
  2,000 feet.

The Anhinga has a snakelike head and neck that make it distinctive among Costa Rican waterbirds. The appearance and posture of this species resemble those of the Neotropic Cormorant, but the cormorant has a shorter and thicker neck. The tip of the bill is hooked on the cormorant and pointed on the Anhinga. The feathers of the Anhinga become waterlogged very quickly. This helps them assume a very low profile when swimming. When only the head and neck are exposed, an Anhinga looks like a snake moving through the water.

This bird inhabits shallow fresh and brackish water of lowland rivers, ponds, marshes, and mangrove lagoons. An Anhinga hunts underwater for small fish among submerged vegetation, paddling slowly with its feet and holding the wings slightly outspread for stability. Modified neck vertebrae allow the neck to be cocked back in an S-shaped profile, enabling the Anhinga to thrust its bill forward to spear its quarry. After swimming, an Anhinga dries its feathers by perching in an upright posture with the wings outspread like a cormorant. Anhingas may also be seen soaring high overhead among vultures and Wood Storks and are distinguished by the long neck extended forward and a widespread fan-shaped tail.

The Anhinga is fairly common in Caribbean lowlands, including canals of Tortuguero NP, in rivers and ponds south to Cahuita NP, and near La Selva, Muelle, Los Chiles, Lake Arenal, and Caño Negro NWR. In the Pacific lowlands, this waterbird is regularly encountered in Palo Verde NP, La Ensenada Lodge, Río Tárcoles, and Carara NP.

Anhinga adult

Anhinga flight profile

MAGNIFICENT FRIGATEBIRD

The Magnificent Frigatebird is aerodynamically stunning. Considering that a frigatebird weighs only as much as a mallard duck, the amount of lift provided by the four-foot-long angular wings demonstrates its perfect flight adaptations for life at sea. The bones are so light that they represent only 5 percent of the bird's body weight and weigh less than the bird's feathers. This low percentage of bone weight is unequaled by any other bird. The deeply forked tail provides great agility in flight. This is the only frigatebird regularly seen along Costa Rican beaches of the Caribbean and the Pacific. This bird has a purplish sheen on its black plumage.

Frigatebirds fly low over the water and dip their head to grasp flying fish, squid, jellyfish, hatchling sea turtles, crabs, and small fish. On land, they prey on the eggs and nestlings of birds, including other frigatebirds. Frigatebirds are well known for aerial piracy. They harass terns, gulls, boobies, and tropicbirds and force them to drop or regurgitate any fish they may be carrying. When the fish falls, the frigatebird acrobatically catches the fish in its bill.

Magnificent Frigatebird adult male displaying

Fregata magnificens
Costa Rican names: *Rabihorcado magno; tijereta del mar; zopilote de mar.*
20/23 trips; 101 sightings.
Status: Permanent resident.
Length: 35.0–44.9 inches.
Weight: 2 pounds 6 ounces–3 pounds 8 ounces (1,100–1,587 grams).
Range: Coastal areas from southern California and Florida to Peru and northern Argentina.
Elevational range: Sea level to 4,000 feet.

Frigatebirds have impressive courtship displays. While sitting on top of a bush in the colony, a male inflates its huge red throat pouch, spreads its wings, points its bill to the sky, and waits for a female to fly overhead. When one is sighted, the male drums its bill against its throat pouch, quivers its wings, and gives a loud "winnowing" sound. Frigatebirds nest only on a few islands along the Pacific coast. The reproductive cycle is longer than for any other seabird. Parental care continues for four and a half to seven months in the nest and for nine to twelve months after the chick leaves the nest.

Frigatebirds may be observed along the beaches of Tortuguero and Cahuita NPs on the Caribbean coast and along the entire Pacific coast. They may even be seen flying overland at sites like La Selva, Poás Volcano NP, and the Wilson Botanical Garden at San Vito as they cross between the Caribbean and the Pacific.

Magnificent Frigatebird in flight

Bare-throated Tiger-Heron adult

Tigrisoma mexicanum
Costa Rican names: *Garza-tigre cuellinuda; martín peña; pájaro vaco.*
19/23 trips; 107 sightings.
Status: Permanent resident.
Length: 28.0–31.9 inches.
Weight: 2 pounds 10 ounces (1,200 grams).
Range: Northern Mexico to Colombia.
Elevational range: Sea level to 3,600 feet.

BARE-THROATED TIGER-HERON

The Bare-throated Tiger-Heron is a large, elegantly marked heron of Caribbean and Pacific marshes, lakes, streams, and mangrove lagoons. This heron often stands in a bitternlike posture along the water's edge and is distinguished by fine gray vermiculations that give a herringbone appearance to its plumage. This is the most common of three tiger-herons in Costa Rica. Others are the Fasciated and Rufescent Tiger-Herons.

A resident of fresh and brackish water habitats, this tiger-heron is usually found in quiet waters of lowland and middle-elevation wetlands. In contrast, the Fasciated Tiger-Heron is typically found amid rocky, fast-flowing streams of the Caribbean lowlands and foothills.

Prey includes small fish, frogs, and crayfish. Feeding occurs primarily in early morning, late evening, and at night. Tiger-herons stand quietly in shallow water and wait for prey to move within striking range of their sharp beak. They may also stalk slowly along wetland edges in search of food. Although usually silent, tiger-herons may squawk loudly when flushed, and the males are known for a loud, booming roar at dusk or at night during the breeding season.

Look for this heron along the canals of Tortuguero NP, Sueño Azul, and Caño Negro NWR on the Caribbean slope. In Pacific lowlands, it may be encountered in wetlands throughout Guanacaste, including those at Palo Verde NP, Hacienda Solimar, La Ensenada Lodge, Caño Negro NWR, and Carara NP, in wetlands near Quepos, Manuel Antonio NP, and in lowland rivers of Corcovado NP. A pair has traditionally nested in the tree overhanging Hotel Villa Lapas near Carara NP.

Bare-throated Tiger-Heron immature

Bare-throated Tiger-Heron in flight

Fasciated Tiger-Heron immature

GREAT BLUE HERON

The Great Blue Heron is the largest of Costa Rica's herons and egrets, standing over three feet high. The bluish-gray plumage could be mistaken for an adult Little Blue Heron or a Tricolored Heron, but there is no white on the head of the smaller Little Blue Heron. The bills of the Little Blue and Tricolored Herons are grayish with a black tip. The bill of the Great Blue Heron is yellowish, and the head is white with a black stripe behind the eyes extending into black plumes.

Great Blue Herons are present from October through April at ponds, canals, and estuaries along the Caribbean coast from Tortuguero NP to Cahuita NP. On the Pacific slope they are found stalking shallow water for fish, small vertebrates, and aquatic invertebrates in wetlands throughout Guanacaste, along the entire Pacific coast, and inland from San Isidro up to premontane levels in lagoons near San Vito. They can also be found at inland streams and lakes on the slopes of the volcanoes surrounding the Central Plateau.

Ardea herodias
Costa Rican name: *Garzón azulado.*
23/23 trips; 103 sightings.
Status: Northern migrant.
Length: 38.2–53.9 inches.
Weight: 4 pounds 10 ounces–5 pounds 8 ounces (2,100–2,500 grams).
Range: Breeds from southeast Alaska to Belize, Guatemala, and the Galápagos Islands; winters from Belize and Guatemala, south to coastal areas of Venezuela, Colombia, and Ecuador.
Elevational range: Sea level to 3,900 feet.

Great Blue Heron adult

GREAT EGRET

Ardea alba (formerly Casmerodius albus)

Costa Rican name: *Garceta grande.*

23/23 trips; 173 sightings.

Status: Neotropical migrant and breeding resident.

Length: 31.5–40.9 inches.

Weight: 1 pound 9 ounces–3 pounds 5 ounces (700–1,500 grams).

Range: Southern Canada to southern Chile. Northern migrants winter in Costa Rica.

Elevational range: Sea level to 5,000 feet.

The Great Egret is the largest of four white wading birds in Costa Rica. The others are the Snowy Egret, Cattle Egret, and immature Little Blue Heron. This egret stands nearly three feet tall; the others are smaller, two feet tall or less. Identification marks include a yellow bill and black feet.

A few Great Egrets nest in Guanacaste Province, but most are wintering migrants from October through April. Great Egrets can be seen hunting for small fish and frogs along the canals and wetlands from Caño Negro NWR southeast to Tortuguero NP and in estuaries and ponds south to Cahuita. This egret is common along the entire Pacific coast, throughout Guanacaste, and in lower and middle-elevation wetlands from San Isidro to San Vito up to flooded pastures at 4,400 feet elevation at Kiri Lodge near the Tapantí NP.

Great Egret

SNOWY EGRET

The Snowy Egret is a stately white wading bird with elegant plumes at the back of the head, on the chest, and over the back. It has a black bill with contrasting yellow face and yellow eyes. The black legs have contrasting yellow feet that give it the nickname "golden slippers." The Great Egret is also white, but stands almost three feet tall; the Snowy Egret is only about two feet tall. The Great Egret has black feet and a yellow bill.

Snowy Egret showing yellow foot

The Snowy Egret is a bird of fresh- and saltwater habitats, including ponds, marshes, mangrove lagoons, estuaries, and coastal beaches. Feeding typically occurs in shallow water in the company of other wading birds. The Snowy Egret uses more feeding strategies than any other heron or egret: It actively moves around to stir up the bottom with its yellow feet to find small fish, shrimp, frogs, and crayfish. It may capture prey during low flights over water. Flocks may also follow livestock to capture insects in a manner similar to that used by Cattle Egrets, so don't assume that all egrets feeding near cattle are Cattle Egrets. Some Snowy Egrets nest in Costa Rica, but most are wintering migrants present from October through March.

This egret is common in Caribbean lowlands from Caño Negro NWR southeast to Tortuguero NP and in estuaries and wetlands south to Cahuita NP. The Snowy Egret is common in the Guanacaste region and along the entire Pacific coast. It is also found inland to San Isidro, along the Río Térraba, San Vito, and in the Central Plateau in the vicinity of the Cachí Reservoir.

Egretta thula
Costa Rican name: *Garceta nivosa.*
21/23 trips; 124 sightings.
Status: A few permanent residents; mostly northern migrants.
Length: 18.7–26.8 inches.
Weight: 13.8 ounces (370 grams).
Range: Northern United States to northern Argentina.
Elevational range: Sea level to 3,900 feet.

Little Blue Heron immature

Egretta caerulea
Costa Rican name: *Garceta azul.*
22/23 trips; 190 sightings.
Status: A few permanent residents; mostly northern migrants.
Length: 20.0–29.9 inches.
Weight: 12.3–12.8 ounces (296–364 grams).
Range: Massachusetts to southern Brazil.
Elevational range: Sea level to 5,000 feet.

LITTLE BLUE HERON

The Little Blue Heron, a common migrant from September through April, offers a challenge in identification. It resembles other herons, and the adults and immatures have different plumages. Adults have slate-blue plumage and a maroon-colored neck. The bill is bluish gray with a black tip. Immature birds are white with bluish-gray, black-tipped bills and often have grayish blotches on the tips of the white scapular feathers over the back. These feathers, as well as the bill color, help distinguish them from other white wading birds such as Snowy Egrets, Great Egrets, and Cattle Egrets. Also, this heron sometimes flies with the neck extended forward, but other herons usually fly with the neck recurved onto their shoulders. The Great Blue Heron, a migrant from North America, can be distinguished from the Little Blue Heron by its height (about three feet) and yellowish bill. The Great Blue Heron also has a white head with a black stripe behind the eyes that extends to plumes behind the head.

The Little Blue Heron is diurnal and feeds by stalking slowly in shallow water or along marshy edges. It may feed singly, in small groups, or in the company of White Ibises. Common food items include small fish, crayfish, crabs, shrimp, frogs, tadpoles, grasshoppers, beetles, and crickets. A few Little Blue Herons nest in Costa Rica from June through September.

This heron may be encountered in the Caribbean lowlands along the canals of Caño Negro NWR, Tortuguero and Cahuita NPs, wetlands near Guapiles and La Selva, and in estuaries along the highway from Limón to Cahuita. The Little Blue Heron can be seen in wetlands, estuaries, and mangrove lagoons in Guanacaste and along the entire length of the Pacific coast.

Little Blue Heron adult

TRICOLORED HERON

The elegantly marked Tricolored Heron is not as common as the Cattle Egret, Little Blue Heron, or Green Heron. It is, however, regularly encountered in lowland wetlands, mangrove lagoons, and estuaries and along beaches of both the Caribbean and Pacific coasts. Although similar to the Little Blue Heron, this heron has a white and chestnut stripe down the front of the neck, and the neck is longer and more slender than that of the Little Blue. The belly is white, in contrast to the uniform bluish-gray belly of the Little Blue.

A diurnal heron, this species feeds alone or in small groups with other wading birds. The Tricolored Heron may stalk slowly in shallow water for small fish, but it also uses other fascinating hunting techniques. It may run, hop, crouch, and spear its quarry, spread its wings to shade the water, and hold its head under a wing to attract and spot prey, or rake the bottom with its feet to flush aquatic prey. In addition to small fish, it eats frogs, grasshoppers, lizards, crayfish, dragonflies, and beetles.

Although a few of these herons nest at Isla Pajaros in the Río Tempisque basin, most are wintering migrants present from October through April.

Among the best places to see the Tricolored Heron are Caño Negro NWR, Tortuguero and Cahuita NPs, La Selva, Sueño Azul Resort, and estuaries along the highway from Limón to Cahuita. On the Pacific coast, it may be seen at Tamarindo, Hacienda Solimar, La Ensenada Lodge, the Puntarenas lagoons, Río Tárcoles estuary, Quepos, Río Sierpe, and Corcovado NP. They also visit the inland wetlands of Guanacaste and the Central Plateau.

Tricolored Heron adult

Egretta tricolor
Costa Rican name: *Garceta tricolor.*
18/23 trips; 56 sightings.
Status: Mostly northern migrants; a few permanent residents.
Length: 19.7–29.9 inches.
Weight: 11.8–14.6 ounces (334–415 grams).
Range: Gulf coast states south to Peru and Brazil.
Elevational range: Sea level to 5,000 feet.

Tricolored Heron hunting posture

CATTLE EGRET

Bubulcus ibis
Costa Rican names: *Garcilla*
bueyera; garza del ganado.
23/23 trips; 322 sightings.
Status: Permanent resident; a few
northern migrants.
Length: 18.1–22.0 inches.
Weight: 11.2–14.4 ounces (340–390
grams).
Range: Southern Canada to
southern Patagonia; southern
Europe, Africa, Asia, and
Australia.
Elevational range: Sea level to
7,000 feet.

The Cattle Egret is the most widespread and adaptable egret in the world. It is a small white egret with a short thick neck, yellowish bill, and buffy to coppery tinges over the head, chest, and back. This egret spread from Africa to northeastern South America in about 1877 and has since dispersed south to Chile and Argentina and northward to Canada. It first appeared in Costa Rica in 1954 and is now the most common egret in the country.

Originally a bird that evolved with roaming herds of African wildlife, the Cattle Egret has adapted to regions occupied by cattle and horses. It accompanies livestock and eats grasshoppers, small lizards, crustaceans, frogs, and invertebrates flushed by grazing animals. It also seeks insects and small creatures flushed by fires or by tractors as people plow or cultivate croplands.

Cattle Egrets roost communally at night in large trees that afford nocturnal protection from predators. The sight of a communal roosting tree adorned with dozens or hundreds of Cattle Egrets is a special treat. In early morning and late evening, small flocks of Cattle Egrets can be seen flying across the countryside between feeding pastures and night roosts. They are normally seen in small flocks of one or two dozen birds during the day. The Cattle Egret may be seen throughout most of Costa Rica, from lowland wetlands and pastures in both Caribbean and Pacific regions to the Central Plateau and highlands where there are mixed forests and pastures.

Cattle Egret adult

Cattle Egret night roost

GREEN HERON (GREEN-BACKED HERON)

The Green Heron, like the Cattle Egret, is widely distributed across tropical and temperate regions. The species in Costa Rica, *Butorides virescens,* is found from southern Canada to Panama. The adult has a black cap and crest, chestnut neck and shoulders, metallic greenish-blue back, a white streak down the center of the breast, yellow eyes, and yellow legs. The

Green Heron adult

immature Green Heron is similar to the adult, but the plumage on the back is dark brownish with less iridescence than on the adult.

This small, common heron is found in lowlands of the Caribbean and Pacific slopes to premontane levels. A solitary heron, it can be found wherever shallow fresh, brackish, and salt water provides an opportunity for capturing small fish, shrimp, insects, and frogs.

Look for the Green Heron in Caribbean lowlands along the edges of canals and ponds in Caño Negro NWR, Tortuguero NP, Puerto Viejo en Sarapiquí, Guapiles, and La Selva. In the Pacific lowlands, it occurs at lagoons in Puntarenas, Carara, and Palo Verde NPs, Río Tárcoles estuary, San Isidro city lagoons, Manuel Antonio NP, and the marshes near the San Vito airport.

Butorides virescens
Costa Rican names: *Garcilla verde;*
 chocuaco; martín peña.
22/23 trips; 139 sightings.
Status: Permanent resident and
 northern migrant.
Length: 13.8–18.9 inches.
Weight: 4.8–8.8 ounces (135–250
 grams).
Range: Southern Canada to
 northern Argentina; Africa,
 Malaysia, India, Galápagos
 Islands, and Australia.
Elevational range: Sea level to
 6,000 feet.

Green Heron immature

CHESTNUT-BELLIED HERON

Agamia agami
Costa Rican name: *Garza*
pechicastaña.
7/23 trips; 9 sightings.
Status: Permanent resident.
Length: 23.6–29.9 inches.
Weight: 1 pound 3.4 ounces (550 grams).
Range: Southern Mexico to central Brazil.
Elevational range: Sea level to 1,000 feet.

Most herons and egrets in Costa Rica are common species that can be seen from the United States south to Brazil, but several are uncommon and eagerly sought by birding enthusiasts, including the Boat-billed Heron, Fasciated Tiger-Heron, and Chestnut-bellied Heron. The Chestnut-bellied Heron has an exceptionally long bill and rich body colors, including dark green on the back, silvery plumes on the chest, a chestnut belly, and a maroon neck. This solitary bird inhabits swampy backwater streams, canals, and lagoons in the Caribbean lowlands and lowlands of the Osa Peninsula and Golfo Dulce region near Panama. It captures fish, frogs, and small lizards by stalking shallow water and wetland edges in daytime and at night.

Six sightings recorded in Costa Rica occurred during boat trips in backwater canals of Tortuguero NP; the other three sightings were in Caño Negro NWR. This rare heron is occasionally encountered at La Selva. It is rare but regular at Laguna del Lagarto Lodge near Boca Tapada, according to birding guide Jay VanderGaast.

Chestnut-bellied Heron immature

YELLOW-CROWNED NIGHT-HERON

The Yellow-crowned Night-Heron is a medium-sized wading bird of Caribbean and Pacific lowlands. The gray body, thick bill, and black-and-white-striped head make it easy to distinguish. The immature bird, brown speckled with white, is similar to a young Black-crowned Night-Heron. In flight, the legs of a Yellow-crowned Night-Heron extend farther beyond the tail because they are proportionally longer than the legs of a Black-crowned Night-Heron.

Preferred habitats include brackish water in mangrove lagoons and freshwater lowland streams, marshes, ponds, and estuaries of rivers of both the Caribbean and the Pacific lowlands. The thick bill is an adaptation for feeding on crabs and crayfish. Frogs, insects, snails, mussels, and fish are also eaten. This night-heron is usually nocturnal or crepuscular but may feed in daytime when tidal water levels are ideal for feeding.

Look for this bird in the Caribbean lowlands in Tortuguero NP and in estuaries along the highway between Limón and Cahuita NP. Along the Pacific coast, it may be seen in mangrove lagoons near Tamarindo, at the mouth of the Río Tárcoles, at Hacienda Solimar and La Ensenada Lodge, at Palo Verde, Carara, Manuel Antonio and Corcovado NPs, along the Río Corobicí near La Pacífica, at Quepos, along the Ríos Térraba and Sierpe, and on islands offshore from the Osa Peninsula.

Yellow-crowned Night-Heron adult

Nyctanassa violacea
Costa Rican name: *Martinete cabecipinto.*
19/23 trips; 73 sightings.
Status: Permanent resident and northern migrant.
Length: 20.0–27.6 inches.
Weight: 1 pound 6 ounces (652 grams).
Range: Central United States to Brazil; Galápagos Islands.
Elevational range: Sea level to 1,000 feet.

Yellow-crowned Night-Heron immature

Boat-billed Heron adult

Cochlearius cochlearius
Costa Rican names: *Pico cuchara;*
chocuacua; cuaca.
18/23 trips; 31 sightings.
Status: Permanent resident.
Length: 17.7–20.0 inches.
Weight: 1 pound 5 ounces (596
grams).
Range: Mexico to northern
Argentina.
Elevational range: Sea level to
1,000 feet.

BOAT-BILLED HERON

The Boat-billed Heron, probably the most memorable of all Costa Rican herons, has a huge, broad bill and enormous eyes that give it an almost comical appearance. This medium-sized wading bird occupies Caribbean and Pacific lowlands in habitats with shallow, quiet, or slow-moving water. This includes mangrove lagoons, ponds, and small streams. It is found in small, noisy colonies that are usually heard before they are seen. Individuals make a variety of croaks, quacks, and squawks, as well as popping noises that are made with the bill.

The large eyes are an adaptation for hunting in shallow water at dawn, dusk, and at night. Standing quietly in shallow water, it looks for prey and uses the bill to scoop up small fish, shrimp, frogs, insects, and even small mammals. This is the only heron that scoops up its prey instead of spearing it with a sharp bill.

Because Boat-billed Heron colonies are often in thick cover, it is generally necessary to have a naturalist guide or boatman locate them. They can be seen in Tortuguero, Carara, and Palo Verde NPs; Caño Negro NWR and the Río Frío region; Hacienda Solimar; La Ensenada Lodge; and along the Río Corobicí near La Pacífica. Care should be taken not to enter nesting colonies because disturbance could cause them to abandon the area. An easily viewed colony is located at the CATIE (Centro Agronómico Tropical de Investigación y Enseñanza) agricultural and forestry education facility near Turrialba. The pond inside the entrance has long been famous for its waterbirds. There is a bamboo thicket on the small island where Boat-billed Herons nest. A $5 fee is required to visit the CATIE grounds for birding. Call ahead at 506-2558-2275 if you have any questions about birding on the grounds there.

Close-up showing bill detail

WHITE IBIS

The White Ibis, a medium-sized wading bird with a white body, red face, and a long, slender, down-curved bill, is regularly encountered in mangrove lagoons and shallow wetlands in Guanacaste and the Pacific coastal region. The male is about 35 percent larger than the female. In flight, the long down-curved bill and black tips on the four outermost primary wing feathers provide good identification marks. The White Ibis flies in lines or V formations. The species is characterized by alternate wing flapping and gliding. Immature White Ibises are brown with white splotches over the head and neck. Their rumps and bellies are white.

This wading bird forages singly or in flocks on mud flats, river estuaries, shallow wetlands, flooded fields, or ponds and among tree roots of mangrove swamps. It picks up crayfish, crabs, shrimp, small fish, snails, small snakes, beetles, and grasshoppers with dexterous movements of its long bill. Nesting and night roosting occurs at colonial sites involving dozens or hundreds of birds.

The White Ibis is most common in the Río Tempisque basin, including Palo Verde NP, Hacienda Solimar, La Ensenada Lodge, Caño Negro NWR, coastal wetlands from the Tamarindo area south to Puntarenas, the Río Tárcoles estuary near Carara NP, Hotel Villa Lapas, Tárcol Lodge, and Playa Hermosa. White Ibises congregate at shrimp-production ponds near Puntarenas. This ibis may be seen on river estuaries near Las Esquinas and along the coast of Corcovado NP.

Eudocimus albus
Costa Rican names: *Ibis blanco; coco.*
19/23 trips; 56 sightings.
Status: Permanent resident.
Length: 22–28 inches.
Weight: 1 pound 10.4 ounces–2 pounds 5.0 ounces (750–1,050 grams).
Range: North Carolina to Venezuela and Peru.
Elevational range: Sea level to 1,000 feet.

White Ibis pair with male on left

GREEN IBIS

Mesembrinibis cayennensis
Costa Rican name: *Ibis verde.*
7/23 trips; 11 sightings.
Status: Permanent resident.
Length: 18.9–22.8 inches.
Weight: 1 pound 9 ounces–1 pound
12 ounces (715–785 grams).
Range: Costa Rica to northeastern
Argentina.
Elevational range: Sea level to
500 feet.

The rare Green Ibis is highly sought-after among birders in Costa Rica. The Green Ibis has dark bronzy-green iridescent plumage and a long decurved bill. The noisy, raucous call is a rapid series of "quoak, quoak, quoak, quoak" sounds that are both ventriloquial and squawky. Part of the call is similar to the "kick-walk" notes of the Gray-necked Wood-Rail. Knowing the call makes it easier to find the ibis perched in trees along the water's edge.

The Green Ibis feeds along the edges of muddy watercourses by probing with its bill to locate worms and other invertebrates. It also eats grasshoppers, beetles, bugs, and some plant matter. A reclusive bird of swampy, Caribbean lowland backwaters, this species is best seen from a boat while exploring Tortuguero NP, along the canal from Tortuguero NP to Limón, and at Caño Negro NWR.

Green Ibis adult

ROSEATE SPOONBILL

The Roseate Spoonbill is a memorable wading bird that is stately, beautiful, and bizarre. The pink body and spoon-shaped bill make identification easy. A close look at the bare facial details reveals prehistoric, almost reptilian, features. Standing nearly three feet tall, this bird is typically seen feeding among other waterbirds in shallow wetlands and flooded fields. The spoonbill feeds alone or in small flocks by walking through shallow water, swinging its head from side to side with the bill slightly open. The bill snaps shut whenever prey is encountered. Food items include shrimp, crayfish, crabs, small fish, aquatic beetles, snails, slugs, plant stems, and roots of sedges.

The greatest concentration of Roseate Spoonbills is in the Río Tempisque basin in the vicinity of Palo Verde NP. This bird may also be seen in wetlands of Caño Negro NWR, Tamarindo, Hacienda Solimar, La Ensenada Lodge, scattered ponds throughout Guanacaste, Puntarenas, Río Tárcoles estuary, Tárcol Lodge, Carara NP, Quepos, and Corcovado NP near the Sirena Biological Station.

Roseate Spoonbill adult

Platalea ajaja (formerly Ajaia ajaja)
Costa Rican names: *Espátula rosada; garza rosada.*
18/23 trips; 40 sightings.
Status: Permanent resident.
Length: 26.8–34.1 inches.
Weight: 3 pounds 1.3 ounces (1,400 grams).
Range: Florida to northern Argentina.
Elevational range: Sea level to 1,000 feet.

Roseate Spoonbill

JABIRU

Jabiru mycteria

Costa Rican names: *Jabirú; galán sin ventura; veterano.*

4/23 trips; 6 sightings.

Status: Permanent resident.

Length: 48.0–55.1 inches.

Weight: 16 pounds 9 ounces (8 kilograms).

Range: Southern Mexico to northern Argentina.

Elevational range: Sea level to 1,000 feet.

Jabiru adult

The stately Jabiru, standing nearly five feet tall and with a wingspread exceeding eight feet, is the largest bird in Costa Rica. It is an endangered species, with only about 70 to 80 birds in Costa Rica. Originally about a dozen nests were known in the country, but in 2008 another ten new nests were discovered. They were primarily on private lands in the general vicinity of the Río Tempisque basin. The population appears to be increasing, but their presence on vast private landholdings makes it very difficult to inventory them.

The Jabiru may be seen soaring high overhead, but unlike the wings of the Wood Stork, which have black tips, the Jabiru's wings are all white. This stork inhabits shallow wetlands and flooded fields of the Guanacaste region. It often feeds in the company of Wood Storks, White Ibises, Roseate Spoonbills, herons, and egrets. Wading through shallow water, the Jabiru uses its huge bill to splash the water and flush prey as well as to clamp shut on fish, frogs, snakes, young caimans, eels, crabs, and small turtles.

The Jabiru nests at the beginning of the dry season so it can capitalize on the availability of aquatic creatures that become stranded as shallow wetlands dry up. Solitary nesters, a pair of Jabiru storks build an enormous stick nest high in a tree. The young are cared for in the nest for eighty to ninety-five days and continue to be fed by the parents for two months after leaving the nest. Jabiru storks have been known to live up to thirty-six years.

Look for the Jabiru in Palo Verde NP. There is also a nest near Caño Negro NWR. The Mata Redonda lagoons in Guanacaste are being managed by Ducks Unlimited; 86 Jabirus were counted there in 2000. A Jabiru also showed up at the wetlands at La Ensenada Lodge in 2000, and several pairs of Jabirus have recently begun nesting in forested pastures near wetlands on Hacienda Solimar.

Jabiru in flight

Jabiru family on treetop nest

WOOD STORK

The Wood Stork is the second tallest bird in Costa Rica—exceeded only by the Jabiru. Although similar to a Great Egret, it is more closely related to vultures than to egrets or herons. Several significant features distinguish it from wading birds. The Wood Stork is larger; the bill is much heavier; the wing tips and secondary feathers are black, whereas all egrets and the immature Little Blue Heron have white wing tips; the head and neck are vulturelike (black and unfeathered); and finally, in flight, storks fly with the neck extended, whereas herons and egrets usually fly with the neck recurved. Since Wood Storks are often seen soaring, the black primaries and secondaries and the extended neck are good identification marks. The most distinctive markings of the Wood Stork at close range are black legs highlighted by pink toes.

Whereas most herons and egrets feed by spearing their prey, the Wood Stork feeds by moving through shallow water with the submerged bill partially open. Whenever the bill comes in contact with prey, the bill snaps shut on it. Sometimes Wood Storks feed in a group. They feed in shallow freshwater and saltwater wetlands, mangrove lagoons, ponds, streams, and flooded fields along the Pacific coast. Prey includes small- to medium-sized fish, crayfish, frogs, insects, snakes, and even hatchling caimans! One pair of Wood Storks and their three or four nestlings will consume 440 pounds of prey during the nesting season.

The Wood Stork is most abundant in the Río Frío and Guanacaste regions, Caño Negro NWR, Palo Verde NP, Hacienda Solimar, La Ensenada Lodge, Puntarenas, and the Río Tárcoles estuary near Carara NP. It can occasionally be encountered in the Caribbean lowlands.

Wood Stork immature

Mycteria americana
Costa Rican names: *Cigueñón; garzón; guairón.*
20/23 trips; 92 sightings.
Status: Permanent resident.
Length: 32.7–40.2 inches.
Weight: 4 pounds 6.5 ounces–6 pounds 9.7 ounces (2,000–3,000 grams).
Range: South Carolina to northern Argentina.
Elevational range: Sea level to 2,500 feet.

Wood Stork adult

Wood Stork in flight

AMERICAN VULTURE FAMILY *(Cathartidae)*

BLACK VULTURE

Coragyps atratus
Costa Rican names: *Zopilote negro; gallinazo; zoncho.*
23/23 trips; 372 sightings.
Status: Permanent resident.
Length: 22.0–26.8 inches.
Weight: 2 pounds 6.8 ounces–4 pounds 3.0 ounces (1,100–1,900 grams).
Range: Southeastern United States to southern Argentina.
Elevational range: Sea level to 9,300 feet.

The Black Vulture is a common scavenger throughout the country and often soars in the company of Turkey Vultures. In flight, this vulture flaps its wings more frequently than the Turkey Vulture and holds its wings horizontally. The short fan-shaped tail is a good identification mark. The head, which is black in contrast to the red head of the Turkey Vulture, helps dissipate body heat. This species has been described as "shameless" because it also urinates onto its legs to cool itself in hot weather.

The Black Vulture hunts by sight and has a poor sense of smell. It is well adapted to life in cities, backyards, and garbage dumps where waste food and meat scraps can be obtained. This is a benefit to some small rural villages, because the vultures perform sanitation duties. In addition to feeding on carrion, this scavenger will kill newborn or weakened prey, including newly hatched sea turtles. Other food items include bananas and fruits of African oil palms. When a dead animal is encountered, Black Vultures dominate Turkey Vultures for feeding preference. Turkey Vultures feed after Black Vultures have eaten their fill. In some cases, dozens or hundreds of Black Vultures will surround a single cow or horse carcass.

Populations of Black Vultures have increased where they have had access to garbage dumps and dead livestock on farms and ranches. This bird may be seen during daylight hours anywhere in the country, but it is most abundant in the lowlands.

Black Vulture flight silhouette

Black Vulture adult

TURKEY VULTURE

The Turkey Vulture is a large black bird with a bare red head that may be seen soaring throughout Costa Rica, from beaches to the highest peaks of the Talamanca Mountains. Although usually not appreciated by humans, vultures are fascinating. Closely related to storks, the Turkey Vulture is one of the only birds with a well-developed sense of smell. It will often fly low over the forest to locate the carcasses of dead animals by smell. Black Vultures and King Vultures may watch the movements of Turkey Vultures to help them locate carrion.

Turkey Vulture adult

Because vultures occur over a broad range of cold and hot climates, they have remarkable adaptations for dealing with extreme temperatures. The bare, wrinkled head is easier to keep clean while eating carrion and also helps radiate excessive body heat. A vulture may also urinate onto its legs because the cooling effect of evaporation on the legs serves to dissipate heat. At night, its body temperature drops to conserve energy, and in the morning, the black body color helps absorb heat from the sun.

The large surface of the wings compared with the relatively light body weight allows a Turkey Vulture to soar for hours without flapping its wings. In flight, the Turkey Vulture holds its wings slightly uplifted in a shallow V profile. This is in contrast to Black Vultures, which hold their wings in a horizontal posture. Also, the tail of the Black Vulture is distinctly shorter and more fan-shaped when viewed in flight. There is a bluish-white band across the back of the head of the resident Turkey Vulture subspecies, *C. aura ruficollis*. The migrant race is red on the back of the head. This scavenger feeds on carcasses of freshly dead animals, primarily mammals. It may go for two weeks without food or water. The digestive system of the Turkey Vulture has the remarkable ability to kill disease organisms associated with carrion—like anthrax and cholera.

Resident Turkey Vultures may be seen throughout Costa Rica all year. Some migratory Turkey Vultures winter in Costa Rica, but most pass through en route to South America from September through October and return north from January through May.

Cathartes aura
Costa Rican names: *Zopilote cabecirrojo; zonchiche; noneca.*
23/23 trips; 384 sightings.
Status: Permanent resident and northern migrant.
Length: 25.1–31.9 inches.
Weight: 1 pound 14 ounces–4 pounds 6.5 ounces (850–2,000 grams).
Range: Southern Canada to southern Argentina.
Elevational range: Sea level to over 10,000 feet.

Turkey Vulture in flight

KING VULTURE

Sarcoramphus papa
Costa Rican names: *Zopilote rey; rey callinazo; rey de zopilotes.*
19/23 trips; 53 sightings.
Status: Permanent resident.
Length: 28.0–31.9 inches.
Weight: 6 pounds 9.7 ounces–8 pounds 4.2 ounces (3,000–3,750 grams).
Range: Southern Mexico to northern Argentina.
Elevational range: Sea level to 4,000 feet.

The sight of a King Vulture circling above the rainforest is one of the highlights of birding in the American tropics. The effortless soaring flight and white body contrasting with the black primaries and secondaries make it easy to identify. The Wood Stork has a similar plumage pattern, but the long neck and legs make soaring Wood Storks distinctive even at great distances. When viewed close-up, the King Vulture's head and neck are an incredible combination of orange, yellow, purple, blue, red, and black patterns amid assorted wattles and wrinkles. Immature King Vultures are black with a small neck ruff and an orange tinge on the bill.

This imposing scavenger, found in Caribbean and Pacific lowlands, may be seen soaring above undisturbed and partially deforested forests where dead mammals can be encountered. Like the Turkey Vulture, this raptor can locate carrion by smell.

The King Vulture may be seen soaring above Tortuguero NP and in the vicinity of La Selva in the Caribbean lowlands. Among the best places to see King Vultures, however, are Corcovado NP, Corcovado Lodge Tent Camp, Lapa Ríos, Carara NP vicinity, Hotel Villa Lapas, Sirena Biological Station, La Cusinga Lodge, Hotel Cristal Ballena, and Tiskita Jungle Lodge.

King Vulture head detail

King Vulture adult

King Vulture in flight

OSPREY

The Osprey is one of the largest and most conspicuous migratory raptors in Costa Rica. It is regularly seen along coastal and inland waters where it can catch fish in shallow water. The brown body, white breast, and brown mask through the eye, and its association with water, make identification easy. In flight, the wings are long and have a distinctive bend at the wrist joint.

As an Osprey hunts, it flies slowly over shallow water and can hover when prey is sighted. It plummets with the wings folded back and the legs extended downward as it strikes the water to capture the fish, which may be a foot or two below the surface. Most fish caught weigh from one-third to two-thirds of a pound. On some occasions, small lizards, mammals, or birds may be taken.

The Osprey has several adaptations for its fish-eating lifestyle. The outer toe of each foot is reversible, in the sense that when a fish is caught, two toes point forward and two point back so the fish can be gripped with the head pointed forward. The fish is carried headfirst for easier flight. The toes have spiny pads that aid in holding slippery fish, the claws are especially long and curved, and the nostrils have valves that shut as the Osprey strikes the water. The Osprey migrates to Costa Rica beginning in September. Some birds stay to winter, but most continue to wintering destinations that range from Panama to Bolivia and Brazil. The return migration occurs from March through April.

Look for wintering Ospreys in the Caribbean lowlands along the beaches of Tortuguero NP, in estuaries and wetlands south to Cahuita NP, and along the Río Sarapiquí near La Selva and Sueño Azul Resort. On the Pacific slope they may be seen in mangrove lagoons and along beaches at Tamarindo, Palo Verde NP, La Ensenada Lodge, along the Río Corobicí near Cañas, and from Playa Doña Ana south to Panama.

Osprey in flight

Pandion haliaetus
Costa Rican names: Aguila
  pescadora; gavilán pescador.
21/23 trips; 98 sightings.
Status: Northern migrant.
Length: 21.7–22.8 inches.
Weight: 2 pounds 10.3 ounces–
  4 pounds 6.5 ounces (1,200–2,000
  grams).
Range: Winters from Florida to
  Argentina.
Elevational range: Sea level to
  5,000 feet.

SWALLOW-TAILED KITE

Elanoides forficatus

Costa Rican names: *Elanio tijereta; tijerilla; gavilán tijerilla.*

21/23 trips; 77 sightings.

Status: Permanent resident, northern migrant, and southern migrant.

Length: 22–26 inches.

Weight: 13.2 ounces (375 grams).

Range: South Carolina to northern Argentina.

Elevational range: Sea level to 6,000 feet; occasionally to 10,000 feet.

The deeply forked tail, graceful flight, and elegant black-and-white markings of the Swallow-tailed Kite make it one of the most impressive raptors in the Americas. With great precision, this bird of prey plucks small creatures on the wing or from treetop foliage. Cicadas, lizards, bats, hummingbirds, small snakes, frogs, and nestling birds are all adeptly snatched from their nests or perches. Fruits are also eaten.

The Swallow-tailed Kite is a breeding resident in wet lowlands of the Caribbean and southern Pacific slopes, including the Monteverde Cloud Forest Reserve and Corcovado NP on the Osa Peninsula. Migratory birds are also present. Some may be northern kites that nest as far north as South Carolina and Florida and migrate to South America. Most are apparently migrants from South America that enter Costa Rica from the southeast in January and February to reproduce in Costa Rica. Those birds leave from July to September. One of the most distinctive behaviors of this raptor is that the wintering birds sleep in communal roosts as a means of protection from predators. Communal roosts have been observed in forests of the Monteverde area (Mariano Arguedas, personal communication 1996).

A few kites may be seen in the Caribbean lowlands from Tortuguero NP and south to Cahuita NP, La Virgen del Socorro, and near Rincón de la Vieja NP. Most sightings are from San Isidro del General south to the Panama border. Some Swallow-tailed Kites may be seen in late January at Villa Mills in Cerro de la Muerte, Vista del Valle Restaurant at kilometer 119 along the Pan American Highway, Savegre Mountain Lodge, Wilson Botanical Garden, Corcovado NP, Lapa Ríos, Talari Mountain Lodge, Los Cusingos, Corcovado Lodge Tent Camp, and Tiskita Jungle Lodge. Mating birds have been observed in late January near San Pedrillo at the northwest end of Corcovado NP.

Swallow-tailed Kite in flight

SNAIL KITE

The Snail Kite, also known as the endangered Everglades Kite in south Florida,
is a raptor that feeds on snails in shallow
freshwater marshes. Although very rare in
Florida, this species has a broad range in the
Americas. It is exceptionally abundant in
the Crooked Tree Lagoon of Belize and in
the Pantanal wetlands of Brazil.

Snail Kite immature

An adult male Snail Kite is slate gray to
black with orange or reddish feet and an
orange or reddish cere between the eyes and
bill. There is a conspicuous white patch at the base of the
tail. The female is dark brown above with a dark stripe
behind the eye, there is a white patch at the base of the
tail, the cere and feet are yellowish orange, and the breast
is heavily streaked with brown. Immatures, which take
four years to mature, are similar to the female.

With a harrier-like flight, the Snail Kite flies low over
marshes looking for snails. When one is spotted, the kite
swoops down to snatch the snail from the water and flies
to a nearby post, piling, or tree branch to extract the snail
from its shell with its slender, sharply curved bill. The snails
most commonly eaten belong to the genera *Pomacea* and
Ampullaria. Dozens of snail shells often lie on the ground
under a well-used perch or post along marsh edges.

The Snail Kite can be seen in shallow wetlands
throughout the Guanacaste and Río Frío regions, including Palo Verde NP, Caño Negro NWR, and Hacienda
Solimar.

Rosthramus sociabilis
Costa Rican names: *Elanio
caracolero; gavilán caracolero.*
5/23 trips; 11 sightings.
Status: Permanent resident.
Length: 15.7–17.7 inches.
Weight: 12.7–13.9 ounces (360–393
grams).
Range: Southern Florida to
northern Argentina.
Elevational range: Sea level to
1,000 feet.

Snail Kite adult

Double-toothed Kite adult

Harpagus bidentatus
Costa Rican name: *Gavilán gorgirrayado.*
21/23 trips; 59 sightings.
Status: Permanent resident.
Length: 13 inches.
Weight: 5.9–8.1 ounces (168–229 grams).
Range: Southern Mexico to southeastern Brazil.
Elevational range: Sea level to 5,000 feet.

DOUBLE-TOOTHED KITE

The attractive Double-toothed Kite is one of the easiest raptors to identify in flight because of the fluffy white feathers on its vent and under-tail coverts. It gives an appearance of having bloomers that are visible even when soaring at great heights. The back is slate gray, and the throat is white with a slender dark stripe down the center of the white throat patch—resembling a slender necktie. The upper chest is chestnut, and the white thighs have rufous barring. This kite spends much time soaring.

The Double-toothed Kite inhabits mature moist and wet lowland and middle-elevation forests and older second-growth forests. It also frequents forest edges and openings, where it watches for prey from a perch and then launches itself like an accipiter to fly down and snatch the unsuspecting creature. Prey items include lizards, frogs, cicadas, bats, and larger insects. This kite follows troops of white-faced and squirrel monkeys so it can catch insects and other creatures that are flushed by the monkeys. The call is a series of several very thin, high-pitched whistled notes.

On the Caribbean slope, the Double-toothed Kite can be seen at La Virgen del Socorro, Tortuga Lodge, Tortuguero NP, Guapiles, Puerto Viejo en Sarapiquí, La Selva, Rainforest Aerial Tram, and lower levels of Braulio Carrillo NP. On the Pacific slope, this kite occurs at Carara and Corcovado NPs, Hotel Villa Lapas, Villa Caletas, Cristal Ballena, San Isidro del General, Los Cusingos, Quepos vicinity, Lapa Ríos, Drake Bay Wilderness Resort, Corcovado Lodge Tent Camp, Tiskita Jungle Lodge, and the Wilson Botanical Garden.

Double-toothed Kite side view

SEMIPLUMBEOUS HAWK

The Semiplumbeous Hawk is a distinctively marked hawk of the Caribbean wet lowland rainforest. It is characterized by a slate-gray back and head, white breast, and bright orange legs and cere. The call is usually a series of two to four ascending high-pitched whistles.

This attractive hawk is most likely to be sighted as it sits motionless in a tree, staring intently at the ground looking for a small lizard, bird, or rodent. It is seldom seen in flight. The Semiplumbeous Hawk will follow swarms of army ants to catch antbirds and other small birds that accompany the ants.

This hawk has been seen perched on the edge of clearings and on the grounds of Tortuga Lodge and in the vicinity of La Selva.

Leucopternis semiplumbeus
Costa Rican name: *Gavilán dorsiplomizo.*
9/23 trips; 15 sightings.
Status: Permanent resident.
Length: 12.2–13.7 inches.
Weight: 9–12 ounces (250–325 grams).
Range: Honduras to northwestern Ecuador.
Elevational range: Sea level to 2,600 feet.

Semiplumbeous Hawk adult

White Hawk adult

Leucopternis albicollis

Costa Rican name: *Gavilán blanco.*

16/23 trips; 28 sightings.

Status: Permanent resident.

Length: 18.2–20.1 inches.

Weight: 1 pound 5.1 ounces–1 pound 6.9 ounces (600–650 grams).

Range: Mexico to central Brazil.

Elevational range: Sea level to 4,600 feet.

WHITE HAWK

Looking like a white phantom in the treetops, the White Hawk is one of Costa Rica's most memorable raptors. Many birds of prey are varying shades of gray or brown, but the White Hawk provides beautiful contrast: snow-white plumage with black wing highlights and a black band across the tip of the tail.

The White Hawk is a raptor of lowland and middle-elevation forests—especially in hilly terrain. It prefers habitats in moist and wet forests of the Caribbean slope and southern Pacific lowlands. From a perch on a vantage point at the edge of the forest, this hawk watches for snakes, lizards, frogs, and small mammals. Snakes make up much of its diet. This hawk is frequently seen soaring above the rainforest. Males defend a territory of about 500 acres. The call is a series of extended buzzy squeals.

The best place to see the White Hawk is at Tiskita Jungle Lodge, where a pair traditionally nests near the lodge. Other sites include Braulio Carrillo NP and the vicinity of the Rainforest Aerial Tram, La Virgen del Socorro, Oro Verde BR, Hotel Villa Lapas, Las Esquinas Rainforest Lodge, Corcovado Lodge Tent Camp, Rara Avis, and Sirena Biological Station.

COMMON BLACK-HAWK

There are two black-hawks in Costa Rica, the Great and the Common, and also a subspecies of the Common Black-Hawk called the Mangrove Black-Hawk. All three are similar in appearance, but the Great Black-Hawk (*Buteogallus urubitinga*) is about four inches taller than the others and has a white patch at the base of the tail. A photo is included here for comparison. The Great Black-Hawk shows fine white barring on the thighs, and it lives near wetlands in Guanacaste, Braulio Carrillo NP, and along the Caribbean coast. All these hawks have a white bar through the middle of the tail. The range of the other black-hawks does not overlap. The Mangrove subspecies of Common Black-Hawk is found only in the mangrove forests along the Pacific coast. The Common Black-Hawk is found along coastal areas of the Caribbean coast. In their coastal and wetland habitats, black-hawks hunt along water for lizards, crabs, birds, snakes, rodents, bats, and frogs.

Great Black-Hawk adult with barring on thighs

Look for the Mangrove subspecies along Pacific coastal forests and mangrove lagoons from Guanacaste to Panama. It has been observed at Tamarindo, Hacienda Solimar, Carara NP, Río Tárcoles estuary and lagoons, Hotel Villa Lapas, Drake Bay Wilderness Resort, Sirena Biological Station, Corcovado Lodge Tent Camp and vicinity, Tiskita Jungle Lodge, Hacienda Barú Natural Reserve, Las Esquinas Rainforest Lodge, and in the Damas Island mangrove forests near Quepos. The Caribbean subspecies of Common Black-Hawk can be observed along the Caribbean coast from Tortuguero NP south to Cahuita NP and Puerto Viejo near the Panama border.

Buteogallus anthracinus
Costa Rican names: *Gavilán negro; aguilucho; gavilán silber.*
17/23 trips; 55 sightings.
Status: Permanent resident.
Length: 15.4–18.5 inches.
Weight: 1 pound 10 ounces–1 pound 6 ounces (750–1,200 grams).
Range: Pacific coast from southern Mexico to northern Peru.
Elevational range: Sea level.

Common Black-Hawk adult

Roadside Hawk immature

Buteo magnirostris
Costa Rican name: *Gavilán*
chapulinero.
22/23 trips; 111 sightings.
Status: Permanent resident.
Length: 13.0–16.1 inches.
Weight: 8.8–10.7 ounces (251–303 grams).
Range: Southern Mexico to northern Argentina.
Elevational range: Sea level to 4,000 feet.

ROADSIDE HAWK

The Roadside Hawk is one of the most common hawks in Costa Rica, and true to its name, it is usually seen perched along roadsides. An adult Roadside Hawk has a pale gray head and shoulders and rusty barring across the breast, whereas an adult Broad-winged Hawk has a dark brown head, a rufous patch on the upper breast area, and variable amounts of rusty barring on the belly. Immatures are similar, but the Roadside Hawk has fine rufous barring on the thighs. In flight, the rufous primaries are conspicuous. The call of the Roadside Hawk is a high-pitched whistle, described as "seeuu."

The Roadside Hawk is found in lowland and middle-elevation deforested areas and has increased as forests were cut to create cropland, pastures, and plantations. It hunts by sitting on a low perch and dropping onto prey such as insects, frogs, snakes, lizards, and small mammals. It may also catch prey escaping from fires or army ants.

Roadside Hawks may be seen in the Caribbean lowlands in the north from Caño Negro NWR and Los Chiles south through Guapiles and Tortuguero NP to Cahuita NP. This raptor is more abundant throughout Guanacaste and the Pacific lowlands to the Panama border. At middle elevations, it may occasionally be observed at the Wilson Botanical Garden, Turrialba, and La Virgen del Socorro.

Roadside Hawk adult

BROAD-WINGED HAWK

The Broad-winged Hawk is the most abundant migratory raptor in Costa Rica and may be seen from late September through March. These hawks pass through Costa Rica en route to wintering sites in South America, but many winter in the country. This hawk soars much more than the Roadside Hawk, and the head and shoulders are more brownish than the grayish head of the Roadside Hawk. The tail has alternating black and white bands, and the upper chest area is rufous. The call is a long, high-pitched whistle.

The Broad-winged Hawk watches ground cover from a tree, post, or power line at the edge of fields, pastures, or forest openings. It swoops down to capture small mammals, lizards, birds, frogs, and insects like grasshoppers and dragonflies.

This hawk can be observed throughout Caribbean and Pacific lowlands in many of the same habitats as the Roadside Hawk. In the Caribbean lowlands, however, it is more common than the Roadside Hawk, and it is much more common in middle- and high-elevation areas like Monteverde, Poás and Braulio Carrillo NPs, Cerro de la Muerte, San Gerardo de Dota Valley, Rancho Naturalista, the Central Plateau, and San Vito. Tens of thousands of Broad-winged Hawks can be seen in mid- to late October each year migrating through Cahuita and Puerto Viejo near the Panama border en route to wintering areas in South America.

Buteo platypterus
Costa Rican names: *Gavilán aludo; gavilán pollero.*
23/23 trips; 130 sightings.
Status: Northern migrant.
Length: 13.4–17.3 inches.
Weight: 9.3 ounces–1 pound 3.7 ounces (265–560 grams).
Range: Breeds Central Canada to Texas; winters Guatemala to Brazil.
Elevational range: Sea level to 6,500 feet.

Broad-winged Hawk adult

Gray Hawk adult

Buteo nitidus (formerly Asturina plagiata)

Costa Rican name: *Gavilán gris.*

19/23 trips; 60 sightings.

Status: Permanent resident.

Length: 15.0–16.9 inches.

Weight: 1 pound 0.4 ounce–1 pound 3.5 ounces (465–554 grams).

Range: Southern Texas to western Ecuador.

Elevational range: Sea level to 3,300 feet.

GRAY HAWK

The fine, pearly gray barring on the breast of the Gray Hawk makes it easy to identify. Primarily a bird of open country and partially forested habitat, this hawk is readily seen as it perches on roadside power lines. The Gray Hawk has a loud whistled call.

This raptor hunts by watching ground cover and vegetation for movements of small lizards, rodents, large insects, or small birds. Very agile in flight, it is able to snatch lizards or birds off their perches. When the nesting season begins in December, mated pairs perform dramatic aerial displays near their nests that include steep climbs, dives, and pursuits.

The Gray Hawk can be seen from Caño Negro NWR to La Selva, Puerto Viejo en Sarapiquí, and La Virgen del Socorro. Look for it at Lost Iguana Resort, Sueño Azul, and Tilajari Resort. It is more abundant on the Pacific slope throughout the Guanacaste region and south to Panama at Carara NP, Hotel Villa Lapas, Quepos, Rancho Casa Grande, Playa Dominical, Hacienda Barú NR, and Manuel Antonio NP. This hawk also occurs at Corcovado Lodge Tent Camp, Lapa Ríos, Tiskita Jungle Lodge, and the Wilson Botanical Garden near San Vito.

Gray Hawk immature

SHORT-TAILED HAWK

Although the Short-tailed Hawk is in the genus *Buteo,* this small hawk hunts like an accipiter. It flies 300 to 600 feet above open and semiopen habitats and dives to snatch small and medium-sized birds, mammals, lizards, and insects from their perches. It may also hover like a kite while scanning for prey. The diet includes birds up to the size of kestrels and mourning doves.

Markings include a dark brown head, cheek area, and back; narrowly barred tail with a dark terminal band; white throat and breast; and a chestnut patch on the lower sides of the neck. The White-tailed Hawk is similar, with a dark brown patch on the sides of the face and a white breast and belly, but the tail is white with a black terminal band. Some Short-tailed Hawks are sooty black "melanistic" birds that are white only on the face.

Short-tailed Hawks are present as residents and as migrants that pass through the Caribbean lowlands. In migration, this bird may be seen flying with Swallow-tailed and Plumbeous Kites. Preferred habitats include the foothills of the Caribbean slope, including areas around La Selva, Sueño Azul Resort, and La Virgen del Socorro. On the Pacific slope, the Short-tailed Hawk may be seen in Guanacaste at La Ensenada Lodge and Palo Verde NWR. Farther south, it occurs at Carara NP, Río Térraba near San Isidro del General, San Vito, Quepos, Las Esquinas Rainforest Lodge, Lapa Ríos, Corcovado Lodge Tent Camp, and Tiskita Jungle Lodge.

Short-tailed Hawk adult

Buteo brachyurus
Costa Rican name: *Gavilán colicorto.*
18/23 trips; 48 sightings.
Status: Permanent resident and northern migrant.
Length: 14.6–18.1 inches.
Weight: 15.9 ounces–1 pound 2.7 ounces (450–530 grams).
Range: Southern Florida and eastern Mexico to northern Argentina.
Elevational range: Sea level to 5,900 feet.

Red-tailed Hawk adult

Buteo jamaicensis
Costa Rican names: *Gavilán colirrojo; gavilán valdivia.*
18/23 trips; 46 sightings.
Status: Permanent resident; a few northern migrants.
Length: 17.7–25.6 inches.
Weight: 1 pound 8 ounces–2 pounds 13 ounces (690–1,300 grams).
Range: Alaska to western Panama.
Elevational range: In Costa Rica, 3,300–10,500 feet.

RED-TAILED HAWK

The Red-tailed Hawk, the most common hawk in North America, demonstrates a remarkable variety of color morphs, ranging from pale whitish and dark rufous to nearly black. A few red-tails migrate through Costa Rica with Broad-winged and Swainson's Hawks. The Costa Rican Red-tailed Hawk, however, is a separate nonmigratory subspecies found at high elevations. It has a dark brown back and head, white chest, and rufous highlights on the sides, thighs, and underwing linings that are distinctive for this subspecies. Several birds characterized as northern temperate species have adapted to fill nonmigratory temperate niches in Costa Rica's higher elevations, including the Red-tailed Hawk, American Dipper, and Hairy Woodpecker.

The Red-tailed Hawk lives in montane forests that have been partially deforested to create pastureland. This hawk watches ground cover from a perch or seeks prey in flight. Prey include voles, squirrels, and rabbits, as well as birds, snakes, and lizards. In Cerro de la Muerte, the red-tail nests in tall trees on open hillsides with expansive views of the surrounding terrain.

This hawk may be seen in mixed forests and pasturelands of Monteverde, but most are seen along the Pan American Highway in mixed montane forest, pastureland, and paramo areas of the Cerro de la Muerte region. Watch for it along the highway from kilometer 66 to 96 at places like Los Chespiritos (km 85), Villa Mills–La Georgina (km 96), the transmission tower site (km 90), and the San Gerardo de Dota Valley.

COLLARED FOREST-FALCON

The Collared Forest-Falcon is an impressive and beauti-ful raptor of Costa Rica's lowland forests. It gives the appearance of a long, upright, slender Cooper's Hawk, but the markings are distinctive: the back and cap are black, and there is a black crescent from the back of the head through the sides of the head. The throat, breast, and belly are white. Some forest-falcons of coastal areas, however, are copper-colored on the throat and breast. There is also a black color morph that has a black body, black tail with narrow white bars, and fine cinnamon barring on the thighs. The skin in front of the eyes (lores) is greenish. Immatures have a cinnamon breast with conspicuous dark barring and narrow cinnamon barring on the tail.

Micrastur semitorquatus
Costa Rican name: *Halcón de monte collarejo.*
10/23 trips; 14 sightings.
Status: Permanent resident.
Length: 18–22 inches.
Weight: 1 pound 5 ounces–1 pound 14 ounces (584–820 grams).
Range: Central Mexico to northern Argentina.
Elevational range: Sea level to 5,000 feet.

This aggressive raptor sits quietly and very upright as it watches the forest understory and ground cover for rodents, squirrels, bats, lizards, snakes, and birds up to the size of chachalacas, guans, owls, and curassows. It will fol-low army ant swarms to capture creatures flushed by the ants. Upon sighting potential prey, it may fly or run along the ground to capture its victim. At dawn and dusk its loud series of five to seven somewhat ventriloquial "owh!" calls can be heard, sounding like the yells of someone who has been injured. The birds also will make an accelerating series of "owh!" calls that increase in frequency and then descend in frequency and pitch at the end.

The Collared Forest-Falcon is found in the lowlands and foothills of both the Carib-bean and Pacific slopes. It may be encoun-tered at Selva Verde Lodge and has also been seen just across the Nicaragua border, near the coast at Río Indio Lodge. On the Pacific slope, it is most common in the dry forests and gallery forests of Guanacaste. It can be encountered at Palo Verde NP, La Pacífica, Hacienda Solimar, Rincón de la Vieja NP, Hotel Villa Lapas, and Carara NP. In the southern Pacific lowlands, it has been seen at La Cusinga Lodge. The main road into Carara NP has been the most depend-able location to see and hear this raptor, just at sunrise.

Collared Forest-Falcon adult

CRESTED CARACARA

Caracara cheriway (formerly Caracara plancus)
Costa Rican names: *Caracara cargahuesos; cargahuesos; querque.*
21/23 trips; 93 sightings.
Status: Permanent resident.
Length: 19.2–23.2 inches.
Weight: 1 pound 13.4 ounces–2 pounds 1.6 ounces (834–953 grams).
Range: Arizona, Texas, and Florida to Tierra del Fuego and the Falkland Islands.
Elevational range: Sea level to 2,500 feet.

Costa Rica has three species of caracara: Crested, Yellow-headed, and Red-throated. The Crested Caracara, the most common, is found primarily throughout Guanacaste and along Pacific coastal areas southeast to Quepos. It continues to spread south. This is the national bird of Mexico—the "Mexican eagle" that was highly regarded as part of the Aztec culture. The Crested Caracara inhabits dry forest and savanna habitats, where it eats dead animals, human garbage, snakes, lizards, turtles, hatchling caimans, small mammals, beetles, crabs, grubs, earthworms, coconut meat, and even nestling egrets and Roseate Spoonbills.

The Crested Caracara sometimes feeds in groups by walking in recently cultivated fields in search of insects, worms, and grubs or by feeding on dead livestock. This opportunistic bird searches for roadkill along highways or will pursue vultures, other caracaras, or pelicans in the air until they regurgitate their food. The acrobatic caracara will catch the falling meal in flight. Preferred habitats include ranchland, pastures, gallery forests, savannas, wet fields, marshes, and brushlands. This caracara may also fly low over an area and catch small animals by stooping at them.

The Crested Caracara can be observed at Guanacaste, Palo Verde, and Santa Rosa NPs, Lomas Barbudal BR, Hotel Borinquen Mountain Resort, La Ensenada Lodge, Hacienda Solimar, La Pacífica, along Pacific coastal areas south to Carara and Manuel Antonio NPs, La Cusinga Lodge, Hacienda Barú NR, Hotel Cristal Ballena, Rancho Casa Grande, Quepos, San Isidro del General, and the Wilson Botanical Garden. Some can be seen in the Central Plateau. Crested Caracaras have dispersed into the Caribbean lowlands and can also be seen at Caño Negro NWR, Los Chiles, Muelle, Tilajari Resort, La Selva, Sueño Azul, Puerto Viejo en Sarapiquí, and at EARTH University near Guapiles.

Crested Caracara adult

Crested Caracara in flight

YELLOW-HEADED CARACARA

The southern Pacific lowlands are of special ornithological significance because some birds of South American origin have extended their range into this region. Examples are the Yellow-headed Caracara, Blue-headed Parrot, Fork-tailed Flycatcher, Crested Oropendola, Southern Lapwing, Pearl Kite, and Smooth-billed Ani. The Yellow-

Yellow-headed Caracara adult

headed Caracara was first recorded in Costa Rica in 1973. It is identified by the dark brown body and yellowish head and breast. Common in southwestern Costa Rica from Carara NP to the Osa Peninsula and Golfo Dulce region, it has recently been expanding into the lowlands and foothills of the Guanacaste region. A pair nested along the road to Monteverde in 1998. In 1999 one was observed along the Pan American Highway south of Cañas, and one was seen at La Ensenada Lodge in 2007. The range has now extended to the Nicaragua border, and this caracara may now be observed in the vicinity of Los Chiles and Caño Negro NWR.

This unusual raptor is adapted to open pastureland, meadows, and cleared forestland where livestock are present. It may sit on the back of horses and cattle to pick ticks from them, or it may search for insects, caterpillars, lizards, frogs, or small rodents that are flushed by grazing animals. Other food items include roadkill, fledglings in bird nests, African oil palm fruits, and corn.

Yellow-headed Caracaras may be observed throughout much of the southern Pacific lowlands and foothills, including cleared areas around Carara NP, San Isidro del General, and the San Vito area; Corcovado Lodge Tent Camp; Corcovado NP; Lapa Ríos; and Tiskita Jungle Lodge. They may also be seen in Guanacaste and in the region around Los Chiles.

Milvago chimachima
Costa Rican name: *Caracara cabigualdo.*
20/23 trips; 80 sightings.
Status: Permanent resident.
Length: 14.7–15.7 inches.
Weight: 11.1–11.8 ounces (315–335 grams).
Range: Costa Rica to northern Argentina.
Elevational range: Sea level to 5,900 feet.

Laughing Falcon adult

Herpetotheres cachinnans
Costa Rican name: *Guaco.*
22/23 trips; 75 sightings.
Status: Permanent resident.
Length: 17.7–20.9 inches.
Weight: 1 pound 4.0 ounces–1
    pound 12.2 ounces (567–800
    grams).
Range: Mexico to northern
    Argentina.
Elevational range: Sea level to
    6,000 feet.

LAUGHING FALCON

The Laughing Falcon is one of the most memorable—and vocal—raptors in Costa Rica. Its loud, wild, raucous calls pierce the woodlands with sounds resembling its local Spanish name, *guaco.* Sometimes a mated pair will call back and forth to each other in a noisy duet. Three features make this raptor easy to identify: the call, the deep chestnut facial mask, and the creamy-buff throat, breast, and belly.

This falcon inhabits savannas and woodland mixed with meadows and pastures. A snake-eating specialist, the Laughing Falcon sits in a tree where it can scan the surrounding tree branches and ground cover for the movement of snakes. When one is spotted, the falcon drops to grasp the snake in its talons and flies back to a perch, where it decapitates the snake with its sharp bill and eats it. Both venomous and nonvenomous snakes are eaten, as well as rodents and lizards.

Beginning in February, the Laughing Falcon lays an egg in a large tree cavity, in a cavity on a cliff face, or in an abandoned hawk nest. After hatching, the young is protected by one adult while the other parent catches snakes and brings them to the nest.

In the Caribbean lowlands, this falcon may be observed in Tortuguero NP, Tortuga Lodge, Caño Negro NWR and vicinity, along the highway from Guapiles to Limón, Rancho Naturalista, and from Limón south to Cahuita NP. It may also be seen in the vicinity of Puerto Viejo en Sarapiquí, La Selva, Sueño Azul Resort, and La Virgen del Socorro. It can be seen in Guanacaste at La Ensenada Lodge, Hacienda Solimar, Palo Verde NWR, Hotel Borinquen Mountain Resort, and Lomas Barbudal BR. Most, however, occur in the moist and wet mixed forest and pastures from Puntarenas south to Carara NP, Hotel Villa Lapas, Rancho Casa Grande, La Cusinga, Oro Verde BR, Quepos, Manuel Antonio NP, San Isidro del General, Talari Mountain Lodge, Wilson Botanical Garden, Lapa Ríos, Corcovado NP, and Tiskita Jungle Lodge.

WHITE-THROATED CRAKE

The elusive White-throated Crake is one of the most widely heard and seldom seen birds in Costa Rica. It is an attractive member of the rail family, with a rufous breast, neck, and head, a gray face, white throat, and black and white bars on the flanks.

This widespread crake occurs in wet grasslands, marshy habitats, and wetland edges. It is extremely tape-responsive and will call back if a recording is played with its call; it is hard to believe that the long, loud, churring sound comes from such a small bird. There is an art to calling this bird out of its heavy cover. If you play the tape next to thick grassy cover, the crake can be calling within two feet of you and you may never see it. The person with the tape should call from the other side of a small opening in the grassy habitat or from the opposite side of a path or trail to encourage the bird to cross the opening to challenge the call. Others should stand or kneel quietly nearby and watch the edges of the opening. Once the bird has been seen, discontinue the calling to avoid excessive disruption of the crake's behavior.

Among the locations where the White-throated Crake can be seen on the Caribbean slope are Tortuguero NP and Caño Negro NWR and in the vicinity of Los Chiles, La Selva, El Gavilán Lodge, Sueño Azul Resort, Rara Avis, and Rancho Naturalista. On the Pacific slope, it can be encountered at Las Esquinas Rainforest Lodge, at the San Vito airport lagoons, and at the Corcovado Lodge Tent Camp.

Laterallus albigularis
Costa Rican name: *Polluela gargantiblanca.*
18/23 trips; 42 sightings.
Status: Permanent resident.
Length: 5.5–6.3 inches.
Weight: 1.6–1.8 ounces (45–50 grams).
Range: Southeastern Honduras to western Ecuador.
Elevational range: Sea level to 5,000 feet.

White-throated Crake adult

Gray-necked Wood-Rail adult

Aramides cajanea

Costa Rican names: *Rascón cuelligrís; chirincoco; pone-pone; pomponé; cocaleca; cacaleo.*

18/23 trips; 51 sightings.

Status: Permanent resident.

Length: 13.0–15.7 inches.

Weight: 12.3 ounces–1 pound 0.4 ounce (350–466 grams).

Range: Central Mexico to northern Argentina.

Elevational range: Sea level to 4,600 feet.

GRAY-NECKED WOOD-RAIL

One of the loudest and most memorable sounds in tropical wetlands and marshy areas comes from the Gray-necked Wood-Rail. Early and late in the day, a ventriloquial, resonant, and somewhat chickenlike call pierces the swamp or marshland. The phrase sounds somewhat like the expression "kick-walk, kick-walk, kick-walk, cow-cow-cow-cow." The size of a small chicken, this rail stands about ten inches high and is seen more often than other rails. The rich earth tones of its olive, gray, and rufous plumage, highlighted by its yellow bill and red eyes and legs, make this one of the most striking waterbirds in the country.

The Gray-necked Wood-Rail is found in swampy forests, edges of forest streams, wet second-growth forests, mangrove forests, marshes, swampy thickets, wet meadows, pastures, and rice and sugarcane fields with standing water. It is resident throughout lowland and middle elevations of both slopes, including the Central Plateau. The diet consists of crabs, snails, spiders, cockroaches, grasshoppers, frogs, small snakes, berries, palm fruits, bananas, rice, and corn. Some feeding occurs at night. This woodrail may follow army ant swarms so it can catch escaping insects, arthropods, and small vertebrates.

Most rails are incredibly hard to spot, but the patchy characteristics of the habitat occupied by this bird provide viewing opportunities as it walks along wetland edges or as it walks from one patch of marshy cover or bamboo thicket to another. Although heard more often than seen, the Gray-necked Wood-Rail can be seen from boats in the canals of Tortuguero NP, on the Tortuga Lodge grounds, at Selva Verde Lodge, Caño Negro NWR, and in pastures at Sueño Azul Resort. On the Pacific slope, it can be seen in wet meadows of Rincón de la Vieja NP, Carara NP, near San Isidro del General, at Talari Mountain Lodge, Las Esquinas Rainforest Lodge, Tiskita Jungle Lodge, Rancho Casa Grande, and the Wilson Botanical Garden by the bamboo thickets near the heliconia garden. They are also common at Zoo Ave at La Garita, where they come out of the forest after four o'clock each afternoon to eat at feeders that have been placed for free-ranging birds on the grounds.

PURPLE GALLINULE

One of Costa Rica's most colorful waterbirds is the Purple Gallinule, which inhabits marshes, ponds, and lake edges with thick emergent vegetation. With its long toes grasping the plants, this gallinule walks among the floating leaves in search of pondweed, sedges, willow leaves, water lily fruits, berries, rice, small fish, frogs, dragonflies, grasshoppers, flies, spiders, insect larvae, and even the eggs and young of Northern Jacanas. It deftly turns over lily pads to feed on invertebrate eggs and larvae attached beneath the leaves.

Nesting occurs during the rainy season in Guanacaste, but in some areas the Purple Gallinule nests every two to four months year-round. The young may be cared for by extended families—both parents and immature birds from previous broods.

This bird is found in marshy wetlands throughout the Caribbean and Pacific slopes at both lowland and middle elevations. Among places where the Purple Gallinule may be seen are Tortuguero NP, wetlands near La Selva, Selva Verde Lodge, on the pond just inside the entrance to the CATIE tropical agricultural education and research center at Turrialba, Palo Verde NP, La Ensenada Lodge, Carara NP, the airport lagoons at San Vito, and wetlands east of Quepos.

Porphyrio martinica (formerly Porphyrula martinica)

Costa Rican names: *Gallareta morada; calamón morada; gallina de agua.*

21/23 trips; 42 sightings.

Status: Permanent resident.

Length: 10.6–14.1 inches.

Weight: 7.2–10.7 ounces (203–305 grams).

Range: Central and eastern United States to northern Argentina.

Elevational range: Sea level to 5,000 feet.

Purple Gallinule adult

SUNGREBE

Heliornis fulica

Costa Rican name: *Pato cantil.*

6/23 trips; 8 sightings.

Status: Permanent resident.

Length: 10.2–13.0 inches.

Weight: 4.2–5.3 ounces (120–150 grams).

Range: Southeastern Mexico to northeastern Argentina.

Elevational range: Sea level.

The elusive Sungrebe is an avian enigma in Costa Rica. It belongs to a family called Heliornithidae, which is also referred to as the family of "finfoots." This family includes only three species worldwide, the African Finfoot from Africa, the Masked Finfoot from Asia, and the Sungrebe in Central and South America. Ironically, the Sungrebe usually is seen swimming along backwater canals of the Caribbean lowlands, where the overhanging vegetation keeps it in the shade. Perhaps it should be called the Shadegrebe. Its markings include black and white stripes on the head and neck. The Sungrebe usually rests fairly low in the water, like a cormorant or the Anhinga.

The male Sungrebe defends a linear territory of about 200 yards along a backwater canal or swamp. Foods include tadpoles, frogs, lizards, nymph stages of dragonflies and midges, spiders, snails, millipedes, and crabs. Sungrebes build a shallow, flimsy nest on branches overhanging the water. Two altricial young hatch after only about 10 to 11 days and are cared for by both parents. If danger threatens, the male can carry a chick in a fold of skin under each wing. It is the only bird in the world with these armpit pockets, where the adult can carry the young, even in flight. The call is a series of several loud barklike chirps.

The best place in Costa Rica to see the Sungrebe is along the backwater canals of Tortuguero NP. Watch under the overhanging vegetation for its elusive swimming movements. It is most active early in the morning and later in the afternoon. At midday it may rest on a low branch overhanging the water.

Sungrebe adult

SUNBITTERN

One of the most unusual and beautiful waterbirds in Costa Rica is the elusive Sunbittern. It is, however, neither a bittern nor a heron. It belongs to an avian family, Eurypygidae, for which there is only one species. The most closely related bird is the bizarre Kagu from New Caledonia near Australia. These two birds had a common ancestor that existed on the supercontinent Gondwanaland in the Mesozoic Period—before continental drift caused the supercontinent to separate into the continents we know today. The most stunning features of the Sunbittern are the eyeball patterns on the primary wing feathers. When the Sunbittern is faced by a threat, it spreads its wings and tail to display the eyeball patterns and intimidate potential predators into thinking the Sunbittern is larger than it really is.

Sunbittern adult

Eurypyga helias
Costa Rican names: *Garza del sol; sol y luna; ave canasta.*
6/23 trips; 8 sightings.
Status: Permanent resident.
Length: 16.9–18.9 inches.
Weight: 6.6 ounces (188.5 grams).
Range: Southern Mexico to central Brazil.
Elevational range: 300–5,000 feet.

The Sunbittern inhabits Caribbean and southern Pacific wet lowlands and middle elevations. It is usually associated with small, rocky, fast-flowing streams in forested foothills about 2,000 to 4,000 feet in elevation. It captures prey by stalking slowly in shallow water and thrusting the bill forward to spear its quarry. Foods include Dobson fly larvae (*Corydalus* sp.), small fish, eels, frogs, toads, snails, shrimp, lizards, earthworms, crayfish, crabs, dragonflies, cockroaches, katydids, beetles, flies, and spiders. This bird may live up to thirty years.

The Sunbittern can be seen rarely along canals in Tortuguero NP, but it is more common on the Caribbean slope along small streams and wetlands in the vicinity of Turrialba and east of Tuís, Rancho Naturalista, Puerto Viejo en Sarapiquí near Selva Verde Lodge, along the river at Sueño Azul Resort, and La Selva Biological Field Station.

Sunbittern with wings outspread

Double-striped Thick-knee adult

DOUBLE-STRIPED THICK-KNEE

The unusual Double-striped Thick-knee is a well-camouflaged bird of the tropical dry forest. It is found in pastures, burned fields, grain stubble, and savanna habitats of the Guanacaste region and south of Lake Nicaragua. It is the only Costa Rican representative in the family Burhinidae, which includes nine species worldwide. The huge eyes (an adaptation for seeing and feeding at night) have an almost comical appearance.

Burhinus bistriatus
Costa Rican names: *Alcaraván*
  americano; alcaraván.
10/23 trips; 21 sightings.
Status: Permanent resident.
Length: 16.9–18.9 inches.
Weight: 1 pound 11.5 ounces (780 grams).
Range: Southern Mexico to northern Brazil.
Elevational range: Sea level to 2,000 feet.

The short, thick bill is adapted for capturing insects, small lizards, frogs, snails, worms, and mollusks on the ground. Thick-knees rest by day in open fields and heavily grazed pastures, and they can be difficult to spot. They are usually encountered as pairs, because they are monogamous and have strong pair bonds. Dozens of birds may sometimes be seen on disked fields where recent cultivation has exposed invertebrates. Because of the medium brown color of the birds and the tendency for pairs to sit on the ground, the best search technique for spotting them is to look for pairs of cow pies out in the pastures. At night, thick-knees are quite vocal and create intriguing trills, cackles, and piping calls that carry for great distances. The sounds resemble the "winnowing" of a Common Snipe.

The Double-striped Thick-knee is found in Guanacaste Province and is one of the distinctive birds of that area. Look for it near Liberia, Cañas, Bebedero, Lomas Barbudal BR, Guanacaste NP, Palo Verde and Santa Rosa NPs, Hacienda Solimar, La Ensenada Lodge, the Hotel Borinquen Mountain Resort vicinity, and pastures south of Los Chiles. The courtyard at Hacienda Solimar is an excellent place to listen for the calling of thick-knees after dark.

SOUTHERN LAPWING

The elegantly marked Southern Lapwing is a relatively new species in Costa Rica. It was first observed there in 1997 and has continued to spread from its main range in South America northward to both the Pacific and Caribbean lowlands of Costa Rica, where extensive cattle pastures provide ideal habitat for this adaptable species. The lapwing is a large member of the plover family, with several black crest feathers and a grayish-brown back that has a bronzy iridescent sheen over the wing coverts. The face, throat, and upper chest are black.

The Southern Lapwing inhabits pastures, wet meadows, and open grassland, where it hunts for earthworms, grasshoppers, and insect larvae.

In the Caribbean lowlands, this species can be observed in pastures in the Muelle vicinity near the Lost Iguana Resort. In the southern Pacific lowlands they have been regularly encountered in a pasture area behind the Playa Hermosa beach and the Río Tarcoles estuary.

Vanellus chilensis
Costa Rican names: *Avefría tero; chorlito.*
2/23 trips; 2 sightings.
Status: Permanent resident.
Length: 12.6–15 inches.
Weight: 8.8–15 ounces (280–425 grams).
Range: Costa Rica to southern Argentina.
Elevational range: Sea level to 2,400 feet.

Southern Lapwing adult

Semipalmated Plover adult

Charadrius semipalmatus
Costa Rican names: *Chorlitejo
semipalmado; chorlito; turillo.*
11/23 trips; 21 sightings.
Status: Northern migrant.
Length: 6.7–7.5 inches.
Weight: 1.0–2.4 ounces (28–69
grams).
Range: Breeds in Alaska and
northern Canada; winters from
southeastern and southwestern
United States to central Chile
and southern Argentina.
Elevational range: Sea level to
5,000 feet.

SEMIPALMATED PLOVER

The Semipalmated Plover is one of seven plovers in Costa Rica. The others are the Killdeer, the Lesser Golden-Plover, and Black-bellied, Wilson's, Snowy, and Collared Plovers. In contrast to sandpipers, plovers have compact, short-necked bodies and short, thick bills. This plover has a short orange bill tipped with black, a single black breast band, a black bar across the forehead, and a black bar across the face above the bill. These marks differentiate it from the larger Killdeer, which has two breast bands; from the Snowy Plover, which has no breast bands; and from the Collared and Wilson's Plovers, which have single breast bands but no orange on the bills. The bill of Wilson's Plover is longer and thicker than that of the Semipalmated Plover, and the profile suggests that Wilson's Plover is smoking a little cigar.

This plover migrates through Costa Rica, primarily along the Pacific coast, from August through November and from March through May. Some winter along both coasts and may be seen on mud flats, sandy and rocky beaches, river estuaries, mangrove lagoons, and even pond or lake edges in the Central Plateau. As these plovers run in small groups, they pause and peck for polychaete worms, gastropods, grasshoppers, beetles, and ants.

This shorebird can be seen along the canals in Tortuguero NP, in river estuaries south of Limón, in Guanacaste at the salt lagoons of La Ensenada Lodge, at Tamarindo, in the Río Tárcoles estuary by Tárcol Lodge, in the Río Sierpe estuary, in rocky tidepools near Sirena Biological Station in Corcovado NP, and in beach tidepools at Tiskita Jungle Lodge.

AMERICAN OYSTERCATCHER

The only large shorebird in Costa Rica with a long, bright red bill is the American Oystercatcher. The black head and neck, dark back, white breast, and short and stout pink legs make this shorebird easy to identify. The bill, usually held pointing downward at a slight angle, is an adaptation for feeding on clams, snails, crabs, limpets, and oysters in coastal tidepools. The thin, bladelike tip of the bill is deftly inserted into the edge of a slightly open clam shell to snip the muscles that hold the clam shut. Then it opens the clam and eats the meat. This shorebird may live more than twenty years.

The American Oystercatcher may be seen singly, as pairs, or in small groups on sandy or gravelly beaches or exposed rocky tidepools at low tide. Feeding occurs during the day or night and appears to match the exposure of prey items in tidepools at low tide.

Look for the American Oystercatcher along beaches of the Guanacaste region, including rocky tidepools in the Tamarindo area and beaches in the Gulf of Nicoya. It can also be seen at tidepools along the coast of Corcovado NP, like the one near the mouth of the Río Llorona. Migrant oystercatchers can be seen along the Caribbean and Pacific coasts from August to October and from April through May.

Haematopus palliatus
Costa Rican name: *Ostrero americano.*
2/23 trips; 3 sightings.
Status: Permanent resident on Pacific coast and northern migrant.
Length: 15.7–17.3 inches.
Weight: 1 pound 4.0 ounces–1 pound 6.5 ounces (567–638 grams).
Range: Coastal northeastern United States and northern Mexico to southern Argentina and Chile.
Elevational range: Sea level.

American Oystercatcher adult

BLACK-NECKED STILT

Himantopus mexicanus
Costa Rican names: *Cigüeñuela cuellinegro; soldadito.*
17/23 trips; 44 sightings.
Status: Permanent resident and northern migrant.
Length: 13.8–15.7 inches.
Weight: 5.9–7.2 ounces (166–205 grams).
Range: Western and southeastern United States to southern Chile and Argentina.
Elevational range: Sea level to 1,000 feet.

The slender, elegant lines and bold black-and-white markings of the Black-necked Stilt make it one of the most conspicuous and memorable shorebirds in the Americas. The long legs, long neck, and long slender bill are all adaptations that allow the stilt to wade in deeper water than most other shorebirds. It feeds in small flocks, striding through the water and sweeping its bill from side to side to capture aquatic insects, mollusks, crustaceans, annelid worms, tadpoles, and small fish. The bill is extremely sensitive and is also used to probe mud for prey.

The Black-necked Stilt is found in Costa Rica's coastal lowland ponds, marshes, mangrove lagoons, estuaries, and tidal mud flats. In addition to the resident population, migrants may be encountered in the lowlands of both the Caribbean and Pacific slopes from October through May.

Black-necked Stilts may be seen in Caribbean coastal areas at the outlet of the Río Reventazón and at Quatro Esquinas, on shallow wetlands throughout the Río Frío region including Caño Negro NWR, in the Guanacaste region at Palo Verde NP, on marshes near Cañas and Bebedero, La Ensenada Lodge, Hacienda Solimar, Carara NP, at the Río Tárcoles estuary, Playa Hermosa, and Quepos vicinity.

Black-necked Stilt adult

NORTHERN JACANA

Northern Jacana adult

One of the most common and interesting waterbirds of Costa Rica's shallow marshy wetlands is the Northern Jacana. The black and russet body is highlighted by yellow wing feathers, a yellow bill, a yellow frontal shield on the forehead, and unusual yellow spurs that are briefly visible at the wrist joint of the wings each time the bird alights. The sexes are identical, but the females are about 40 percent larger than the males.

Young jacanas are colored so differently that they look like a different species. The back is pale brown, the throat and breast are white, and the cap and back of the neck are dark brown. The wing feathers are yellow like those of the adult.

The jacana has extremely long toes and toenails that enable it to walk on lily pads and floating vegetation as it searches for aquatic insects and other invertebrates, tiny fish, snails, and water lily seeds that have been exposed by Purple Gallinules. The most unusual feature of the jacana is that the females are polyandrous. Each female defends a marshy area that contains enough territory to support one to four males. She mates with all of them, and each male incubates four eggs on small, wet, floating platform nests of aquatic vegetation. The female defends the males as they incubate the eggs, and each male raises the young that hatch in his nest.

The Northern Jacana is readily seen in shallow wetlands of both coasts and in marshes of the Central Plateau. In the Caribbean lowlands, it is common in the Río Frío region, Caño Negro NWR, Lost Iguana Resort and Spa, Tilajari Resort, Tortuguero NP, the outlet of the Río Reventazón, La Selva, and Sueño Azul Resort. In Guanacaste, jacanas are common throughout the wetlands of Palo Verde NP, Hacienda Solimar, La Ensenada Lodge, and Carara NP. In the southern Pacific lowlands, they can be found in low- to middle-elevation wetlands and at the San Vito lagoons near the airport.

Jacana spinosa
Costa Rican names: *Jacana centroamericana; cirujano; gallito de agua; mulita.*
23/23 trips; 140 sightings.
Status: Permanent resident.
Length: 6.7–9.1 inches.
Weight: 3.2–5.7 ounces (91–161 grams).
Range: Southern Texas to western Panama.
Elevational range: Sea level to 5,000 feet.

Northern Jacana immature

Spotted Sandpiper, winter plumage

Actitis macularius
Costa Rican names: *Andarríos maculado; alzacolita; piririza; tigüiza.*
23/23 trips; 154 sightings.
Status: Northern migrant.
Length: 7.1–7.9 inches.
Weight: 1.3–1.4 ounces (37–40 grams).
Range: Breeds from Alaska to central United States; winters from southern United States to northern Argentina.
Elevational range: Sea level to 7,200 feet.

SPOTTED SANDPIPER

The Spotted Sandpiper is the most common sandpiper in Costa Rica. In the northern breeding range, this bird is distinctly marked with black spots on the breast and is characterized by continual "rump-bobbing." When wintering in Costa Rica, however, the Spotted Sandpiper becomes the "spotless sandpiper," because the bird's winter plumage includes a white, unmarked breast. Nevertheless, the rump-bobbing behavior readily identifies the bird. Other identification marks include brownish smudges on the sides of the upper breast, a light horizontal stripe through the top of the eye, and a brownish bill that is yellow at the base.

Unlike many other sandpipers found on marine beaches, the Spotted Sandpiper is also found along the edges of freshwater inland ponds, marshes, and lakes of lowlands, middle elevations, and highlands up to 7,200 feet. The Spotted Sandpiper runs along the water's edge and on beaches to pursue crustaceans, mollusks, fish, fly larvae, beetles, grasshoppers, and caterpillars.

Studies have revealed that Spotted Sandpipers, on their northern nesting grounds in the United States and Canada, are polyandrous, like Northern Jacanas and tinamous. The females are larger and defend territories where they mate with three to four males. Each male has its own nest, where it incubates the eggs and raises about four young.

Some Spotted Sandpipers migrate through Costa Rica en route to Panama and South America from August through October and return through Costa Rica from April to May. Many winter in the country and may be seen along both coasts, at wetlands throughout the Guanacaste region and the San Isidro Valley, in inland wetlands of the Caribbean lowlands, and along highland streams like the Río Savegre in the San Gerardo de Dota Valley.

WANDERING TATTLER

The Wandering Tattler nests along mountain streams of Alaska and northwestern Canada. It can be confused with the Spotted Sandpiper on wintering grounds because it also bobs its rump while running along marine beaches of the southern Pacific lowlands. The Wandering Tattler is much less common than the Spotted Sandpiper, and it is enthusiastically sought by birders.

This sandpiper is eleven inches long, quite a bit larger than the seven- or eight-inch Spotted Sandpiper. Other marks help distinguish it from the Spotted Sandpiper: the body is grayish (brownish on the Spotted Sandpiper) and the chest and upper breast area is grayish (white on the Spotted Sandpiper). The call is a high-pitched whistle.

The Wandering Tattler searches for crustaceans, mollusks, small fish, and marine invertebrates among the tidepools of exposed rocky beaches at low tide on the Pacific coast and on rocky beaches of offshore islands.

Migrants pass along Costa Rica's coastlines from September through November and again from March through April. Some Wandering Tattlers spend the winter along the country's Pacific coast from December through March. Sightings can be expected at Manuel Antonio and Corcovado NPs and at Tiskita Jungle Lodge.

Tringa incana (formerly Heteroscelus incanus)
Costa Rican name: *Correlimos vagamundo.*
5/23 trips; 6 sightings.
Status: Northern migrant.
Length: 10.2–11.4 inches.
Weight: 3.9–7.5 ounces (110–213 grams).
Range: Northeastern Siberia, Alaska, Yukon, and northwestern British Columbia; winters along Pacific coast from coastal southwestern United States south to Ecuador and Galápagos Islands.
Elevational range: Sea level.

Wandering Tattler adult

Willet adult in flight showing white wing bars

Tringa semipalmatus (formerly Catoptrophorus semipalmatus)

Costa Rican name: *Pigüilo.*

18/23 trips; 46 sightings.

Status: Northern migrant.

Length: 13.0–16.1 inches.

Weight: 6.1–13.2 ounces (173–375 grams).

Range: Southern and eastern Canada to northern United States and Gulf Coast; winters from southern United States to Galápagos Islands, northern Chile, and Brazil.

Elevational range: Sea level.

WILLET

The Willet is a large, pale gray sandpiper with a straight, thick bill and prominent black and white bars on the wings. It is among the most common sandpipers of Costa Rica's Caribbean and Pacific beaches. The Willet has a noisy repertoire of loud shrieking "keeek" or "whreek" sounds.

This sandpiper migrates through Costa Rica from August through September and from March through May as it travels to and from wintering sites in Panama and the coasts of South America. Some Willets winter along Costa Rica's beaches.

The Willet lives on mud flats, mangrove lagoons, river estuaries, and rocky shorelines. It may walk in shallow water, pecking and probing for fiddler crabs, marine worms, and aquatic insects. It may also run through shallow water swishing the bill from side to side to capture small fish.

A few Willets may be encountered on the Caribbean coast at Tortuguero NP, at the Río Reventazón estuary, and on estuaries south of Limón, but most occur along Pacific beaches. Good places to observe them include Sugar Beach, Tamarindo, salt ponds at La Ensenada Lodge, Puntarenas, Playa Doña Ana, the Río Tárcoles estuary at Tárcol Lodge, Quepos, Manuel Antonio and Corcovado NPs, Río Sierpe estuary, Sirena Biological Station, and beaches at Tiskita Jungle Lodge.

Willet adult, winter plumage

WHIMBREL

No sandpipers nest in Costa Rica, but twenty-nine species migrate through the country en route to South American wintering grounds. Some winter in the country. One of the largest and most common shorebirds is the Whimbrel. It has a long, down-curved bill (2.9–4.1 inches long) and black and white stripes through the head that differentiate it from other large sandpipers.

The Whimbrel is a type of curlew that migrates along Costa Rica's coasts from August to September and from March to May. Some Whimbrels winter along the country's coastline and wetland edges. It is usually seen singly or in small numbers as it walks along the water's edge in search of ghost and fiddler crabs, crayfish, mollusks, polychaete worms, small fish, and lizards. The long bill is used to reach into fiddler crab (*Uca* sp.) burrows in search of the crabs. The curvature of the Whimbrel's bill matches the curvature of fiddler crab burrows. Its calls include loud piping notes, whistled calls, and trills.

This shorebird can be seen along the beaches of Tortuguero NP and along the Caribbean coastline, including Cahuita NP. Along the Pacific coast, Whimbrels are regularly seen at Sugar Beach, Tamarindo, Río Abangares estuary at La Ensenada Lodge, Playa Doña Ana near Puntarenas, Río Tárcoles estuary, mangrove lagoons at Quepos, Hacienda Barú Natural Reserve, La Cusinga, along the beaches of Corcovado NP, and at Tiskita Jungle Lodge.

Numenius phaeopus
Costa Rican names: *Zarapito trinador; cherelá.*
17/23 trips; 45 sightings.
Status: Northern migrant.
Length: 15.7–18.1 inches.
Weight: 9.4 ounces–1 pound 3.4 ounces (268–550 grams).
Range: Breeds Alaska, northern Canada, and Eurasia; winters southwestern and southeastern United States to southern Brazil and Chile.
Elevational range: Sea level.

Whimbrel adult

RUDDY TURNSTONE

Arenaria interpres
Costa Rican name: *Vuelvepiedras rojizo.*
12/23 trips; 18 sightings.
Status: Northern migrant.
Length: 8.3–10.2 inches.
Weight: 3.0–6.7 ounces (84–190 grams).
Range: Breeds Alaska and northern Canada; winters from both U.S. coasts to Tierra del Fuego.
Elevational range: Sea level.

While the Ruddy Turnstone is in breeding plumage, it is one of the most distinctly marked of all sandpipers. Its nonbreeding plumage on its wintering grounds, however, is much more cryptic. The back and head are grayish brown, the belly is white, and the breast is grayish. The bill, short and thick at the base, is slightly upturned and is adapted for turning over rocks and seaweed to expose marine invertebrates.

The Ruddy Turnstone winters singly or in small flocks along Caribbean and Pacific beaches. It may be encountered on mud flats at river estuaries, on rocky or sandy beaches, or on shallow wetlands and fields near coastal beaches. A flock of a dozen or more birds will walk along the shoreline and flip over stones and other debris in search of crustaceans, mollusks, worms, and insects. They will also eat small fish, eggs of fish and birds, human food scraps, and dead creatures that have washed up on the beach.

This sandpiper migrates along Costa Rica's coastlines from August through October en route to wintering sites in Panama and South America. It returns north from March through May. Small numbers remain on the country's coasts. They can be seen in rocky tidepools at low tide at La Ensenada Lodge, at Tamarindo, at Río Tárcoles estuary near Tárcol Lodge, at Quepos, and along the beaches of Corcovado NP.

Ruddy Turnstone, winter plumage

LAUGHING GULL

The Laughing Gull is the most com-
mon migrant gull in Costa Rica.
Other gulls in the country are the
Ring-billed, Herring, Franklin's,
Bonaparte's, Heermann's, and Sabine's
Gulls. Don't look for the conspicuous
black head and wing tips that are typi-
cal of this bird in breeding plumage.
In winter, adults have a white head
and grayish hood on the back of the

Laughing Gull first-year subadult, left,
and second-year subadult, right

head. The back is gray, the bill and legs are black, the primaries and secondaries are dark, and the tail is white.

First-year subadults have a light brownish to speckled
head and are brownish gray over the back, with a white
rump, a white trailing edge on the wings, and a broad,
black terminal band across the tail. First-year subadults do
not have a well-defined light gray hood over the back of
the head. Second-year subadults have a whitish head with
a pale gray hood over the back of the head.

Laughing Gulls are found on both coasts from September through May but are more abundant on the Pacific
coast. They are commonly seen on sandy beaches and mud
flats. The Laughing Gull catches small fish, aquatic insects,
and shrimp in shallow water; it also captures insects on the
wing, pursues crabs on the beach, scavenges waste materials and fish parts from fishing boats, eats carrion and garbage in seacoast communities, and follows tractors in fields
to capture worms and grubs exposed by cultivation. It will
land on the head of a Brown Pelican that has just dived for
a fish and try to grab the fish out of the pelican's bill as the
pelican raises its head from the water.

The Laughing Gull winters in Costa Rica and also
migrates through Costa Rica from September through
November en route to wintering sites in Panama and
South America. It returns north from April through May.
On the Caribbean coast, these gulls may be seen migrating or wintering along the beach from Tortuguero NP
south to Limón and Cahuita NP. They are common from
September through May on Pacific beaches from Nicaragua to Panama.

*Leucophaeus atricilla (formerly
Larus atricilla)*
Costa Rican name: *Gaviota reidora.*
16/23 trips; 38 sightings.
Status: Northern migrant.
Length: 15.3–18.1 inches.
Weight: 8.5–14.1 ounces (240–400
grams).
Range: Breeds from eastern
Canada and southern California
to Texas, West Indies, and
Venezuela; winters from North
Carolina to southern Peru.
Elevational range: Sea level.

Laughing Gull adult, winter plumage

Royal Tern, winter plumage

Thalasseus maximus (formerly Sterna maxima)

Costa Rican name: *Pagaza real.*

17/23 trips; 49 sightings.

Status: Northern migrant and permanent resident.

Length: 17.7–20.0 inches.

Weight: 11.3 ounces–1 pound 1.6 ounces (320–500 grams).

Range: Breeds from southwestern and eastern United States to Mexico and Uruguay; winters from southern United States to Peru and Argentina.

Elevational range: Sea level.

ROYAL TERN

The Royal Tern is the most common of fifteen terns in Costa Rica. In breeding plumage, the top of the Royal Tern's head, including the eyes, is black, and the bill is bright orange. In winter plumage, the forehead is white, and the crest on the top and back of the head is black, but the black does not extend forward to the eye. Other characteristics include a large orange bill, black feet, and a deeply forked tail.

In comparison, the similar Caspian Tern has black streaking over the crest and forehead, a thick red bill, and a tail that is not deeply forked. The Elegant Tern has a long orange bill that is more slender than that of the Royal Tern and a black crest with a black stripe that extends forward to the eyes. The second most abundant tern in Costa Rica, the Sandwich Tern, is often present with Royal Terns. Smaller than the Royal Tern, it has a black bill with a yellow tip and a short tail.

The Royal Tern feeds by flying over shallow coastline waters and estuaries in search of small fish, squid, shrimp, and crabs. From a height of 15 to 30 feet above the water, the tern plunge-dives to capture its prey but does not submerge. It may also skim the surface and dip its head to capture fish.

The Royal Tern is not known to breed in Costa Rica, but some birds in breeding and nonbreeding plumage are present from May to August. From September through December, migrants pass along the coasts to Panama and South America. Some Royal Terns remain in Costa Rica from December through March. In April and May the terns migrate back to Mexico and the United States.

This bird may be seen along the Caribbean coast on the beaches of Tortuguero NP, at the Río Reventazón estuary, and along estuaries and beaches from Limón to Cahuita NP. More common on the Pacific coast, the Royal Tern is regularly seen at Guanacaste beaches, Puntarenas, Río Tárcoles estuary, Quepos, and Corcovado NP.

SANDWICH TERN

The Sandwich Tern is an attractive, slender tern of the Caribbean and Pacific coasts that is regularly encountered with Laughing Gulls and Royal Terns. It is distinguished by its black bill, which usually has a yellow tip. The Elegant Tern is similar but has a slender orange bill and is uncommon. The Royal Tern is significantly larger and has a thicker orange bill. The very large Caspian Tern has a reddish bill.

When hunting, the Sandwich Tern plunge-dives for small fish, shrimp, and squid at the surface. Migrants are common along both coasts from September through November and from April through May. Some winter on Costa Rica's coasts, and some nonbreeding birds remain in the country during the remainder of the year.

Look for the Sandwich Tern from Limón southeast to Cahuita at estuaries where streams flow into the Caribbean, like Quebrada Westfalia. More common on the Pacific coast, it may be seen on the beaches at Tamarindo, Playa Grande, La Ensenada Lodge, Puntarenas, Río Tárcoles estuary near Tárcol Lodge, Hacienda Barú Natural Reserve, Playa Hermosa, Damas Island mangrove lagoons near Quepos, and along beaches of the Osa Peninsula, including those near Carate and Corcovado Lodge Tent Camp.

Thalasseus sandvicensis (formerly Sterna sandvicensis)
Costa Rican name: *Pagaza puntiamarilla.*
13/23 trips; 27 sightings.
Status: Northern migrant; nonbreeding summer resident.
Length: 16 inches.
Weight: 6.7 ounces (190 grams).
Range: Eastern U.S. coast to Uruguay; British Isles to Caspian Sea; Pacific coast from Oaxaca, Mexico, to Peru.
Elevational range: Sea level.

Sandwich Tern showing black bill with yellow tip

PALE-VENTED PIGEON

Patagioenas cayennensis (formerly Columba cayennensis)
Costa Rican name: *Paloma colorada.*
19/23 trips; 59 sightings.
Status: Permanent resident.
Length: 10.0–10.4 inches.
Weight: 5.9–9.2 ounces (167–262 grams).
Range: Southern Mexico to northern Argentina.
Elevational range: Sea level to 2,000 feet.

The Pale-vented Pigeon is a large member of the pigeon family found in the Caribbean and southern Pacific wet lowlands. It has a rufous-purple color over the back with a gray head, black bill, and a pale to whitish vent area. The Short-billed Pigeon lives in similar habitats and has a similar body color, but it is smaller and does not have a gray head or pale vent.

This pigeon is most frequently seen at the edge of forests; in second-growth forests, plantations, and pastures with scattered trees; in mangrove forests; and along riverbanks. It is not common in mature unbroken rainforest. Pale-vented Pigeons are typically found high in the canopy, where they forage for berries and fruits of *Miconia*, *Byrsonima*, *Solanum*, *Trema*, and *Conostegia*.

In the Caribbean lowlands, the Pale-vented Pigeon may be encountered from Caño Negro NWR near Los Chiles at the Nicaragua border to Tortuguero NP, Tortuga Lodge, Puerto Viejo en Sarapiquí, Monteverde, La Selva, Sueño Azul Resort, and south to Cahuita NP. In the southern Pacific lowlands, it may be seen at Carara NP, Hotel Villa Lapas, Villa Caletas, Manuel Antonio NP, Quepos vicinity, Rancho Casa Grande, and the Wilson Botanical Garden.

Pale-vented Pigeon adult

SCALED PIGEON

The Scaled Pigeon is the most attractively marked pigeon in Costa Rica. The throat and breast are richly marked, with scalloped edges on the feathers that are iridescent green to dark purplish. The head is purplish brown and the back and wings are reddish purple. The bill is red with a white tip.

This pigeon is found in moist to wet lowlands of the Caribbean slope, including mature forest, forest edges, and forest openings and pastures with scattered trees. They are usually spotted in treetops singly or as pairs or trios. Scaled Pigeons forage for small fruits in the forest canopy.

In the Caribbean lowlands, this pigeon may be encountered at Caño Negro NWR, in the Río Frío region, La Selva, and Sueño Azul Resort grounds. In the southern Pacific lowlands, it is more prevalent at middle elevations, such as the Wilson Botanical Garden and San Vito area, but it also can be seen at La Cusinga Lodge and on the grounds of Hotel Cristal Ballena.

Patagioenas speciosa (formerly Columba speciosa)
Costa Rican name: *Paloma esacamosa.*
12/23 trips; 24 sightings.
Status: Permanent resident.
Length: 11.0–13.4 inches.
Weight: 8.0–12.3 ounces (225–350 grams).
Range: Southern Mexico to southern Brazil.
Elevational range: Sea level to 4,000 feet.

Scaled Pigeon adult

Red-billed Pigeon adult

RED-BILLED PIGEON

The Red-billed Pigeon is a large pigeon with a white to whitish-yellow bill that is pinkish red at the base. The head, neck, and breast are a deep wine-red color, the back is grayish, the shoulders are brownish, the tail is black, and the feet are red. The iris is deep orange. Males are larger than females, and the wine red of the head and neck area is a richer color than that of the female.

Patagioenas flavirostris (formerly Columba flavirostris)

Costa Rican names: *Paloma morada; paloma piquirroja.*

22/23 trips; 100 sightings.

Status: Permanent resident.

Length: 12 inches.

Weight: 9.4–14.9 ounces (268–424 grams).

Range: Northwestern Mexico to Costa Rica.

Elevational range: Sea level to 7,000 feet.

This pigeon inhabits open and agricultural country. It is most common in the dry forests and brushy pastures of Guanacaste Province, the Central Plateau, and middle elevations of Poás, Irazú, and Barva volcanoes and nearby foothills. Single birds, pairs, or small flocks may be seen perched in trees while feeding on berries, buds, figs (*Ficus*), and guava (*Psidium guajava*). Ground foraging is also common. In Guanacaste, flocks may be seen eating spilled grain along the Pan American Highway. In agricultural sites, it may be considered a pest because it eats new sprouts of corn and sorghum.

The Red-billed Pigeon is common throughout Guanacaste and southeast to Carara NP, Villa Caletas, and Hotel Villa Lapas. It has been recorded at Quepos and Rancho Casa Grande. In the highlands and Central Plateau, it occurs at Monteverde, San José de la Montaña, San José, Sarchí, Xandari Plantation Resort, Orosi, Curridabat, La Paz Waterfall Gardens, Hotel Bougainvillea, and even Savegre Mountain Lodge. On the Caribbean slope, this pigeon is found from Caño Negro NWR near Los Chiles to La Virgen del Socorro, Rancho Naturalista, Puerto Viejo en Sarapiquí, La Selva Biological Field Station, El Gavilán Lodge, Sueño Azul Resort, and Selva Verde Lodge.

BAND-TAILED PIGEON

The dove and pigeon family is well represented in Costa Rica, with twenty-five doves, pigeons, and quail-doves. The large Band-tailed Pigeon lives in mountainous regions. This handsome bird has a grayish-purple body, a white bar across the back of the neck, and an iridescent greenish patch below the white neck bar. Although this pigeon is found from Canada through Argentina, the Band-tailed Pigeon of Costa Rica and western Panama is a darker, separate subspecies (*Patagioenas fasciata crissalis*). On this subspecies, the bill is yellow with a pale grayish tip, and the more northern subspecies has a black-tipped bill.

The Band-tailed Pigeon is usually seen as a high, fast-flying flock of ten to thirty birds passing over forested regions of the volcanoes surrounding the Central Plateau and montane forests of Cerro de la Muerte and the Talamanca Mountains. When perched, this pigeon usually sits at the top of a tree. It is easy to identify because it is the only pigeon with a white bar across the back of the neck. Acorns are a preferred food, as well as fruits of bayberry (*Myrica*) and pokeweed (*Phytolacca*).

Look for flocks of Band-tailed Pigeons on Poás and Barva volcanoes, at Monteverde, along the Pan American Highway in Cerro de la Muerte from kilometers 62 to 96, and in the San Gerardo de Dota Valley. In January and February, Band-tailed Pigeons sometimes descend to the Pacific coast in the vicinity of Carara NP, Hotel Villa Lapas, and Villa Caletas.

Patagioenas fasciata
Costa Rican name: *Paloma collareja.*
20/23 trips; 75 sightings.
Status: Permanent resident.
Length: 13.0–15.7 inches.
Weight: 8.0 ounces–1 pound 0.2 ounce (226–460 grams).
Range: Southwestern Canada to northern Argentina.
Elevational range: 3,000–10,000 feet.

Band-tailed Pigeon adult showing yellow bill with grayish tip and white neck collar

SHORT-BILLED PIGEON

Patagioenas nigrirostris (formerly Columba nigrirostris)
Costa Rican name: *Paloma piquicorta.*
23/23 trips; 131 sightings.
Status: Permanent resident.
Length: 10.2–12.2 inches.
Weight: 4.5–8.3 ounces (128–236 grams).
Range: Southern Mexico to northwestern Colombia.
Elevational range: Sea level to 4,800 feet.

The Short-billed Pigeon gives a special touch to the rain-forest with its "Who-cooks-for-you" call. This pigeon of Costa Rica's moist and wet Caribbean and southern Pacific lowlands is a deep wine-red color. A closely related species, the Ruddy Pigeon, is found in the highlands and is also a deep wine-red color.

The preferred habitat includes mature rainforest, older second growth, and forest edges. This pigeon forages mainly at middle to upper levels of the canopy for fruits and berries, like mistletoe berries and *Cecropia* catkins. It will also descend to lower levels to eat pokeberries (*Phytolacca* sp.) and to forage for fruits that have fallen to the ground.

In the Caribbean lowlands, Short-billed Pigeons can be seen and heard at locations like Tortuguero NP, Tortuga Lodge, La Selva, Selva Verde Lodge, El Gavilán Lodge, and Sueño Azul Resort. They are found up to middle eleva-tions on the Caribbean slope at Rancho Naturalista and at lower levels of Braulio Carrillo NP. This pigeon is com-mon in the southern Pacific lowlands from Carara NP to the Panama border and inland to San Vito.

Short-billed Pigeon pair

WHITE-WINGED DOVE

The White-winged Dove is characteristic of the Guanacaste dry forest. It is sandy brown with conspicuous white patches on the wings that are visible both at rest and in flight. Flocks may be seen flying over savannas, shrubby areas, pastures, and grain fields as they search for waste grain and seeds on the ground. The species roosts in large flocks in scattered trees.

The White-winged Dove feeds by walking on the ground and foraging for grit, small seeds, rice, and corn. The resident nesting population of White-winged Doves is a nonmigratory subspecies that occurs only in Costa Rica and western Panama (*Zenaida asiatica australis*). Migratory doves from the Río Grande Valley of Texas and northern Mexico arrive in Guanacaste in November and depart in May.

The White-winged Dove is common throughout most of Guanacaste south to Puntarenas and Orotina. It is particularly tame and common around Puntarenas. Its range has recently expanded to the Central Plateau and San José.

Zenaida asiatica
Costa Rican name: *Paloma aliblanca.*
18/23 trips; 47 sightings.
Status: Permanent resident and northern migrant.
Length: 9.8–12.2 inches.
Weight: 4.4–6.6 ounces (125–187 grams).
Range: Southwestern United States to Panama.
Elevational range: Sea level to 1,650 feet.

White-winged Dove adult

INCA DOVE

Columbina inca

Costa Rican names: *Tortolita colilarga; San Juan.*

21/23 trips; 77 sightings.

Status: Permanent resident.

Length: 7.4–8.7 inches.

Weight: 1.1–2.0 ounces (30–58 grams).

Range: Southwestern United States to northwestern and central Costa Rica.

Elevational range: Sea level to 4,500 feet.

Only two members of the dove and pigeon family in Costa Rica have a strongly scaled plumage—the Scaled Pigeon, which is a large, reddish woodland species, and the small, pale gray Inca Dove. The Inca Dove is a tropical dry forest bird that expanded its range into Costa Rica from the north in 1928. Since then it has spread throughout Guanacaste, south to Quepos, and east to Cartago and Paraíso in the Central Plateau. This small dove has a loud two-note call described as "cow-coo."

The Inca Dove inhabits open terrain of dry forests, second-growth scrubland, backyards, woodlots, and grassy areas. It searches the ground for small seeds, waste grain, and grit and feeds singly or in small numbers. Nesting occurs primarily during the rainy season.

The Inca Dove is a common bird that can be encountered on ranches and around residences throughout Guanacaste and south to Puntarenas, Quepos, and the vicinity of Las Esquinas Rainforest Lodge. Its range continues to expand through the Central Plateau and Caribbean lowlands eastward to the vicinity of La Selva and Sueño Azul Resort.

Inca Dove adult

RUDDY GROUND-DOVE

The small, rust-colored Ruddy Ground-Dove is a common and easily identified dove that frequents yards, gardens, roadsides, and pastures of Costa Rica. The male has a rufous body and a bluish-gray cap. The female is browner and less distinctive, but it is frequently seen in association with the male. They may perch so closely that they touch each other. The call is described as "kitty-woo."

The Ruddy Ground-Dove is present in the Caribbean lowlands, including Guapiles, and from Caño Negro NWR and Los Chiles south to Muelle, the Arenal volcano area, and Puerto Viejo en Sarapiquí. It is most common in the moist Pacific lowlands south of the Gulf of Nicoya. Look for it in Cañas, Puntarenas, Carara NP, Quepos, Manuel Antonio NP, San Isidro del General, La Ensenada Lodge, Hotel Villa Lapas, Rancho Casa Grande, Lapa Ríos, Corcovado Lodge Tent Camp, and Tiskita Jungle Lodge.

Ruddy Ground-Dove male

Columbina talpacoti
Costa Rican names: *Tortolita rojiza; tortolita; palomita colorada.*
23/23 trips; 141 sightings.
Status: Permanent resident.
Length: 5.5–7.1 inches.
Weight: 1.2–2.0 ounces (35–56 grams).
Range: Mexico to northern Argentina.
Elevational range: Sea level to 4,600 feet.

Ruddy Ground-Dove female

White-tipped Dove adult

Leptotila verreauxi
Costa Rican names: *Paloma coliblanca; yuré; coliblanca.*
23/23 trips; 161 sightings.
Status: Permanent resident.
Length: 9.3–11.6 inches.
Weight: 3.4–5.5 ounces (96–157 grams).
Range: Southern Texas to central Argentina.
Elevational range: Sea level to 7,200 feet.

WHITE-TIPPED DOVE

Common throughout the American tropics, the White-tipped Dove is a medium-sized bird with a plain gray-brown body, black bill, red legs, blue eye-ring, and orange iris. The outer feathers of the tail are tipped with white and are the source of the bird's name. These white tips show up well in flight. The White-tipped Dove occurs throughout the Central Plateau, along the Pacific lowlands from Nicaragua to Panama, and east from the Central Plateau into northern regions of the Caribbean slope. This dove is adapted to disturbed habitats like second-growth forest, brushlands, farms, and backyards. It can be quite tame. It does not occur in undisturbed forest. The White-tipped Dove walks on the ground in search of small seeds, berries, and insects. Sorghum and corn are included in the diet. The call of this dove is a ventriloquial "hoop" that simulates the sound of blowing across the mouth of a bottle.

In the Caribbean lowlands, look for the White-tipped Dove at Caño Negro NWR, La Selva, and Sueño Azul Resort. In Guanacaste, it is common at Guanacaste, Palo Verde, and Santa Rosa NPs; Lomas Barbudal BR; the Hotel Borinquen Mountain Resort; and the Cañas vicinity. It is more common in the southern Pacific lowlands. It is very tame along the beaches of Manuel Antonio NP. Some White-tipped Doves can be seen in the highlands at Savegre Mountain Lodge, Bosque de Paz, La Paz Waterfall Gardens, and nearby Sarchí and Rancho Naturalista.

SULPHUR-WINGED PARAKEET

Costa Rica is home to sixteen members of the parrot family, including two macaws, six parakeets, one parrotlet, and seven parrots. These birds add a wonderful tropical dimension to the forests of Costa Rica, and seeing them is always a highlight for tourists. Most of these birds have a broad range in Latin America, but two are endemic to the mountains of Costa Rica and western Panama, the Sulphur-winged Parakeet and the Red-fronted Parrotlet. One other parakeet is endemic from southeastern Nicaragua to western Panama, the Crimson-fronted Parakeet.

The Sulphur-winged Parakeet is distinguished by red ear markings, and in flight the underside of the wings is mostly yellow. It is found in highland oak forests of the Talamanca Mountains and is regularly seen in the San Gerardo de Dota Valley. This adaptable parakeet occurs in small flocks and frequents mature forests, cutover forests, forest edges, and highland apple orchards. Its preferred foods include *Ficus, Croton, Myrtus, Miconia,* and apples. Outside the breeding season, these flocks range to lower elevations in the Central Plateau and south to San Isidro del General.

This parakeet may be encountered at Tapantí NP and in Cerro de la Muerte. The best place to observe it is in the vicinity of the apple orchards in the San Gerardo de Dota Valley.

Sulphur-winged Parakeet adult

Pyrrhura hoffmanni
Costa Rican name: *Perico aliazufrado.*
15/23 trips; 38 sightings.
Status: Permanent resident.
Length: 9.1–9.5 inches.
Weight: 2.6–2.9 ounces (75–82 grams).
Range: Endemic to southern Costa Rica and western Panama.
Elevational range: 2,300–10,000 feet.

Parakeets and parrots are green because their feathers contain both blue and yellow structural layers. This Crimson-fronted Parakeet is blue because it lacks the yellow structural layer.

Aratinga finschi
Costa Rican name: *Perico frentirrojo.*
22/23 trips; 78 sightings.
Status: Permanent resident.
Length: 11 inches.
Weight: 5.3 ounces (150 grams).
Range: Endemic from southeastern Nicaragua to western Panama.
Elevational range: Sea level to 5,000 feet.

CRIMSON-FRONTED PARAKEET

The Crimson-fronted Parakeet has a restricted range but can be very common in the San José area, including downtown San José, where it roosts in the Parque Central. It occurs in the northern Caribbean lowlands and foothills, and in the southern Pacific lowlands to the Panama border. This is the most commonly seen parakeet in the San José area. The call consists of short, squeaky squawks, often heard as the birds are in flight. The adaptable Crimson-fronted Parakeet has learned to feed on agricultural crops like corn and sorghum and thrives in cutover forests, second growth, gardens, and coffee plantations. Other foods include *Erythrina, Inga, Croton,* and wild figs.

Distinguishing marks include a long pointed tail and bright red forehead. In flight, this parakeet has red under the leading edge of the wing at the wrist joint. Populations of this parakeet have been increasing and expanding to new areas of Costa Rica as tropical forests have been cut and converted to agricultural crop production.

The green coloration of parrots is caused not by pigments in the feathers but by two structural layers in the feathers. The base layer creates a blue color through refraction. The light then passes through a transparent layer that creates yellow through refraction of light. This combination creates the green coloration of parrots and parakeets. Rarely, a parakeet or parrot will have the genes for only one of those structural layers. If the yellow layer is missing, the bird will be blue. If the blue layer is missing, the bird will be yellow.

Look for the Crimson-fronted Parakeet from the Nicaragua border at Caño Negro NWR and Los Chiles south to Muelle, Tilajari Resort, La Selva, Selva Verde Lodge, Guapiles, El Pizote Lodge, and Rancho Naturalista, throughout San José and the Central Plateau, and in the southern Pacific region at the Wilson Botanical Garden, San Vito, Carara NP, Tiskita Jungle Lodge, and Playa Hermosa.

Crimson-fronted Parakeet adult

OLIVE-THROATED PARAKEET

The Olive-throated Parakeet is a common parakeet of the humid Caribbean lowlands from Los Chiles and Caño Negro NWR southeast to the Panama border. It is green overall with a green head and an olive-colored throat. In flight, blue primary and secondary feathers can be seen.

This parakeet usually occurs in small flocks in primary forest, forest edges, gardens, plantations, and forest openings along rivers. It eats native and cultivated fruits, seeds, and flowers, including corn, guava, figs, *Inga, Hura,* and *Hieronyma*. The call consists of high-pitched screeches and a two-note chirp in which the second note is slightly higher than the first. The Olive-throated Parakeet creates a cavity in an arboreal termite mound, usually near a forest edge, for use as a nesting site. The termitary creates a waterproof shelter for incubating and raising three to four young from April through May.

Look for the Olive-throated Parakeet in Caño Negro NWR and southeast through La Selva, to Sueño Azul Resort, east to Tortuguero NP, and south to Guapiles, Limón, Puerto Viejo, and Cahuita.

Aratinga nana
Costa Rican name: *Perico azteco.*
12/23 trips; 25 sightings.
Status: Permanent resident.
Length: 8.7–10.2 inches.
Weight: 2.5–3.0 ounces (72–85 grams).
Range: East central Mexico to western Panama.
Elevational range: Sea level to 3,300 feet.

Olive-throated Parakeet adult

Orange-fronted Parakeet, head detail

Aratinga canicularis
Costa Rican names: *Catano; periquito; zapoyol; perico frentinaranja.*
15/23 trips; 40 sightings.
Status: Permanent resident.
Length: 9.1–9.8 inches.
Weight: 2.4–3.8 ounces (68–180 grams).
Range: Western Mexico to central Costa Rica.
Elevational range: Sea level to 3,300 feet.

ORANGE-FRONTED PARAKEET

Three members of the parrot family have a reference to "fronted" in their common name: White-fronted Parrot, Crimson-fronted Parakeet, and Orange-fronted Parakeet. In each case, "front" refers to the forehead. The Orange-fronted Parakeet has a bright orange forehead and blue on top of the head. The tail is long and pointed.

A common bird of the dry forest, this parakeet is found in savannas, pastures, and deciduous forests. It eats fruits of *Ficus, Bursera,* and *Brosimum* trees; flowers of *Combretum* and *Gliricidia;* and seeds of *Ceiba* and *Inga* trees. As with other parakeets, this bird sleeps in communal roosts that may contain hundreds of individuals.

The Orange-fronted Parakeet is one of many Costa Rican birds that excavates a nest cavity within a termite nest. These are the large gray structures commonly seen on the side of a tree trunk or atop a fence post. The benefits of this nesting structure include protection from rain and insulation from hot weather. Chicks are often stolen from their nest by local residents who use them as pets. This parakeet can be seen throughout Guanacaste, along the road that leads from the Pan American Highway to Monteverde and south through Carara NP to Quepos.

Orange-fronted Parakeet at the entrance to its nest in a termite nest

GREAT GREEN MACAW

The Great Green Macaw is an endangered and beautiful bird of Caribbean lowland rainforests. Its last stronghold appears to be along the Nicaraguan border near Laguna del Lagarto Lodge and Tortuguero NP. The intense green and blue of the body, highlighted by red tail feathers, make this imposing member of the parrot family a stunning symbol of the country's diminishing rainforests. It is a victim of both deforestation and the illegal pet trade. This macaw ranges widely across the Caribbean lowlands in search of food, but the amount of suitable remaining nesting habitat appears very small, the number of feeding trees is declining, and the number of birds left is probably only thirty to thirty-five pairs. The nationwide population count declined from 549 in 1998 to 210 in 2000.

Ara ambiguus
Costa Rican names: *Lapa verde; guacamayo verde mayor.*
6/23 trips; 13 sightings.
Status: Permanent resident.
Length: 33.5–35.4 inches.
Weight: 2 pounds 12.6 ounces–3 pounds 2.4 ounces (1,265–1,430 grams).
Range: Eastern Honduras to western Ecuador.
Elevational range: Sea level to 2,500 feet.

The bill of this macaw is larger than that of the Scarlet Macaw and is adapted to cracking open the very tough nuts of the swamp almond tree (*Dipteryx panamensis*). The life cycle of this macaw appears to be tied very closely to *Dipteryx* trees; it nests in hollow cavities of this tree and depends on the nuts as a major food.

These macaws may live more than sixty years. The only places that offer a fair opportunity to see the Great Green Macaw are Tortuguero NP, Boca Tapada, Laguna del Lagarto Lodge, La Selva, EARTH University near Guapiles, Rara Avis, the Rainforest Aerial Tram property, and the Costa Rican Amphibian Research Center near Guayacán. The Tropical Science Center is working to save the last nesting areas of this species through research and creation of a new reserve called Maguenque NP. More information can be obtained by contacting the Tropical Science Center at 506-2253-3267 (lapa@cct.or.cr).

Great Green Macaw adult

SCARLET MACAW

Ara macao
Costa Rican names: *Lapa roja; lapa colorada.*
16/23 trips; 76 sightings.
Status: Permanent resident.
Length: 33.1–35.0 inches.
Weight: 1 pound 15.7 ounces–3 pounds 4.5 ounces (900–1,490 grams).
Range: Southeastern Mexico to central Brazil.
Elevational range: Sea level to 2,600 feet.

One of the most spectacular and beautiful birds in Costa Rica is the endangered Scarlet Macaw. Its large size and gaudy colors make it a favorite of even the most casual tourist. The Scarlet Macaw is usually heard before it is seen. Its coarse, raucous squawks carry great distances as mated pairs fly from roosts and nesting sites to trees ripe with fruits and nuts.

The Scarlet Macaw has been ruthlessly endangered by people who have sought it only as a pretty bird to be taken from the wild for use as a pet. For decades, nesting trees have been cut down and the chicks stolen to sell to the local and international pet trade. Costa Rica is, however, a place where it is once again possible to see this magnificent species in flight, squawking back and forth with its lifetime mate and raising its young in huge hollow trees.

Scarlet Macaws live in dry, moist, and wet tropical lowland forests of the Pacific slope where large mature trees provide nesting cavities and diverse crops of wild nuts, fruits, and flowers. Macaws eat fruits and flowers of *Jacaranda, Hymenaea, Guarea, Hura,* wild beach almond

Scarlet Macaw adult

(*Terminalia catappa*), *Virola, Erythrina,* balsa (*Ochroma*), *Spondias, Eschweilera, Inga, Bursera,* fig (*Ficus*), *Dipteryx,* and *Enterolobium.* The heavy bill of the macaw is very efficient for breaking open nuts and palm fruit. Scarlet Macaws mate for life and may live more than sixty years in captivity but less in the wild.

A few remaining pairs of Scarlet Macaws are found in protected dry forests of Guanacaste, like those in Palo Verde NP. In addition, a few Scarlet Macaws were first sighted in early 1999 in Tortuguero NP. They may represent birds dispersing from rainforests of southeastern Nicaragua. If so, these are the first Scarlet Macaws to occur in the Caribbean lowlands in decades. Sightings have continued there in 2000 and 2001.

There are several places to see these birds in the southern Pacific lowlands. If you arrive at the bridge over the Río Tárcoles by the entrance to Carara NP at sunrise, it is possible to see and hear pairs of Scarlet Macaws leaving their roosting areas and dispersing over the forest. Within that national park and at nearby Villa Lapas and Villa Caletas, it is possible to see them feeding in fruiting trees and attending their nest cavities. The best place to see them in abundance is at Sirena Biological Station in Corcovado NP, Drake Bay Wilderness Resort, Luna Lodge, Lapa Ríos, and Corcovado Lodge Tent Camp. Along the beaches, they can be observed feeding on wild beach almond (*Terminalia catappa*) fruit.

In recent years, hand-reared Scarlet Macaws have been reintroduced to the Tiskita area, east of the Golfo Dulce near the Panama border, where they had been extirpated for decades. This effort was organized by Margo and Richard Frisius, who founded the Asociación Amigos de las Aves near San José in 1992. Since 2002, fifty-two macaws have been hand-raised and subsequently released at Tiskita Jungle Lodge. Four chicks were hatched in the wild in 2008 and give promise for the future recovery of the species in that region.

ORANGE-CHINNED PARAKEET

Brotogeris jugularis
Costa Rican names: Catano;
zapoyolito; perico; periquito
barbinaranja.
22/23 trips; 100 sightings.
Status: Permanent resident.
Length: 7.1–7.5 inches.
Weight: 1.9–2.3 ounces (53–65
grams).
Range: Southwestern Mexico to
Colombia and Venezuela.
Elevational range: Sea level to
4,000 feet.

The Orange-chinned Parakeet is one of the most common and smallest members of the parrot family in Costa Rica. This parakeet has a small orange patch on the "chin," but that patch often is not visible. More conspicuous identification features include a short, compact appearance; brownish shoulder areas; a very short, pointed tail; and yellow linings under the wings, which are visible in flight. This parakeet is often seen in flocks of four to five individuals.

The Orange-chinned Parakeet was originally a bird of open, savanna-like habitat in dry forests, pastures with scattered trees, and gallery forests of the Guanacaste region. Many of the fruits and flowers it eats, however, grow in deforested areas. Lowland and middle-elevation moist and wet forests of the Caribbean and Pacific slopes that have been cleared for pastures, fields, and plantations now provide habitat for the Orange-chinned Parakeet. Foods include fruits and seeds of figs (*Ficus*), *Ceiba, Byrsonima, Cecropia, Bombax,* and *Muntingia* and the flowers and nectar of *Erythrina,* guava (*Psidium guajava*), *Bombacopsis,* and balsa (*Ochroma lagopus*).

Orange-chinned Parakeets may be observed in the Caribbean lowlands at Caño Negro NWR, La Selva, Sueño Azul Resort, and Guapiles. They come to the feeders at Tilajari Resort, near Muelle, to eat papayas. On the Pacific slope, this bird is common throughout Guanacaste, Carara NP, Quepos, San Isidro, San Vito, Corcovado NP, Corcovado Lodge Tent Camp, and Tiskita Jungle Lodge. Small flocks can be seen flying around San José, including the grounds of the University of Costa Rica, Hotel Bougainvillea, and Parque Central.

Orange-chinned Parakeet adult

BLUE-HEADED PARROT

The Blue-headed Parrot is the only parrot with a blue head. A small parrot of South American origin, it has expanded into Costa Rica within the last one hundred years. This parrot is in the same genus as the White-crowned Parrot, but in flight the Blue-headed Parrot's wing beat is shallower.

This parrot is adapted to life in lowland rainforests but also thrives in deciduous forests, second-growth forests, pastures, plantations, and woodlands. It expanded into Costa Rica in association with the cutting of lowland rainforests because it eats seeds and fruits of plants that grow after mature forests are cut. Among its foods are palm fruits and seeds of *Anacardium, Hura, Clusia,* wild avocado (*Persea*), *Inga, Brosimum,* and fig (*Ficus*), as well as flowers of *Erythrina* and *Psidium.*

Look for this distinctive parrot in Cahuita NP and along the highway from Limón to Cahuita. It is also present in the vicinity of the Wilson Botanical Garden and the San Vito area.

Pionus menstruus
Costa Rican names: *Chucuyo; loro cabeciazul.*
9/23 trips; 22 sightings.
Status: Permanent resident.
Length: 9.5–11.0 inches.
Weight: 7.4–10.4 ounces (209–295 grams).
Range: Eastern Costa Rica to eastern Brazil.
Elevational range: Sea level to 3,900 feet.

Blue-headed Parrot adult

WHITE-CROWNED PARROT

Pionus senilis

Costa Rican names: *Chucuyo; loro coroniblanco.*

22/23 trips; 143 sightings.

Status: Permanent resident.

Length: 9.4 inches.

Weight: 6.8–8.1 ounces (193–229 grams).

Range: Northeastern Mexico to western Panama.

Elevational range: Sea level to 5,250 feet.

The seven parrots found in Costa Rica are the Brown-hooded, White-crowned, Blue-headed, White-fronted, Red-lored, Yellow-naped, and Mealy. The White-crowned Parrot is a conspicuous and abundant small parrot of the humid lowlands in the Caribbean and southern Pacific slopes. It frequently sits atop a palm tree in an upright "Maltese falcon" pose. The white crown is distinctive, the head is dark bluish green, and the shoulders are coppery brown. In flight, the wing beats show deeper strokes than most other parrots, which have shallow wing beats. It frequently travels in flocks of more than fifty birds.

This parrot usually keeps to the treetops and is associated with second-growth forests, forest openings, plantations, and croplands. Foods include palm fruits and seeds of *Dendropanax, Inga,* and *Erythrina.* The White-crowned Parrot is sometimes considered a pest by farmers because it eats corn, grain sorghum, and pejivalle palm fruits.

White-crowned Parrots may be observed in the Caribbean lowlands at Caño Negro NWR, Guapiles, Puerto Viejo en Sarapiquí, La Selva, La Virgen del Socorro, Tortuguero and Cahuita NPs, and Limón. In the Pacific lowlands, sightings are common in San Isidro del General, Wilson Botanical Garden, and Carara, Manuel Antonio, and Corcovado NPs. These birds also range to the Central Plateau outside the breeding season in search of food and may be seen at middle and higher elevations, at sites like Rara Avis, Rancho Naturalista, and the Sarchí area.

White-crowned Parrot adult

WHITE-FRONTED PARROT

The names "White-fronted" and "White-crowned" are so similar that one would expect those two parrots to be easily confused with each other; however, there is a significant difference. The White-crowned Parrot is primarily a bird of the wet Caribbean lowlands and the southern Pacific lowlands. The White-fronted Parrot is a species of Mexican origin that reaches the southern limit of its range in the tropical dry forests of northwestern Costa Rica. There is little or no overlap in the ranges of these two species.

The White-fronted Parrot has a white forehead; the white does not extend to the top of the head as it does on the White-crowned Parrot. There are red highlights at the base of the bill, and on the male the red surrounds the eyes. The top of the head is blue. In flight, it is possible to see red at the bend of the wing and blue on the secondary feathers. This parrot inhabits tropical dry forest, gallery forests, and ranchland with scattered trees and woodlots in Guanacaste. It roosts at night in communal flocks that disperse into small groups or flocks of thirty to fifty during the day to locate trees with ripe fruits, nuts, and flowers. Among the foods eaten are figs (*Ficus*), *Inga, Croton,* wild almond (*Terminalia*) and cactus. Mangoes and corn are also eaten.

Like most other parrots and parakeets in Guanacaste, White-fronted Parrots nest during the dry season from December through March. Monogamous pairs select nest sites in tree cavities and vacant woodpecker holes.

The White-fronted Parrot can be encountered throughout most of Guanacaste, including Guanacaste, Palo Verde, and Santa Rosa NPs; in Lomas Barbudal BR; and south to Carara NP. It occurs in the Liberia and Cañas vicinities; along Pacific coastal areas like Playa Doña Ana, Tamarindo, and Sugar Beach; and in pasturelands approaching Monteverde.

White-fronted Parrot

Amazona albifrons
Costa Rican names: *Lora; Loro frentiblanco.*
14/23 trips; 41 sightings.
Status: Permanent resident.
Length: 9.8–11.4 inches.
Weight: 6.2–8.5 ounces (176–242 grams).
Range: Northwestern Mexico to northwestern Costa Rica.
Elevational range: Sea level to 3,500 feet.

Parrots are green because of blue and yellow structural layers in the feathers. This Red-lored Parrot lacks the blue structural layer, making it appear yellow.

Amazona autumnalis
Costa Rican names: *Lora; loro frentirrojo.*
18/23 trips; 86 sightings.
Status: Permanent resident.
Length: 12.6–13.8 inches.
Weight: 11.1 ounces–1 pound 1.1 ounces (314–485 grams).
Range: Eastern Mexico to northwestern Brazil.
Elevational range: Sea level to 3,300 feet.

RED-LORED PARROT

Many tropical birds play a role in dispersing seeds of rainforest plants by swallowing fruits whole and regurgitating the seeds or passing the intact seeds in their droppings. Parrots, macaws, and parakeets, including the Red-lored Parrot, are, however, seed destroyers—like peccaries. They crush the seeds in order to digest the nutrients. The Red-lored Parrot is a large parrot that has a conspicuous red forehead and blue on top of the head, and in flight, it is possible to see red patches in the secondary wing feathers.

In addition to the image of a Red-lored Parrot with normal plumage shown here, another photo has been included of a rare yellow phase of the species. The green coloration of parrots is caused not by pigments in the feathers but by two structural layers in the feathers, as described under "Crimson-fronted Parakeet." If the feathers lack the layer that creates the blue color, the bird will be yellow. These rare color phases may occur in any species of parrots or parakeets.

This parrot inhabits moist and wet lowland forests and adjacent middle elevations of the Caribbean and southern Pacific slopes. Preferred habitats include forest openings, second growth, pastures, and plantations mixed with forests. Foods include palm fruits, figs (*Ficus*), *Virola, Casearia, Protium, Cordia lutea, Stemmadenia, Spondias,* mangoes, and oranges. These parrots have regularly been poached for use as pets.

On the Caribbean slope, look for the Red-lored Parrot in treetop feeding sites in the vicinity of Cahuita and Tortuguero NPs, Puerto Viejo en Sarapiquí, La Selva, and in tropical lowlands south and east from Caño Negro NWR. On the southern Pacific slope, this parrot can be seen near Quepos, Manuel Antonio, Carara, and Corcovado NPs and at Drake Bay Wilderness Resort, Corcovado Lodge Tent Camp, Lapa Ríos, Hotel Villa Lapas, Rancho Casa Grande, Las Esquinas Rainforest Lodge, and Tiskita Jungle Lodge.

Red-lored Parrot

MEALY PARROT

The Mealy Parrot, the largest parrot in Costa Rica, is a green parrot whose identification marks are a conspicuous whitish eye-ring and a narrow black cere above the bill. A bird of undisturbed lowland rainforests of the Caribbean and southern Pacific slopes, the Mealy Parrot has a distribution similar to that of the Red-lored Parrot. The Mealy Parrot, however, declines as an area is deforested whereas the Red-lored Parrot increases. This parrot may be encountered as pairs or in small flocks. During the rainy season, Mealy Parrots roost at night in communal flocks exceeding one hundred birds. Foods include fruits, nuts, and seeds of palms (*Euterpe*), figs (*Ficus*), *Cecropia, Brosimum, Inga, Pithecellobium,* buttercup trees (*Cochlospermum vitifolium*), *Virola,* and *Casearia.*

Look for the Mealy Parrot in Tortuguero and Cahuita NPs, Selva Verde Lodge, La Selva, and Sueño Azul Resort on the Caribbean slope. On the southern Pacific slope, this parrot can be seen at Carara NP, Hotel Villa Lapas, Villa Caletas, Hotel Cristal Ballena, Las Esquinas Rainforest Lodge, Rancho Casa Grande, and south to Tiskita Jungle Lodge.

Mealy Parrot, head detail

Amazona farinosa
Costa Rican names: *Lora; lora verde.*
17/23 trips; 63 sightings.
Status: Permanent resident.
Length: 15.0–16.9 inches.
Weight: 1 pound 2.9 ounces–1 pound 11.0 ounces (535–766 grams).
Range: Southeastern Mexico to southeastern Brazil.
Elevational range: Sea level to 1,600 feet.

Mealy Parrot adult

Yellow-naped Parrot pair

Amazona auropalliata
Costa Rican names: *Lora; lora de nuca amarilla.*
13/23 trips; 27 sightings.
Status: Permanent resident.
Length: 13.8–15.0 inches.
Weight: 12.0 ounces–1 pound 2.9 ounces (340–535 grams).
Range: Southern Mexico to northwestern Costa Rica.
Elevational range: Sea level to 2,000 feet.

YELLOW-NAPED PARROT

The Yellow-naped Parrot is one of ten closely related but distinctive Yellow-crowned Parrots (*Amazona ochrocephala*) found from Mexico to Brazil and Peru. Some taxonomists consider this a subspecies of the Yellow-crowned Parrot (*Amazona o. auropalliata*), but the Yellow-naped Parrot is treated here as a separate species. Identification marks include a yellow nape, black cere, and pale eye-ring. In flight, red patches are visible on the secondary wing feathers. The wing beats are characterized by very shallow strokes that make it appear as if only the wing tips are beating. Because this bird is considered a good talking parrot, it has been ruthlessly stolen from the wild by poachers who cut down or climb nesting trees to remove young from the nests.

Like the White-fronted Parrot, the Yellow-naped Parrot is found only in lowland dry forests, mangrove forests, gallery forests, savannas, mixed pastures, and woodlots of Guanacaste southeast to Carara NP. Foods eaten include the wild almond (*Terminalia*), *Acacia, Tabebuia,* buttercup tree (*Cochlospermum vitifolium*), *Curatella,* figs (*Ficus*), and *Erythrina*. Some cultivated crops are also eaten, including corn, mangoes, lemons, avocados, and green bananas.

This parrot has declined where it is not protected from people who poach it for use as pets. It may be seen in protected Guanacaste dry forests and mangrove lagoons of Las Baulas, Guanacaste, Palo Verde, Santa Rosa, and Carara NPs and Lomas Barbudal BR. It can be seen in the vicinity of La Ensenada Lodge, Hotel Borinquen Mountain Resort, La Pacífica, and the Río Tárcoles estuary.

SQUIRREL CUCKOO

There are eleven members of the cuckoo family in Costa Rica, including two northern migrants (Black-billed and Yellow-billed Cuckoos), one endemic species on Cocos Island (Cocos Cuckoo), and eight permanent residents: Mangrove, Squirrel, Striped, and Pheasant Cuckoos; Lesser and Rufous-vented Ground-Cuckoos; and Groove-billed and Smooth-billed Anis. The Squirrel Cuckoo is a widespread, common, and conspicuous bird whose bright rufous plumage is readily sighted in treetop foliage.

This adaptable bird is found in dry, moist, and wet forests; gallery and mangrove forests; forest edges; woodlots; shade coffee plantations; and pastures with scattered trees. Foraging singly or in pairs, the Squirrel Cuckoo searches leaf cover for caterpillars, grasshoppers, moths, beetles, ants, katydids, small lizards, and spiders. Occasionally it will follow army ant swarms to capture escaping creatures. One of its common sounds is an extended series of twenty or more loud robinlike chirps given at the same pitch and frequency.

The Squirrel Cuckoo is common in the forests of Tortuguero NP, along the coast from Limón to Cahuita NP, and in the forests of La Selva, Selva Verde Lodge, and El Gavilán Lodge. It is very common in shade coffee plantations of the Central Plateau. The Squirrel Cuckoo may be seen throughout Guanacaste and at middle and higher elevations, including Monteverde Cloud Forest Reserve, Rara Avis, Rancho Naturalista, Rainforest Aerial Tram, Braulio Carrillo NP, and the Wilson Botanical Garden near San Vito.

Piaya cayana
Costa Rican names: *Bobo chiso;*
  cuco ardilla.
23/23 trips; 156 sightings.
Status: Permanent resident.
Length: 18 inches.
Weight: 3.5 ounces (98 grams).
Range: Northwestern Mexico to northern Argentina.
Elevational range: Sea level to 8,000 feet.

Squirrel Cuckoo adult

Mangrove Cuckoo adult

Coccyzus minor
Costa Rican names: *Cucillo de antifaz; orejinegro.*
6/23 trips; 11 sightings.
Status: Permanent resident.
Length: 11.0–12.6 inches.
Weight: 2.3–2.5 ounces (65–70 grams).
Range: Southern Mexico coastal areas south to eastern Brazil.
Elevational range: Sea level to 3,600 feet.

MANGROVE CUCKOO

The Mangrove Cuckoo is one of those mangrove-specialty birds sought by birders in Costa Rica, along with the Mangrove Hummingbird, the Mangrove Vireo, and the mangrove race of the Yellow Warbler. The Mangrove Cuckoo inhabits lowland mangrove and Pacific coast riparian and scrub-type dry and moist forests from Guanacaste south to the Panama border. This cuckoo is distinguished by a black mask and buffy breast. The bill has a black maxilla (upper bill) and yellow mandible (lower bill) with a black tip. In addition to mangrove habitats, it may be seen inland through much of the Guanacaste Province and in the Río Frío region as well as on the Osa Peninsula.

Foods of this cuckoo include caterpillars, spiders, grasshoppers, walkingsticks, flies, beetles, frogs, fruits, berries, and eggs and nestlings of small birds. The Mangrove Cuckoo hops along branches of trees in mangroves and scrub forests, where it gleans its prey from leaves and twigs.

This cuckoo is found only along the Pacific coastal region and Río Frío area, including Caño Negro NWR. It can be seen in the forests at Palo Verde NP, Tamarindo and Playa Grande NPs, Río Corobicí at La Pacífica, Playa Doña Ana south of Puntarenas, Damas Island estuary at Quepos, and Corcovado Lodge Tent Camp vicinity on the Osa Peninsula.

SMOOTH-BILLED ANI

The Smooth-billed Ani is a recent addition to Costa Rica's avifauna. It is distinguished by a huge high-arching bill that lacks the grooves of the Groove-billed Ani. It was first recorded in the country in 1931, when it extended its range from Panama. It is now found throughout the southern Pacific lowlands and continues to extend its range into the foothills approaching the Central Plateau and southern portions of Guanacaste.

This large, black, floppy-tailed member of the cuckoo family is usually seen in flocks in brushy roadsides and pasture areas. It feeds on small lizards, frogs, bird eggs and nestlings, snakes, and small invertebrates. Flocks will typically follow herds of cattle to eat creatures flushed by the cattle, and they will also accompany swarms of army ants for the same purpose. Several females will lay their eggs in the same nest, so one nest may contain more than fifteen eggs. A pair of anis may share chick-rearing duties with other members of their social group.

This species was introduced to the Galápagos Islands in 1962 by farmers who thought the anis would eat ticks from their cattle, but they became a terrible exotic nuisance species, eating the eggs and young of the endangered Darwin's finches there.

Look for the Smooth-billed Ani in the southern Pacific lowlands along roadsides from Quepos to the Panama border and from coastal areas inland to Talari Mountain Lodge and the Wilson Botanical Garden.

Crotophaga ani
Costa Rican name: *Garrapatero piquiliso.*
12/23 trips; 40 sightings.
Status: Permanent resident.
Length: 14 inches.
Weight: 3.3–4.0 ounces (95–115 grams).
Range: Central Florida to northern Argentina.
Elevational range: Sea level to 4,000 feet.

Smooth-billed Ani adult

Groove-billed Ani adult

Crotophaga sulcirostris
Costa Rican names: *Tijo; zopilotillo; garrapatero piquiestriado.*
22/23 trips; 194 sightings.
Status: Permanent resident.
Length: 12 inches.
Weight: 2.5–2.8 ounces (70–80 grams).
Range: Central Texas to northwestern Argentina.
Elevational range: Sea level to 7,500 feet.

GROOVE-BILLED ANI

The Groove-billed Ani is a conspicuous black bird of tropical lowlands that is not in the blackbird family (Icteridae). A cuckoo, this social bird lives in small groups that include two or three monogamous pairs and their young in a territory that may encompass 2.5 to 25 acres. All members of the flock cooperate in nesting and raising young. This ani is named for prominent grooves along the curving contour of the bill. The Costa Rican name for this bird is "tijo," derived from its call, "tee-ho, tee-ho, tee-ho."

The Groove-billed Ani is a common, adaptable bird of open country, roadsides, plantations, and pastures. Groups of anis forage for grasshoppers, flies, wasps, ants, cicadas, *Norops* lizards, and cockroaches. Like Cattle Egrets, anis accompany livestock and capture insects flushed by cows or horses. Sometimes anis will pick ticks from the skin of these animals, and they also follow army ants to catch insects flushed by them.

Anis frequently seek prey in wet foliage and subsequently dry themselves by sunning in an upright pose with outstretched wings. This sunning behavior may also help raise their body temperature in the morning, because at night their body temperature drops from 105 to 93 degrees Fahrenheit.

Nesting is a cooperative activity carried out by the entire flock of anis from June through November. All the females lay their eggs in the nest, with the most dominant female laying her eggs last, on top of the others. Those last eggs have the greatest chance of hatching. The nest eventually contains twelve to fifteen eggs. All of the males and females take part in incubation. The entire group of anis feeds the young, and the group may renest several times in one season.

Look for the Groove-billed Ani in lowland and middle elevations of the Caribbean lowlands, Guanacaste Province, and the Central Plateau. At higher elevations, it occurs near Monteverde, San José de la Montaña on Barva volcano, Tapantí NP, and Rancho Naturalista.

PACIFIC SCREECH-OWL

Four screech-owls are found in Costa Rica: the Tropical, Pacific, Vermiculated, and Bare-shanked. The Bare-shanked Screech-Owl is found at higher elevations, the Pacific and Vermiculated Screech-Owls are found at lowland elevations, and the Tropical Screech-Owl is a bird of foothills and middle elevations. The Pacific Screech-Owl is limited primarily to the Guanacaste region.

This owl is found in mangrove forests, riparian forests, woodlots, farm groves, and savannas. At night it hunts primarily for large insects like beetles, moths, and katydids. Like the Tropical Screech-Owl, the Pacific Screech-Owl has ear tufts and fine vertical black streaking on the breast.

Pacific Screech-Owl young

The Pacific Screech-Owl gives a staccato series of five to fifteen sharp, hooting notes in its call, with the last notes in the series louder, at a higher pitch, and slower than the first notes. It is tape-responsive and will come to the recorded sound of its call. This owl nests in hollow trees and vacant woodpecker cavities during the dry season. It can be encountered on the grounds of La Pacífica, Tárcol Lodge, and Hacienda Solimar.

Megascops cooperi (formerly Otus cooperi)

Costa Rican name: *Lechucita sabanera.*

9/23 trips; 17 sightings.

Status: Permanent resident.

Length: 7.9–10.0 inches.

Weight: 5.1–6.0 ounces (145–170 grams).

Range: Pacific southern Mexico to northwestern Costa Rica.

Elevational range: Sea level to 3,300 feet.

Pacific Screech-Owl adult

Tropical Screech-Owl adult

Megascops choliba (formerly Otus choliba)

Costa Rican names: *Lechucita neotropical; estucurú; sorococa.*

6/23 trips; 9 sightings.

Status: Permanent resident.

Length: 7.9–9.4 inches.

Weight: 3.4–5.6 ounces (97–160 grams).

Range: Costa Rica to Paraguay.

Elevational range: 1,300–5,000 feet.

TROPICAL SCREECH-OWL

The Tropical Screech-Owl is the common screech-owl of the Central Plateau and premontane forests from the Tilarán Mountains south to the Panama border. This owl has a pair of conspicuous ear tufts. The Tropical Screech-Owl occurs only in a grayish-brown color phase; it does not have a rufous color phase, as some other screech-owls do. It makes several calls, including a rapid high-pitched trill ending with a higher-pitched "toot-toot," a slower extended trill, and an extended "cooo-cooo-cooo-cooo-tooka-tooka-tooka-took-took" phrase.

The Tropical Screech-Owl inhabits mixed woodland, open areas, farms, woodlots, plantations, orchards, second-growth forests, and urban areas. It hunts at night by perching on low tree branches and watching for insects, spiders, beetles, crickets, snakes, scorpions, rodents, and bats. Sometimes this owl will hunt near security lights to capture katydids and moths attracted to the lights.

The Tropical Screech-Owl can sometimes be attracted by playing a tape of its call or by taping and playing back its call. The use of such playbacks should be discontinued after the owl comes to the tape to avoid disrupting normal territorial behavior. This owl is regularly encountered at the Wilson Botanical Garden near San Vito, Talari Mountain Lodge near San Isidro del General, Xandari Plantation Resort, and in shade coffee plantations of the Central Plateau.

VERMICULATED SCREECH-OWL

The Vermiculated Screech-Owl occurs in wet tropical lowlands of the Caribbean slope and the southern Pacific slope to elevations of 3,300 feet, so the range does not overlap with that of the Pacific Screech-Owl. The Vermiculated Screech-Owl has inconspicuous ear tufts and occurs in grayish-brown and rufous-brown color phases. This screech-owl does not have vertical streaking on the breast. The call is a resonant trill that extends over five to ten seconds. The volume increases toward the middle and decreases toward the end of the call.

The Vermiculated Screech-Owl hunts at night near forest openings or in tall second-growth forests. Food items include moths, beetles, and katydids. Nesting occurs from March through April in old trogon nesting cavities in dead trees. It is present at La Selva Biological Field Station in the Arboretum area.

Megascops guatemalae (formerly Otus guatemalae)
Costa Rican name: *Lechucita vermiculada.*
2/23 trips; 2 sightings.
Status: Permanent resident.
Length: 7.9–9.1 inches.
Weight: 3.5–3.9 ounces (100–110 grams).
Range: Northeastern Costa Rica to northern Bolivia.
Elevational range: Sea level to 3,300 feet.

Vermiculated Screech-Owl adult

Crested Owl pair

Lophostrix cristata
Costa Rican name: *Buho penachudo.*
8/23 trips; 11 sightings.
Status: Permanent resident.
Length: 14.2–16.9 inches.
Weight: 14.0 ounces–1 pound 5.1 ounces (400–600 grams).
Range: Southern Mexico to northeastern Argentina.
Elevational range: Sea level to 5,000 feet.

CRESTED OWL

The Crested Owl is one of Costa Rica's most impressive owls. Its white markings above the eyes, sharply angled like Mr. Spock's eyebrows, are unlike those of any other owl. Although nocturnal, it can sometimes be seen during the day in a day roost beneath overgrown tangles of vines within fifteen feet of the ground. This owl occurs in two color phases. The darker color phase is usually found near wetter habitats and is characterized by a darker grayish-brown head and shoulders and dark cinnamon to ochraceous brown over the back. The lighter phase is sandy to buffy brown and is associated with drier environments.

The Crested Owl is a medium-sized nocturnal raptor that eats beetles, katydids, grasshoppers, caterpillars, and cockroaches. It lives in tropical lowland rainforests and middle-elevation forests that have not been significantly logged. Frequently it lives at the edges of forests, along stream banks, and near Pacific beaches. When heard in the tropical nighttime, the call is a heart-stopping, resonant growl that increases in volume in the middle; the call lasts only about a second or two.

On the Caribbean slope, look for the Crested Owl in Tortuguero NP, along the back trail at Tortuga Lodge, in the Arboretum at La Selva, and at Rancho Naturalista at night along the trail to the hummingbird meadow. If searching for this bird at night, you may need to play its call to get it to respond and come to the call. As with other species, please limit calling to avoid disrupting the owl's hunting activities more than a few minutes. On the Pacific slope, you may be able to locate a day roost along the overgrown beach trail near Corcovado Lodge Tent Camp or at Oro Verde BR. It can also be seen at La Cusinga and at the Wilson Botanical Garden along the river trail.

SPECTACLED OWL

The Spectacled Owl is the largest owl in Costa Rica's forests. Adults feature white highlights around the dark brown facial disks that surround each eye, giving the owl its name. Even the downy white young have a spectacled appearance because of their brown facial disks. In Peru, this owl has a local name meaning "the undertaker," because one of its most common calls is a muffled series of seven to nine staccato, ventriloquial notes that are likened to the sound of an undertaker pounding nails into a coffin. The notes descend slightly in pitch and accelerate in frequency toward the end of the call. Sometimes a pair of these owls will call back and forth to each other.

The Spectacled Owl inhabits dry, moist, and wet tropical forests throughout the lowlands and middle elevations of both slopes. It may be encountered in primary forest, secondary forest, gallery forest, and shade coffee plantations and along forest and stream edges. Hunting occurs at night when the owl perches at mid-canopy levels and watches for the movement of grasshoppers, opossums, katydids, lizards, skunks, jays, bats, crabs, and mice.

This widespread owl may be found in forests of Tortuguero, Corcovado, Tapantí, Guanacaste, Santa Rosa, Carara, and Palo Verde NPs. It has been observed along the canals of Tortuguero NP and along trails of the Sirena Biological Station. It has also been seen at Selva Verde Lodge, El Gavilán Lodge, Monteverde, and on the grounds of Villa Lapas near Carara NP.

Spectacled Owl chick

Pulsatrix perspicillata
Costa Rican names: *Buho de anteojos; oropopo; olopopo.*
5/23 trips; 8 sightings.
Status: Permanent resident.
Length: 16.9–20.4 inches.
Weight: 1 pound 5 ounces–2 pounds 12 ounces (590–1,250 grams).
Range: Southern Mexico to northern Argentina.
Elevational range: Sea level to 5,000 feet.

Spectacled Owl adult

Costa Rican Pygmy-Owl adult

Glaucidium costaricanum (formerly Glaucidium jardinii)
Costa Rican name: *Mochuelo montañero.*
9/23 trips; 9 sightings.
Status: Permanent resident.
Length: 6 inches.
Weight: 2.3 ounces (65 grams).
Range: Endemic to Costa Rica and western Panama.
Elevational range: 3,000–10,000 feet.

COSTA RICAN PYGMY-OWL

Three tiny owls called pygmy-owls occur in Costa Rica: Central American, Costa Rican, and Ferruginous. The Central American Pygmy-Owl is found in the Caribbean lowlands, the Costa Rican Pygmy-Owl occurs in the highlands, and the Ferruginous Pygmy-Owl lives in the Guanacaste lowlands and the Central Plateau.

The tiny Costa Rican Pygmy-Owl was formerly considered a race of the more widely distributed Andean Pygmy-Owl. Recently it has been divided into its own species. This reaffirms that the reproductive isolation of this owl in the oak-dominated highlands of Costa Rica and western Panama has resulted in the creation of an individual species from a formerly widespread ancestor found throughout montane forests from Mexico through the Andes of South America.

This highland owl occurs in two color morphs, dark brown and cinnamon rufous. It hunts during the day and will take small birds, so its presence is often betrayed by hummingbirds, warblers, and other species that scold it to drive it away. The call is an extended series of paired, high-pitched, hornlike "toot-toot, toot-toot, toot-toot" calls. The calls can sometimes be played in the highlands to attract songbirds and hummingbirds that come to scold the owl, and sometimes the call will also attract the owl itself. When perched quietly on an epiphyte-festooned horizontal tree branch, this owl looks no larger than a tennis ball with eyes. It feeds on insects, small birds, and lizards like those of the genus *Norops*. The Costa Rican Pygmy-Owl is a cavity nester and uses a former woodpecker hole, like that of the Acorn Woodpecker, for its nest.

The Costa Rican Pygmy-Owl can be observed at Tapantí NP, on the volcanoes surrounding the Central Plateau, and in the Talamanca Mountains including the San Gerardo de Dota region. It is regularly observed along the mountain trails above Savegre Mountain Lodge.

FERRUGINOUS PYGMY-OWL

The Ferruginous Pygmy-Owl is the most common of the three pygmy-owls. No more than six inches tall, it is more frequently seen and heard during the day than other owls. The call is distinctive, an extended series of high-pitched "toots."

The adaptable Ferruginous Pygmy-Owl is a dry-forest species found mainly in the savannas, riparian areas, and dry forests of Guanacaste and pastures, woodlands, coffee plantations, and suburban areas of the Central Plateau. This owl hunts primarily at dawn and dusk but also in daytime and at night. It perches and waits to spot its prey and then makes a swift flight to capture it. The relatively long tail provides great maneuverability for capturing prey, including small birds, grasshoppers, katydids, mice, and small lizards. Because this bird is a predator of songbirds, small birds mob it whenever it is discovered. In fact, the call of this owl is sometimes mimicked by birders by whistling or by use of a tape recording to attract hummingbirds and songbirds for viewing.

This owl may be observed throughout Guanacaste, including Santa Rosa, Guanacaste, and Palo Verde NPs, Palo Verde NWR, ranchland woodlots, and Hacienda Solimar. Toward San José and its suburbs, the owl can also be observed in backyards and scattered woods. It occurs on the grounds of Hotel Aeropuerto at Alajuela, Xandari Plantation Resort, and Hotel Bougainvillea.

Ferruginous Pygmy-Owl adult

Glaucidium brasilianum
Costa Rican names: *Mochuelo común; cuatro ojos; mahafierro.*
13/23 trips; 37 sightings.
Status: Permanent resident.
Length: 6 inches.
Weight: 2.5 ounces (70 grams).
Range: Southwestern United States to southern Argentina.
Elevational range: Sea level to 5,000 feet.

MOTTLED OWL

Ciccaba virgata

Costa Rican names: *Lechuza café; hu de león.*

13/23 trips; 26 sightings.

Status: Permanent resident.

Length: 11.4–15.0 inches.

Weight: 6.2–11.3 ounces (175–320 grams).

Range: Northern Mexico to northern Argentina.

Elevational range: Sea level to 7,200 feet.

The Mottled Owl, a widespread and common owl of Costa Rica's lowland and middle elevations, is distinguished from smaller screech-owls by its lack of ear tufts and its more heavily mottled breast. One of its distinctive calls is a series of about six ventriloquial-sounding notes that are each best described as "whoOOoo," with more emphasis and volume in the middle of each note.

This owl inhabits forest edges and openings, shade coffee plantations, and second growth. Hunting takes place at night for prey including cockroaches, grasshoppers, beetles, katydids, small rodents, bats, tree frogs, salamanders, lizards, and small snakes. It has been observed coming to security lights at night to feed on insects attracted to the lights.

This bird, found in lowland and middle elevations of the Caribbean slope, occurs regularly at Rancho Naturalista. In Guanacaste, it is found in gallery forests, like those along the Río Corobicí at La Pacífica, and in moist and wet forests of the southern Pacific lowlands and middle elevations. It has been observed there at the Wilson Botanical Garden and Savegre Mountain Lodge.

Mottled Owl adult

BLACK-AND-WHITE OWL

The Black-and-white Owl is a striking and beautiful rainforest species highlighted by fine black-and-white vermiculations on the breast. Although typically associated with mature rainforests of both Caribbean and southern Pacific lowlands, this adaptable owl is also found in mangrove forests, forest edges, gardens, lodges, and city parks where large quantities of insects and bats are attracted to lights at night.

At Tortuga Lodge on the Caribbean coast, Black-and-white Owls regularly visited the dock at night for years because bulldog fishing bats (*Noctilio* sp.) came to feed on top-minnows that were attracted to feed under the security lights along the shore. Between 1990 and 1991, a Black-and-white Owl cleaned out an entire group of about fifteen bulldog fishing bats that had regularly fed at Tortuga Lodge.

Black-and-white Owl adult

This owl feeds on beetles, grasshoppers, crickets, and rodents, as well as bats. The call consists of four to eight rapidly ascending hoots "hoo—hoo—hoo—hoo—hoo" followed by a final emphatic note "HOOH." It also makes a loud two-note ascending hoot-type call.

In the Caribbean lowlands, this owl can be seen or called in at night with the limited use of recordings of its call (if permissible) at Tortuguero NP, Tortuga Lodge grounds, El Gavilán Lodge, and La Selva (Arboretum Trail). In the Pacific lowlands it can be encountered at Carara NP, Hotel Villa Lapas courtyard and grounds, and the Wilson Botanical Garden. The best place to see this owl is in the city park of Orotina northeast of Carara NP. A pair of owls has lived in that park for many years. They feed on bats and insects that are attracted to the city lights at night. You will find the owls in the trees, during the daytime, directly above the owl "whitewash" that you will see on the sidewalk at the park.

Ciccaba nigrolineata
Costa Rican name: *Lechuza blanco y negro.*
13/23 trips; 21 sightings.
Status: Permanent resident.
Length: 13.0–17.7 inches.
Weight: 15.3 ounces–1 pound 2.9 ounces (434–536 grams).
Range: Central Mexico to northwestern Peru.
Elevational range: Sea level to 5,000 feet.

Striped Owl adult

*Pseudoscops clamator (formerly
   Asio clamator)*
Costa Rican name: *Buho listado.*
7/23 trips; 8 sightings.
Status: Permanent resident.
Length: 11.8–15.0 inches.
Weight: 11.3 ounces to 1 pound 1.6
   ounces (320–500 grams).
Range: Southern Mexico to
   northern Argentina.
Elevational range: Sea level to
   4,500 feet.

STRIPED OWL

The Striped Owl has long blackish ear tufts, a facial disk edged with black, and a white to buffy breast heavily streaked with brownish black. The back is tawny buff and streaked with irregular black marks. Closely related to the Short-eared Owl, this is the only medium-sized owl in Costa Rica with ear tufts and heavy streaking on the breast. Its calls include high-pitched screams and squeals, a series of barking doglike hoots, a series of about seven low muffled hoots, and an extended single hoot with a rising inflection in the middle of the call.

An inhabitant of farms, pastures, scattered woodlots, savannas, marshes, rice fields, and grasslands with thickets of brush and trees, this owl rests during the day in the thick cover of woodlots and brush. It comes out at dusk and hunts by perching on power lines or fence posts, along roadsides, or on tree branches where it watches for prey. It may also hunt at night in a manner similar to that used by the diurnal Short-eared Owl—by flying low over open grassy or marshy areas. Prey includes small mammals, birds, large insects, and some reptiles.

This owl has been sighted in the Puerto Viejo area near Selva Verde Lodge, San Isidro del General, and in the northern Caribbean lowlands. It is widely distributed in the lowlands and middle elevations of the Pacific slope.

Striped Owl, front view

LESSER NIGHTHAWK

Ten members of the nighthawk family are known from Costa Rica. The Short-tailed Nighthawk, Common Pauraque, Ocellated Poorwill and Rufous, Dusky and White-tailed Nightjars are all resident breeding birds. The Chuck-will's-Widow and Whippoor-will are rare migrants from October to April. The Common Nighthawk and Lesser Nighthawk are both breeding residents

Lesser Nighthawk adult

and migrants from the north. The reference to the Lesser Nighthawk as the "trilling" nighthawk refers to this bird's habit of producing a toadlike trill when perched on the ground during the nesting season.

This nighthawk, a species of dry forests, savannas, and arid habitats, is found in open areas and pastures where there are scattered trees and nearby wetlands, wet meadows, or rivers. At dusk and dawn this nighthawk makes low, erratic flights near the ground to capture beetles, wasps, flying ants, craneflies, and dragonflies.

The Lesser Nighthawk nests in the Pacific coastal lowlands on open areas of grass or sand just beyond the beach. It can sometimes be found roosting on the ground in loosely assembled colonies of more than ten birds from March through June. Two eggs are laid on the bare ground when nesting. If intruders approach the nest, the adults put on a broken-wing act to lead the potential predator away.

Although the Lesser Nighthawk can be encountered throughout the year along the Pacific slope and up to the Central Plateau, northern migrants enter Costa Rica in September and can become locally abundant as they migrate along the Pacific and Caribbean coastal regions. They return north in March and April. Look for this bird in Guanacaste near Cañas, Bebedero, Palo Verde, and Santa Rosa NPs and above the high-tide line on the beach near Tárcol Lodge. At sunset, dozens can be seen hunting over the mangroves there and at La Ensenada Lodge.

Chordeiles acutipennis
Costa Rican name: *Añapero menor.*
12/23 trips; 23 sightings.
Status: Permanent resident and northern migrant.
Length: 7.5–9.1 inches.
Weight: 1.2–2.3 ounces (34–64 grams).
Range: Southwestern United States to southern Brazil.
Elevational range: Sea level to 8,200 feet.

COMMON PAURAQUE

Nyctidromus albicollis
Costa Rican name: *Cuyeo.*
23/23 trips; 99 sightings.
Status: Permanent resident.
Length: 8.7–11.0 inches.
Weight: 1.5–3.2 ounces (43–90 grams).
Range: Southern Texas to northern Argentina.
Elevational range: Sea level to 5,600 feet.

One of the great sounds associated with sunset in the American tropics is the call of the Common Pauraque. The call of this tropical nighthawk resembles its local name, "cuyeo." Other descriptions of its memorable songs are "Who-are-you?" and "hip-hip, hip-hip, hip-hip hooray." At night, the eyes reflect like glowing reddish-orange coals when a flashlight or the headlights of a car are focused on this bird as it rests on roads, lawns, or footpaths.

The Common Pauraque inhabits second-growth forest, shade coffee plantations, forest edges, and pastures with scattered trees and shrubs. During the day it rests on the ground amid brushy cover, where it is nearly invisible because of its cryptic markings. Sometimes it rests on branches near the ground. At dusk it flies low over the landscape to catch moths, butterflies, wasps, winged ants, beetles, and other insects. It frequently rests on roads and trails where it can be viewed. In flight, the male has a white bar visible near its wing tips, but the wings are wider than on the Lesser Nighthawk. The female has buffy wing bars. The Common Pauraque's longer tail is rounded at the tip, but the tip of the Lesser Nighthawk's narrow tail is notched.

The most common nighthawk in the country, the Common Pauraque is readily observed or heard throughout lowland and middle elevations of the Caribbean and Pacific slopes. It can often be encountered on the grounds of rural tourism lodges and along country roads after dark.

Common Pauraque nest and egg

Common Pauraque adult

GREAT POTOO

Potoos are among the most interesting, unusual, and almost mystical birds of Costa Rica's forests. They spend most of their life in consummate camouflage; perched upright on an upward-sloping tree limb, the bird looks like a dead branch. The Great Potoo is a rare, huge bird, almost as large as a Great Horned Owl. Because of the scary sound that it makes at night, the Great Potoo has been given the local names *leona,* meaning "lioness," and *bruja,* meaning "witch." The call is a loud, extended guttural roar that penetrates great distances through the tropical night. Potoos look like owls, but they are more closely related to nighthawks. The tail is proportionately longer than an owl's, which allows the bird to use its tail as a brace while perching vertically on tree branches; the long tail also provides additional agility when pursuing prey on the wing. Potoos have huge eyes and an enormous mouth that help them capture prey in flight at night.

Great Potoo adult (Photo of mounted specimen, courtesy of the Milwaukee Public Museum)

Nyctibius grandis
Costa Rican names: *Leona; bruja; nictibio grande.*
6/23 trips; 8 sightings.
Status: Permanent resident.
Length: 17.7–21.7 inches.
Weight: 1 pound 1.6 ounces–1 pound 5.9 ounces (500–620 grams).
Range: Guatemala to southeastern Brazil.
Elevational range: Sea level to 5,000 feet.

The Great Potoo is a nocturnal bird of the rainforest canopy in the Caribbean and southern Pacific lowlands. It spends the day resting on tree branches, and if alarmed it slowly stretches its body upward and tilts its bill up. From a perch high in the canopy, the potoo makes short nocturnal flights to capture bats, moths, and beetles and then returns to its perch.

One of the most amazing features of potoo natural history is the nesting story. On a high branch that slopes upward at an angle of 20 to 40 degrees, the potoo locates a small circular scar of wood that has swollen on the top of a main limb where an old branch has broken off. The potoo carefully lays an egg within that circular branch scar and incubates the egg for at least thirty-three days. One parent incubates by day and the other at night. After hatching, the chick remains at the nesting site and is cared for by both parents for at least seven weeks.

The Great Potoo is found in Caribbean lowland rainforests, in the Pacific lowlands of Corcovado NP, and in the forests of Golfo Dulce near Panama. The best locations to look for this potoo are in Tortuguero NP, Caño Negro NWR, and in the Arboretum forest at La Selva.

Common Potoo adult

Nyctibius griseus
Costa Rican names: *Pájaro estaca;*
pájaro palo; nictibio común.
8/23 trips; 9 sightings.
Status: Permanent resident.
Length: 13–15 inches.
Weight: 5.1–7.1 ounces (145–202
grams).
Range: Nicaragua to northern
Argentina.
Elevational range: Sea level to
4,100 feet.

COMMON POTOO

The Common Potoo is found across a broad range of lowland and middle-elevation habitats, particularly in the lowlands of the Caribbean slope and southern Pacific slope. The Northern Potoo (*Nyctibius jamaicensis*), which is very similar but slightly larger, is found in similar habitats from southern Mexico to the Guanacaste region of Costa Rica. The Common Potoo has one of the most intriguing bird calls in Costa Rica. The song of the Common Potoo is a mournful series of four to six descending flutelike tones. When the call of the potoo is heard amid the shadows of a tropical forest on a moonlit night, the rainforest takes on a nearly mystical quality.

For many years, this eerie song was attributed to sloths, because when people used lights to locate the source of the call, the potoo was overlooked and sloths were sometimes spotted in the same tree. In South America, the Common Potoo has the nickname *alma perdida,* meaning "lost soul," because its song is so melancholy.

Common Potoos are found in rainforest edges, dry and mangrove forests, open woodlands, mixed woods, pastures, plantations, savannas, and forest openings with scattered trees and fence posts that serve as perches for hunting. The potoo spends the day asleep on a branch or post, camouflaged as a wooden stump or branch. At dusk it becomes active and begins hunting. The diet includes beetles, flying ants, flying termites, praying mantises, cicadas, grasshoppers, bugs, leafhoppers, and moths.

Nesting behavior is similar to that of the Great Potoo. A single egg is laid within a circular branch scar on the top of an upward-sloping branch. The male incubates the egg during the day and the female incubates at night. The egg hatches after thirty-three days, and the fledgling period is forty-seven to fifty-one days. This long period at the nest is the second-longest known for land birds in tropical America, exceeded only by the Black Vulture.

The Common Potoo is widespread throughout Caribbean and Pacific lowland and middle elevations, but it is not commonly seen. It can be seen and heard along the canals of Tortuguero NP, Caño Negro NWR, La Selva, Selva Verde Lodge, Rancho Naturalista, the Quepos airstrip, Monteverde Lodge, and the Wilson Botanical Garden.

BRONZY HERMIT

One of the greatest delights while exploring Costa Rica is viewing the beauty, abundance, and diversity of the hummingbirds. About twenty-three hummingbirds are known from the entire United States, but Costa Rica has fifty-two species! This high diversity is significant because hummingbirds are important flower pollinators. The Bronzy Hermit is one of six hermit hummingbirds whose feeding habits are tied closely to *Heliconia* flowers in the rainforest. The Bronzy Hermit has a greenish back, a rufous breast and belly, a dark eye mask, and a long, moderately decurved bill.

The Bronzy Hermit, found in the wet lowlands of the Caribbean and southern Pacific slopes, is a bird of rainforest second growth, swamps, and forest and stream edges. As with other hermits, it feeds on the nectar of *Heliconia* and banana (*Musa*) flowers. Additional nutrition is provided by plucking small insects and spiders from leaves.

The Bronzy Hermit starts nesting in January under the fronds of palm trees. It can be seen in the Caribbean lowlands at Caño Negro NWR, Lost Iguana Resort and Spa, El Pizote Lodge, La Selva, Tortuga Lodge, Tortuguero NP, and Rancho Naturalista. In the southern Pacific lowlands, this hummingbird can be seen at Carara NP, Hotel Villa Lapas, Tiskita Jungle Lodge, La Cusinga Lodge, Hotel Cristal Ballena, Las Esquinas Rainforest Lodge, Sirena Biological Station, and Drake Bay Wilderness Resort.

Glaucis aenea

Costa Rican name: *Ermitaño bronceado.*

15/23 trips; 42 sightings.

Status: Permanent resident.

Length: 3.5–3.9 inches.

Weight: 0.11–0.23 ounce (3–7 grams).

Range: Eastern Nicaragua to Ecuador.

Elevational range: Sea level to 2,500 feet.

Bronzy Hermit showing bill profile

Bronzy Hermit adult at *Heliconia* flowers

GREEN HERMIT

Phaethornis guy
Costa Rican name: *Ermitaño verde.*
19/23 trips; 63 sightings.
Status: Permanent resident.
Length: 5.1–6.0 inches.
Weight: 0.14–0.17 ounce (4–7 grams).
Range: Costa Rica to southeastern Peru.
Elevational range: 1,650–6,500 feet.

The Green Hermit is a dark green, middle-elevation species closely related to the Long-billed Hermit of the lowlands. It has a long, decurved bill and a long tail like the Long-billed Hermit, but the Long-billed Hermit is found at lower elevations. The female has long, central white tail feathers, and the male has shorter white-tipped tail feathers. There is also a dark mask that is prominent on the lighter green female but less conspicuous on the male because of its dark green plumage. This hummingbird, which is about five inches long, is fairly common in moist and wet forests of premontane sites. Lek behavior by groups of displaying and calling males is also characteristic of the Green Hermit. The call is a monotonous single note.

The Green Hermit occurs in the forest understory, tall second growth, and forest edges along the length of the Caribbean and Pacific slopes. It feeds by traplining (repeatedly visiting the same flowers within a territory) for the nectar of *Heliconia, Costus, Canna,* banana (*Musa*), *Centropogon, Pachystachys, Razisea,* and *Columnea* in a territory that it defends from others of its species. This hummingbird may be observed on the Caribbean slope at Rancho Naturalista, La Virgen del Socorro, the Hummingbird Gallery at Monteverde, Catarata de la Paz (Peace Waterfall), La Paz Waterfall Gardens, Rainforest Aerial Tram, and mid-levels of Braulio Carrillo NP. The Green Hermit occurs in Monteverde and along the Palm and River Trails of the Wilson Botanical Garden.

Green Hermit adult

LONG-BILLED HERMIT (LONG-TAILED HERMIT)

Identification of Costa Rica's fifty-two hummingbirds can be challenging, but some species are easy to identify because of obvious marks or geographic distribution that excludes similar species. The Long-billed Hermit is a large hummingbird of wet lowlands with a very long, decurved bill, a dark eye mask, a brownish body, and very long, white-tipped central tail feathers. The Green Hermit is similar but occurs at higher elevations.

The Long-billed Hermit is a rainforest species associated with sun-dappled forest edges, older second growth, and streams that pass through the forest understory where there is enough sunlight for the plants they depend

Long-billed Hermit at *Heliconia* flower

on for nectar: *Heliconia pogonantha, Costus, Aphelandra,* and passionflower (*Passiflora vitifolia*). Like many other hermits, it feeds by traplining—repeatedly visiting the same flowers over a large area. Small insects and spiders are also gleaned from vegetation.

This hermit forms leks, or singing assemblies. From ten to twenty-five males perch at eye level in understory vegetation and call to attract females with a note described as "sree." The call note is given at a higher pitch and then at a lower pitch, with a one-note-per-second frequency. Since the long tail flicks with each call, that movement should be looked for when trying to spot this bird in the undergrowth. The leks at La Selva are particularly well known.

In the Caribbean lowlands, the Long-billed Hermit can be seen at Tortuguero NP, La Selva, Lost Iguana Resort, and El Pizote Lodge. In the southern Pacific lowlands, it occurs at Carara NP, Hotel Villa Lapas, Lapa Ríos, Esquinas Rainforest Lodge, Corcovado Lodge Tent Camp, Tiskita Jungle Lodge, and Sirena Biological Station in Corcovado NP.

Phaethornis longirostris (formerly Phaethornis superciliosus)

Costa Rican name: *Ermitaño colilargo.*

14/23 trips; 51 sightings.

Status: Permanent resident.

Length: 5.1–6.3 inches.

Weight: 0.14–0.26 ounce (4–8 grams).

Range: Southern Mexico to central Brazil.

Elevational range: Sea level to 3,300 feet.

Stripe-throated Hermit

Nest of the Stripe-throated Hermit

Phaethornis striigularis (formerly Phaethornis longuemareus)
Costa Rican name: *Ermitaño enano.*
20/23 trips; 75 sightings.
Status: Permanent resident.
Length: 3.75 inches.
Weight: 0.08–0.11 ounce (2–3 grams).
Range: Southern Mexico to northern Brazil.
Elevational range: Sea level to 5,000 feet.

STRIPE-THROATED HERMIT (LITTLE HERMIT)

The Stripe-throated Hermit, formerly known as the Little Hermit, is one of Costa Rica's smallest hummingbirds, and it is easy to identify. Identification marks include a conspicuous dark facial mask bordered above by a whitish stripe, cinnamon-brown to bronzy-green body color, a long and slightly decurved bill, and central tail feathers that are buffy white. This hermit is found in many of the same habitats and regions as the much larger Long-billed Hermit.

The Stripe-throated Hermit is found in moist and wet lowland and middle-elevation forest edges, young secondary forests, gallery forests, shade coffee plantations, flowering hedges, gardens, and parks. This bold little hummingbird is a common backyard species and will even fly into open rooms of rural homes to feed on the nectar of blooming house plants. Feeding by traplining, it visits *Canna, Scutellaria,* shrimp plant (*Justicia brandegeana*), and other small flowers. It will also eat spiders and small insects. This hummingbird punctures large flowers at the base of the corolla to steal the nectar, taking it without pollinating the flower.

The Stripe-throated Hermit usually forages singly, but throughout much of the year it is possible to encounter leks, or singing assemblies, of up to twenty-five males that perch within three feet of the ground in very thick brush. One song of the males consists of a ventriloquial five-note phrase of thin, high-pitched squeaks that Slud (1964:145) described as "squick, squick, squick-squick-squick," with the first two notes long and the remaining three quick and descending. The long, white-tipped tail pumps up and down as the bird sings. The ventriloquial sound makes you look higher in the foliage than the bird's actual location.

The Stripe-throated Hermit is common on the Caribbean slope from Tortuguero NP inland to La Selva, Selva Verde Lodge, El Gavilán Lodge, Lost Iguana Resort, Sueño Azul Resort, the Rainforest Aerial Tram, lower levels of Braulio Carrillo NP, and Rancho Naturalista. On the southern Pacific slope, this hermit can be seen at Los Cusingos, Vista del Valle Restaurant, Manuel Antonio NP, Sirena Biological Station in Corcovado NP, Lapa Ríos, Corcovado Lodge Tent Camp, Las Esquinas Rainforest Lodge, Tiskita Jungle Lodge, and the Wilson Botanical Garden. A few are found in gallery forests of Guanacaste.

SCALY-BREASTED HUMMINGBIRD

The Scaly-breasted Hummingbird is not the most colorful hummingbird in Costa Rica. In fact, its markings are rather nondescript. It is dull green, with a scaly pattern on the breast that gives the hummingbird its name. The most distinguishing features are the white corners of the outspread tail. Most hummingbirds have only a limited vocabulary of assorted chirp sounds, but the Scaly-breasted Hummingbird, considered the most vocal and musically inclined of all Costa Rican hummingbirds, is known for extended phrases that Slud (1964:147) described as assorted chips, rattling notes, buzzes, trills, and twitters.

Scaly-breasted Hummingbird adult

The Scaly-breasted Hummingbird feeds on the nectar of flowers common in the drier forests of lowlands and middle elevations of the entire Pacific slope, from Nicaragua to Panama, and the Caribbean slope of northern Costa Rica near Lake Arenal. It feeds on the nectar of *Genipa, Inga,* and *Erythrina* flowers, the large terrestrial bromeliad called *Bromelia pinguin,* and flowers of the Pacific mangrove, *Pelliciera* sp. This hummingbird also gleans small insects and spiders, and it sallies from perches to catch insects in the air.

The preferred habitat includes forest edges, second-growth forests, pastures with scattered trees, mangrove forests, gardens, and fencerows with living fence posts of *Erythrina.*

This hummingbird may be encountered at the Lost Iguana Resort and Spa and in the vicinity of Lake Arenal on the Caribbean slope. On the Pacific slope, it is more common in the southern Pacific region and may be seen at Carara NP, Villa Lapas, Corcovado Lodge Tent Camp, Tiskita Jungle Lodge, Talari Mountain Lodge, Las Esquinas Rainforest Lodge, San Isidro del General, Los Cusingos, and the Wilson Botanical Garden.

Phaeochroa cuvierii
Costa Rican name: *Colibrí pechiescamado.*
13/23 trips; 41 sightings.
Status: Permanent resident.
Length: 4.5–5.1 inches.
Weight: 0.30–0.36 ounce (9–10 grams).
Range: Southeastern Mexico to northern Colombia.
Elevational range: Sea level to 4,000 feet.

Violet Sabrewing male

Campylopterus hemileucurus
Costa Rican name: *Ala de sable violáceo.*
17/23 trips; 45 sightings.
Status: Permanent resident.
Length: 6 inches.
Weight: 0.33–0.42 ounce (9–12 grams).
Range: Southern Mexico to western Panama.
Elevational range: 3,300–8,000 feet.

VIOLET SABREWING

The striking Violet Sabrewing, one of the larger hummingbirds in Costa Rica, is a species of foothills and middle-elevation forests. The Violet Sabrewing male is rich bluish violet on the head, back, and upper chest and has a long tail with conspicuous white spots on the outer edges. The long bill is strongly decurved. The female's back is green, the chest is gray, the gorget is blue, and the tail is similar to that of the male. The subspecies found in Costa Rica and western Panama, *Campylopterus hemileucurus mellitus,* is different from the subspecies found from southern Mexico to Nicaragua.

The Violet Sabrewing inhabits forest edges, second-growth forest, banana plantations, and flower gardens. It visits flowers of heliconias, banana (*Musa*), ornamental banana (*M. coccinea),* hot lips (*Cephaelis),* and *Palicourea.*

Violet Sabrewings can be regularly encountered at mid-level and highland sites like Monteverde, Bosque de Paz, La Paz Waterfall Gardens, Rancho Naturalista, and Savegre Mountain Lodge. On the Pacific slope, the birds occur at Carara NP, Vista del Valle Restaurant at kilometer 119 on the Pan American Highway, and along the River Trail at the Wilson Botanical Garden. They visit nectar feeders at many of these lodges and are very aggressive in chasing other hummingbirds from the feeders. Some birders have dubbed them the "violent" sabrewing.

Violet Sabrewing female

WHITE-NECKED JACOBIN

The White-necked Jacobin, with its iridescent blue, green, and white markings, is one of the most beautiful of Costa Rica's hummingbirds. The male has a short, straight bill, a deep blue head and throat, a white breast, and a rich green back highlighted by a white collar on the back of the neck. The female lacks the blue head and white collar and has a scaly pattern on its bluish-green throat.

A resident of moist and wet tropical forests, the White-necked Jacobin pollinates flowers of *Inga, Vochysia, Symphonia, Bauhinia, Heliconia,* and *Erythrina* trees and the flowers of epiphytic plants like *Norantea* and *Columnea.* Small insects are captured on the wing.

White-necked Jacobin female

The White-necked Jacobin inhabits lowland and middle elevations of the Caribbean slope and can be seen in Tortuguero NP, La Selva, El Gavilán Lodge, Selva Verde Lodge, Lost Iguana Resort, Sueño Azul, and Cahuita NP; at the Rainforest Aerial Tram; and at lower levels of Braulio Carrillo NP. It is common at Rancho Naturalista. On the Pacific slope, it can be seen at Corcovado Lodge Tent Camp, La Cusinga, Hotel Villa Lapas, Hotel Cristal Ballena, Oro Verde BR, Las Esquinas Rainforest Lodge, Sirena Biological Station, Lapa Ríos, Corcovado NP, and on the grounds of Tiskita Jungle Lodge.

Florisuga mellivora
Costa Rican name: *Jacobino nuquiblanco.*
18/23 trips; 92 sightings.
Status: Permanent resident.
Length: 4.3–4.7 inches.
Weight: 0.23–0.26 ounce (6–7 grams).
Range: Southern Mexico to Brazil.
Elevational range: Sea level to 4,000 feet.

White-necked Jacobin male

Brown Violet-ear adult

Colibri delphinae
Costa Rican name: *Colibrí*
orejivioláceo pardo.
4/23 trips; 5 sightings.
Status: Permanent resident.
Length: 4.3–4.7 inches.
Weight: 0.21–0.24 ounce
(6–7 grams).
Range: Guatemala to northern
Bolivia and northern Brazil.
Elevational range: 1,300–5,200 feet.

BROWN VIOLET-EAR

The Brown Violet-ear is a specialty hummingbird of the middle elevations in Costa Rica's mountains. In contrast to the iridescent green body colors of most hummingbirds, this species is brown with an iridescent violet to purplish ear marking that distinguishes it as one of the violet-ear hummingbirds. The only other violet-ear in Costa Rica is the Green Violet-ear, which is found at higher elevations.

This hummingbird ranges from ground-level shrubs to forest canopy and edges, where it feeds on nectar from trees like *Inga, Calliandra, Symphonia, Erythrina,* and *Warszewiczia;* shrubs like *Clusia, Cephaelis,* and *Stachytarpheta;* and vines like *Gurania.* Since the bird's bill is short and straight, the plants the bird visits have relatively small flowers that allow it to access the nectar. The hummingbird will also capture insects in flight.

Nesting occurs late in the rainy season, from November through May. Brown Violet-ear males form a lek from which three to eight males display about 30 to 60 yards apart to attract females. The nest typically straddles a small horizontal twig of a low shrub, and the typical clutch contains two eggs.

The Brown Violet-ear is uncommon, but it may be encountered at premontane to lower montane levels on both slopes and on the Osa Peninsula. It may be seen at Rancho Naturalista, La Virgen del Socorro, lower levels of Braulio Carrillo NP, and La Paz Waterfall Gardens. It is especially abundant at La Paz Waterfall Gardens in July and August.

GREEN VIOLET-EAR

The Green Violet-ear is a common highland hummingbird; its name describes its markings. It is iridescent green
with a bluish-violet mask that passes through the lower
portion of the eye and to the "ear." The bill is slightly
decurved, and there is a conspicuous blue band across the
tail. The most vocal of highland hummingbirds, the Green
Violet-ear is often heard before it is seen—and is often
heard but unseen. The call is a repetitious series of high-
pitched chirps, with each phrase usually consisting of a
higher note and two lower notes.

This hummingbird inhabits pasture and forest edges,
second growth, gardens, and backyards. Among the flowers it visits are *Salvia, Lobelia, Cirsium, Centropogon,* hot
lips (*Cephaelis*), *Besleria, Cuphea, Stachytarpheta, Columnea, Inga, Clusia,* and *Erythrina.* It also captures insects on
the wing.

Green Violet-ear nest suspended under
cut bank along roadside

The Green Violet-ear can be encountered on the
slopes of Barva and Poás volcanoes, Bosque de Paz, La
Paz Waterfall Gardens, Monteverde, Savegre Mountain
Lodge, Talamanca Mountains, San Gerardo de Dota Val-
ley, and at kilometers 66, 77, 80, 86, and 96 in Cerro de la
Muerte.

Colibri thalassinus cabanidis
Costa Rican name: *Colibrí
orejivioláceo verde.*
23/23 trips; 52 sightings.
Status: Permanent resident.
Length: 4.2–4.5 inches.
Weight: 0.17–0.20 ounce (5–6
grams).
Range: Central Mexico to Bolivia
(subspecies endemic to
highlands).
Elevational range: 3,300–10,000
feet.

Green Violet-ear adult

Green-breasted Mango male

Anthracothorax prevostii
Costa Rican name: *Manguito pechiverde.*
17/23 trips; 59 sightings.
Status: Permanent resident.
Length: 4.3–4.7 inches.
Weight: 0.24–0.25 ounce (7 grams).
Range: Northeastern Mexico to northwestern Peru.
Elevational range: Sea level to 3,200 feet.

GREEN-BREASTED MANGO

In a country with fifty-two different hummingbirds, it is reassuring that some are easy to identify. The Green-breasted Mango is such a species. The greenish female has a white breast with a blackish-green marking on the throat and center of the breast, like a necktie. The male is darker green and has a similar but broader black necktie marking on the throat and center of the breast. It has a purplish tail. The bill is long and slightly decurved on both sexes, and the dark tail is tipped with white on the female.

The Green-breasted Mango lives in dry and moist lowland and middle-elevation grasslands; savannas; dry, gallery, and mangrove forests; mature second growth; shade coffee plantations; forest edges; and fencerows planted with flowering trees and shrubs. Among the flowers it visits are *Inga, Bauhinia, Ceiba, Calycophyllum, Combretum, Ipomoea, Hibiscus, Erythrina,* and *Caesalpinia.* Insects are captured in flight.

The Green-breasted Mango can be seen on the Caribbean slope at Caño Negro NWR, La Selva, Turrialba, and Rancho Naturalista, where it visits the nectar feeders. On the Pacific slope, it is most abundant in Guanacaste Province, including La Ensenada Lodge, Santa Rosa and Palo Verde NPs, Tamarindo, Hacienda Solimar, along the road from the Pan American Highway near Río Lagarto to Monteverde, and southeast to Playa Doña Ana, Carara NP, Hotel Villa Lapas, Tárcol Lodge, Talari Mountain Lodge, and Manuel Antonio NP.

Green-breasted Mango female

GREEN THORNTAIL

The Green Thorntail is a rare elfin spirit of Costa Rica's forests that is a delight to watch. The male is dark green with a conspicuous white band over the rump, a short straight bill, and a long, straight, spikelike tail that gives the bird its name. It is closely related to the coquettes, which also have a white rump band. As the Green Thorntail appears to levitate in front of a flower or feeder, the long slender tail is cocked upward at a sharp angle. The female lacks the long tail but also has a white rump band and a distinctive white malar stripe that extends from the back of the bill across the face below the eye.

Green Thorntail male

This is a foothill species, found at middle elevations, mainly 2,300 to 4,600 feet, on the Caribbean slope. During the rainy season it ranges down the Caribbean foothills to elevations as low as 200 feet. It feeds on the nectar of *Inga, Pithecellobium, Warszewiczia,* and *Clusia* trees, and also catches insects on the wing. It also feeds on cultivated flowers, like *Stachytarpheta,* and it visits nectar feeders.

Two of the best places to see Green Thorntails are La Paz Waterfall Gardens and Rancho Naturalista, where they visit the hummingbird feeders.

Discosura conversii
Costa Rican name: *Colicerda verde.*
10/23 trips; 33 sightings.
Status: Permanent resident.
Length: 2.6–3.9 inches.
Weight: 0.11 ounce (3 grams).
Range: Costa Rica to western Ecuador.
Elevational range: 200–4,600 feet.

Green Thorntail female

VIOLET-CROWNED WOODNYMPH

Thalurania colombica venusta
Costa Rican name: *Ninfa violeta y verde.*
17/23 trips; 85 sightings.
Status: Permanent resident.
Length: 3.3–4.3 inches.
Weight: 0.14–0.16 ounce (4–5 grams).
Range: Central Mexico to northern Colombia and western Venezuela.
Elevational range: Sea level to 4,000 feet.

A hummingbird that almost glows with deep iridescent tones is the Violet-crowned Woodnymph. This medium-sized hummingbird is bluish violet on the crown and over the shoulders. The huge gorget, which extends further down onto the chest than on most hummingbirds, is bright green on the male and white on the female.

The Violet-crowned Woodnymph inhabits wet lowland and middle-elevation rainforests, older second growth, forest edges, and light gaps in mature forest. Males forage in the upper canopy for nectar of bromeliads, *Columnea, Inga,* and plants of the blueberry family (Ericaceae). Females forage near the ground on understory flowers of *Heliconia, Costus, Hamelia, Cornutia, Besleria,* and hot lips (*Cephaelis*). Insects and spiders are captured on leaf cover, and some insects are captured in flight.

In Caribbean lowlands, this bird can be encountered at La Selva, Selva Verde Lodge, Lost Iguana Resort, El Gavilán Lodge, La Virgen del Socorro, Rara Avis, Rancho Naturalista, Rainforest Aerial Tram, La Paz Waterfall Gardens, and lower levels of Braulio Carrillo NP. On the southern Pacific slope, it occurs at Corcovado NP, Sirena Biological Station, Lapa Ríos, La Cusinga Lodge, Corcovado Lodge Tent Camp, Tiskita Jungle Lodge, and the Wilson Botanical Garden.

Violet-crowned Woodnymph female

Violet-crowned Woodnymph male

Violet-crowned Woodnymph male displaying gorget

FIERY-THROATED HUMMINGBIRD

The Fiery-throated Hummingbird is one of the most stunning hummingbirds of Costa Rica's forested highlands. This medium-sized hummingbird is dark green with a blue tail, but its most striking feature is the throat, which is an intense iridescent red in the central portion, surrounded by iridescent orange. The crown is deep blue. Sexes are identical.

This aggressive hummingbird visits flowers of *Cavendishia, Macleania, Clusia, Centropogon, Tropaeolum, Gaiadendron, Vaccinium, Cestrum, Fuchsia,* and *Bomarea.* It may pierce flowers that have a corolla that is too long for their bill, like *Centropogon* or *Fuchsia,* or use holes that have been previously made at the base of those flowers by bumblebees or Slaty Flowerpiercers. Small insects are also eaten.

The Fiery-throated Hummingbird may be seen at Poás Volcano NP, Talamanca Mountains, San Gerardo de Dota Valley, Savegre Mountain Lodge, and Cerro de la Muerte at kilometers 66, 86, and 96 and at the transmission tower site (km 90).

Panterpe insignis
Costa Rican name: *Colibrí garganta de fuego.*
18/23 trips; 32 sightings.
Status: Permanent resident.
Length: 4.25 inches.
Weight: 0.17–0.22 ounce (5–6 grams).
Range: Endemic to highlands of Costa Rica and western Panama.
Elevational range: 4,600–9,000 feet.

Fiery-throated Hummingbird adult

The gorget of the Fiery-throated Hummingbird

Rufous-tailed Hummingbird adult

Amazilia tzacatl
Costa Rican name: *Amazilia rabirrufa.*
23/23 trips; 251 sightings.
Status: Permanent resident.
Length: 3.2–4.3 inches.
Weight: 0.18–0.19 ounce (5–6 grams).
Range: Northeastern Mexico to western Ecuador.
Elevational range: Sea level to 5,000 feet.

RUFOUS-TAILED HUMMINGBIRD

The Rufous-tailed Hummingbird is the most common hummingbird in Costa Rica. It is often seen visiting backyard flower gardens throughout the country. It is a medium-sized green hummingbird with a reddish bill and a rusty-colored tail.

This hummingbird inhabits disturbed forest, forest edges, meadows, pastures interspersed with brush, woodlots, second-growth forest, shade coffee plantations, and urban and rural backyards. The Rufous-tailed Hummingbird visits flowers that are both native and introduced, including *Hamelia, Tabebuia, Lantana, Costus,* banana (*Musa*), coffee (*Coffea arabica*), *Heliconia, Stachytarpheta,* and hot lips (*Cephaelis*). Insects and spiders are also eaten. Where abundant flowers provide a good source of nectar, this hummingbird is aggressive and chases away other hummingbirds, bees, and butterflies.

This common hummingbird can be seen throughout lowland and middle elevations of the Caribbean and Pacific slopes and throughout premontane levels, including San José and suburbs of the Central Plateau, the Turrialba region, Rancho Naturalista, and the Wilson Botanical Garden. Few sightings occur above 4,000 feet in elevation. It is less common in the dry forests of Guanacaste, where it is largely replaced by the Cinnamon Hummingbird.

Rufous-tailed Hummingbird on nest

STRIPE-TAILED HUMMINGBIRD

Two hummingbirds in Costa Rica's highlands have a copper-colored shoulder patch—the Black-bellied Hummingbird and the Stripe-tailed Hummingbird. The Black-bellied Hummingbird male has a black face and breast. The male Stripe-tailed Hummingbird, however, has a dark green breast. The female Stripe-tailed Hummingbird shows less white on the edges of the tail than the female Black-bellied Hummingbird.

The Stripe-tailed Hummingbird is found in mature wet montane forests, forest edges, and in second growth. It feeds on the nectar of trees and shrubs like *Inga, Clusia, Besleria,* and *Salvia.* It gleans insects from leaves and tree bark and sallies to catch insects on the wing.

Look for this uncommon hummingbird at Monteverde, Peace Waterfall, La Paz Waterfall Gardens, and in the Talamanca Mountains at the Savegre Mountain Lodge.

Eupherusa eximia
Costa Rican name: *Colibrí colirrayado.*
7/23 trips; 8 sightings.
Status: Permanent resident.
Length: 3.5–4.1 inches.
Weight: 0.14–0.17 ounce (4–5 grams).
Range: Eastern Mexico to central Panama.
Elevational range: 2,600–6,500 feet.

Stripe-tailed Hummingbird showing bronzy wing patch

BLACK-BELLIED HUMMINGBIRD

Eupherusa nigriventris
Costa Rican name: *Colibrí pechinegro.*
6/23 trips; 7 sightings.
Status: Permanent resident.
Length: 3.0–3.3 inches.
Weight: 0.12–0.13 ounce (3–4 grams).
Range: Endemic to highlands of Costa Rica and western Panama.
Elevational range: 2,000–6,500 feet.

The rare Black-bellied Hummingbird, Costa Rica's only black hummingbird, is endemic to Costa Rica and western Panama. It is found nowhere else in the world. This species is found only in the highland forests on the Caribbean slopes of the Central Cordillera and Talamanca Mountains.

The male has a black face and breast that is unique among Costa Rican hummingbirds. The bill is short and straight, the copper shoulder patch is conspicuous, and the outer three feathers on each side of the dark tail are white. The female has a whitish throat and breast and also has the copper shoulder patch.

Among the favored habitats of the Black-bellied Hummingbird are montane oak forests, cloud forests, forest edges, mature shade coffee plantations, gardens, and pastures with scattered trees. Among the preferred nectar sources are trees (*Pithecellobium* and *Inga*), epiphytes (*Columnea, Elleanthus,* and *Norantea*), and shrubs (*Cephaelis, Witheringia,* and *Besleria*). It will glean insects from leaves and sally for insects that it captures on the wing.

Look for this rare hummingbird at La Virgen del Socorro, Tapantí NP, and La Paz Waterfall Gardens, where it comes to the hummingbird feeders.

Black-bellied Hummingbird female

Black-bellied Hummingbird male

WHITE-TAILED EMERALD

The White-tailed Emerald is another gem of Costa Rica's tropical forests. It is an endemic species whose range is limited to the foothills of the southern Pacific slope and adjacent areas of western Panama. This hummingbird has a short, straight bill. The male has an emerald-green body with a white belly, and the tail's outer three feathers on each side are white with a black band at the tip. The female has a green body with a white tail, a distinctive black bar near the tip, and a white tip. The throat, breast, and belly are white, and there is green speckling on the throat.

White-tailed Emerald female

This uncommon hummingbird is found in moist to wet mountain forests, gardens, second growth, and coffee plantations. It feeds on the nectar of *Symphonia, Inga,* and *Quararibea* trees, *Stachytarpheta* and *Palicourea* shrubs, and epiphytes like *Clusia, Satyria,* and *Cavendishia.* It also catches insects on the wing.

The White-tailed Emerald can be seen from the balcony at Vista del Valle Restaurant, at Wilson Botanical Garden, and at Tiskita Jungle Lodge.

Elvira chionura
Costa Rican name: *Esmeralda coliblanca.*
8/23 trips; 13 sightings.
Status: Permanent resident.
Length: 3.0–3.1 inches.
Weight: 0.11–0.12 ounce (3 grams).
Range: Endemic to middle elevations from southern Costa Rica to central Panama.
Elevational range: 2,500–6,500 feet.

White-tailed Emerald male

COPPERY-HEADED EMERALD

There are only two birds endemic to Costa Rica, the Black-cheeked Ant-Tanager and the Coppery-headed Emerald. The Coppery-headed Emerald is found only at middle elevations of the Caribbean slope from the Tilarán Mountains to the Reventazón Valley. The male Coppery-headed Emerald has a coppery sheen over the head, rump, and central tail feathers. The throat and breast are green, and the outer tail feathers are white. This is similar to the tail pattern of the White-tailed Emerald of southern Costa Rica, but their ranges do not overlap. Also, the bill of the Coppery-headed Emerald is slightly decurved, but the bill of the White-tailed Emerald is straight.

This special hummingbird is found in wet mountain forests from the understory to the upper canopy at the forest edge and in forest openings. Since it has such a short bill, it is adapted to feed on small flowers, like those of *Guarea, Quararibea, Pithecellobium, Clusia, Satyria, Cavendishia,* and *Besleria.*

Look for the Coppery-headed Emerald at the Hummingbird Gallery at Monteverde, at the hummingbird feeders at La Paz Waterfall Gardens, and in Tapantí NP.

Coppery-headed Emerald male

Elvira cupreiceps

Costa Rican name: *Esmeralda de coronilla cobriza.*

5/23 trips; 8 sightings.

Status: Permanent resident.

Length: 3 inches.

Weight: 0.11–0.12 ounce (3 grams).

Range: Endemic to highlands of northern and central Costa Rica.

Elevational range: 1,000–5,000 feet.

Coppery-headed Emerald female

SNOWCAP

The Snowcap is one of the smallest of Costa Rica's fifty-two hummingbirds. Only the Scintillant Hummingbird is smaller. It is also one of the most beautiful and eagerly sought species for birders visiting Central America. Like a jewel in the rainforest, its iridescent purple body and snow-white cap make a first sighting a lifetime memory. Young male Snowcaps molting into adult plumage exhibit a calico pattern of purplish splotches on bronzy green. The female is bronzy green above and dull white below and has a white spot behind the eye.

This hummingbird lives in middle-elevation wet forests along the Caribbean slope. It inhabits the rainforest canopy, where it feeds on nectar of epiphytes like *Norantea, Columnea,* and *Cavendishia* and on the flowers of *Warszewiczia, Inga,* and *Pithecellobium* trees. In forest edges and openings, the Snowcap feeds near the ground on the flowers of shrubs and vines like those of *Hamelia,* hot lips (*Cephaelis*), *Psychotria, Besleria, Stachytarpheta,* and *Gurania.*

The Snowcap is rare, but it is consistently observed at Rara Avis and in the hummingbird meadow at Rancho Naturalista, where it visits the feeders. It has also been seen at the Tapir Trail site at the eastern lower levels of Braulio Carrillo NP.

Microchera albocoronata
Costa Rican name: *Copete de nieve.*
9/23 trips; 49 sightings.
Status: Permanent resident.
Length: 2.4–2.6 inches.
Weight: 0.09 ounce (2–3 grams).
Range: Honduras to western Panama.
Elevational range: 1,000–4,600 feet.

Snowcap female

Snowcap male in flight

Snowcap immature male plumage

BRONZE-TAILED PLUMELETEER (RED-FOOTED PLUMELETEER)

Bronze-tailed Plumeleteer in flight

Chalybura urochrysia
Costa Rican name: *Colibrí patirrojo.*
9/23 trips; 18 sightings.
Status: Permanent resident.
Length: 4.1–4.7 inches.
Weight: 0.21–0.25 ounce (6–7 grams).
Range: Eastern Nicaragua to southwestern Ecuador.
Elevational range: Sea level to 2,300 feet.

The Bronze-tailed Plumeleteer, formerly called the Red-footed Plumeleteer, has been named for its two most distinctive characteristics. The feet are pinkish red, the long tail is purplish bronze, and the throat and upper chest are green. The medium-length bill is slightly decurved, an adaptation for feeding on *Heliconia* blossoms. The female has a white throat and chest, pinkish-red feet, and pale to whitish tips on the outer tail feathers.

This hummingbird inhabits wet forests of the Caribbean lowlands and feeds on small rainforest flowers like those of *Heliconia* and *Cephaelis* (hot lips). It is most often seen at forest edges, clearings, stream banks, and in second-growth along roads where *Heliconia* is found. It can often be located because of its noisy calling, which Slud (1964:159) described as loud trills, twitters, and "a weak gurgling 'churk' followed by a little roll."

The Bronze-tailed Plumeleteer can be seen in Tortuguero NP, Tortuga Lodge, La Selva, at lower levels of Braulio Carrillo NP (Tapir Trail), and at the hummingbird meadow at Rancho Naturalista.

Bronze-tailed Plumeleteer perched

WHITE-BELLIED MOUNTAIN-GEM

Another of Costa Rica's highland endemic species is the White-bellied Mountain-gem. This attractive hummingbird is found at middle elevations in the montane forests of the Caribbean slope from the Tilarán Mountains to western Panama. Like other mountain-gems, the White-bellied Mountain-gem has a conspicuous white stripe behind the eye (called the postocular stripe). It is the only mountain-gem with a white breast and belly and a violet gorget. The range of the Purple-throated Mountain-gem overlaps with this species, but that species has a green upper chest and a purple gorget. The female Purple-throated Mountain-gem has a copper-colored breast, and the female White-bellied Mountain-gem has a white breast.

The short, straight bill of this hummingbird is adapted for feeding on the nectar of small flowers of high-elevation trees (*Inga, Clusia,* and *Calliandra*) and epiphytes (*Cavendishia, Columnea,* and *Thibaudia*). It sallies to catch insects on the wing and gleans insects from plants. The White-bellied Mountain-gem is most frequently found in forest openings because that is where most of the flowers are found that provide its food supply. The best place to look for it is at the hummingbird feeding plaza at La Paz Waterfall Gardens.

White-bellied Mountain-gem, showing gorget detail

Lampornis hemileucus
Costa Rican name: *Colibrí montañés vientriblanco.*
4/23 trips; 5 sightings.
Status: Permanent resident.
Length: 3.9–4.3 inches.
Weight: 0.18–0.22 ounce (5–6 grams).
Range: Endemic in highlands from north-central Costa Rica to western Panama.
Elevational range: 2,300–4,600 feet.

White-bellied Mountain-gem adult

PURPLE-THROATED MOUNTAIN-GEM

Purple-throated Mountain-gem male

Lampornis calolaemus
Costa Rican name: *Colibrí
    montañés gorgimorado.*
11/23 trips; 19 sightings.
Status: Permanent resident.
Length: 3.9–4.5 inches.
Weight: 0.17–0.22 ounce (5–6
    grams).
Range: Endemic to highlands from
    southern Nicaragua to central
    Costa Rica.
Elevational range: 2,600–8,200 feet.

Any visitor to Monteverde will quickly be attracted by the abundant and beautiful Purple-throated Mountain-gem, a frequent visitor at feeders. The male has a purple gorget and a white streak behind the eye. The female has a similar white streak behind the eye, but it has a cinnamon-colored throat and breast. The female is identical to the female White-throated Mountain-gem. The Purple-throated Mountain-gem is found in middle- and high-elevation forests of northern Costa Rica. It visits flowers of *Satyria* and *Cavendishia* in the blueberry family, as well as those of *Columnea, Clusia, Stachytarpheta,* and hot lips (*Cephaelis*).

The Purple-throated Mountain-gem lives at middle and upper elevations of mountains from Tenorio to the Monteverde region, La Virgen del Socorro, volcanoes surrounding the Central Plateau, and the northern end of the Talamanca Mountains at Kiri Lodge and Tapantí NP. The best place to view it is at the hummingbird feeders at the Monteverde Cloud Forest Reserve, at the nearby Hummingbird Gallery, at feeders of tourism lodges in the Monteverde community, at Bosque de Paz, and at La Paz Waterfall Gardens.

Purple-throated Mountain-gem female

WHITE-THROATED MOUNTAIN-GEM (GRAY-TAILED MOUNTAIN-GEM)

The White-throated Mountain-gem has resulted from differentiation through natural selection from a common mountain-gem ancestor that was geographically separated by the mountains in northern Costa Rica and the Talamanca Mountains to the south. The species in the north became the Purple-throated Mountain-gem, and in the Talamanca Mountains, the white-throated species developed a white gorget, instead of a purple one, and a gray tail. The tail is blue-black on the purple-throated species.

The white-throated species has become further differentiated, with a gray-tailed subspecies in the Costa Rican mountains and a blue-tailed subspecies in western Panama. Females are identical to the female Purple-throated Mountain-gem. Epiphytic plants visited for nectar include *Cavendishia, Satyria, Centropogon,* and *Alloplectus.*

This mountain-gem is regularly encountered in the San Gerardo de Dota region along the road that leads from the Pan American Highway to Savegre Mountain Lodge at kilometer 80 and on the lodge balcony, where it visits the hummingbird feeders. It can also be observed at Tapantí NP and along the private road in Cerro de la Muerte at kilometer 66 on the Pan American Highway.

White-throated Mountain-gem female

Lampornis castaneoventris (formerly Lampornis cinereicauda)

Costa Rican name: *Colibrí montañés coligrís.*

18/23 trips; 55 sightings.

Status: Permanent resident.

Length: 3.9–4.5 inches.

Weight: 0.18–0.22 ounce (5–6 grams).

Range: Endemic to highlands from southern Costa Rica to western Panama.

Elevational range: 2,300–6,600 feet.

White-throated Mountain-gem male

GREEN-CROWNED BRILLIANT

Heliodoxa jacula

Costa Rican name: *Brillante frentiverde.*

17/23 trips; 51 sightings.

Status: Permanent resident.

Length: 4.1–5.1 inches.

Weight: 0.29–0.33 ounce (8–9 grams).

Range: Costa Rica to western Ecuador.

Elevational range: 2,300–6,600 feet.

The Green-crowned Brilliant is a medium-sized hummingbird with a short, straight bill, a dark green body, a small purple spot on the throat, and a white spot behind the eye. The female has a green body and a white breast speckled with green. It is one of the most common hummingbirds in the cloud forests of Monteverde.

This is a hummingbird of cloud, premontane, and montane forests. It visits epiphytic flowers in the canopy, like *Marcgravia,* and plants of forest edges, like *Heliconia,* hot lips (*Cephaelis*), and *Drymonia conchocalyx.* Al-though most hummingbirds feed while hovering at a flower, this bird perches on the flower or feeder while feeding.

The Green-crowned Brilliant is found at mid-level locations along the Caribbean and Pacific slopes. Among the best places to see it are along the trails at the Monteverde Cloud Forest Reserve, at feeders by the reserve head-quarters, and at the nearby Hummingbird Gallery. It can also be observed in Braulio Carrillo NP, La Paz Waterfall Gardens, Tapantí NP, the hummingbird meadow at Rancho Naturalista, Savegre Mountain Lodge, and from the balcony at Vista del Valle Restaurant.

Green-crowned Brilliant male

MAGNIFICENT HUMMINGBIRD

Magnificent Hummingbird male

The Magnificent Hummingbird is the largest hummingbird of Costa Rica's mountains. It has a long, straight bill
(1.2–1.5 inches long), a dark green body with a bright
green gorget, a violet forehead, and a white spot behind
the eye. This hummingbird is found from Arizona to
western Panama. The subspecies found in Costa Rica and
western Panama (*E. fulgens spectabilis*) is endemic to that
region and is larger and lighter than the subspecies found
from Arizona to Nicaragua.

A bird of montane forests, the Magnificent Hummingbird visits epiphytes in oak trees (*Satyria* and *Cavendishia*), passionflowers (*Passiflora*), and flowers of forest
openings, roadsides, pastures, and disturbed sites like
giant thistle (*Cirsium*), *Penstemon, Bomarea costaricensis,
Fuchsia, Centropogon, Erythrina, Lobelia,* and *Cestrum.*
The Magnificent Hummingbird will aggressively defend
nectar sources like giant thistles from other hummingbirds and has been known to grab large bumblebees from
these thistles and toss them from the flowers.

The Magnificent Hummingbird occurs in the mountains at the Monteverde Cloud Forest Reserve, La Virgen
del Socorro, Bosque de Paz, Poás volcano, La Paz Waterfall
Gardens, and southward to the Talamanca Mountains and
the Panama border. Among the best places to view it are in
Poás Volcano NP, along the Pan American Highway in the
Talamanca Mountains, and in Cerro de la Muerte, including locations at kilometers 66, 80, 86, and 96 and the transmission tower site (km 90). It comes to the hummingbird
feeders at Savegre Mountain Lodge in the San Gerardo de
Dota Valley and at Vista del Valle Restaurant.

Eugenes fulgens
Costa Rican name: *Colibrí
magnífico.*
23/23 trips; 85 sightings.
Status: Permanent resident.
Length: 4.7–5.5 inches.
Weight: 0.30–0.35 ounce (8–10
grams).
Range: Arizona to western Panama
(subspecies endemic to Costa
Rica).
Elevational range: 6,000–10,000
feet.

Magnificent Hummingbird female

VOLCANO HUMMINGBIRD

Selasphorus flammula
Costa Rican names: *Chispitas;*
  chispita volcanera; colibrí
  moscá.
19/23 trips; 78 sightings.
Status: Permanent resident.
Length: 3.0–3.1 inches.
Weight: 0.09–0.10 ounce (2–3
  grams).
Range: Endemic to highlands of
  Costa Rica and western Panama.
Elevational range: 6,000–10,000
  feet.

The Volcano Hummingbird is an endemic species found only on the volcanoes of the Central Plateau (Irazú, Poás, and Barva) and south through the Talamanca Mountains to Barú volcano in western Panama. This tiny humming-bird is one of the most attractive hummingbirds in the mountains. The colorful gorget is flared at the lower sides and features different colors in different regions. Males living on the Poás and Barva volcanoes have rosy-red gorgets; males of the Talamanca Mountains have lavender or pur-plish-gray gorgets; and males living on the Irazú and Tur-rialba volcanoes have dull purple gorgets. The female has a white breast and a speckled throat, and the outer three tail feathers on each side of the tail have white to buffy tips.

A resident of montane forests, paramo, and stunted forests of high elevations near the treeline, the Volcano Hummingbird visits flowers of *Fuchsia, Salvia, Bomarea,* foxglove (*Digitalis*), Indian paintbrush (*Castilleja*), blue-berry (*Vaccinium*), blackberry (*Rubus*), and *Miconia*. It feeds through holes at the base of *Centropogon* flowers that have been pierced by Slaty Flowerpiercers.

The Volcano Hummingbird is common at the summit of the Irazú, Poás, and Barva volcanoes and in Amistad NP; it can be observed in the Talamanca Mountains and along the Pan American Highway in Cerro de la Muerte at kilometers 66, 80, 86, and 96, the transmission tower site (km 90), and in the San Gerardo de Dota Valley at loca-tions like Savegre Mountain Lodge.

Volcano Hummingbird male

Volcano Hummingbird female

SCINTILLANT HUMMINGBIRD

The Scintillant Hummingbird is the smallest humming-bird in Costa Rica. Like the Volcano Hummingbird, this bird is endemic to Costa Rica and western Panama. Similar in appearance to the Volcano Hummingbird, it is found in premontane forests up to the level of montane forests. It is not as abundant in higher paramo habitats. The gorget flares at the sides, like that of the Volcano Hummingbird, but it is orangish red. The breast, sides, and belly are rufous, and there is much rufous color in the tail.

The female is similar in size and profile to the Volcano Hummingbird, but it also shows more rufous on the breast, sides, and tail than the female Volcano Hummingbird. Since it has such a short bill, it visits small flowers of *Salvia, Lantana, Hyptis,* blackberry (*Rubus*), and *Stachytarpheta.*

The Scintillant Hummingbird may be observed on Barva, Irazú, and Poás volcanoes; in the Monteverde Cloud Forest Reserve; and along the Pan American Highway in Cerro de la Muerte at kilometers 66, 80, and 96. It regularly visits nectar feeders and flowers on the grounds of Bosque de Paz, La Paz Waterfall Gardens, Savegre Mountain Lodge, and Vista del Valle Restaurant.

Selasphorus scintilla
Costa Rican name: *Chispita gorginaranja.*
19/23 trips; 73 sightings.
Status: Permanent resident.
Length: 2.6–2.8 inches.
Weight: 0.07–0.08 ounce (2 grams).
Range: Endemic to highlands of Costa Rica and western Panama.
Elevational range: 3,000–8,000 feet.

Scintillant Hummingbird male

Scintillant Hummingbird female at *Fuchsia* flowers

Black-headed Trogon male

Black-headed Trogon female

Trogon melanocephalus
Costa Rican name: *Trogón*
cabecinegro.
17/23 trips; 46 sightings.
Status: Permanent resident.
Length: 10.6 inches.
Weight: 2.4–3.2 ounces (69–91 grams).
Range: Southeastern Mexico to northwestern Costa Rica.
Elevational range: Sea level to about 1,000 feet.

BLACK-HEADED TROGON

For newcomers to Costa Rica, encountering a trogon is an enchanting and memorable experience. There are ten different species of trogon in the country, and they all create an essence of the tropical forest that provides lasting memories of their stunning iridescence and bright colors. To distinguish trogons, look carefully for the color of the breast, the presence or absence of a white band between the throat and breast, the pattern on the underside of the tail, and the color of the eye-ring. The Black-headed Trogon is characteristic of the dry forests in the Guanacaste Province of northwestern Costa Rica and the Río Frío region in the vicinity of Los Chiles and Caño Negro NWR.

This beautiful trogon has a black head, bright lemon-yellow breast and belly, greenish-black back, and, perhaps most important, blue eye-rings and a bluish-gray bill. When viewed from the front, the underside of the tail shows white-tipped tail feathers without the black-and-white vermiculated pattern characteristic of the tails of the Violaceous and Black-throated Trogons. The female is similar to the male but the body is more grayish than black. The call is a series of quickly accelerating clucks that rise in pitch to a trill and then descend as a cackle.

The Black-headed Trogon is a bird of tropical dry forest, gallery forest, shrubby thickets, pastures with scattered trees, gardens, and forest edges. As with other trogons, this species will sit quietly on a horizontal limb and watch its surroundings for an insect (grasshopper, dragonfly, praying mantis, or caterpillar) or a fruit or berry. Then it will fly from its perch and snatch its prey while on the wing. It will eat *Cecropia* catkins and oranges that have been opened by other birds.

When the nesting season arrives in March, this trogon excavates a cavity in a termitary that is in a tree or on a fence post. This protects the eggs and young from hot temperatures and rainfall. The three eggs hatch after nineteen days, and the young fledge after sixteen to seventeen days.

Look for this distinctive dry-forest trogon at Caño Negro NWR, Los Chiles, Hotel Borinquen Mountain Resort, Palo Verde NP, La Ensenada Lodge, Puntarenas, La Pacífica, Hacienda Solimar, Carara NP, and Hotel Villa Lapas.

BAIRD'S TROGON

Like the Slaty-tailed Trogon, Baird's Trogon is an attractive trogon with a red breast and no white neck collar. The underside of the tail is white on the male, and the head is purplish, instead of greenish as on the Slaty-tailed Trogon. The female has a gray breast, a red vent, and fine white lines on the underside of the black tail. In contrast, the female Slaty-tailed Trogon has a red breast. The bill and eye-ring of this trogon are gray. This unique species is known only from the lowlands and middle elevations of the southern Pacific slope and adjacent lands in Panama. This is an example of how mountains and drier regions can isolate a population geographically and genetically and contribute to the creation of species through natural selection.

This trogon occurs in mature rainforest, second growth, and forest edges where additional sunlight contributes to the growth of fruiting shrubs. Baird's Trogon eats fruits, small lizards, and insects. Nesting occurs from April through August in the cavity of a large, rotten tree trunk. The entrance hole, perhaps an old woodpecker hole, may be from six to 50 feet above the ground.

The distribution of Baird's Trogon almost perfectly defines the limits of the southern Pacific lowlands, and the bird is found in many of the same habitats as the Slaty-tailed Trogon. Baird's Trogon occurs as far north as the Carara NP and as high as the Wilson Botanical Garden, at an elevation of 3,900 feet. It can also be encountered in Manuel Antonio NP, Los Cusingos, La Cusinga Lodge, Las Esquinas Rainforest Lodge, Tiskita Jungle Lodge, Corcovado Lodge Tent Camp, lodges throughout the Osa Peninsula, and Corcovado NP.

Baird's Trogon male

Trogon bairdii
Costa Rican name: *Trogón vientribermejo.*
15/23 trips; 28 sightings.
Status: Permanent resident.
Length: 9.8–11 inches.
Weight: 3.3 ounces (94–95 grams).
Range: Endemic to southwestern Costa Rica and western Panama.
Elevational range: Sea level to 4,000 feet.

Baird's Trogon female

Violaceous Trogon male

Trogon violaceus
Costa Rican name: *Trogón*
violáceo.
19/23 trips; 71 sightings.
Status: Permanent resident.
Length: 9 inches.
Weight: 2.0–2.3 ounces (56–66 grams).
Range: Southern Mexico to northern Bolivia and western Brazil.
Elevational range: Sea level to 4,000 feet.

VIOLACEOUS TROGON

The Violaceous Trogon, the most common and widespread trogon in Costa Rica, is one of three yellow-breasted trogons in the country. It has a violet-blue head and is the only yellow-breasted trogon with a yellow eye-ring. The others have gray eye-rings. The male has fine barring on the tail, with broader white tips on the underside of the tail feathers. The female is gray with a yellow breast and has an incomplete white eye-ring. The call is a series of about forty to fifty strong, thrushlike chirps at about the same pitch, given at a frequency of about two per second.

This adaptable and widespread trogon is found in the Guanacaste dry forest, especially in riparian forests. It is also found in moist and wet forests of lower and middle elevations throughout the Caribbean and southern Pacific slopes. This trogon frequents moist and wet forest edges, second-growth forest, and openings with scattered trees. It usually sits quietly on a horizontal branch high in the canopy. From its perch it will fly out to pluck a fruit, insect, or lizard while hovering. It is also known to perch near wasp nests and fly out to capture wasps on the wing. Nests are excavated within wasp nests.

On the Caribbean slope, look for this trogon at La Selva, Sueño Azul, Selva Verde Lodge, along the coast from Limón to Cahuita, El Pizote Lodge, Rancho Naturalista, the Rainforest Aerial Tram, and lower levels of Braulio Carrillo NP. In Guanacaste, the Violaceous Trogon can be seen in Palo Verde and Santa Rosa NPs, Lomas Barbudal BR, La Pacífica, La Ensenada Lodge, Hotel Villa Lapas, Carara NP, and Playa Doña Ana south of Puntarenas. On the southern Pacific slope, it is present at Tárcol Lodge, the Wilson Botanical Garden, Manuel Antonio NP, Rancho Casa Grande, Las Esquinas Rainforest Lodge, Corcovado Lodge Tent Camp, and Tiskita Jungle Lodge.

Violaceous Trogon female

COLLARED TROGON

Although upstaged in beauty by the Resplendent Quetzal, the Collared Trogon is one of the spectacular sights in Costa Rica's highlands. The male has a cherry-red breast edged above by a white line; an iridescent green back, head, and upper chest; no eye-ring; and a black face and black throat. The tail has narrow black-and-white barring, with the tip featuring a slightly wider white bar. The bill is yellow.

The attractive female has a reddish-orange breast, narrow white bar above the breast, medium-brown head and shoulders, black upper chest and face, and no eye-ring. The tail has no barring. It is grayish rufous, with feather tips that have narrow black and white bars. The bill of the female is bright yellow with a black stripe along the top edge.

The Collared Trogon is a bird of mature cloud forests and montane forests. It sits quietly in the understory or at forest edges watching for insects and fruits. Prey consists of caterpillars, bugs, beetles, and other insects. This trogon may accompany mixed flocks and capture insects as they try to escape.

The call is usually a series of two to five high-pitched squeals, with approximately the same pitch and sound as the call of a Chestnut-mandibled Toucan.

Look for the Collared Trogon in highland forests at Tapantí NP, La Virgen del Socorro, Bosque de Paz, La Paz Waterfall Gardens, Rancho Naturalista, and the Wilson Botanical Garden; along the trail at kilometer 66 of the Pan American Highway in Cerro de la Muerte; and in the San Gerardo de Dota Valley along the road that descends from the Pan American Highway to Savegre Mountain Lodge.

Collared Trogon female

Trogon collaris

Costa Rican names: *Trogón collarejo; viuda roja; quetzal macho.*

16/23 trips; 40 sightings.

Status: Permanent resident.

Length: 10 inches.

Weight: 2.2–2.5 ounces (63–79 grams).

Range: Southern Mexico to southeastern Brazil.

Elevational range: 2,300–8,200 feet.

Collared Trogon male

Black-throated Trogon female

Trogon rufus

Costa Rican name: *Trogón*
  cabeciverde.

19/23 trips; 37 sightings.

Status: Permanent resident.

Length: 9 inches.

Weight: 2 ounces (57 grams).

Range: Honduras to northeastern
  Argentina.

Elevational range: Sea level to
  3,300 feet.

BLACK-THROATED TROGON

The Black-throated Trogon is a yellow-breasted trogon with a green head, yellow bill, and bluish-gray eye-ring. Barring on the tail is similar to that of the Violaceous Trogon. The female is brown with a yellow breast. The call is a series of three to four identical notes, which each drop in pitch and sound like "e-oo, e-oo, e-oo, e-oo." The notes are given at a rate of about one per second.

In contrast to the Violaceous Trogon, which inhabits the upper canopy of disturbed forests, the Black-throated Trogon inhabits the shaded lower canopy of mature lowland rainforest. It will sit quietly on a horizontal branch for long periods and occasionally fly out to snatch an insect or fruit on the wing. Nesting occurs from February through June. A pair of trogons will excavate the nest cavity in the base of a rotten tree stump with their bills and share incubation duties.

In the Caribbean lowlands, the Black-throated Trogon can be observed in rainforests at Tortuga Lodge, Tortuguero NP, Lost Iguana Resort, La Selva, and Rancho Naturalista. In the southern Pacific lowlands, it occurs at Carara NP, Hotel Villa Lapas, Los Cusingos, La Cusinga Lodge, the Wilson Botanical Garden, and Corcovado NP, including Sirena Biological Station, Lapa Ríos, Corcovado Lodge Tent Camp, and Tiskita Jungle Lodge.

Black-throated Trogon male

SLATY-TAILED TROGON

The Slaty-tailed Trogon is a large, colorful member of the trogon family. Like most trogons, it usually sits quietly on horizontal branches in the lower canopy. The Slaty-tailed Trogon has a red breast but no white upper breast band, the underside of the tail is dark gray with no white markings, and the bill and eye-ring are orange. This trogon is often heard before it is seen, because it makes a repetitious call of the same note, repeated about once or twice per second: "Kuow-kuow-kuow-kuow."

This trogon inhabits mature forest, second growth, and forest edges. It is diurnal and usually solitary, except during the nesting season. Like other trogons, it sits quietly and watches for fruit, katydids, caterpillars, or lizards. Once food is spotted, it flies from its perch, hovers momentarily as it snatches the food item, and then returns to the perch. Fruits eaten include small palm fruits, *Coussarea, Hamelia, Virola, Didymopanax,* and *Guatteria.* This trogon may also follow troops of monkeys and capture insects flushed by them.

A resident of moist and wet lowland forests of Caribbean and southern Pacific slopes, the Slaty-tailed Trogon can be seen along the canals of Caño Negro NWR, at Tortuguero NP, on the grounds of Tortuga Lodge, and at La Selva. In the southern Pacific lowlands, it can be encountered at Carara NP, Hotel Villa Lapas, Hotel Cristal Ballena, Oro Verde BR, Las Esquinas Rainforest Lodge, Wilson Botanical Garden, Lapa Ríos, Corcovado Lodge Tent Camp, Tiskita Jungle Lodge, Sirena Biological Station, and Corcovado NP.

Slaty-tailed Trogon male

Trogon massena
Costa Rican name: *Trogón coliplomizo.*
20/23 trips; 70 sightings.
Status: Permanent resident.
Length: 12–14 inches.
Weight: 5.1 ounces (145 grams).
Range: Southeastern Mexico to northwestern Ecuador.
Elevational range: Sea level to 4,000 feet.

Slaty-tailed Trogon female

Resplendent Quetzal male, head detail

Pharomachrus mocinno
Costa Rican name: *Quetzal.*
23/23 trips; 66 sightings.
Status: Permanent resident.
Length: 14 inches (plus 19–32-inch
tail on males).
Weight: 7.2–8.3 ounces (206–236
grams).
Range: Southern Mexico to
western Panama (subspecies
endemic to Costa Rica and
western Panama).
Elevational range: 3,900–9,800 feet.

RESPLENDENT QUETZAL

The Resplendent Quetzal (pronounced "ket-sál")
is one of the most stunning and beautiful birds
in the world. The iridescent green body, fluffy-
looking crown, cherry-red breast, and shimmering two-foot or longer green tail that shimmers
like a satin ribbon provide a vision of tropical
beauty that most people will never forget. The
long green tail on the male consists of four
upper-tail covert feathers that grow from above
the base of the real tail. The actual tail is much
shorter—about seven to eight inches long—and
is white when viewed from below. The male quetzal is also adorned with elongated green, satiny
wing covert feathers that drape over the sides.

The quetzal is the national bird of Guatemala
and is featured as the standard of currency there,
but it is very rare in that country. The Resplendent Quetzal of Costa Rica is a different subspecies
(*Pharomachrus m. costaricensis*) and is found only in the
mountains of Costa Rica and western Panama.

The quetzal is one of ten trogons found in Costa Rica,
but it is the only one with the extraordinary tail feathers. It

Resplendent Quetzal adult female

is a bird of cloud forests in the Monteverde area and montane forests surrounding the Central Plateau and Talamanca Mountains. A quetzal will sit quietly in an upright posture on a horizontal branch for long periods, watching for a blackberry, fig, wild avocado, or small lizard. The food item is frequently plucked from its stem or perch as the bird hovers, and then the quetzal returns to its perch.

Because the iridescent green or blue of this bird is a structural color caused by refraction of light on the feathers, the plumage is dull and hard to spot in the shade—and spectacular when viewed in sunlight. When flushed, the male quetzal drops backward off its perch to avoid damage to its tail feathers.

Nesting occurs from March through June. A cavity or abandoned woodpecker hole is selected in a dead, rotten tree. The male defends an area with a radius of about 1,100 feet around the nesting tree. The young are fed golden beetles (*Plusiotis resplendens*), fruits, lizards, snails, and caterpillars.

The Resplendent Quetzal may be observed in the Monteverde Cloud Forest Reserve and vicinity and in the montane forests of Poás Volcano NP, Vara Blanca, and Barva volcano. It is also found in the Talamanca Mountains and San Gerardo de Dota Valley, including the Savegre Mountain Lodge grounds and vicinity. Along the Pan American Highway in Cerro de la Muerte, the quetzal may sometimes be seen, with permission and for a fee, along the private road at kilometer 66 and at other private reserves that advertise along the highway.

Resplendent Quetzal adult male

This remarkable photo shows a quetzal at the moment that it has just regurgitated a wild avocado seed, which is falling in front of the bird's breast. This is how quetzals help disperse tree seeds in the forest.

The "blue crown" of the Blue-crowned Motmot

Momotus momota
Costa Rican names: *Pájaro bobo; momoto común.*
22/23 trips; 141 sightings.
Status: Permanent resident.
Length: 15–17 inches.
Weight: 4.2 ounces (120 grams).
Range: Northeastern Mexico to northern Argentina.
Elevational range: Sea level to 7,000 feet.

BLUE-CROWNED MOTMOT

One of the most delightful experiences for tourists exploring Costa Rica's wildlands is encountering birds unlike anything ever seen before. Motmots are such birds. They leave the observer with lasting memories of their form, beauty, and rich colors. The Blue-crowned Motmot is one of six motmots in the country, and it is perhaps the most beautiful and widespread. The others are the Tody, Broad-billed, Keel-billed, Rufous, and Turquoise-browed Motmots.

The Blue-crowned Motmot inhabits backyards and gardens throughout the country. Early in the morning, its deep, ventriloquial "whoot-whoot" call is one of the country's most memorable bird sounds. Since the top of the head is crowned with an iridescent pale blue circle, Dr. Alexander Skutch called this bird the "Blue-diademed Motmot." The long, racquet-tipped tail often swings from side to side as the bird quietly sits in the shady understory. This is apparently a ruse that tricks lizards into looking up at the tail so that their movement reveals their location to the motmot.

This motmot is found in riparian forests in Guanacaste, moist and wet forests of low and middle elevations, second growth, shade coffee plantations, mixed woodland, pastures, wooded ravines, wooded backyards, and residential areas of the Central Plateau. The Blue-crowned Motmot sits quietly on horizontal branches in the understory, where it watches for small lizards, beetles, walkingsticks, cicadas, katydids, spiders, nestling birds, and small snakes. Once prey is spotted, the motmot flies out, captures the creature, and returns to a perch. This motmot may follow army ants to capture prey flushed by the ants. Sometimes it visits bird feeders to eat bananas, papayas, and watermelon.

Nesting occurs from March through May in burrows that are excavated in cut banks along creeks or rivers, roadsides, or steep hillsides. The burrow may be five to fourteen feet back from the entrance and have three to four eggs inside. Both parents incubate the eggs and care for the young.

The Blue-crowned Motmot's unusual distribution includes the Central Plateau and surrounding suburbs of San José, Monteverde Cloud Forest Reserve, San José de la Montaña, Poás Volcano NP, Bosque de Paz, and Rancho Naturalista. It inhabits gallery forests of Guanacaste but is absent in the Caribbean lowlands. In the southern Pacific lowlands, it occurs at Manuel Antonio and Corcovado NPs and is common on the grounds of most lodges from the coast to inland sites like Talari Mountain Lodge and the Wilson Botanical Garden.

Among the best places to see this motmot are the Wilson Botanical Garden, Hotel Bougainvillea, Rancho Naturalista, and Xandari Plantation Resort. Since this bird is difficult to spot, walk slowly, stop often, and scan the low horizontal branches. One will frequently materialize before your eyes.

Blue-crowned Motmot adult

Rufous Motmot adult

RUFOUS MOTMOT

At eighteen inches, the Rufous Motmot is the largest motmot in Costa Rica and also the most impressive. It sports the long racquet tail of other motmots, a black mask through the eyes, a green back, and an attractive orange-rufous color on the head, chest, and belly. The Broad-billed Motmot also has an orange color over the head and upper chest, but the color does not extend down to the belly, and the bird is much shorter, only about twelve inches. The call is a delightfully distinctive sound of the Caribbean lowland rainforest, a bubbling roll of hoots that can best be described as a bouncing-ball effect with a ventriloquial quality. The call consists of three quick notes followed by two slower notes at a slightly higher pitch and three or four final notes at the same pitch and frequency as the first three: "doo-doo-doo hoot-hoot doo-doo-doo."

Baryphthengus martii
Costa Rican name: *Momoto canelo mayor.*
9/23 trips; 21 sightings.
Status: Permanent resident.
Length: 16.5–18.5 inches.
Weight: 5.1–6.8 ounces (146–193 grams).
Range: Northeastern Honduras to Brazil.
Elevational range: Sea level to 4,600 feet.

The Rufous Motmot is a species of mature lowland rainforest and foothills on the Caribbean slope. It will sit quietly on a horizontal branch, usually at mid- to lower levels of the canopy, and watch for the movements of insects, small lizards, and frogs. At the water's edge, this motmot will dive for fish and crabs, and within the forest it will follow army ants to capture creatures flushed by the ants. As with other motmots, it nests in burrows that are excavated into vertical cut banks, like those along stream banks or roadsides.

It takes patience and persistence to see a Rufous Motmot. Listen for the distinctive call at sunrise, or try playing the call and waiting for a response. If one is heard, quietly approach the area, looking through the foliage. The bird will normally be sitting quietly, perhaps twitching its tail back and forth like a pendulum. Look for this motmot at the Lost Iguana Resort and the Hanging Bridges site, La Selva, and along the forest trails at Rancho Naturalista.

BROAD-BILLED MOTMOT

Like the Rufous Motmot, the Broad-billed Motmot is a species of the Caribbean lowlands and foothills. It appears to be a miniature version of the Rufous Motmot, but the orange on the head and upper chest does not extend to the belly. It is also shorter. The huge Rufous Motmot is about eighteen inches long, and the Broad-billed Motmot is only about twelve inches long. The call is like the distant whistle of a train, with a deep ventriloquial effect that is similar to that of the Turquoise-browed Motmot.

Broad-billed Motmot adult

The Broad-billed Motmot inhabits moist and wet forest, second growth, forest edges, and openings, where it may be encountered singly, in pairs, or in small groups. It feeds on small lizards, frogs, cicadas, scorpions, centipedes, butterflies, and dragonflies. This motmot also eats the notorious *Parapona,* or bullet ant, and will follow army ants to capture creatures flushed by the ants. Fruits are a small part of its diet, including *Heliconia* fruit. Nesting begins in February. This motmot excavates a burrow into a vertical cut bank and lays two or three eggs, which are incubated by both parents.

Look for this motmot at low to middle levels of the understory along forest trails at Lost Iguana Resort, La Selva, and Rancho Naturalista. Listen for the call, or try playing the call and listening for a response. Do not call excessively, and discontinue use of the tape recording after viewing the motmot.

Electron platyrhynchum
Costa Rican name: *Momoto piquiancho.*
12/23 trips; 26 sightings.
Status: Permanent resident.
Length: 12.2–15.4 inches.
Weight: 2.0–2.3 ounces (56–66 grams).
Range: Northern Honduras to central Brazil.
Elevational range: Sea level to 5,000 feet.

Turquoise-browed Motmot adult

Eumomota superciliosa
Costa Rican names: *Pájaro bobo;*
   momoto cejiceleste.
14/23 trips; 36 sightings.
Status: Permanent resident.
Length: 13–15 inches.
Weight: 2.3 ounces (65 grams).
Range: Southeastern Mexico to
   northwestern Costa Rica.
Elevational range: Sea level to
   2,600 feet.

TURQUOISE-BROWED MOTMOT

The Turquoise-browed Motmot has a slender greenish and turquoise body with a rufous back and breast, a black mask and bill, a black throat patch edged by turquoise, bright iridescent turquoise stripes over the eyes, and a long, slender tail with bare central veins above "racquet tips" on the two central tail feathers. When alarmed, the motmot twitches its tail back and forth like a pendulum.

The Turquoise-browed Motmot lives in dry forests of Guanacaste. Sitting quietly in the cover of brushy thickets and small trees, it watches for small lizards, snakes, beetles, spiders, grasshoppers, katydids, butterflies, dragonflies, and bees. When prey is spotted, the motmot flies out and snatches the creature from its perch or in flight. The motmot flies back to its perch, thrashes the creature against the perch to dispatch it, and subsequently swallows it. Its call is a series of single notes, spaced at intervals of five to ten seconds, that have the quality of a coarse, brief, distant train whistle.

The Turquoise-browed Motmot is found throughout forests of Guanacaste, including Palo Verde, Guanacaste, Santa Rosa, and Carara NPs and Lomas Barbudal BR. It can be seen at La Pacífica, Hacienda Solimar, La Ensenada Lodge, Hotel Borinquen Mountain Resort, and in other dry forest habitats. The trick to spotting this motmot is to look into forest thickets and small trees, four to eight feet above the ground, and watch for the movement of the pendulum-like tail feathers.

RINGED KINGFISHER

The Ringed Kingfisher is the largest kingfisher in the Americas. The male has a thick, bushy crest, large bill, white collar, bluish head and back, and rufous breast and belly. The female has a blue band across the upper chest. It is much larger than the Belted Kingfisher, which has white on the belly.

This kingfisher can be observed perching on dead trees, branches, or power lines adjacent to or over rivers, lakes, lagoons, mangrove swamps, and flooded tidal marshes. Often it will perch fifteen to thirty-five feet above the water, which is higher than other kingfishers usually perch. When prey is sighted, it dives headfirst into the water and captures small fish, frogs, and small snakes. It does not hover above the water to spot prey as Belted and Amazon Kingfishers do.

The Ringed Kingfisher nests from January through March. A burrow is excavated in the cut bank of a river, road bank, or eroded hillside. The horizontal burrow is six inches high, four inches wide, and six to eight feet deep.

This kingfisher is common and can be found along watercourse edges throughout the length of the Caribbean and Pacific lowlands, including Guanacaste. Among the best places to see it are Palo Verde, Carara, and Manuel Antonio NPs, Hotel Villa Lapas, the Damas Island mangrove lagoons at Quepos, Sueño Azul Resort, Caño Negro NWR, and Tortuguero NP.

Megaceryle torquata (formerly Ceryle torquata)
Costa Rican name: *Martín pescador collarejo.*
22/23 trips; 109 sightings.
Status: Permanent resident.
Length: 16 inches.
Weight: 10.2 ounces (290 grams).
Range: Southern Texas to Tierra del Fuego.
Elevational range: Sea level to 3,000 feet.

Ringed Kingfisher female

Ringed Kingfisher male

AMAZON KINGFISHER

Chloroceryle amazona
Costa Rican name: *Martín pescador amazónico.*
22/23 trips; 72 sightings.
Status: Permanent resident.
Length: 11.5 inches.
Weight: 3.9 ounces (110 grams).
Range: Southern Mexico to northern Argentina.
Elevational range: Sea level to 3,000 feet.

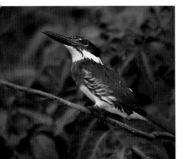

Six kingfishers are found in the Americas, and all six are found in Costa Rica. Almost a foot long, the Amazon Kingfisher is the largest of the dark green kingfishers and has an extremely long, thick bill. The male has a wide rufous band across the chest and a white belly. The female has a white throat and breast that is speckled with green on the sides. The Amazon Kingfisher inhabits the edges of both fast-flowing and slow-moving streams and rivers, mangrove lagoons, and lakeshores where the forest canopy is not closed over the water. It perches or hovers above the water to spot its quarry and dives headfirst to capture fish.

The Amazon Kingfisher can be found along the length of the Caribbean and Pacific slopes. It can be seen at Caño Negro NWR, Tortuguero and Cahuita NPs, and along rivers, canals, and estuaries from Tortuguero south to Cahuita. Inland it can be seen at La Selva and Sueño Azul. On the Pacific slope, this kingfisher occurs in mangrove lagoons near Tamarindo, at Punta Morales, at La Ensenada Lodge, in lagoons at Puntarenas, along the Río Tárcoles, at Hotel Villa Lapas, in the San Isidro del General valley, at Los Cusingos, along the Río Térraba, in Quepos, and near the Sirena Biological Station in Corcovado NP.

Amazon Kingfisher male

Amazon Kingfisher female

GREEN KINGFISHER

The Green Kingfisher resembles a miniature Amazon Kingfisher. The male is dark green with a white collar and a rufous breast band. The female has a white throat and white belly that are highlighted with two incomplete, speckled green breast bands and green speckles on the sides. The wing coverts of both sexes have white speckles, which are absent on the Amazon. The bill is not as thick as that of the Amazon Kingfisher. At only about seven inches long, this bird is much shorter than the nearly foot-long Amazon Kingfisher.

The Green Kingfisher inhabits the edges of quiet or slow-moving woodland streams, pools, and canals. It perches on wires, rocks, or overhanging twigs one to fifteen feet above the water and dives headfirst to capture small fish and aquatic invertebrates. Nesting occurs from February through April when the monogamous pair of kingfishers excavates a burrow into a cut bank along a stream or river.

The Green Kingfisher is found along river and wetland edges throughout lowland and middle elevations of the Caribbean and Pacific slopes. It is one of the most common kingfishers in Costa Rica.

Chloroceryle americana
Costa Rican name: *Martín pescador verde.*
21/23 trips; 101 sightings.
Status: Permanent resident.
Length: 7.1–7.9 inches.
Weight: 1.0–1.2 ounces (29–55 grams).
Range: Texas to central Argentina and Chile.
Elevational range: Sea level to 4,000 feet.

Green Kingfisher male

Green Kingfisher female

GREEN-AND-RUFOUS KINGFISHER

Chloroceryle inda
Costa Rican name: *Martín pescador vientrirrufo.*
7/23 trips; 17 sightings.
Status: Permanent resident.
Length: 9.4 inches.
Weight: 1.4–2.2 ounces (40–62 grams).
Range: Southeastern Nicaragua to central Brazil.
Elevational range: Sea level to 500 feet.

The Green-and-rufous Kingfisher's name describes the bird. It is green above and completely rufous below, with no white on the belly as on other medium and small kingfishers. There are fine white to buffy speckles on the wings of both the male and female. The male has a plain rufous breast; the female has a green breast band across the breast with white speckles. This is the least common kingfisher in Costa Rica.

This kingfisher inhabits shady forested swamps of the Caribbean lowlands. It sits on low perches above the water and dives to catch small fish and insects.

The best place to observe the Green-and-rufous Kingfisher is along the canals of Tortuguero NP, including Caño La Palma, and on the grounds of Tortuga Lodge. It can be sometimes seen at Caño Negro NWR in the Río Frío region, along the Río Sarapiquí at La Selva, and in the Cahuita area.

Green-and-rufous Kingfisher male

AMERICAN PYGMY KINGFISHER

The American Pygmy Kingfisher is the smallest kingfisher in the Americas—only about five inches long. It appears to be a miniature version of the Green-and-rufous Kingfisher. The male is iridescent green above and rufous below, but it has a white belly. The belly of the Green-and-rufous Kingfisher is rufous. The female has a green breast band with fine white speckles. In Spanish, it is called *martín pescador enano,* meaning "dwarf kingfisher."

This tiny kingfisher inhabits shallow forested wetlands, including backwater ponds, pools, puddles, and mangrove lagoons. It is extremely difficult to see because it frequently sits in thick, shady, streamside brush, no more than a foot or two above the water, as it watches for small fish and insects. It may dive headfirst for its prey or fly out to capture insects on the wing.

The best place to see this kingfisher is in Tortuguero NP. It can be seen along canals during the day, often perched just above the water among foliage on the edge of a backwater canal like Caño Harold. Other places where it has been observed include small streams in Caño Negro NWR, Carara NP, and mangrove forests at La Ensenada Lodge and along the Río Tárcoles near Tárcol Lodge.

Chloroceryle aenea
Costa Rican name: *Martín pescador enano.*
13/23 trips; 25 sightings.
Status: Permanent resident.
Length: 5 inches.
Weight: 0.6 ounce (18 grams).
Range: Southern Mexico to central Brazil.
Elevational range: Sea level to 2,000 feet.

American Pygmy Kingfisher male

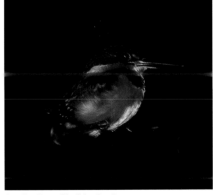

American Pygmy Kingfisher female

WHITE-NECKED PUFFBIRD

Notharchus macrorhynchos
(formerly Bucco macrorhynchos)
Costa Rican name: *Buco collarejo.*
17/23 trips; 28 sightings.
Status: Permanent resident.
Length: 9.5–10 inches.
Weight: 3.7 ounces (105 grams).
Range: Southern Mexico to
northeastern Argentina.
Elevational range: Sea level to
2,000 feet.

Puffbirds are like motmots and jacamars in their perching and hunting behavior, but they lack iridescent colors. Five puffbirds occur in Costa Rica: the White-necked, Pied, and White-whiskered Puffbirds; the Lanceolated Monklet; and the White-fronted Nunbird. The White-necked Puffbird is easily identified by its short, rounded body; thick, straight bill; and bold black and white markings that include a black cap and a black bar across the chest.

The White-necked Puffbird inhabits dry to wet forests in the lowlands of both slopes. It is usually found at forest edges and in forest clearings where scattered tall trees or power lines provide conspicuous hunting perches. This bird perches in the open and sits quietly for long periods as it scans the surrounding area for insects and small lizards. With its large keen eyes, it can spot small insects up to sixty feet away. After prey is captured, the puffbird returns to its perch and beats the prey against the branch to dispatch it before eating it.

In the Caribbean lowlands, the White-necked Puffbird may be seen along the canals of Tortuguero NP, at La Selva, and on the grounds of tourism lodges adjacent to mature forest, like Tortuga Lodge and El Pizote Lodge. Along the entire Pacific slope, this puffbird can be encountered at locations like Hacienda Solimar, La Cusinga, Hotel Cristal Ballena, and Tiskita Jungle Lodge and at Palo Verde, Santa Rosa, Manuel Antonio, and Corcovado NPs and Lomas Barbudal BR.

White-necked Puffbird adult

WHITE-WHISKERED PUFFBIRD

The diminutive White-whiskered Puffbird creates an elfin image in the lowland forests of Costa Rica. It usually sits quietly on a horizontal branch at eye level amid epiphytes that help it blend into the surrounding vegetation. This puffbird has a short, squatty, appearance highlighted by bright red eyes, a huge head, a long heavy bill, and a very short tail. The male is bright cinnamon brown with a lightly streaked breast and white feathers behind the bill that give a whiskered look. The female is darker brown with similar markings. The call of this bird is a high-pitched, soft buzz, but it seldom calls.

Watching quietly from its perch in a manner similar to that of motmots, it sallies from its perch to capture centipedes, small lizards, small snakes, frogs, spiders, insects, scorpions, cockroaches, mantises, crickets, beetles, grasshoppers, caterpillars, and termites. It will thrash its victim against its perch to kill it and then swallow it. This puffbird may follow swarms of army ants to capture creatures flushed by the ants, and it may hunt in mixed flocks with other birds.

Look for this fascinating species in mature moist and wet lowland and middle-elevation forest edges on the Caribbean slope and southern Pacific slope at Tortuguero NP, Sueño Azul Resort (the pasture trail near the river), Carara NP, Hotel Villa Lapas, and Sirena Biological Station.

Malacoptila panamensis
Costa Rican name: *Buco barbón.*
6/23 trips; 10 sightings.
Status: Permanent resident.
Length: 7.1–8.3 inches.
Weight: 1.2–1.6 ounces (33–46 grams).
Range: Southeastern Mexico to western Ecuador.
Elevational range: Sea level to 3,000 feet.

White-whiskered Puffbird male; the female is more grayish.

White-fronted Nunbird pair

Monasa morphoeus
Costa Rican name: *Monja frentiblanca.*
9/23 trips; 15 sightings.
Status: Permanent resident.
Length: 8.3–11.4 inches.
Weight: 3.2–3.4 ounces (90–101 grams).
Range: Eastern Honduras to southeastern Brazil.
Elevational range: Sea level to 2,400 feet.

WHITE-FRONTED NUNBIRD

One of the most delightful and entertaining sounds of the tropical rainforest is the chattering, barking, jabbering, chirping conversation of a flock of White-fronted Nunbirds. There is no mistaking these birds. They travel in social flocks of up to about ten birds and noisily announce their arrival as they sit together and chatter away. This species might better be named the babbling nunbirds. Nunbirds obviously have much to say and not enough time to say it in. White-fronted Nunbirds are black with a lipstick-red bill and a white chin and forehead.

This is a bird of mature rainforests. It nests on the ground in tunnels that it pushes up under the leaf litter on the forest floor. Ironically, where better law enforcement has provided better protection for game animals from poachers, the nunbirds may have suffered. In areas like La Selva, greatly increased numbers of peccaries may be foraging on the eggs and young of nunbirds hidden in the forest floor. Their numbers have decreased in recent years as the peccaries have recovered from the former effects of subsistence hunting and poaching.

The diet of nunbirds includes beetles, praying mantises, crickets, cicadas, caterpillars, moths, butterflies, dragonflies, centipedes, frogs, small lizards, spiders, and fruits. A very adaptable and opportunistic species, the White-fronted Nunbird may follow swarms of army ants, foraging flocks of caciques and oropendolas, and troops of monkeys to capture small creatures trying to escape from them. This declining species may be encountered on the grounds of Tortuga Lodge, in Tortuguero NP, and in the Arboretum at La Selva.

RUFOUS-TAILED JACAMAR

A large number of Costa Rican birds have stunning iridescent colors. Trogons, hummingbirds, and motmots provide vibrant and colorful rainforest memories, but if you ever see a Rufous-tailed Jacamar in full sunlight, you will have seen the magic of iridescence at its finest. The metallic green back and throat band nearly glow and at times take on shimmering bronzy to coppery tones. The iridescent effect is not caused by pigment in the feathers, which are actually dull brown to gray. The structure of the feathers refracts sunlight like a prism to create the colors you see. The throat of the male is white and that of the female is buffy. Jacamars look like enormous hummingbirds with long, straight bills held at an upturned angle. Because of the unusual position of the eyes, when the bill is upturned the bird is actually looking forward.

Rufous-tailed Jacamar female

Galbula ruficauda
Costa Rican names: *Gorrión de montaña; jacamar rabirrufo.*
19/23 trips; 47 sightings.
Status: Permanent resident.
Length: 9 inches.
Weight: 1 ounce (27 grams).
Range: Southern Mexico to northeastern Argentina.
Elevational range: Sea level to 4,000 feet.

The Rufous-tailed Jacamar is a bird of the forest edge, second growth, streamsides, and forests with an open understory. A jacamar will sit quietly on a favorite perch within two to fifteen feet of the ground and watch for passing butterflies, dragonflies, bees, and beetles. When one is spotted, the jacamar flies out from its perch and grasps the insect in flight with its long bill. It then returns to its perch, removes the insect's wings, and eats it. A well-used perch will have many butterfly wings on the ground below. Jacamars are partial to perches that overlook a muddy or sandy streamside bank that is visited by butterflies or to perches overlooking rotten, fallen fruit that is attracting butterflies.

The reproductive behavior of jacamars is similar to motmots and kingfishers. Both parents excavate a burrow into a cut bank or termitary and share the duties of incubation. On observing the emergence of young jacamars from an earthen burrow, Dr. Alexander Skutch wrote: "They were truly gems from the earth, as scintillating as any diamond, emerald, or other precious stone."

The Rufous-tailed Jacamar inhabits moist and wet lowlands and foothills of the Caribbean and southern Pacific

slopes. On the Caribbean slope, it occurs at La Selva, Sueño Azul, Rara Avis, and Rancho Naturalista. On the southern Pacific slope, this jacamar can be encountered along trails at Carara NP, Hotel Villa Lapas, Sirena Biological Station in Corcovado NP, and the Wilson Botanical Garden. One of the best ways to find this bird is to learn its various calls: the single, high-pitched squeaks that sound like a baby's squeaky toy, a series of about twelve to fifteen high-pitched squeaks at the same pitch given in rapid succession, and a high-pitched trill that descends in pitch over several seconds.

Rufous-tailed Jacamar male

RED-HEADED BARBET

The Red-headed Barbet is one of the most colorful and easily identified birds in Costa Rica's mountains. The male has a cherry-red head, orangish breast, green back, and huge yellow bill. The attractive female has a green back, yellowish breast and belly streaked with green, large yellow bill, black forehead, and prominent gray "ear" patch below and behind the eye. Recently the New World barbets were reclassified into the toucan family; they can generally be considered the first cousins of their larger toucan relatives.

This barbet inhabits wet montane forests and forest edges where it explores tangles of vines looking for insects hidden among the leaves. It especially likes to explore curled-up brown dead leaves for insects or pupae hidden inside. Slud (1964:182) described the foraging movements of the Red-headed Barbet: "clinging, hanging, stretching, or hopping, climbing, fluttering, this bird seems too intent on its search to be disturbed by close observation." This barbet may travel in a mixed flock as it forages for insects and will eat fruits of the bayberry (*Myrica*) and blueberry family, like *Satyria* and *Cavendishia*. It will also visit feeders for guavas, bananas, and papayas. The call of the male is a brief medium-pitched trill.

The Red-headed Barbet can be seen in montane forests of the Caribbean slope at La Virgen del Socorro and La Paz Waterfall Gardens. In the Pacific highlands and middle elevations, it may be encountered at Tapantí NP and Los Cusingos, and it regularly visits the feeders at Vista del Valle Restaurant.

Eubucco bourcierii
Costa Rican name: *Barbudo cabecirrojo.*
11/23 trips; 11 sightings.
Status: Permanent resident.
Length: 6.3 inches.
Weight: 1.1–1.6 ounces (30–45 grams).
Range: Costa Rica to northeastern Peru.
Elevational range: 1,200–6,000 feet.

Red-headed Barbet male

Red-headed Barbet female

PRONG-BILLED BARBET

Semnornis frantzii

Costa Rican name: *Barbudo cocoro.*

12/23 trips; 15 sightings.

Status: Permanent resident.

Length: 7.1 inches.

Weight: 1.9–2.5 ounces (55–72 grams).

Range: Endemic to highlands of Costa Rica and western Panama.

Elevational range: 2,400–8,000 feet.

Costa Rica's other barbet, the Prong-billed Barbet, is not as colorful as the Red-headed Barbet, but it is also a special bird of the highlands. This stocky bird is olive over the back, with golden brown over the head and chest, and the face is black. The male has a small tuft of black, glossy feathers on the back of its head. The thick, bluish-gray bill has two sharp prongs at the tip. This may be an aid in excavating tree cavities for nesting. The Prong-billed Barbet is endemic in the mountains from central Costa Rica to western Panama. Although the Red-headed Barbet is usually quiet, the Prong-billed Barbet is a chatterbox. Its song is an extended series of resonant toots, about three to four per second, up to a minute in duration. The tooting serenade is often enhanced by a pair or group of barbets calling together. This is a very social species that can occur in flocks of up to sixteen birds, and at night up to nineteen have been found sleeping together in the same tree cavity.

This barbet has a big appetite for fruit of trees, shrubs, and epiphytes, including *Clusia, Miconia, Ocotea,* and *Rubus* (blackberry); it also eats flower nectar and some insects. It has a unique manner of using its large bill to squeeze a fruit so that it can swallow the juice and discard the skin and seeds.

The Prong-billed Barbet may be encountered at Monteverde, Savegre Mountain Lodge, Bosque de Paz, and Tapantí NP. It regularly comes to the feeders at La Paz Waterfall Gardens.

Prong-billed Barbet adult

EMERALD TOUCANET

Among the favorite birds of Costa Rica's forests are toucans. Their bright and varied colors, interesting calls, and outrageous bill design always steal the show during a rainforest outing. Toucan family members include Keel-billed and Chestnut-mandibled Toucans and four smaller species, the Emerald and Yellow-eared Toucanets and the Collared and Fiery-billed Aracaris. The Emerald Toucanet is easily distinguished by its bright green plumage. Only about a foot long, it is the smallest toucan in the country and is found only at middle and higher elevations. In contrast, others occupy lowland and middle elevations. In the highlands of Costa Rica and western Panama, this toucanet is geographically isolated and has a blue throat. It is a separate subspecies (*A. p. caeruleogularis*) from Emerald Toucanets in Mexico, which have a white throat.

Emerald Toucanet adult

The Emerald Toucanet is found in cloud forests, montane forests, second growth, forest edges, mixed pastures, and woodlands. It is frequently encountered in small flocks of six to eight that roam the forest in search of fruiting trees, lizards, and insects. This toucanet is frequently mobbed and scolded by songbirds because it eats eggs and young from other birds' nests. The call is a low-pitched chirp that resembles the bark of a small dog.

Look for the Emerald Toucanet at Monteverde, La Virgen del Socorro, San José de la Montaña on Barva volcano, Bosque de Paz, La Paz Waterfall Gardens, Poás Volcano NP, Tapantí NP, Savegre Mountain Lodge, and in the San Gerardo de Dota Valley. It can be seen in forests along the Pan American Highway at kilometers 66 and 96 and is also found at the Wilson Botanical Garden.

Aulacorhynchus prasinus
Costa Rican names: *Curré;*
  tucancillo verde.
23/23 trips; 73 sightings.
Status: Permanent resident.
Length: 12.5–14.5 inches.
Weight: 6.3 ounces (180 grams).
Range: Southern Mexico to
  eastern Peru (subspecies
  endemic to highlands).
Elevational range: 2,600–8,000
  feet.

COLLARED ARACARI

Pteroglossus torquatus

Costa Rican names: *Cusingo; tití; félix; tucancillo collarejo.*

18/23 trips; 96 sightings.

Status: Permanent resident.

Length: 15–17 inches.

Weight: 8.1 ounces (230 grams).

Range: Southern Mexico to western Ecuador.

Elevational range: Sea level to 3,900 feet.

Aracaris (pronounced "ara-sorry") are the most colorful members of the toucan family in Costa Rica. It is suspected that the two aracaris in this country have a common ancestor; however, geographic isolation caused by the country's mountain ranges has separated the birds for so long that natural selection has resulted in the development of two separate species. The one in the Caribbean lowlands, the Collared Aracari, is black over the back and tail and has a colorful pattern of yellow, red, and black on the breast. The call is a shrill, two-note "cheep-eep" in which the second note is higher than the first.

The Collared Aracari travels in small flocks of six to fifteen in second growth, forest edges, and openings with scattered trees. The additional sunlight in these areas stimulates fruiting of trees and shrubs that provide foods, including fruits of *Protium,* palms, and *Cecropia.* These birds roost at night as family groups in tree cavities.

Look for this bird at Caño Negro NWR, Tortuguero NP, Tortuga Lodge, La Selva, El Gavilán Lodge, Sueño Azul Resort, and in the Caribbean lowlands at Guacimo, Guapiles, Limón, and south along the coast to Cahuita NP. At Rancho Naturalista they regularly visit the feeders to eat bananas. Some sightings occur in Guanacaste in the vicinity of Rincón de la Vieja NP, on the grounds of Hotel Borinquen Mountain Resort, and eastern portions of Santa Rosa NP.

Collared Aracari adult

FIERY-BILLED ARACARI

The Fiery-billed Aracari has a stunning orangish-red, yellow, and black bill that leaves little doubt about its identity. The bright yellow breast is highlighted by reddish smudges, a red breast band edged with black, and a black central spot. The call is similar to the two-note call of the Collared Aracari. The Fiery-billed Aracari is found only in Costa Rica's Pacific southern lowlands and adjacent areas of western Panama.

This colorful member of the toucan family inhabits the upper canopy of mature forests, forest edges, and pastures with scattered trees. It travels through the forest in flocks of about six to ten birds. Among fruits eaten are those of *Protium, Dipterodendron, Lacistema, Souroubea,* and pokeweed (*Phytolacca*). The aracari's long bill aids in reaching ripe fruits. This bird also raids the nests of other birds and eats their eggs and young. At night, families of aracaris roost in the same tree cavity.

The Fiery-billed Aracari may be encountered in Carara, Corcovado, and Manuel Antonio NPs and Drake Bay Wilderness Resort, Rancho Casa Grande, La Cusinga, Lapa Ríos, Hotel Villa Lapas, Villa Caletas, Las Esquinas Rainforest Lodge, Corcovado Lodge Tent Camp, and Tiskita Jungle Lodge. Other locations include San Isidro del General and Los Cusingos, which is named after the Fiery-billed Aracari. It also occurs at middle elevations in areas like San Vito and the Wilson Botanical Garden.

Pteroglossus frantzii
Costa Rican names: *Cusingo;*
 tucancillo piquianaranjado.
16/23 trips; 59 sightings.
Status: Permanent resident.
Length: 15–17 inches.
Weight: 8.8 ounces (250 grams).
Range: Endemic to southwestern
 Costa Rica and western Panama.
Elevational range: Sea level to
 5,000 feet.

Fiery-billed Aracari adult

Keel-billed Toucan adult

Ramphastos sulfuratus
Costa Rican names: *Curré negro;*
   tucán pico iris.
18/23 trips; 110 sightings.
Status: Permanent resident.
Length: 20–23 inches.
Weight: 1 pound 1.6 ounces (500
   grams).
Range: Southern Mexico to
   Colombia and Venezuela.
Elevational range: Sea level to
   4,000 feet.

KEEL-BILLED TOUCAN

The large and beautiful Keel-billed Toucan is one of the most memorable birds in Costa Rica. Referred to as the Rainbow-billed Toucan by ornithologist Alexander Skutch, this toucan has a huge bill that is a fascinating blend of yellow, orange, lime-green, and pastel blue with a cherry-red tip. Although the bill looks thick and clumsy, it has a slender profile when viewed from above and is used with great precision when plucking ripe fruits. The call is a series of shrill, ascending trilled chirps that sound more like the call of a giant cricket than a bird.

This toucan inhabits Caribbean lowland and middle-elevation forests, including older second growth and pastures interspersed with mature trees. The Keel-billed Toucan travels through the canopy in small flocks of up to six birds. The diet includes fruits of *Virola, Protium, Alchornea,* figs (*Ficus*), *Cupania, Cnestidium, Didymopanax,* and palm fruits (*Astrocaryum* and *Iriartea*). Small lizards, spiders, snakes, insects, and the eggs and nestlings of small birds are also eaten.

The Keel-billed Toucan is regularly encountered in the Caribbean lowlands, including Tortuguero and Cahuita NPs, Muelle, Los Chiles, La Selva, and Sueño Azul. At middle elevations, it is common in the Monteverde area and at Rancho Naturalista. The range extends to the Guanacaste region in the vicinity of Rincón de la Vieja NP and Hotel Borinquen Mountain Resort.

Narrow vertical profile of a toucan's bill

CHESTNUT-MANDIBLED TOUCAN

The Chestnut-mandibled Toucan is the largest toucan in Costa Rica. It is easily distinguished from the Keel-billed Toucan by the large bill that is chestnut brown below and bright yellow above. The call is a repetitious series of ascending squeals, each followed by two ascending squeaks.

The habits of this toucan are similar to those of the Keel-billed Toucan. Small flocks roam the canopy of mature forest searching for fruiting trees, insects, small vertebrates, and eggs and nestlings of small birds. This toucan can often be seen calling from the tops of canopy trees.

This bird is found throughout the Caribbean lowlands at Tortuguero and Cahuita NPs, Muelle, Lost Iguana Resort, La Selva, Selva Verde Lodge, and Sueño Azul. It is also found throughout the southern Pacific lowlands up to the elevation of Talari Mountain Lodge and the Wilson Botanical Garden. It should be noted that the Keel-billed Toucan is not found in the southern Pacific lowlands.

Ramphastos swainsonii
Costa Rican names: *Quioro; dios-te-dé; gran curré negro; tucán de Swainson.*
21/23 trips; 151 sightings.
Status: Permanent resident.
Length: 22 inches.
Weight: 1 pound 10.4 ounces (750 grams).
Range: Eastern Honduras to northern Colombia.
Elevational range: Sea level to 6,000 feet.

Chestnut-mandibled Toucan adult

ACORN WOODPECKER

Melanerpes formicivorus
Costa Rican name: *Carpintero careto.*
18/23 trips; 71 sightings.
Status: Permanent resident.
Length: 8.3–9.3 inches.
Weight: 3 ounces (85 grams).
Range: Western United States to Colombia.
Elevational range: 5,000–10,000 feet.

High in the montane forests of Cerro de la Muerte and the Talamanca Mountains is a boldly marked woodpecker well known for its ecological relationship to oaks—the Acorn Woodpecker. The clownlike facial markings of black, white, yellow, and red are unique among Costa Rica's woodpeckers. Only three other woodpeckers occur in the highlands: a local nonmigratory subspecies of Hairy Woodpecker, the Golden-olive Woodpecker, and the uncommon, migratory Yellow-bellied Sapsucker.

The Acorn Woodpecker inhabits high-elevation oak woodlands and adjacent pastures where there are scattered trees. Acorns and insects are the most common foods. It excavates small holes in tree bark, power poles, and even fence posts as caches for those acorns. Holes are also drilled into the bark of live trees so it can feed on the sap that drains from those holes. This woodpecker also flies out to capture insects on the wing. A social species, it lives in groups of three to eight individuals that include offspring from previous nestings.

Nesting is an extended-family activity that occurs from April through August. A pair of woodpeckers excavates a hole high in a dead tree or a telephone pole. Nests usually contain three to five eggs, but sometimes more than one female in the family group lays eggs, so up to thirteen have been recorded. Both parents incubate the eggs. The young are cared for by the parents and by young from the previous one or two years' broods.

The Acorn Woodpecker can be observed in forests and pastures with scattered oak trees in Cerro de la Muerte, the Talamanca Mountains, and San Gerardo de Dota Valley. Along the Pan American Highway, it can be encountered at kilometers 66 and 80 and on the grounds of Savegre Mountain Lodge.

Cache of acorns stored in the top of a fence post by an Acorn Woodpecker

Acorn Woodpecker at nest hole

Acorn Woodpecker adult

GOLDEN-NAPED WOODPECKER

The Golden-naped Woodpecker is one of several pairs of rainforest species that have one counterpart in the Caribbean lowlands and one in the southern Pacific lowlands. They have a common ancestor and have been geographically separated by the country's mountains for so long that they have developed through natural selection into separate species. The Golden-naped Woodpecker's corresponding Caribbean lowland species is the Black-cheeked Woodpecker. Both birds have a black stripe through the eye, a creamy-buff breast, a horizontal yellow bar across the face above the bill, a reddish-orange belly, and a red cap. However, the back of the Golden-naped Woodpecker's head (the nape) is bright yellowish gold. The back is black with white down the center, and the tertial feathers are tipped with white.

Living in family groups of three to six, this bird occupies the upper and middle canopy of moist and wet forests in the southern Pacific lowlands. It also occurs in adjacent forest openings and pastures that have scattered trees. The Golden-naped Woodpecker's diet includes insect larvae and beetles that live under the bark and in the wood of rainforest trees. A variety of fruits are also eaten, including *Cecropia* and bananas.

Nesting occurs from March through June in the trunk of a tall dead tree. This is one of the few birds whose nesting habit is for both parents to spend the night together on the nest. After fledging, the young stay with the parents until the following year's nesting season. They all sleep together in a tree cavity or in the nesting tree. Sometimes this woodpecker nests twice in the same breeding season. When it does, the four-month-old females from the first brood help care for the second brood.

The Golden-naped Woodpecker, endemic to southwestern Costa Rica and western Panama, inhabits Carara, Manuel Antonio, and Corcovado NPs. It can be seen at Hotel Villa Lapas, La Cusinga, Hotel Cristal Ballena, Playa Hermosa, Oro Verde BR, Sirena Biological Station within Corcovado NP, Lapa Ríos, Rancho Casa Grande, Drake Bay Wilderness Resort, Corcovado Lodge Tent Camp, and Tiskita Jungle Lodge. In the San Isidro del General area, this woodpecker can be observed at Los Cusingos and at the Wilson Botanical Garden.

Melanerpes chrysauchen
Costa Rican name: *Carpintero nuquidorado.*
16/23 trips; 36 sightings.
Status: Permanent resident.
Length: 7 inches.
Weight: 2.1 ounces (60 grams).
Range: Endemic to lowlands of southern Costa Rica and western Panama.
Elevational range: Sea level to 500 feet.

Golden-naped Woodpecker male

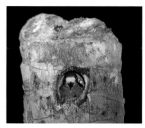

Golden-naped Woodpecker in nest cavity

Black-cheeked Woodpecker male

Melanerpes pucherani
Costa Rican name: *Carpintero carinegro.*
18/23 trips; 72 sightings.
Status: Permanent resident.
Length: 7.0–7.5 inches.
Weight: 2.2 ounces (63 grams).
Range: Southeastern Mexico to western Ecuador.
Elevational range: Sea level to 3,900 feet.

BLACK-CHEEKED WOODPECKER

The Black-cheeked Woodpecker is the common rainforest species of the Caribbean slope that is closely related to the Golden-naped Woodpecker of the southern Pacific lowland forests. It has a black stripe through the eye and cheek area, a yellow bar in front of the eyes, a creamy-buff breast, and a reddish-orange belly. It differs from the Golden-naped Woodpecker in having a red crown that extends all the way down the back of the head. The back has a ladder pattern of white lines on a black background.

This woodpecker inhabits all levels of mature moist and wet forests, older second growth, and adjacent pastures that have scattered live or dead trees. It explores dead wood, epiphytes, and tree trunks for insect larvae, beetles, termites, and ants. Flying insects are also spotted from a perch and captured on the wing. The diverse diet includes nectar from balsa (*Ochroma*) and kapok (*Ceiba*) flowers, fruits, berries, and *Cecropia* fruits. At the bird feeders of Rancho Naturalista, this bird is attracted to cooked rice, and at the Tilajari Resort it comes to the feeders for papayas.

The Black-cheeked Woodpecker, found only on the Caribbean slope, can be observed at Caño Negro NWR and Lodge, Tilajari Resort, Los Chiles, Muelle, Lost Iguana Resort, La Selva, Sueño Azul, El Gavilán Lodge, Tortuguero NP, and southeast along the Caribbean coast to Cahuita NP. At middle elevations, it occurs at the Rainforest Aerial Tram property, lower levels of Braulio Carrillo NP, and Rancho Naturalista.

RED-CROWNED WOODPECKER

The most common woodpecker of the southern Pacific lowlands is the Red-crowned Woodpecker. It is the tropical moist-forest relative of the dry-forest Hoffmann's Woodpecker, found in Guanacaste and the Central Plateau. At first glance it looks like the Red-bellied Woodpecker from the United States. The male has a red crown and nape and reddish belly. The female has a red nape and yellow bar in front of the eyes. In contrast, the male Hoffmann's Woodpecker has red on the top of the head and yellow on the nape. The female has yel-

Red-crowned Woodpecker female

low in front of the eyes and yellow on the nape. The range of these two species meets in the region from Carara NP to Quepos. Many Red-crowned Woodpeckers in that region are hybrids with Hoffmann's Woodpecker. Male hybrids have a red crown and orange nape and an orange patch on the belly.

The Red-crowned Woodpecker is a common wood-pecker of developed urban and rural areas that has ben-efited from forest clearing. It is found in forest openings, second-growth forest, plantations, backyards, gardens, and mangrove forests. This woodpecker feeds on ants, beetles, and grubs that it discovers in rotting wood, and it also gleans spiders and other invertebrates from tree bark and foliage. It visits balsa (*Ochroma*) trees to feed on flower nectar and eats fruit, including bananas, at bird feeders.

This woodpecker can be observed at most national parks and lodges and gardens in southwestern Costa Rica, including Carara NP, Hotel Villa Lapas, Corcovado Lodge Tent Camp, Tiskita Jungle Lodge, La Cusinga, Oro Verde BR, Hotel Cristal Ballena, Las Esquinas Rainforest Lodge, Rancho Casa Grande, Talari Mountain Lodge, San Isidro del General, Los Cusingos, and the Wilson Botanical Garden.

Melanerpes rubricapillus
Costa Rican name: *Carpintero nuquirrojo.*
17/23 trips; 82 sightings.
Status: Permanent resident.
Length: 6.3–7.3 inches.
Weight: 1.4–2.3 ounces (40–65 grams).
Range: Southwestern Costa Rica to northwestern Venezuela.
Elevational range: Sea level to 5,300 feet.

Hoffmann's Woodpecker feeding on nectar at a balsa flower

Melanerpes hoffmannii
Costa Rican name: *Carpintero de Hoffmann.*
22/23 trips; 120 sightings.
Status: Permanent resident.
Length: 7.5–8.0 inches.
Weight: 2.4 ounces (68 grams).
Range: Southern Honduras to Costa Rica.
Elevational range: Sea level to 7,000 feet.

HOFFMANN'S WOODPECKER

Hoffmann's Woodpecker, the most common woodpecker of Guanacaste and the Central Plateau, resembles the Red-bellied Woodpecker of the eastern United States, except that the nape is yellow. The crown is red, the black back has a ladder pattern, the breast is creamy tan, and the belly is yellowish. The female lacks the red crown. Hoffmann's Woodpecker is closely related to the Red-crowned Woodpecker of the southern Pacific slope. In Carara NP and at Hotel Villa Lapas, the ranges of the two species overlap, so in that area it is possible to see hybrid woodpeckers intermediate in characteristics between the two species.

Hoffmann's Woodpecker occurs in tropical dry forest and surrounding woodlands that have been cleared as pastures, shade coffee plantations, ranches, backyards, and gardens. It explores dead wood and bark for insect larvae, ants, and beetles. Fruits, including bananas, berries, and *Cecropia*, are eaten, as well as the nectar of balsa (*Ochroma*) and African tulip tree (*Spathodea campanulata*) flowers.

The distribution of Hoffmann's Woodpecker encompasses most of the Guanacaste region. It also occurs in the Monteverde area, at Hotel Borinquen Mountain Resort, throughout the Central Plateau, south to Carara NP, Hotel Villa Lapas, and Orotina, and east to the Turrialba area and Rancho Naturalista. This woodpecker is readily attracted to a tape recording of the Ferruginous Pygmy-Owl.

Hoffmann's Woodpecker female

Hoffmann's Woodpecker male

HAIRY WOODPECKER

A casual look at the bird list of Costa Rica will reveal two familiar woodpeckers for the North American birder: the Yellow-bellied Sapsucker, which is a rare North American migrant mainly encountered in the highlands, and the Hairy Woodpecker. The Hairy Woodpecker, however, is not a migrant. Technically, the same species occurs across North America, but the Costa Rican birds represent the southernmost of fourteen subspecies of Hairy Woodpecker distributed from Alaska to the mountains of western Panama. The Hairy Woodpeckers of the subspecies *Picoides villosus sanctorum* occur in the mountains of southern Mexico to Panama. The woodpeckers of Costa Rica, however, are geographically isolated from those found farther north in Guatemala and Mexico and could be considered a regional endemic subspecies.
The Costa Rica subspecies is significantly different from the larger North American Hairy Woodpeckers. They are darker and about one-third smaller, and the upper breast is dingy white. The male has red on the back of the head, and the female is black on the back of the head.

Hairy Woodpecker male, with red on the back of the head

Picoides villosus

Costa Rican names: *Carpintero serranero; carpintero velloso.*

10/23 trips; 18 sightings.

Status: Permanent resident.

Length: 6.5 inches.

Weight: 1.5 ounces (42 grams).

Range: Alaska to western Panama (subspecies endemic to highlands).

Elevational range: 4,000–10,000 feet.

The Costa Rican Hairy Woodpecker lives in highland oak forests and in forest openings, pastures with scattered trees, and gardens where it comes to bird feeders for bananas. It feeds on beetles, grubs, spiders, and some fruits.

Look for this woodpecker in the Talamanca Mountains, in San Gerardo de Dota Valley, at Savegre Mountain Lodge, at Bosque de Paz, at Vara Blanca, in Poás Volcano NP, and in Cerro de la Muerte at kilometer 66.

Chestnut-colored Woodpecker male, distinguished by a red mustache mark

Celeus castaneus
Costa Rican name: *Carpintero castaño.*
8/23 trips; 14 sightings.
Status: Permanent resident.
Length: 9.1–9.8 inches.
Weight: 2.8–3.7 ounces (80–105 grams).
Range: Southern Mexico to northwestern Panama.
Elevational range: Sea level to 2,500 feet.

CHESTNUT-COLORED WOODPECKER

There are two large chestnut-brown woodpeckers in rainforests of the Caribbean lowlands, the Cinnamon Woodpecker and the Chestnut-colored Woodpecker. At first glance, they appear similar. Both are around nine inches long and have a conspicuous crest, but the Cinnamon Woodpecker has a pale breast and belly. The Chestnut-colored Woodpecker is more uniformly chestnut on the back and breast. The male has a red mustache mark behind the bill. That mark is missing on the female.

The preferred habitat of this impressive woodpecker is the middle and upper canopy of mature rainforest and older second growth. It may descend to lower levels to feed in gardens, forest edges, and cacao plantations. The diet of the Chestnut-colored Woodpecker comprises ants, termites, and other insects that it finds by foraging and pecking into termitaries, foliage, and *Cecropia* tree trunks. It may travel in mixed-species flocks. Look for this woodpecker in Tortuguero NP, in the vicinity of Tortuga Lodge, and at La Selva.

Chestnut-colored Woodpecker head detail

LINEATED WOODPECKER

The two largest woodpeckers in Costa Rica are the Lineated and the Pale-billed Woodpeckers. Obvious differences make these large-crested birds easy to distinguish. The bright red color of the crest on the Lineated Woodpecker does not include the entire head; below the top of the head, the area around the eyes is black. The Lineated Woodpecker has a white stripe on each side of the neck that extends across the face to the base of the bill. Finally, the white lines on the upper back do not meet to form a V on the Lineated Woodpecker, but they do form a V on the back of the Pale-billed Woodpecker. The loud, resonant pecking of the Lineated Woodpecker consists of a staccato, rapid-fire burst of pecks given during a two- to three-second interval.

The Lineated Woodpecker occurs at forest edges and in gallery forests, second growth, mixed woodlands, pastures, wooded plantations, and gardens. Food items include insect larvae, beetles, ants, and *Heliconia* fruits. It may open the trunks of *Cecropia* trees and eat the *Azteca* ants within. Lineated Woodpeckers live as mated pairs but sleep separately in different tree cavities. This woodpecker is found in gallery forests of Guanacaste and lowland moist and wet forests along the length of both the Caribbean and the Pacific slopes.

Dryocopus lineatus
Costa Rican names: *Carpintero lineado; picamadero barbirrayado.*
21/23 trips; 69 sightings.
Status: Permanent resident.
Length: 12.5–13.5 inches.
Weight: 6.9 ounces (197 grams).
Range: Northern Mexico to northern Argentina.
Elevational range: Sea level to 3,900 feet.

Lineated Woodpecker, distinguished from the Pale-billed Woodpecker by the white stripe from the base of the bill to the back of the neck. The red mustache mark behind the bill identifies this as a male.

Lineated Woodpecker female, with white stripe through the face but no red on the "chin" area

Pale-billed Woodpecker male, with an all-red head. The female has a black stripe over the top of the head. Notice that the white V meets at the center of the back on the Pale-billed Woodpecker.

Campephilus guatemalensis
Costa Rican names: *Carpintero picoplata; dos golpes.*
20/23 trips; 58 sightings.
Status: Permanent resident.
Length: 14–15 inches.
Weight: 9 ounces (255 grams).
Range: Northern Mexico to western Panama.
Elevational range: Sea level to 5,000 feet.

PALE-BILLED WOODPECKER

The Pale-billed Woodpecker, the largest woodpecker in Costa Rica, is responsible for one of the distinctive sounds of the rainforest: a rapid double tap that characterizes its pecking into the dead wood of rainforest trees. This is the source of one of its local Spanish names, *dos golpes*, meaning "two blows." This woodpecker has a large red bushy crest, an ivory-colored bill, and a red head, including red around the eyes and to the top of the neck. The female is black in front of the red crest. There is no white stripe through the side of the face, as there is on the Lineated Woodpecker. The white lines of the upper back converge to form a V pattern.

Lineated and Pale-billed Woodpeckers coexist in the same habitats and may be found in mature forests, forest edges, and solitary trees in clearings and pastures. In Guanacaste, the Pale-billed Woodpecker occurs in riparian forests. With its large body and powerful ivory-colored bill, it opens up cavities in dead wood to expose insect larvae of long-horned and scarab beetles. Some fruits and berries are also eaten. Foraging may occur in trees from near the ground to the upper canopy.

The Pale-billed Woodpecker nests from August through December high in a large tree. Both sexes participate in incubating two eggs and rearing the young. This species is often observed as pairs or in groups of four, which may be family groups of the parents and two fledged young. At night each woodpecker sleeps in a separate tree cavity.

This woodpecker is regularly encountered throughout the Caribbean lowlands, including Tortuguero NP, Tortuga Lodge, Monteverde, lower elevations of Braulio Carrillo NP, and La Selva. On the Pacific slope, it may be seen in riparian forests of Santa Rosa, Palo Verde, Guanacaste, Carara, Manuel Antonio, and Corcovado NPs and at La Cusinga Lodge, Sirena Biological Station, Corcovado Lodge Tent Camp, and Tiskita Jungle Lodge.

SLATY SPINETAIL

The Slaty Spinetail is one of eighteen tropical ovenbirds that occur in Costa Rica. They should not be confused with the Ovenbird (*Seiurus aurocapilla*) that nests in northern forests in the United States. The Ovenbird is actually a warbler that winters in Costa Rica. The family Furnariidae includes birds with strange-sounding names like "spinetail," "barbtail," "treerunner," "tuftedcheek," "foliage-gleaner," "leaftosser," "xenops," and "treehunter." These interesting birds are typically brownish to grayish and have a long tail.

Slaty Spinetail adult

Each tail feather has a strong spine that helps support the bird as it works its way up tree trunks to glean insects and invertebrates from tree bark, leaves, and moss. The slender Slaty Spinetail is dark gray with a rufous crown, rufous wings, and a long tail.

This spinetail inhabits thick second-growth cover at forest edges, pasture edges, and roadsides. It inspects leaf litter, curled dead leaves, branches, and foliage in a wren-like manner to glean insects, caterpillars, spiders, and other invertebrates. Pairs remain together all year. Nesting occurs from January to September. The unusual nest is a huge globular structure in a shrub or vine-covered tree. It can be up to fourteen inches high and seventeen inches long. A horizontal entryway is lined with downy leaves, cobwebs, and snake skins. The nest has resulted in the nickname "Slaty Castlebuilder" for this bird. Two or three eggs are laid in a nest, and both parents care for the young. The call is a series of medium-pitch, descending churry trills.

An inhabitant of moist and wet lowland and middle-elevation forests, the Slaty Spinetail is found mainly throughout the lowlands and middle elevations of the Caribbean slope. Sightings have been made at Caño Negro NWR, Lost Iguana Resort and Spa, La Selva, and Rancho Naturalista. It is also found in the southern Pacific region from Carara NP inland to elevations of about 4,000 feet. The most consistent sightings on the Pacific slope have been on the grounds of Talari Mountain Lodge near San Isidro del General.

Synallaxis brachyura
Costa Rican name: *Arquitecto plomizo.*
11/23 trips; 16 sightings.
Status: Permanent resident.
Length: 6 inches.
Weight: 0.65 ounce (18 grams).
Range: Northern Honduras to Brazil.
Elevational range: Sea level to 5,000 feet.

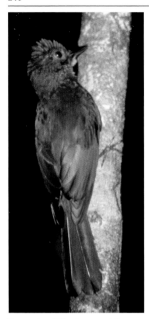

Tawny-winged Woodcreeper adult

Dendrocincla anabatina
Costa Rican name: *Trepador alirrubio.*
9/23 trips; 13 sightings.
Status: Permanent resident.
Length: 6.7–7.5 inches.
Weight: 1.0–1.5 ounces (28–43 grams).
Range: Southeastern Mexico to western Panama.
Elevational range: Sea level to 5,000 feet.

TAWNY-WINGED WOODCREEPER

There are sixteen species of woodcreeper in Costa Rica. Since birders from temperate lands are not experienced with this family of birds, they might appear difficult to identify. They are typically found hopping up a tree trunk like a woodpecker. They have beaks especially adapted for finding insects hidden in tree bark and among epiphytes. Look closely; pay attention to the length and profile of the bill, and look for streaks, spots, or barring on the breast and back and the presence or absence of a light stripe behind the eye.

The Tawny-winged Woodcreeper is an ant follower, found in the southern Pacific lowlands. If you see a Tawny-winged Woodcreeper, there will likely be antbirds and other birds following the army ants. This woodcreeper has a plain body with no spotting or streaking. The bill is black and straight. The upper part of the body is olive-brown, and the tail and wings are light rufous. While following army ants, the Tawny-winged Woodcreeper catches escaping insects, small lizards, spiders, and other invertebrates. Most woodcreepers are extremely responsive to tape recordings and can be called in for close observation for a few moments. If you use a tape recording to observe woodcreepers, please use discretion and limit the tape play to a few minutes, just until the woodcreeper responds, so it does not significantly disrupt the behavior of the bird.

Look for this woodcreeper in mature moist and wet forests and mangrove forests at Carara NP (the figure-eight loop trail), Hotel Villa Lapas skywalk, Corcovado Lodge Tent Camp, La Cusinga, Los Cusingos, and the Wilson Botanical Garden.

RUDDY WOODCREEPER

The Ruddy Woodcreeper is another army ant follower. It will typically be found in mixed flocks in both dry forests and humid lowland forests, catching insects and other invertebrates that are attempting to escape from the ants. This woodcreeper has no stripes, spots, or other markings. It is all deep rufous to chestnut-colored. The bill is pale brown and straight, and the lore (the area between the eyes and bill) is gray. The top of the head and nape have a ruffled look, like a bad hair day.

Among the creatures eaten by this woodcreeper are cockroaches, spiders, beetles, grasshoppers, and wasps. It appears to be more common from premontane to montane forest elevations and is sometimes seen in the company of Tawny-winged Woodcreepers at army ant swarms. The Ruddy Woodcreeper will perch on a vertical trunk of a tree or shrub near the ground, watching for prey. Upon sighting a victim, it flies down and captures it. The call is a loud, brief, descending trill that lasts several seconds.

Look for the Ruddy Woodcreeper at Rincón de la Vieja NP, Monteverde, and Savegre Mountain Lodge.

Dendrocincla homochroa
Costa Rican name: *Trepador rojizo.*
4/23 trips; 4 sightings.
Status: Permanent resident.
Length: 6.9–8.0 inches.
Weight: 1.3–1.6 ounces (37–45 grams).
Range: Southern Mexico to northern Venezuela.
Elevational range: Sea level to 5,000 feet.

Ruddy Woodcreeper adult

Wedge-billed Woodcreeper adult

Glyphorhynchus spirurus
Costa Rican name: *Trepadorcito pico de cuña.*
18/23 trips; 48 sightings.
Status: Permanent resident.
Length: 5.1–6.3 inches.
Weight: 0.4–0.7 ounces (11–21 grams).
Range: Southern Mexico to central Brazil.
Elevational range: Sea level to 5,000 feet.

WEDGE-BILLED WOODCREEPER

The Wedge-billed Woodcreeper is a small bird with a plain olive-gray head and a rich cinnamon-rufous back and tail. Sexes are identical. The bill is short, with a straight, wedge-shaped profile. The throat is buffy, and there is a buff-colored stripe over the eye. The upper chest has fine buffy vertical streaking. This is one of the most common woodcreepers in the country. The Wedge-billed Woodcreeper has a fast, high-pitched warbling whistle that consists of about seven interconnected notes.

This woodcreeper inhabits lowland moist and wet forests, older second growth, forest edges, and partially cleared forest openings. It forages for small insects and spiders by hopping upward on thick tree trunks. It feeds by using its wedge-shaped bill to pry up pieces of bark, moss, and lichen to expose prey underneath. At night this woodcreeper sleeps in vertical cracks in tree stumps just a few feet above the ground.

This woodcreeper occurs in Caribbean and southern Pacific lowlands. On the Caribbean slope, it is regularly encountered at La Selva, Lost Iguana Resort, Rancho Naturalista, lower levels of Braulio Carrillo NP (Tapir Trail), and La Paz Waterfall Gardens. On the Pacific slope, it can be observed at Carara NP, Wilson Botanical Garden, Las Esquinas Rainforest Lodge, Corcovado NP, Sirena Biological Station, Lapa Ríos, Hotel Villa Lapas, Corcovado Lodge Tent Camp, and Tiskita Jungle Lodge.

NORTHERN BARRED-WOODCREEPER

One of Costa Rica's largest woodcreepers, the Northern Barred-Woodcreeper is also the only woodcreeper with barring across the back of the head and upper back. This impressive bird is olive-brown on the head, breast, and shoulders and cinnamon-brown on the wings and tail. The dark bill is straight and thick. The most distinguishing marks, however, are the fine barring over the entire head and shoulder region and across the breast and belly. The Black-banded Woodcreeper is the only other woodcreeper that has barring, but that barring is present only on the belly, and most of its middle-elevation range does not overlap with the lowland range of the Northern Barred-Woodcreeper. The call of this woodcreeper sounds like someone letting an extended series of bursts of air out of a balloon that has the opening stretched tight; the brief squealing, ascending notes are each about one second long.

This woodcreeper is primarily a species of mature lowland moist and wet forests on both the Caribbean and Pacific lowlands. Sometimes it ranges out to forest edges and clearings. It hunts singly, in pairs, and sometimes as trios for beetles, cockroaches, and spiders, but it also catches small lizards and frogs by perching quietly on tree trunks at lower to mid-levels of the canopy and flying down to catch its victim. This woodcreeper often accompanies army ant swarms.

On the Caribbean slope, the Northern Barred-Woodcreeper may be seen in Tortuguero NP, Tortuga Lodge, La Selva, and Rancho Naturalista. In the Pacific lowlands, it can be observed at Hotel Borinquen Mountain Resort, Santa Rosa, Palo Verde, Rincón de la Vieja, Carara and Corcovado NPs, Sirena Biological Station, and Corcovado Lodge Tent Camp.

Northern Barred-Woodcreeper adult

Dendrocolaptes sanctithomae (formerly Dendrocolaptes certhia)

Costa Rican name: *Trepador barreteado.*

16/23 trips; 41 sightings.

Status: Permanent resident.

Length: 9.8–11.4 inches.

Weight: 2.5–2.9 ounces (71–83 grams).

Range: Southern Mexico to northern Brazil.

Elevational range: Sea level to 4,200 feet.

BLACK-BANDED WOODCREEPER

Dendrocolaptes picumnus
Costa Rican name: *Trepador vientribareteado.*
2/23 trips; 3 sightings.
Status: Permanent resident.
Length: 9.4–12.0 inches.
Weight: 2.1–2.3 ounces (61–64 grams).
Range: Southern Mexico to northwestern Argentina.
Elevational range: 3,000–6,500 feet.

The Black-banded Woodcreeper is the only other wood-creeper in Costa Rica, besides the Northern Barred-Woodcreeper, with barring. Its horizontal barring is present only on the lower chest and belly. The upper portion of the chest is vertically streaked, and the back of the head is finely marked with streaks that extend to the scapular feathers. The dark bill is thick and straight. Found on higher elevations of both the Caribbean and Pacific slopes, the Black-banded Woodcreeper range does not significantly overlap with the Northern Barred-Woodcreeper.

The Black-banded Woodcreeper occurs mainly in mature moist and wet forests at premontane and lower montane elevations. It can also be found at forest edges and in plantations and may be found in association with army ant swarms. Perching quietly on small vertical tree trunks, this woodcreeper watches the ground for beetles, scorpions, spiders, frogs, lizards, cockroaches, and centipedes that are escaping from the ants. Away from army ant swarms, it will explore tree bark and foliage in search of food. The call, about three seconds long, is a rapid series of twelve to fifteen short squeals. They descend slightly in pitch and volume from the beginning to the end of the call. This rare species has been encountered by the author only at Bosque de Paz on the Caribbean slope.

Black-banded Woodcreeper adult

COCOA WOODCREEPER (BUFF-THROATED WOODCREEPER)

The Cocoa Woodcreeper, one of the most common Costa Rican woodcreepers, is typically encountered in moist and wet forests of the Caribbean and Pacific lowlands. It is more common in the southern Pacific lowlands. The most conspicuous feature is its long and slightly decurved bill, which has a dark upper mandible and light lower mandible. The head, neck, and upper chest are streaked. Formerly known as the Buff-throated Woodcreeper, this species has a distinctive call, consisting of a series of twenty or more sharply ascending high-pitched whistles given over five seconds, that sounds like someone whistling for a dog. The call increases in volume and then decreases in volume at the end. It can also give a rapid buzzy trill that descends in pitch and volume at the end.

This woodcreeper may be encountered in mature forests as well as second-growth forests, forest openings, and gardens. It is usually seen hopping up tree trunks and exploring for invertebrates hidden in the bark and among epiphytes. The long, stout bill is especially adapted for probing for insects in tree bark and prying bits of bark loose to reveal prey. It does not usually follow army ant swarms. Prey include beetles, katydids, cockroaches, spiders, caterpillars, and some small lizards and frogs.

Look for this woodcreeper at Tortuguero NP, La Selva, the Sueño Azul pasture area, and Rancho Naturalista. In the southern Pacific lowlands, it may be found in Carara, Manuel Antonio, and Corcovado NPs and at Hotel Villa Lapas skywalk, Sirena Biological Station, Corcovado Lodge Tent Camp, Tiskita Jungle Lodge, La Cusinga, Las Esquinas Rainforest Lodge, Oro Verde BR, Hotel Cristal Ballena, Rancho Casa Grande, and Los Cusingos. It can be found up to middle elevations at Rancho Naturalista on the Caribbean slope and the Wilson Botanical Garden on the Pacific slope.

Cocoa Woodcreeper adult

Xiphorhynchus sussurrans (formerly Xiphorhynchus guttatus)
Costa Rican name: *Trepador gorgianteado.*
20/23 trips; 69 sightings.
Status: Permanent resident.
Length: 8.9–10.0 inches.
Weight: 1.4–2.0 ounces (41–58 grams).
Range: Eastern Guatemala to Brazil.
Elevational range: Sea level to 3,000 feet.

Spotted Woodcreeper adult

Xiphorhynchus erythropygius
Costa Rican name: *Trepador manchado.*
12/23 trips; 29 sightings.
Status: Permanent resident.
Length: 7.5–9.4 inches.
Weight: 1.4–1.9 ounces (40–54 grams).
Range: Southern Mexico to western Ecuador.
Elevational range: 2,300–5,600 feet.

SPOTTED WOODCREEPER

The key to identification of the Spotted Woodcreeper is the presence of buffy-colored spots on its brownish breast. If you can see the spots on the breast, the identification choices are narrowed from sixteen down to only two woodcreepers—the rare Long-tailed Woodcreeper and the Spotted Woodcreeper. The Long-tailed Woodcreeper has a buffy stripe behind the eye, a plain brown back, and a slender bill. The Spotted Woodcreeper has an eye-ring, pale buffy streaking on the back, and a thick, straight bill that is dark above and light below.

This woodcreeper may follow army ant swarms or join mixed flocks of other rainforest birds, like Golden-crowned Warblers, Common Bush-Tanagers, and Lineated Foliage-gleaners. It feeds singly or in pairs by gleaning invertebrates on vertical trunks or, more commonly, as it travels in a spiraling manner around epiphyte-laden horizontal limbs in search of prey. It may hang upside down or lean down from above to search for hidden insects in the manner of a Black-and-white Warbler. The short legs with long claws and the long, heavy bill are adaptations for this acrobatic style of foraging. Prey include beetles, katydids, spiders, earwigs, cockroaches, frogs, and small salamanders. Upon capturing a struggling victim, the bird thrashes it against the branch to kill it and then eats it. The call of this woodcreeper is a series of several high-pitched sharply descending, tremulous, whistles that are each about a second in duration.

The Spotted Woodcreeper is found at middle-elevation moist to wet forests where there is an abundance of epiphytes. It can be encountered on the Caribbean slope at Monteverde, La Paz Waterfall Gardens, and Rancho Naturalista. On the Pacific slope, it occurs at Tapantí NP and the Wilson Botanical Garden (River Trail).

STREAK-HEADED WOODCREEPER

The widespread Streak-headed Woodcreeper is probably the most common woodcreeper in Costa Rica. This is a slender and medium-sized woodcreeper. The breast, head, and upper back are all streaked. The bill is fairly long, slender, slightly decurved, and pinkish brown. Two other woodcreepers have streaking on the head and breast, but each has a long, thick bill—the Cocoa Woodcreeper and the Ivory-billed Woodcreeper. The Ivory-billed Woodcreeper is found only in Guanacaste and in the Río Frío region, so its range does not overlap with the main range of the Streak-headed Woodcreeper. The Spot-crowned Woodcreeper is the highland equivalent of the Streak-headed Woodcreeper, but it has small spots on top of the head instead of streaks, and their ranges do not overlap.

The Streak-headed Woodcreeper could be considered antisocial among woodcreepers. It does not join in mixed-species foraging flocks, and it does not follow army ant swarms. Instead, it is a solitary hunter that uses its long, slender bill for gleaning beetles, ants, cockroaches, caterpillars, bees, termites, scorpions, millipedes, and wasps from hidden nooks and crannies among tree bark and epiphytes. The bill is used to move leaves in search of food. The bird will spiral up a tree trunk as it searches for prey. The call is a loud, high-pitched, descending trill that lasts about two seconds.

This woodcreeper is found in forest edges, openings, gardens, gallery forests, and mangrove forests. On the Caribbean slope, it is found from lowlands to montane forests at Cahuita, Puerto Viejo, Caño Negro NWR and Lodge, Lost Iguana Resort, La Selva, Selva Verde Lodge, Rancho Gavilán, Sueño Azul, Rancho Naturalista, and La Paz Waterfall Gardens. It is uncommon in Guanacaste, but it can be encountered at Hotel Borinquen Mountain Resort. In the southern Pacific region, it can be seen at Carara NP, Hotel Villa Lapas skywalk, Hotel Cristal Ballena, La Cusinga, Las Esquinas Rainforest Lodge, Talari Mountain Lodge, Los Cusingos, and the Wilson Botanical Garden.

Streak-headed Woodcreeper adult

Lepidocolaptes souleyetii
Costa Rican name: *Trepador cabecirrayado.*
23/23 trips; 100 sightings.
Status: Permanent resident.
Length: 6.7–8.7 inches.
Weight: 0.8–1.2 ounces (22–34 grams).
Range: Southern Mexico to northern Brazil.
Elevational range: Sea level to 5,000 feet.

SPOT-CROWNED WOODCREEPER

Lepidocolaptes affinis

Costa Rican name: *Trepador cabecipunteado.*

18/23 trips; 41 sightings.

Status: Permanent resident.

Length: 8.0–8.5 inches.

Weight: 1.2 ounces (35 grams).

Range: Central Mexico to northern Bolivia.

Elevational range: 3,300–10,000 feet.

Most woodcreepers live in tropical lowlands, but the Spot-crowned Woodcreeper is found primarily from 5,000 feet to the timberline. The crown of this chestnut-cinnamon woodcreeper has small, oval buffy spots. There are elongated buffy streaks on the back of the head and the sides of the face, neck, and upper breast. The bill is pale, the throat is pale buffy, and the call is a high-pitched trill.

This woodcreeper lives in the same montane forests as the Acorn Woodpecker. It climbs trees in forests and forest edges and is also found in scattered trees in pastures. The long, slightly decurved bill is used to probe bark, lichens, mosses, and epiphytes for insects and insect larvae. Sometimes this bird joins mixed flocks of Common or Sooty-capped Bush-Tanagers as they forage in the canopy.

The most dependable sites to see this bird are at Bosque de Paz on the Caribbean slope of Poás volcano, in the Talamanca Mountains at kilometers 66 and 76 of the Pan American Highway in Cerro de la Muerte, and in the San Gerardo de Dota Valley, including the Savegre Mountain Lodge.

Spot-crowned Woodcreeper adult

GREAT ANTSHRIKE

Among the highlights of birding in a tropical rainforest is the opportunity to see and hear birds found nowhere else. In the American tropics there are 250 members of the antbird family (Thamnophilidae), including antshrikes, antbirds, antvireos, and antwrens. These birds do not command attention the way toucans, macaws, and quetzals do, but they provide a vital essence to the spirit and diversity of the rainforest. Antbirds get their name because many members of this interesting family fol-low swarms of army ants, often as mixed flocks, and they capture escaping insects and other invertebrates. Not all antbirds, however, follow army ants.

Great Antshrike female

Costa Rica has twenty-two species of antbirds, the largest of which is the distinctive Great Antshrike. The male has a black head and crest and is black over the back and tail. There are narrow white wing bars. The throat and breast are white, the bill has a pronounced hook at the tip, and the eye is bright red. The female is also quite attractive, with a bright rufous-brown head and back, a white throat and breast, a strongly hooked tip on the bill, and red eyes, but no wing bars. The call is memorable, an accelerating, bouncing-ball progression of chirps that descends in pitch and volume and ends with a squalling churr at the end.

The Great Antshrike lives in thick, tangled lowland forest and riverbank edges characterized by plants like *Heliconia* and *Calathea*. It hunts in pairs or in mixed flocks and may attend army ant swarms in search of bee-tles, katydids, cockroaches, caterpillars, spiders, lizards, frogs, and even small mammals. It stalks its prey either on the ground or from low perches in thick foliage, stop-ping and scanning for prey, then jumping up, sallying, or hopping down to capture the victim, even including minnows underwater. The Great Antshrike is more easily heard than seen, and it may be necessary to play a tape

Taraba major
Costa Rican name: *Batará grande.*
12/23 trips; 15 sightings.
Status: Permanent resident.
Length: 7.4–7.8 inches.
Weight: 1.8–2.5 ounces (50–70 grams).
Range: Southeastern Mexico to northeastern Argentina.
Elevational range: Sea level to 3,300 feet.

recording of the call to get it to appear, even momentarily, for a sighting. Discontinue playing the call after sighting the bird to avoid excessive disturbance.

The Great Antshrike is found in the Caribbean lowlands in locations like Puerto Viejo near Cahuita, Lost Iguana Resort, Caño Negro Lodge and NWR, Tortuguero NP, and along the entry road at La Selva. In the southern Pacific lowlands, it may be observed at Hotel Villa Lapas, Las Esquinas Rainforest Lodge, Sirena Biological Station, and Corcovado and Manuel Antonio NPs.

Great Antshrike male

BARRED ANTSHRIKE

The Barred Antshrike is one of the most easily identified members of the antbird family. The male has a pronounced bushy crest and fine zebra-striped barring over the entire body. The female has a prominent rufous crest and is rufous over the wings, tail, and back. The breast of the female is pale cinnamon, and the sides of the face and back of the neck have fine black stripes. The call is one of the great sounds of the rainforest. It is an accelerating series of staccato nasal notes, given over a five-second period, that increase in frequency as they are given. The call ends with a higher-pitched squeak.

Barred Antshrike female

The Barred Antshrike inhabits brushy thickets and second growth of humid lowland forests and gallery forests. It eats beetles, caterpillars, spiders, and other insects. Sometimes it follows army ant swarms.

It occurs in the Caribbean lowlands at Caño Negro Lodge grounds and NWR, Lost Iguana Resort, Tortuga Lodge, La Selva, Sueño Azul, and EARTH University near Guapiles. On the Pacific slope, this antshrike can be encountered in gallery forests of Guanacaste, Lomas Barbudal BR, Santa Rosa and Carara NPs, Los Cusingos, Hotel Villa Lapas, and Tiskita Jungle Lodge. It is usually necessary to record and play back the call of this antbird in order to get it to emerge briefly from thick underbrush so it can be seen. Some Costa Rican naturalist guides carry a tape recorder and directional microphone to attract and provide viewing opportunities for these seldom-seen birds.

Thamnophilus doliatus
Costa Rican name: *Batará barreteado.*
19/23 trips; 40 sightings.
Status: Permanent resident.
Length: 5.9–6.3 inches.
Weight: 0.8 –1.1 ounces (24–30 grams).
Range: Northeastern Mexico to northeastern Argentina.
Elevational range: Sea level to 4,600 feet.

Barred Antshrike male

Black-hooded Antshrike female

Thamnophilus bridgesi
Costa Rican name: *Batará negruzco.*
17/23 trips; 65 sightings.
Status: Permanent resident.
Length: 6.3–6.5 inches.
Weight: 0.9–1.0 ounces (26–27 grams).
Range: Endemic to southwestern Costa Rica and western Panama.
Elevational range: Sea level to 3,600 feet.

BLACK-HOODED ANTSHRIKE

The Black-hooded Antshrike is a short, stocky member of the antbird family. The male is black with white speckles on the wings. The female is sooty brown above with a black head and neck that are finely streaked with white. Its breast and belly are olive-grayish with longitudinal whitish streaking on the upper breast.

The habitat of this antshrike includes brushy edges along fields and roads, thick second growth, and forest interior, and this is one of the only antbirds to inhabit mangrove forests. Foods include insects and spiders, which are gleaned from ground cover and foliage. The call is typically a plaintive, brief, three-note cawing phrase in which each note drops slightly in volume and pitch at the end.

This is the most common antbird of southern Pacific lowland forests and middle-elevation forests. It is an endemic species found only in southwestern Costa Rica and western Panama. More conspicuous than other antbirds, it is often easily approached for a closer view. It responds well to recording and playback of its call or to squeaking to arouse its curiosity.

It can be regularly observed at Carara, Manuel Antonio, and Corcovado NPs, the Villa Lapas skywalk, Villa Caletas, La Cusinga, Hotel Cristal Ballena, Oro Verde BR, Rancho Casa Grande, Sirena Biological Station, Corcovado Lodge Tent Camp, Tiskita Jungle Lodge, the Wilson Botanical Garden, Los Cusingos, and Las Esquinas Rainforest Lodge.

Black-hooded Antshrike male

CHESTNUT-BACKED ANTBIRD

One of the distinctive calls of Costa Rica's lowland moist and wet forests is the plaintive whistle of the Chestnut-backed Antbird. In this two-note whistle, the first sharp, short, high-pitched note is followed by a brief second note that drops in pitch. The male has a short, rounded chestnut-brown body and black head. The female's head is dark rufous. A fleshy area surrounding the eyes extends forward to the bill and makes the bird look like it has blue goggles.

Chestnut-backed Antbird female. Males have a grayish head and breast.

The Chestnut-backed Antbird inhabits thick, brushy forest edges along trails and streams and in rainforest light gaps where additional sunlight stimulates plant growth. There it lurks on or near the ground, searching for insects, spiders, frogs, and small lizards. It may follow army ant swarms or join mixed flocks of foraging birds.

The distribution includes both the Caribbean and southern Pacific lowlands. On the Caribbean slope, it can be heard and sometimes seen in Tortuguero and Cahuita NPs, Tortuga Lodge, and La Selva (Sendero Tres Ríos). On the Pacific slope, the Chestnut-backed Antbird occurs at Carara (the figure-eight loop trail), Manuel Antonio and Corcovado NPs, the Hotel Villa Lapas skywalk, La Cusinga, Las Esquinas Rainforest Lodge, Hotel Cristal Ballena, Sirena Biological Station, Drake Bay Wilderness Resort, Corcovado Lodge Tent Camp, and Tiskita Jungle Lodge.

Viewing this antbird will probably require the use of tape recording and playbacks to get the antbird to emerge from heavy cover. Such calling should be limited to a few minutes to avoid disrupting the behavior of the birds.

Myrmeciza exsul
Costa Rican name: *Hormiguero dorsicastaño.*
20/23 trips; 73 sightings.
Status: Permanent resident.
Length: 5.3–5.7 inches.
Weight: 0.9–1.1 ounces (25–30 grams).
Range: Eastern Nicaragua to western Ecuador.
Elevational range: Sea level to 3,000 feet.

DULL-MANTLED ANTBIRD

Myrmeciza laemosticta
Costa Rican name: *Hormiguero alimaculado.*
7/23 trips; 14 sightings.
Status: Permanent resident.
Length: 5.1–5.5 inches.
Weight: 0.8 ounce (24 grams).
Range: Costa Rica to northwestern Ecuador.
Elevational range: 1,000–3,300 feet.

The Dull-mantled Antbird is a foothill species of the Caribbean slope found mainly at premontane levels in moist and wet forests. The limited range makes it a Costa Rican specialty that is a prize to observe. It is dark brown over the back with a gray head, gray breast, red eyes, and white speckles on the leading edge of the wing. The female has white speckles on the throat. This antbird has a short, rounded appearance, like that of a stunted robin.

This terrestrial antbird is found mostly in undisturbed rainforest, inhabiting the ground level of thick understory vegetation, often along streams and slopes of moist and wet forests. It gleans invertebrates, such as beetles, cockroaches, crickets, spiders, and sowbugs, by turning over leaf litter and exploring ground-level foliage. Sometimes this antbird follows army ant swarms. The call consists of a series of about four high-pitched whistled notes followed by two or three notes that descend in pitch. It may also give individual sharp buzzy chirps.

This uncommon antbird can be observed at Rancho Naturalista (forest loop trail, hummingbird meadow, and hummingbird pools) and at the Hanging Bridges property near the Lost Iguana Resort.

Dull-mantled Antbird adult. Notice the red eyes and pale spots on the shoulders.

IMMACULATE ANTBIRD

In addition to the Dull-mantled Antbird, the Immaculate Antbird is also found in the Caribbean foothills, and occasionally it is seen in the middle elevations of the southern Pacific slope. The Immaculate Antbird has the blue-goggles characteristic of many antbirds. Its distinguishing feature, however, is its uniform color with no wing bars, spots, or streaking. The male is black with red eyes and the female is dark reddish brown with a grayish face and tail.

Like the Dull-mantled Antbird, this antbird gleans invertebrates at ground level by hopping among foliage and vine tangles to capture grasshoppers, katydids, cockroaches, beetles, and small lizards and frogs. It constantly raises and lowers its tail as it hunts. Perhaps this movement helps flush hidden insects. Small groups of this antbird will also follow army ant swarms and perch above the ants, watching for escaping invertebrates that can be caught by sallying from low horizontal perches. The call is a rapid series of about eight to ten short, high-pitched, whistled notes. The series lasts about three seconds.

An inhabitant of wet mature forests and older second-growth forests, this uncommon antbird may be encountered at Rancho Naturalista (bug light and hummingbird meadow) and La Paz Waterfall Gardens (forest trail).

Myrmeciza immaculata
Costa Rican name: *Hormiguero immaculado.*
4/23 trips; 4 sightings.
Status: Permanent resident.
Length: 7.1 inches.
Weight: 1.3–1.5 ounces (38–43 grams).
Range: Northern Honduras to western Ecuador.
Elevational range: 1,000–5,600 feet.

Immaculate Antbird female. Males are black with blue goggles.

BICOLORED ANTBIRD

Gymnopithys leucaspis
Costa Rican name: *Hormiguero bicolor.*
2/15 trips; 3 sightings.
Status: Permanent resident.
Length: 5.5–5.8 inches.
Weight: 1.1 ounces (30 grams).
Range: Northern Honduras to western Brazil.
Elevational range: Sea level to 5,600 feet.

The Bicolored Antbird is the only small antbird with a pure white breast. The back is dark brown, and it has the blue goggles that also characterize Chestnut-backed and Immaculate Antbirds. This antbird follows swarms of army ants, often in the company of Tawny-winged Woodcreepers. This bird moves ahead of advancing ants, perching on low twigs and exposed roots. When a small creature tries to escape, the antbird flies down to snatch the insect or spider. It does not eat the ants.

The Bicolored Antbird inhabits moist and wet lowland and middle-elevation forests. It occurs in mature forest, second growth, and adjacent openings. The call is a good one to learn because it usually indicates that a swarm of army ants is present, and that may provide the opportunity to see other rarely seen rainforest birds following the ants. The call is a loud, brief, churry, buzzing note.

The distribution of this uncommon antbird includes the Caribbean and southern Pacific lowlands and middle elevations. It has been observed along the main entrance road at Carara NP, at the Wilson Botanical Garden, and on the hillside forest trail behind Corcovado Lodge Tent Camp.

Bicolored Antbird adult

TORRENT TYRANNULET

Three birds are typically associated with the streams of Costa Rica's foothills and mountains: the Black Phoebe, the Torrent Tyrannulet, and the American Dipper. The Torrent Tyrannulet is a small, slender, pearly gray flycatcher with a black cap, black wings, and black tail. It lives along fast-flowing, boulder-strewn streams, where it perches on rocks or on branches that extend over the water. From these perches, it sallies out to capture insects such as flies, damselflies, and stoneflies that may be in flight or perched on streamside vegetation.

The Torrent Tyrannulet is found in foothills and higher elevations along streams of both the Caribbean and Pacific slopes. It can be seen on the Caribbean slope from the bridge at La Virgen del Socorro and at the bridge crossing by the Catarata de la Paz (Peace Waterfall) and at La Paz Waterfall Gardens. On the Pacific slope, it can be observed along the Río Macho and Río Grande de Orosi in Tapantí NP and along the Río Savegre in the San Gerardo de Dota Valley.

Serpophaga cinerea
Costa Rican name: *Mosquerito guardarríos.*
22/23 trips; 47 sightings.
Status: Permanent resident.
Length: 4 inches.
Weight: 0.3 ounce (8 grams).
Range: Costa Rica to northern Bolivia.
Elevational range: 800–6,500 feet.

Torrent Tyrannulet nest tucked into a notch in a boulder. Notice the whitewash.

Torrent Tyrannulet adult

Ochre-bellied Flycatcher adult

Ochre-bellied Flycatcher feeding on nectar at a *Heliconia*

Mionectes oleagineus
Costa Rican name: *Mosquerito aceitunado.*
16/23 trips; 32 sightings.
Status: Permanent resident.
Length: 5 inches.
Weight: 0.5 ounce (13 grams).
Range: Mexico to central Brazil, Trinidad, and Tobago.
Elevational range: Sea level to 4,000 feet.

OCHRE-BELLIED FLYCATCHER

The Ochre-bellied Flycatcher is interesting among flycatchers because its diet comprises mainly fruits and berries, not insects. The body is grayish olive-green without any stripes or wing bars. The belly has a distinctive ochraceous color that is apparent under the wings when the bird is in flight.

Its habitat includes lowland wet forests, second growth, courtyard areas, and clearings adjacent to forests. This incredibly agile flycatcher flies from a perch and plucks fruits from *Heliconia, Clusia, Faramea, Alchornea, Siparuna, Zanthoxylum,* mistletoe (*Gaiadendron*), palms, and members of the family Araceae. A few insects are also taken. Sometimes this bird forages as part of a mixed flock.

The reproductive behavior is quite different from most flycatchers. The males are promiscuous and do not form pair bonds. They form a leklike assembly of up to half a dozen males that are spaced in the midcanopy about 50 to 160 feet apart. They sing and display by alternately raising each wing to display their ochre-colored "armpits." This wing-flipping behavior takes place up to seven months of the year. The call is a series of short double-chirp notes in which the second note is higher in pitch. After mating, the female leaves the male and raises two or three young by herself in an elaborate pendulous sac-shaped nest that is about a foot high and four inches wide.

In the Caribbean lowlands, the Ochre-bellied Flycatcher can be observed in Cahuita NP, La Selva, Selva Verde Lodge, and Rancho Naturalista. In the southern Pacific lowlands, this bird can be seen at Carara, Manuel Antonio, and Corcovado NPs, Lapa Ríos, the Hotel Villa Lapas skywalk, Hotel Cristal Ballena, Rancho Casa Grande, La Cusinga, Las Esquinas Rainforest Lodge, Corcovado Lodge Tent Camp, Tiskita Jungle Lodge, Sirena Biological Station, and the Wilson Botanical Garden.

COMMON TODY-FLYCATCHER

One of the smallest flycatchers in Costa Rica is the Common Tody-Flycatcher. Less than four inches long, it is identified by the black hood that extends over pale yellowish eyes, giving it a sinister hooded appearance. It also has a dark gray back, black tail, and bright yellow throat, breast, and belly. The black wing feathers have yellowish edges. Unique behaviors include constantly flipping the tail upward and walking sideways along branches while looking for prey.

The Common Tody-Flycatcher is regularly encountered in backyards, courtyards, forest and wetland edges, and ornamental shrubbery of urban and rural homes. It occurs in second-growth lowland forests, plantations, and gallery and mangrove forests. This tody-flycatcher makes quick flights from its perch to trap flies, beetles, ants, wasps, and other insects against the foliage they are resting on. The relatively large, wide bill is an effective tool for such a hunting technique.

A bird of moist and wet lowland and middle-elevation habitats, the Common Tody-Flycatcher is found on both Caribbean and southern Pacific slopes. In the Caribbean region, it can be found in Cahuita and Tortuguero NPs, Limón, Tilajari Resort, Guapiles, Guacimo, La Selva, Puerto Viejo en Sarapiquí, Sueño Azul, Rara Avis, and Rancho Naturalista. In the Pacific lowlands, it is common throughout the region up to the elevations of Talari Mountain Lodge and Wilson Botanical Garden.

Todirostrum cinereum
Costa Rican names: *Espatulilla común; pechita; tontilla.*
22/23 trips; 113 sightings.
Status: Permanent resident.
Length: 3.75 inches.
Weight: 0.2 ounce (6.5 grams).
Range: Mexico to southern Brazil.
Elevational range: Sea level to 5,000 feet.

Common Tody-Flycatcher adult

BRAN-COLORED FLYCATCHER

Myiophobus fasciatus
Costa Rican name: *Mosquerito pechirrayado.*
3/23 trips; 4 sightings.
Status: Permanent resident.
Length: 4.75–5.00 inches.
Weight: 0.3–0.4 ounce (9–11 grams).
Range: Southwestern Costa Rica to Central Argentina.
Elevational range: 1,000–4,000 feet.

The Bran-colored Flycatcher has distinguishing marks that make it easier to identify than many other flycatchers. It is rich cinnamon-ochraceous brown over the back with buffy wing bars and buffy to whitish edging on the secondary feathers when at rest. Those feathers merge to form a white patch on the wing. The breast is marked with vertical grayish-brown streaks, and a yellow crown is visible when the bird is agitated or displaying.

Typical habitat for the Bran-colored Flycatcher includes broken forest and pasture edges, brushy fence-lines, and roadsides. Perching in the open, it sallies to catch insects on the wing or snatches them from nearby vegetation. Included in its diet are beetles, ants, wasps, flies, and a few berries.

This uncommon flycatcher is found only at middle elevations of the southern Pacific slope. It may be encountered on the grounds of Talari Mountain Lodge, along the roadside from San Vito to Sabalito near the Panama border, and in the vicinity of San Vito las Cruces.

Bran-colored Flycatcher adult

TAWNY-CHESTED FLYCATCHER

Many of Costa Rica's flycatchers are found over a broad range, but the Tawny-chested Flycatcher is an endemic specialty found only in eastern Nicaragua and the Caribbean slope of Costa Rica. This flycatcher has a grayish head, a white eye-ring that is open at the front and back, an olive-greenish back with ochraceous wing bars, a white throat, a white spot in front of the eye, a yellowish belly, and a distinctive ochraceous upper chest, from which it gets its name. The head of the female is olive-grayish.

Tawny-chested Flycatcher adult

This rare species is found in the eastern Caribbean lowlands and at middle elevations, where it occurs at openings in mature forest or near streams where the vegetation is very dense.

The Tawny-chested Flycatcher hunts near the ground. From that low perspective, it has a special technique of looking upward to spot beetles, bugs, ants, and other invertebrates hiding on the underside of leaves and twigs. When it sees prey, it sallies or leaps upward to capture its victim.

The only place where this species is regularly encountered is at Rancho Naturalista (hummingbird meadow, bug light, and forest loop trail).

Aphanotriccus capitalis
Costa Rican name: *Mosquerito pechileonado.*
6/23 trips; 11 sightings.
Status: Permanent resident.
Length: 4.7 inches.
Weight: 0.4 ounce (11 grams).
Range: Endemic to eastern Nicaragua and northern Costa Rica.
Elevational range: Sea level to 3,300 feet.

TUFTED FLYCATCHER

Mitrephanes phaeocercus
Costa Rican name: *Mosquerito moñudo.*
20/23 trips; 58 sightings.
Status: Permanent resident.
Length: 4.7–5.3 inches.
Weight: 0.3 ounce (9 grams).
Range: Northwestern Mexico to eastern Bolivia.
Elevational range: 2,300–10,000 feet.

The Tufted Flycatcher is one of three friendly flycatchers that can be observed in Costa Rica's mountains. The other two are the Yellowish Flycatcher and the Black-capped Flycatcher. These small birds are easily approached. The prominent crest and ochraceous color make this bird easy to identify.

In montane forests, this flycatcher occurs at forest edges, in pastures, and in light gaps within the forest. The Tufted Flycatcher watches the surrounding area from a favorite perch on a tree or shrub. When an insect passes, the bird flies out, captures it on the wing, and returns to its perch.

The Tufted Flycatcher occurs along the foothills and higher elevations of both slopes. It can be seen at La Virgen del Socorro, Monteverde, Bosque de Paz, La Paz Waterfall Gardens, and Braulio Carrillo and Tapantí NPs on the Caribbean slope. It also occurs in the Talamanca Mountains and in Cerro de la Muerte at kilometers 66 and 80, and in the San Gerardo de Dota Valley.

Tufted Flycatcher adult

YELLOWISH FLYCATCHER

Most small flycatchers of the genus *Empidonax* are difficult to identify, but the friendly Yellowish Flycatcher of Costa Rica's mountains is easily approached. It has the most conspicuous whitish-yellow eye-ring of all *Empidonax* flycatchers. The back is yellowish olive, the breast is yellow, and there are two prominent yellowish wing bars.

The Yellowish Flycatcher inhabits montane forests, mountain pastures, and forest edges. Amid relatively open understory, it sits on perches that are sometimes no more than two feet from the ground. It flies out to pluck insects from foliage and on the ground. Small berries are sometimes eaten.

This bird occurs in mountainous regions through the length of the country. It has been observed at Monteverde, Bosque de Paz, La Paz Waterfall Gardens, Xandari Plantation Resort, San José de la Montaña, Tapantí NP, and in the San Gerardo de Dota Valley.

Empidonax flavescens
Costa Rican name: *Mosquerito amarillento.*
14/23 trips; 36 sightings.
Status: Permanent resident.
Length: 4.9–5.5 inches.
Weight: 0.4 ounce (12 grams).
Range: Southeastern Mexico to western Panama.
Elevational range: 2,600–8,000 feet.

Yellowish Flycatcher nest tucked into a cut bank along a road

Yellowish Flycatcher adult

BLACK-CAPPED FLYCATCHER

Empidonax atriceps
Costa Rican name: *Mosquerito cabecinegro.*
19/23 trips; 44 sightings.
Status: Permanent resident.
Length: 4.5 inches.
Weight: 0.3 ounce (9 grams).
Range: Endemic to highlands of Costa Rica and western Panama.
Elevational range: 6,000–11,000 feet.

The Black-capped Flycatcher is the third of Costa Rica's friendly flycatchers in the mountains. It has a black cap, dark brown back and wings, brownish-tan chest, yellowish belly, and two brownish wing bars. The only other flycatcher with an obvious black cap is the Torrent Tyrannulet, which is silvery gray with dark wings and tail.

The Black-capped Flycatcher, often observed in pairs, is characteristic of montane forests, pastures, trails, and clearings. It perches on posts and branches where it has a view of the surrounding area. When an insect is sighted, the bird flies out to capture it on the wing and then returns to the same perch. Beetles, flies, and butterflies are among the prey eaten.

Endemic to the mountains surrounding the Central Plateau through the Talamanca Mountains to western Panama, this flycatcher can be observed in Poás Volcano and Irazú Volcano NPs, at higher elevations of the Talamanca Mountains, and in Cerro de la Muerte at sites like the transmission tower at kilometer 90. Along the Pan American Highway, it can be observed at kilometers 66, 77, 80, and 86. The Black-capped Flycatcher is regularly seen in the San Gerardo de Dota Valley.

Black-capped Flycatcher adult

BLACK PHOEBE

Costa Rica's avifauna includes seventy-nine flycatchers, many of which are difficult to identify. The Black Phoebe, however, has distinctive markings, behavior, and habitat. This medium-sized flycatcher is black with white in the lower central portion of the belly. Its tail-bobbing behavior and tendency to perch along wetland edges resembles the behavior of the Eastern Phoebe in North America. It is typically found along stream edges, where it sallies from perches to capture insects.

The Black Phoebe is found at middle and higher elevations along boulder-strewn streams. It frequently perches on buildings and power lines near streams. Food, including flies, wasps, bees, beetles, crickets, caterpillars, grasshoppers, and an occasional small fish, is caught by sallying from perches.

In the Caribbean foothills, the Black Phoebe occurs along the main highway to Limón on the Río Roca, on the Río Blanco, and at the Río Sucio bridge between Guacimo and La Selva, Bosque de Paz, Lost Iguana Resort, and Sueño Azul. In the southern Pacific foothills and mountains, it can be seen at Tapantí NP, along the Río Chirripó Pacífico between San Isidro del General and Los Cusingos, and along the Río Savegre in San Gerardo de Dota Valley.

Sayornis nigricans
Costa Rican name: *Mosquero de agua.*
22/23 trips; 79 sightings.
Status: Permanent resident.
Length: 5.9–7.1 inches.
Weight: 0.7 ounce (21 grams).
Range: Southwestern United States to northwestern Argentina.
Elevational range: 2,000–7,200 feet.

Black Phoebe adult

Distinctive profile of a Long-tailed Tyrant adult male

Colonia colonus
Costa Rican name: *Mosquero coludo.*
11/23 trips; 29 sightings.
Status: Permanent resident.
Length: 5 inches, plus 4–4.75-inch-long tail feathers.
Weight: 0.5 ounce (15 grams).
Range: Northeastern Honduras to northeastern Argentina.
Elevational range: Sea level to 2,000 feet.

LONG-TAILED TYRANT

The Long-tailed Tyrant is another easily identified fly-catcher. Small and black, it has a grayish cap that extends to the nape and merges into a whitish stripe down the back. A white horizontal stripe extends from above the bill past the eye. The male has two long, stringlike feathers that extend four to five inches beyond the tail. The female is similar but does not have the long tail feathers. The Long-tailed Tyrant perches in an upright posture so the tail feathers hang straight down. The profile is unique and conspicuous even at a distance.

An inhabitant of tropical Caribbean lowlands, this flycatcher sits conspicuously on the highest branches of dead trees and on power lines in forest openings, mead-ows, plantations, stream edges, and in recently cleared forest lands. It flies out to capture flies, bees, and other insects on the wing and then returns to its perch. With the two long tail feathers streaming behind, it is a delight to watch. Pairs are often observed perching together. Stingless bees (*Trigona* sp.) and flying termites are com-mon food items.

The Long-tailed Tyrant may be observed in Cahuita NP, Cahuita and Puerto Viejo, Limón, Tortuguero NP, La Selva (River Trail and entry road), Sueño Azul pastures, Puerto Viejo en Sarapiquí, Rara Avis, and lower levels of Braulio Carrillo NP (Sendero Botarama).

BRIGHT-RUMPED ATTILA

The Bright-rumped Attila is one of the most frequently heard but hard-to-see birds in Costa Rica. Its call is a loud "Wheedeep-wheedeep-wheedeep-wheeee," often given from the top of the dense tree canopy, where the bird can be frustratingly hard to see. Sometimes it will come to more open meadows and gardens where it is more easily observed. This flycatcher has a bright yellow rump that is usually not visible when the wings are at rest. The head and back are olive-brown, the eye is red, and the tail is rufous-brown. The throat is pale and lightly streaked, and the upper chest is pale yellowish or olive-brownish, fading to white on the belly. The bill is quite thick and straight, with a hook at the tip.

This flycatcher is endemic in a region from Nicaragua to Panama. It is found over much of Costa Rica in both dry and wet lowland mature forests, meadows, and back-yard gardens up to lower montane levels. It forages at all levels, from the top of the canopy to the ground, in search of cicadas, beetles, spiders, lizards, frogs, and toads. It sits quietly on a branch until prey is spotted and then sallies to catch its victim on a nearby leaf, branch, or on the ground.

This common flycatcher occurs in lowland and middle elevations from Muelle to Tortuguero NP, Limón, and south to Cahuita, inland to La Selva, Monteverde, Bosque de Paz, Rancho Naturalista, and lower levels of Braulio Carrillo NP. On the Pacific slope, it is common from Carara NP south to the Osa Peninsula and Golfo Dulce region and inland to the Wilson Botanical Garden and San Isidro del General.

Attila spadiceus
Costa Rican name: *Atila lomiamarilla.*
22/23 trips; 94 sightings.
Status: Permanent resident.
Length: 6.7–8.5 inches.
Weight: 1.1–1.6 ounces (31–44 grams).
Range: Northwestern Mexico to southeastern Brazil.
Elevational range: Sea level to 6,000 feet.

Bright-rumped Attila adult

GREAT KISKADEE

Pitangus sulphuratus
Costa Rican names: *Bienteveo grande; cristofué; pechoamarillo.*
23/23 trips; 284 sightings.
Status: Permanent resident.
Length: 8.1–9.3 inches.
Weight: 1.9–2.4 ounces (53–68 grams).
Range: Southern Texas to central Argentina.
Elevational range: Sea level to 5,000 feet.

Like the Tropical Kingbird, the Great Kiskadee is one of the most common birds in Costa Rica. It is also one of the most vocal, announcing its presence from prominent perches with a loud "kis-ka-dee" call. This bird is easy to identify because it tells you its name! The bold markings include a bright yellow breast, a black mask, a white stripe above the eyes that extends to the back of the head, a black cap that usually conceals a yellow crown-patch, and an olive-brownish body. Distinguishing marks include rufous edges on the primary and secondary wing feathers and rufous tail feathers. The similar Boat-billed Flycatcher has a broader bill and lacks rufous markings on the wing and tail feathers; its call is also very different, sounding like an extended series of squeaks from an infant's squeaky toy.

The Great Kiskadee is found in pastures, agricultural lands, forest edges, cities, suburban backyards, woodlands, and wetland edges. With its large size and formidable bill, it may sally from a perch to take small fruits, catch insects on the wing, or fly to the ground to catch lizards, small snakes, mice, earthworms, spiders, grasshoppers, and beetles. It may plunge into shallow water to capture frogs, tadpoles, insects, and small fish. At feeders it will eat bananas. The Great Kiskadee may raid the nests of smaller birds and eat their eggs or young. Although the Great Kiskadee will commonly catch insects at ground level, the similar Boat-billed Flycatcher catches its insect prey at middle to higher levels of the forest canopy and rarely comes to the ground to catch insects.

From lowland to middle elevations of both slopes, Great Kiskadees are present on the grounds and court-yards of most hotels, roadside restaurants, and wilderness lodges. Just listen for their "kis-ka-dee" call.

Great Kiskadee nest with young

Great Kiskadee adult

SOCIAL FLYCATCHER

The Social Flycatcher is one of several yellow-breasted flycatchers in Costa Rica. It is smaller than the Tropical Kingbird and is distinguished from kingbirds by the white stripe over its eyes. It has a gray cap and gray mask, and the head appears small in proportion to the body. The bill also appears proportionately smaller than on Tropical Kingbirds or Great Kiskadees. A reddish-orange crown patch is usually concealed. The Boat-billed Flycatcher and Great Kiskadee both have similar facial patterns but are larger with much heavier bills. Similar species that could be confused with the Social Flycatcher are the Gray-capped and White-ringed Flycatchers. The Gray-capped Flycatcher has a white forehead instead of a white eyebrow, and the White-ringed Flycatcher has a longer bill and the white eyebrow marking extends all the way around the back of the head. The call is a series of squeaks and chirps.

Social Flycatcher adult

A common species, the Social Flycatcher is found in backyards, gardens, courtyards, pastures, and cities as well as forest and wetland edges. It perches in the open and flies out to capture insects on the wing or flies to the ground to capture its prey. It may go into shallow water to catch tadpoles, and it will eat small fruits and berries while perched or on the wing.

Like the Tropical Kingbird, the Social Flycatcher can be seen nearly anywhere in the country, from the lowlands to middle elevations of both slopes.

Myiozetetes similis
Costa Rican names: *Mosquero cejiblanco; pecho amarillo.*
23/23 trips; 198 sightings.
Status: Permanent resident.
Length: 6.3–7.3 inches.
Weight: 0.8–1.0 ounce (24–27 grams).
Range: Northwestern Mexico to northeastern Argentina.
Elevational range: Sea level to 5,600 feet.

Gray-capped Flycatcher adult

Myiozetetes granadensis
Costa Rican name: *Mosquero cabecigrís.*
15/23 trips; 75 sightings.
Status: Permanent resident.
Length: 6.3–7.1 inches.
Weight: 1.0–1.1 ounces (28–30 grams).
Range: Eastern Honduras to western Brazil.
Elevational range: Sea level to 5,500 feet.

GRAY-CAPPED FLYCATCHER

The three smaller tyrant flycatchers that have a black eye mask, yellow breast, white throat, and short bill are the White-ringed, Social, and Gray-capped Flycatchers. The key to identifying them is the extent of the white line above the eye, which is called a superciliary line.

The White-Ringed Flycatcher is a Caribbean lowland species. Its broad white superciliary line extends from each eye and meets on the back of the head. On the Social Flycatcher, the broad white superciliary line extends behind the eye but does not meet on the back of the head. The Gray-capped Flycatcher can be identified by its grayish puffy looking head and nape and the thin white superciliaries that stop just above and behind the eye.

The Gray-capped Flycatcher lives in open areas, gardens, pastures with scattered trees, second-growth forests, and forest edges, especially along rivers and streams. It can be quite tame and easy to approach. Often occurring in pairs or small family groups, this species sallies to capture insects in flight or resting on nearby vegetation. It will also eat berries. The call is a series of sharp, high-pitched robinlike chirps.

Look for this flycatcher on the Caribbean slope at Caño Negro NWR and Lodge, La Selva, Sueño Azul, Selva Verde Lodge, Cahuita and Tortuguero NPs, and Rancho Naturalista. On the Pacific slope, it can be seen in the Hotel Villa Lapas courtyard along the river, Carara NP, La Cusinga, Las Esquinas Rainforest Lodge, Hotel Cristal Ballena, Talari Mountain Lodge, Tiskita Jungle Lodge, Corcovado Lodge Tent Camp, Sirena Biological Station, and Drake Bay Wilderness Resort.

STREAKED FLYCATCHER

The Streaked Flycatcher is a boldly marked species characterized by a black mask, brownish back with black streaking, rusty tail, and a pale yellowish to white breast with vertical streaking. It has a buffy white superciliary line above the eye, a white malar stripe below the black eye mask, and a uniquely pink mandible (lower bill) that is black at the tip. Only one other flycatcher, the Sulphur-bellied Flycatcher, is similar, but it has a black bill with no pink on the lower bill, a white (not buffy) superciliary stripe over the eye, and (as the name implies) a yellowish belly.

This flycatcher sallies from perches to catch flying prey like cicadas, wasps, and other invertebrates. It may also fly from perches to capture invertebrates and small lizards and to secure berries and other fruits. Some Streaked Flycatchers are residents in Costa Rica. Others migrate from Mexico and Guatemala to Costa Rica from February to March. The call of this flycatcher is a sharp whistled "pichhoo" or "pichihoo" or a sharp "quick" call.

The Streaked Flycatcher is found in the Caño Negro NWR and Los Chiles region and along the Pacific coastal lowlands, including the dry forest habitats of Guanacaste and the moist and wet forested lowlands of the southern Pacific slope. It can be seen at Tamarindo, Palo Verde and Carara NPs, Hotel Villa Lapas grounds and skywalk, Villa Caletas, La Cusinga, Playa Hermosa, Talari Mountain Lodge, Tiskita Jungle Lodge, Rancho Casa Grande, and on Caño Island.

Myiodynastes maculatus
Costa Rican name: *Mosquero listado.*
12/23 trips; 28 trips.
Status: Permanent resident and tropical migrant from Mexico.
Length: 7.7–9.1 inches.
Weight: 1.5–1.6 ounces (43–45 grams).
Range: Southern Mexico to northern Argentina.
Elevational range: Sea level to 5,000 feet.

Streaked Flycatcher adult

Streaked Flycatcher, showing the broad bill and yellow spot on top of the head

Tropical Kingbird adult

Tyrannus melancholicus
Costa Rican names: *Tirano tropical;*
pecho amarillo.
23/23 trips; 348 sightings.
Status: Permanent resident.
Length: 7.2–9.4 inches.
Weight: 1.1–1.5 ounces (32–42
grams).
Range: Southeastern Arizona to
central Argentina.
Elevational range: Sea level to
8,000 feet.

TROPICAL KINGBIRD

The ever present Tropical Kingbird, or "TK" as it is often called by birders, is one of the most common birds in Costa Rica. Its bright yellow breast and tendency to sit on prominent perches in open areas make it easy to observe. Since there are several other flycatchers with yellow breasts that also sit in open areas, care should be taken to distinguish them from Tropical Kingbirds. Among the most common are the Great Kiskadee, Boat-billed Flycatcher, Social Flycatcher, and Gray-capped Flycatcher. The Boat-billed Flycatcher and Great Kiskadee have distinctive calls; they are larger and have a black mask with a white stripe above the eyes. The Tropical Kingbird does not. The Social Flycatcher is smaller and has a proportionally smaller head. It has a gray stripe through the eyes and a white stripe above each eye. The Gray-capped Flycatcher is similar to the Social Flycatcher but has a white forehead and lacks the white stripe above the eye. The Tropical Kingbird also has a deeply notched tail.

The Tropical Kingbird is present in all regions of Costa Rica and adapts well to cities, farms, backyards, river edges, and cleared lands. The TK may fly out from its favorite perch to catch bees, dragonflies, beetles, wasps, and moths on the wing and then return to its perch. Several prey items may be captured on a single flight. The Tropical Kingbird may perch near flowers or mud puddles to capture butterflies. It has also been observed capturing prey from the surface of water and flying to the ground to capture insects or spiders. Wherever you stay in Costa Rica, there will probably be a Tropical Kingbird nearby. It is probably the easiest of all birds to encounter.

CINNAMON BECARD

Costa Rica's fauna includes five becards: Barred, Cinnamon, White-winged, Black-and-white, and Rose-throated. As the name implies, the Cinnamon Becard is cinnamon-colored, and the sexes are identical. Three other tropical birds share that cinnamon hue and appearance: the Rufous Piha, the Rufous Mourner, and the female White-lined Tanager. The first two species are larger than the Cinnamon Becard and frequent the upper forest canopy, where they are more often heard than seen. The female White-lined Tanager is similar in size and color but is often accompanied by the black male.

The Cinnamon Becard frequents lower levels of primary and secondary forest edges along streams and clearings and in mangrove lagoons. Pairs often can be seen foraging together in small trees. This insectivorous species plucks caterpillars, beetles, katydids, ants, and spiders from foliage while on the wing. Berries are also eaten.

Nesting occurs from March through July. A globe-shaped nest comprising plant fibers, rootlets, and moss is suspended from the tip of a drooping tree branch. There is often a wasp nest nearby that helps provide protection from arboreal predators.

This becard inhabits Caribbean lowlands and foothills and, along the Pacific coast, mangrove lagoons from the Gulf of Nicoya to Panama. Among the best places to view it are Caño Negro NWR and Lodge, La Selva, Selva Verde Lodge, Sueño Azul, and Rancho Naturalista. It may sometimes be encountered at Carara NP, the Hotel Villa Lapas skywalk, and Tárcol Lodge.

Pachyramphus cinnamomeus
Costa Rican name: *Cabezón canelo.*
13/23 trips; 26 sightings.
Status: Permanent resident.
Length: 5.5–5.9 inches.
Weight: 0.6–0.8 ounces (17–22 grams).
Range: Southeastern Mexico to northwestern Ecuador.
Elevational range: Sea level to 3,200 feet.

Cinnamon Becard adult

* Taxonomy in flux. The evolutionary relationship of tityras and becards to each other and to other birds is currently under scientific review. DNA samples are being examined to resolve the issue. Tityras and becards were previously in their own family, called Tityridae. They may be reassigned to a new subfamily, Tityrinae, in the Tyrant-flycatcher family or to another classification.

Masked Tityra male

Tityra semifasciata
Costa Rican name: *Tityra carirroja.*
23/23 trips; 118 sightings.
Status: Permanent resident.
Length: 7.9–9.4 inches.
Weight: 2.7–3.1 ounces (77–88
  grams).
Range: Northern Mexico to Brazil.
Elevational range: Sea level to
  6,000 feet.

MASKED TITYRA

For many birders visiting Costa Rica, the first impression created by a tityra is that it looks like a chunky shrike. Primarily, however, it is a fruit-eating bird rather than a predatory songbird. There are two tityras in Costa Rica, the Black-crowned Tityra (described in the next account) and the Masked Tityra. The main difference between these two widespread species is that the male Black-crowned Tityra is black over the top half of the head, including the eyes, with a black bill. The female is more dusky white over the back with a black cap, black bill, and brown on the sides of the face. The male Masked Tityra has a black forehead and black encircling a fleshy red circle around each eye, like spectacles. The bill is red with a black tip. The female Masked Tityra has a dusky head and back with fleshy red spectacles around the eyes and a red bill tipped with black.

This species forages in the canopy of dry, moist, and wet forests throughout most of Costa Rica, except in highland forests. It is common at forest edges, forest openings, gardens, and plantations. It frequently perches in open areas, which makes it easy to spot. It sits in an upright posture and sallies from a perch to snatch a fruit, insect, or small lizard from a nearby leaf or branch. It may also work its way along a branch in search of food. Fruits compose most of the diet, including *Casearia, Trichilia, Virola,* figs, wild avocados, and *Guarea.* When seeds pass through its digestive system, they are dispersed in the forest, so the bird is an important agent in the propagation and dispersal of plants in tropical forests. The call is a series of brief, mechanical, two-note buzzy squawks that sound more like a cricket than a bird.

The Masked Tityra may be encountered on the Caribbean slope at La Selva, Selva Verde Lodge, Sueño Azul pastures, Tortuguero NP, Tortuga Lodge, south to Cahuita and Puerto Viejo, and inland to Monteverde and Rancho Naturalista, and in the Central Plateau at Xandari Plantation Resort. On the Pacific slope, it can be observed at Santa Rosa NP, La Pacífica, La Ensenada Lodge, from Carara NP throughout the southern lowlands, and inland to Talari Mountain Lodge and the Wilson Botanical Garden.

Masked Tityra female

BLACK-CROWNED TITYRA

The male Black-crowned Tityra is black over the top half of the head, including the eyes, and it has a black bill. The female is more dusky white over the back with a black cap, black bill, and brown on the sides of the face. Like the Masked Tityra, it has a short, rounded profile and a relatively short tail. Its habitat includes forest edges and clearings with scattered trees, from which the tityra scans the surrounding terrain for insects or fruit. When a food item is sighted, the tityra flies out and snatches it while on the wing. This bird is usually sighted in pairs or as family groups and is often in the company of Masked Tityras.

The Black-crowned Tityra can be observed in the Caribbean lowlands to premontane levels, including Caño Negro NWR and Lodge, Cahuita and Tortuguero NPs, La Selva, Sueño Azul, and Rancho Naturalista. It is also found at Hacienda Solimar, La Ensenada Lodge, Carara and Manuel Antonio NPs, Hotel Villa Lapas, La Cusinga, Hotel Cristal Ballena, Oro Verde BR, Las Esquinas Rainforest Lodge, Talari Mountain Lodge, and the Wilson Botanical Garden on the Pacific slope.

Tityra inquisitor
Costa Rican name: *Tityra coroninegra.*
15/23 trips; 37 sightings.
Status: Permanent resident.
Length: 6.7–8.1 inches.
Weight: 1.4–1.8 ounces (40–50 grams).
Range: Central Mexico to northeastern Argentina.
Elevational range: Sea level to 4,000 feet.

Black-crowned Tityra male

Purple-throated Fruitcrow adult

Purple-throated Fruitcrow displaying

Querula purpurata
Costa Rican name: *Quérula gorgimorada.*
12/23 trips; 24 sightings.
Status: Permanent resident.
Length: 9.8–11.8 inches.
Weight: 3.3–4.3 ounces (93–122 grams).
Range: Costa Rica to Brazil.
Elevational range: Sea level to 2,000 feet.

PURPLE-THROATED FRUITCROW

The family of cotingas includes seven species in Costa Rica, including the Yellow-billed and Turquoise Cotingas in the southern Pacific lowlands, the rare Bare-necked Umbrellabird and Lovely Cotinga in the Caribbean foothills, the Three-wattled Bellbird, and two species in the Caribbean lowlands, the Snowy Cotinga and the Purple-throated Fruitcrow. The male Snowy Cotinga is pure white with a yellow bill, and the female is grayish with a white breast. The Purple-throated Fruitcrow is less colorful than most cotingas, since most of the body is black, but the throat of the male can be flared during displays to show a stunning iridescent purple throat. The female is black. The bill of both sexes is pale grayish.

The Purple-throated Fruitcrow is a bird of mature lowland rainforests; it is most often seen at forest edges and gardens. This is a very social species, usually encountered in small, active flocks of birds. Often this bird is heard before it is seen. It has a distinctive querulous (wavering) series of churring whistles. The feeding technique, similar to that of a trogon, involves sitting quietly on a horizontal branch and watching its surroundings for fruits or insects. It eats katydids, cicadas, praying mantises, caterpillars, and fruits of *Heliconia* and *Hamelia*. When it spots a fruit or insect, the fruitcrow sallies out to take its food on the wing. This species will sometimes come to recordings of its call. During the nesting season, May to August, a social group of three to eight individual birds may attend the parent birds to assist in the care of the single young until it fledges.

Among locations where the Purple-throated Fruitcrow can be seen in the Caribbean lowlands are rainforest sites at La Selva (Sendero Tres Ríos and the Arboretum), Tortuguero NP, the courtyard at Tortuga Lodge, and El Pizote Lodge near Cahuita.

WHITE-COLLARED MANAKIN

White-collared Manakin female

The White-collared Manakin adds a spritelike presence to Caribbean lowland rainforests. The male has a black cap; white throat, neck, and shoulders; black wings; yellow belly; and bright orange legs. When the male is displaying, the throat feathers are extended so far forward that the bill almost disappears amid them. The female is greenish with a yellow belly and orange legs.

In the southern Pacific lowlands is a geographically isolated species closely related to the White-collared Manakin: the Orange-collared Manakin. These two birds appear to have had a common ancestor. The habitat for the White-collared Manakin includes primary and secondary rainforest understory, brushy forest margins, and stream edges. Preferred foods consist of small fruits like *Hamelia* and insects. These foods are plucked while the bird is on the wing.

The breeding season is from April through August. Several males display in leks in the thick understory. Each male establishes a display area and clears all debris from the ground in a four-foot-diameter plot that has several vertical saplings. As each male leaps back and forth from one stem to the other, the throat feathers are extended forward and the wings snap loudly with each jump. When a female enters the display area, the pair jumps simultaneously, like avian popcorn, passing in midjump. When the males are on a lek, they produce a sharp, loud finger-snapping sound with their wings that travels far through the forest understory.

Among the best places to observe White-collared Manakins are along the nature trail behind Tortuga Lodge, at Tortuguero and Cahuita NPs, Lost Iguana Resort (Hanging Bridges), Caño Negro Lodge and vicinity, Selva Verde Lodge, La Selva, and Rancho Naturalista. Listen for their snapping sounds, then get low and peer through the underbrush to spot the males.

White-collared Manakin male

Manacus candei
Costa Rican names: *Bailarín; saltarín cuelliblanco.*
17/23 trips; 55 sightings.
Status: Permanent resident.
Length: 4.25 inches.
Weight: 0.7 ounce (18 grams).
Range: Southeastern Mexico to western Panama.
Elevational range: Sea level to 3,200 feet.

Long-tailed Manakin male

Chiroxiphia linearis
Costa Rican names: *Toledo;*
  saltarín toledo; saltanix colilargo.
11/23 trips; 26 sightings.
Status: Permanent resident.
Length: 4.5 inches (plus two 4- to
  6-inch tail feathers on the male).
Weight: 0.7 ounce (19 grams).
Range: Southern Mexico to Costa
  Rica.
Elevational range: Sea level to
  5,000 feet.

LONG-TAILED MANAKIN

One of the most stunning birds in Costa Rica is the ornately marked Long-tailed Manakin. It is one of eight manakins in the country. The others are the Red-capped, Blue-crowned, White-crowned, Lance-tailed, White-ruffed, Orange-collared, and White-collared Manakins. Manakins are well known for their lek display behavior, and the Long-tailed Manakin takes that behavior to the extreme.

The male Long-tailed Manakin has a small, rounded black body highlighted by a red crest, powder-blue back, bright orange legs, and two long, slender black tail feathers. The female is olive-green above with paler greenish hues below. Young males resemble the females and do not acquire adult plumage until about four years of age. The three-note call, referred to as "to-le-do," rises from the original note to a higher pitch and then drops back to the original pitch. This whistled call, given synchronously by two males displaying on a lek, has a rich resonance and a harmonic quality that sounds like the bird is whistling from the bottom of a well.

Most manakins live in lowland rainforests, but the Long-tailed Manakin is found primarily in dry forests and gallery forests of Guanacaste and western portions of the Central Plateau south to Carara NP. It also occurs in second-growth and mangrove forests, where these birds eat small fruits that they pluck while on the wing. Preferred fruits include *Ardisia revoluta, Cecropia peltata, Cocoloba caracasana, Trichilia cuneata, Trema micrantha, Muntingia calabura,* and *Psychotria* sp.

Mating season extends from March through September. The courtship ritual is incredible and bizarre. Pairs of bonded males associate with each other throughout the year, although no mating is involved. When mating season arrives, leks form that are multiple arenas, each occupied by a pair, or sometimes a trio, of displaying males. The pairs of males give synchronous "toledo" vocalizations until a female arrives. With both males facing the female, they alternately jump into the air in an acrobatic display that may include a hundred alternating jumps!

The dominant of the two males eventually mates with the female. Then the female leaves to build the nest, lay the eggs, and raise the young by herself, while the two males continue their life together, singing their three-note to-le-do song.

Look for the Long-tailed Manakin in forests of Santa Rosa, Guanacaste, Palo Verde, Rincón de la Vieja (Los Pailos Trail), and Carara NPs and Lomas Barbudal BR; at La Ensenada Lodge, Hacienda Solimar, La Pacífica, and Monteverde at the Ecological Farm and Children's Rainforest. It is typically observed low in thick shrubbery and at mid-levels of the forest canopy. In the Central Plateau, it can be encountered at La Universidad de la Paz in El Rodeo near Ciudad Colón and on the grounds of the Xandari Plantation Resort. Near Carara NP it can be seen along the Hotel Villa Lapas skywalk near the second and fourth bridges.

Long-tailed Manakin female

BLUE-CROWNED MANAKIN

The Blue-crowned Manakin is one of those special birds of the mature rainforest in the southern Pacific lowlands of Costa Rica that cannot be mistaken for other manakins. The male is all black with a powder-blue cap. This species is also found in the Caribbean lowlands near the Panama border. The White-crowned Manakin has a white cap, and the Red-capped Manakin has a bright red cap. The male White-ruffed Manakin is black and has a white throat. The female Blue-crowned Manakin is darker green than other female manakins, which are more olive-green, and has a grayish-green throat.

The Blue-crowned Manakin inhabits the lower canopy of mature forests. It typically perches on slender horizontal twigs no more than a few yards above the ground, where it sallies to snatch insects or berries from nearby leaves and twigs. The males, like other manakins, display lek behavior to attract females, although their performances are not as elaborate as those of some manakins. Several males may occur in a lek. One male will quickly jump around on the perch, make a 180-degree turn, and flick its wings as it jumps to nearby perches and then back to the original perch.

This manakin can be seen at Carara NP (the figure-eight loop trail), Corcovado Lodge Tent Camp (the trail behind the lodge), Tiskita Jungle Lodge, Manuel Antonio NP, La Cusinga, Los Cusingos, and at the Wilson Botanical Garden along the river trail.

Blue-crowned Manakin female

Pipra coronata
Costa Rican name: *Saltarín coroniceleste.*
14/23 trips; 33 sightings.
Status: Permanent resident.
Length: 3.1–3.5 inches.
Weight: 0.3 ounce (8.5 grams).
Range: Costa Rica to Brazil.
Elevational range: Sea level to 4,500 feet.

Blue-crowned Manakin male

YELLOW-WINGED VIREO

The Yellow-winged Vireo is a highland endemic species found on the volcanoes of the Central Cordillera and in the Talamanca Mountains of southern Costa Rica. This vireo is easy to distinguish because of its yellow wing bars, yellow breast and belly, and an incomplete eye-ring that is open at the front and rear edge. The superciliary line above the eye is broad and yellowish. The migratory Yellow-throated Vireo has a white belly and white wing bars, but it is found at lower elevations. The only other highland vireo is the Brown-capped Vireo. It is brown above with a broad white superciliary line, a white throat, and a pale yellowish wash on the belly; it has no wing bars.

The Yellow-winged Vireo is found in mature montane oak forests as well as in shrubby pastures with scattered trees, along mountain roadsides, orchards, and gardens. It eats insects, spiders, and berries by gleaning them from vegetation. The song typically consists of short, high-pitched whistles of two or three notes, reminiscent of the song of the Eastern Wood-Pewee.

Look for the Yellow-winged Vireo in Poás Volcano NP, on the slopes of the Central Cordillera at Bosque de Paz, and at La Paz Waterfall Gardens. In the Talamanca Mountains it may be seen at locations like the San Gerardo de Dota Valley, Savegre Mountain Lodge, Cerro de la Muerte at kilometer 66, and along the road from the Pan American Highway to Providencia at kilometer 76.

Vireo carmioli
Costa Rican name: *Vireo aliamarillo.*
15/23 trips; 24 sightings.
Status: Permanent resident.
Length: 4.5 inches.
Weight: 0.4 ounce (13 grams).
Range: Endemic to Costa Rica and western Panama.
Elevational range: 5,000–10,000 feet.

Yellow-winged Vireo adult

White-throated Magpie-Jay adult

Calocitta formosa
Costa Rican names: *Urraca*
  copetona; urraca; piapia azul.
14/23 trips; 57 sightings.
Status: Permanent resident.
Length: 18 inches.
Weight: 7.2 ounces (205 grams).
Range: Central Mexico to Costa
  Rica.
Elevational range: Sea level to
  4,000 feet.

WHITE-THROATED MAGPIE-JAY

One of the largest and most conspicuous songbirds in Guanacaste is the White-throated Magpie-Jay. This social and vocal bird is normally seen in family groups of five to ten birds and is quite attractive. The blue body, white breast, exceptionally long blue tail, and tall, forward-curving topknot feathers on its head make it unmistakable. A closely related species, the Black-throated Magpie-Jay, is found in Mexico.

The White-throated Magpie-Jay is found in savannas, dry forests, gallery forests, farmsteads, ranches, backyards, and woodlots. Roaming in family groups, these intelligent and omnivorous jays search for small lizards, caterpillars, frogs, beetles, grasshoppers, katydids, and cockroaches. Other foods include fruits, corn, eggs, the young of other birds, and the nectar of balsa (*Ochroma*) flowers. At La Ensenada Lodge, they boldly enter the open-air restaurant to pick up fallen food scraps.

Nesting season occurs from February through July. While incubating, the female is visited by several family members and the male, who all take turns feeding her. The young are fed by the parents and by young from previous broods.

The White-throated Magpie-Jay can be found in Guanacaste's NPs—Guanacaste, Palo Verde, Santa Rosa, and Las Baulas—and in the Lomas Barbudal BR. It can also be seen at Sugar Beach, Tamarindo, Hacienda Solimar, La Ensenada Lodge, Playa Doña Ana, La Pacífica, east to Hotel Borinquen Mountain Resort, and southeast to Tárcol Lodge at the mouth of the Río Tárcoles.

White-throated Magpie-Jay head detail

BROWN JAY

The Brown Jay is the most common and wide-spread jay in Costa Rica. It is found from lowland to high elevations—often in disturbed and developed habitats. Other jays in this country are tied to more specific habitats: the White-throated Magpie-Jay in the Guanacaste dry forest, the Black-chested Jay in the lowlands and foothills of the southeastern Caribbean slope, the Azure-hooded Jay in cloud forests and wet mountain forests, and the rare Silvery-throated Jay in high mountain forests. Costa Rica's other jays are quite colorful, but the Brown Jay is a plain dark brown above and white below. Immature jays have varying amounts of yellow on the bill. The bill of adults is dark brown.

Brown Jay adult

Cyanocorax morio
Costa Rican names: *Urraca parda*;
   piapia.
23/23 trips; 124 sightings.
Status: Permanent resident.
Length: 15.5 inches.
Weight: 8.3 ounces (235 grams).
Range: Southern Texas to western
   Panama.
Elevational range: Sea level to
   8,200 feet.

Habitats occupied by the Brown Jay include natural forests, second-growth forests, shade coffee and banana plantations, ranches, pastures, urban woodlots, and wooded backyards. The diet of this omnivorous bird includes small lizards, frogs, insects, spiders, dragonflies, *Cecropia*, corn, balsa (*Ochroma*) nectar, banana (*Musa*) flowers, and eggs and nestlings of smaller birds. It comes to bird feeders for cooked rice.

The Brown Jay lives in family groups of six to ten birds throughout the year. Some groups of more than twenty are occasionally encountered and may represent two family groups. Nesting begins in January and extends to June. The oldest birds build a nest in an isolated tree. More than one female may lay eggs, so the clutch size may vary from two to seven. Up to five females may take turns incubating the eggs. While on the nest, the female and nearby females give a loud whining call to beg other family members to feed them. After hatching, the young are fed by up to ten family members.

In the Caribbean lowlands, the Brown Jay may be observed in Guacimo and Guapiles, Selva Verde Lodge, Sueño Azul, Lost Iguana Resort, Puerto Viejo en Sarapiquí near La Selva, La Virgen del Socorro, Turrialba, and Rancho Naturalista. In Guanacaste, it occurs on the properties of La Pacífica and Hacienda Solimar and in Palo Verde, Guanacaste, Santa Rosa, and Carara NPs. The Brown Jay is present from Carara NP southeast to Manuel Antonio NP. At higher elevations, the Brown Jay is common at Monteverde, on the Central Plateau, and on volcanoes surrounding the Central Plateau.

Gray-breasted Martin adult

Progne chalybea
Costa Rican name: *Martín
    pechigrís.*
21/23 trips; 82 sightings.
Status: Permanent resident.
Length: 6.3–7.1 inches.
Weight: 1.2–1.8 ounces (33–50
    grams).
Range: Northern Mexico to
    northern Argentina.
Elevational range: Sea level to
    5,600 feet.

GRAY-BREASTED MARTIN

The Gray-breasted Martin is the largest member of the swallow family in Costa Rica. The head, back, wings, and tail are a dark steel-blue, the breast is grayish, and the belly is whitish. The Brown-chested Martin has been recorded only a few times in Costa Rica, and the Purple Martin is primarily a migrant that passes through Costa Rica between breeding areas in North America and wintering areas in Brazil.

The Gray-breasted Martin inhabits open areas throughout the country where there are abundant high perches on power lines, dead trees, or girders in open buildings like airport hangars and gas stations. This gregarious species is normally encountered by the dozens at such perching sites. A strong flier, it captures flies, bees, dragonflies, beetles, mayflies, and other insects on the wing.

The Gray-breasted Martin nests in abandoned woodpecker holes from March through May. In settled areas, where it is most abundant, it also nests on building girders and bridge supports, in birdhouses, and on other human structures. Nesting may also occur among rocks.

This martin is partial to airports. It can be seen around the hangars at the Tobias Bolaños Airport at Pavas, the Liberia airport, the International Airport and the Guapiles airport. Other locations in the Caribbean lowlands include Cahuita and Tortuguero NPs, Puerto Viejo, La Selva, Rancho Naturalista, and the Limón area. On the Pacific slope, the Gray-breasted Martin occurs at Carara NP, Puntarenas, San Isidro del General, Manuel Antonio NP, Quepos, Playa Dominical, the Osa Peninsula, and the Wilson Botanical Garden.

MANGROVE SWALLOW

Complementing the distribution of the Blue-and-white Swallow in the highlands, the Mangrove Swallow inhabits Caribbean and Pacific lowlands. This swallow is dark iridescent green above and snow-white on the throat, chest, and belly. It has a white rump patch and a slender white line above each eye.

The Mangrove Swallow inhabits lowland canals, lakes, marshes, and mangrove lagoons, where it frequently perches in large groups on dead trees and stumps that project from the water. It forages over water and captures insects on the wing.

In the Caribbean lowlands, the Mangrove Swallow can be seen along the canals of Tortuguero NP, in wetlands of the Puerto Viejo en Sarapiquí area, at La Selva, and from Limón to Cahuita. On the Pacific slope, it is widespread in wetlands of Guanacaste, along the entire coast, and inland to the Río Térraba valley. It is present in Carara, Palo Verde, Corcovado, Santa Rosa, Guanacaste, and Manuel Antonio NPs.

Tachycineta albilinea
Costa Rican name: *Golondrina lomiblanca.*
22/23 trips; 91 sightings.
Status: Permanent resident.
Length: 4.3–4.7 inches.
Weight: 0.4–0.6 ounce (10–16 grams).
Range: Northern Mexico to northern Peru.
Elevational range: Sea level to 3,900 feet.

Mangrove Swallow adult

BLUE-AND-WHITE SWALLOW

*Pygochelidon cyanoleuca
(formerly Notiochelidon
cyanoleuca)*

Costa Rican name: *Golondrina azul
y blanco.*

23/23 trips; 191 sightings.

Status: Permanent resident; some
southern migrants.

Length: 4.7–5.1 inches.

Weight: 0.3–0.5 ounce (9–15
grams).

Range: Nicaragua to Tierra del
Fuego.

Elevational range: Sea level to
10,000 feet.

The most common swallow in Costa Rica is the Blue-and-white Swallow. The breast is snow-white, and the top half of the head, the back, and the tail are deep glossy blue. This swallow is commonly seen resting on power lines and telephone wires outside homes and buildings at middle and higher elevations. Most are permanent residents, but from May through September some South American migrants are present.

In natural habitats, the Blue-and-white Swallow may be seen "flycatching" over openings and wetlands in montane and premontane forests. It is far more abundant, however, in settled areas and around buildings. Among insects that are caught on the wing are beetles, flies, and wasps.

This monogamous swallow raises two broods of young from March through June. After fledging, the young return to the nest each night to sleep with the parents until they are two months old.

The Blue-and-white Swallow is widespread in middle and high elevations but uncommon on the Caribbean coast and Pacific coastal lowlands. There are some records at sea level at the outlet of the Río Barú at Playa Dominical.

Blue-and-white Swallow

RUFOUS-NAPED WREN

The wren family is well represented in Costa Rica's avifauna, with twenty-two species present. They live in habitats ranging from tropical dry forests to lowland wet forests and montane forests at the timberline. The largest wren is the seven-inch-long Rufous-naped Wren. This songbird of the Guanacaste dry forest is easily seen and readily identified because family groups of three or more individuals continuously call to each other as they boldly explore garden shrubs and vines for food. The bright rufous colors of the neck, the rufous-checked back, the white breast, and the cream-colored superciliary stripe are distinctive.

Rufous-naped Wren adult

Campylorhynchus rufinucha
Costa Rican names: *Soterrey nuquirrufo; chico piojo; salta piñuela; soterrey matraquero.*
19/23 trips; 82 sightings.
Status: Permanent resident.
Length: 5.9–7.4 inches.
Weight: 1.0–1.1 ounces (29–32 grams).
Range: Central Mexico to Costa Rica.
Elevational range: Sea level to 2,600 feet.

A close relative of the Cactus Wren in the southwestern United States, the Rufous-naped Wren inhabits Guanacaste's dry forests, savannas, gallery forests, second-growth forests, small woodlots, backyards, and gardens. Each group of wrens includes a mated pair and young from the previous year. They eat beetles, cockroaches, crickets, and other invertebrates like spiders.

A pair of Rufous-naped Wrens defends a territory throughout the year and maintains a globe-shaped nest made of grasses and plant fibers. This nest is most frequently in a bullhorn acacia (*Acacia collinsi*). The thorns provide protection from predators. The bullhorn acacia ants (*Pseudomyrmex*) attack any creatures that approach the nest. The young are cared for by both parents. After fledging, young stay with the parents until the subsequent breeding season.

The Rufous-naped Wren is found throughout Guanacaste from the Nicaragua border to Carara NP, east to Hotel Borinquen Mountain Resort near Rincón de la Vieja, in the Central Plateau at Alajuela, Xandari Plantation Resort, Hotel Bougainvillea, and the grounds of Zoo Ave at La Garita near the Juan Santamaría International Airport.

Rufous-naped Wren and nest in an acacia tree

STRIPE-BREASTED WREN

Thryothorus thoracicus
Costa Rican name: *Soterrey pechirrayado.*
15/23 trips; 31 sightings.
Status: Permanent resident.
Length: 4.5 inches.
Weight: 0.6 ounce (17 grams).
Range: Nicaragua to central Panama.
Elevational range: Sea level to 3,300 feet.

There are eight wrens characteristic of the Caribbean lowlands and foothills: the Band-backed, Bay, Plain, Black-throated, House, Song, and Stripe-breasted Wrens and the White-breasted Wood-Wren. The Stripe-breasted Wren is the only wren with a striped throat and breast.

The habitat of this wren includes the brushy edges of forests, gardens, plantations, and riverbanks, where it is usually present in pairs. It explores leaves, epiphytes, moss, and dead tangles of foliage in search of insects and spiders. The calls and songs include short whistled notes and a melodic series of whistled phrases sounding like "whichy go for me here—whichy go for me here." Tape recordings may be used to call this wren out of heavy cover to provide a brief viewing experience.

The Stripe-breasted Wren can be encountered near Muelle at the Lost Iguana Resort and nearby Hanging Bridges site, at Tortuguero NP, along the loop trail at Tortuga Lodge, at La Selva, El Pizote Lodge near Cahuita, Rancho Naturalista, and lower levels of Braulio Carrillo NP like Sendero Botarama.

Stripe-breasted Wren adult

BAY WREN

The Bay Wren is among the most attractive of Costa Rica's wrens. The body and breast are chestnut brown, the throat is white, and the head is black highlighted by white stripes. Sexes are similar. Like most rainforest wrens, it is seldom seen, but its beautiful songs of warbling whistles and trills mark its presence in the underbrush. One of its songs sounds like "What a day it is—what a day it is—what a day it is."

This wren is usually found in the forest understory near streams or rivers in the Caribbean lowlands and foothills from Nicaragua to Panama. Sightings usually include pairs or family groups of parents and offspring foraging together. They feed by searching foliage and masses of vines for insects, caterpillars, and spiders.

Look for this distinctive wren at Caño Negro NWR, in the vicinity of Caño Negro Lodge, at La Selva, along the pasture trail near the river at Sueño Azul Resort, in Tortuguero NP, and at La Virgen del Socorro.

Thryothorus nigricapillus
Costa Rican name: *Soterrey castaño.*
16/23 trips; 49 sightings.
Status: Permanent resident.
Length: 5.7 inches.
Weight: 0.6–0.9 ounce (18–26 grams).
Range: Eastern Nicaragua to western Ecuador.
Elevational range: Sea level to 3,300 feet.

Bay Wren adult

HOUSE WREN

Troglodytes aedon intermedius and
T. a. inquietus

Costa Rican names: *Soterrey*
cucarachero; soterrey; zoterré;
cucarachero; ratonerita.

23/23 trips; 205 sightings.

Status: Permanent resident.

Length: 4.5–4.9 inches.

Weight: 0.4 ounce (12 grams).

Range: Southern Canada to Tierra
del Fuego; *T. a. intermedius,*
southern Mexico to central
Costa Rica; *T. a. inquietus,*
extreme southwestern Costa
Rica to eastern Panama.

Elevational range: Sea level to
9,000 feet.

The ubiquitous House Wren is found around homes and backyards throughout Costa Rica. Some taxonomists consider this the same species throughout North and South America, but other taxonomists consider House Wrens from southern Mexico through Tierra del Fuego a separate species, the Southern House Wren. The bubbling, musical song of the wren adds a warm sense of familiarity to birders from North America.

The House Wren inhabits brushy areas, plantations, farm woodlots, ornamental tree and shrub plantings, weedy pastures, river edges, and backyards. These wrens are constantly singing to defend their territories from other wrens. They are easily noticed as they search for small insects and invertebrates. They sleep in tree cavities, nest boxes, or other nooks and crannies in natural vegetation and buildings.

Although the northern race of House Wren is migratory and often polygamous, the southern subspecies is nonmigratory and monogamous. Both parents care for the young. They renest to raise a second and third brood in the same season. The young may stay in the territory to help care for the young of the subsequent brood. House Wrens can be found around lodges, farm buildings, backyards, and resorts throughout the country.

House Wren adult

WHITE-BREASTED WOOD-WREN

The White-breasted Wood-Wren, a small wren of rainforest lowlands and middle elevations, is characterized by a white eye-stripe, white throat, white breast, and very short tail that is typically cocked upward. It is closely related to the Gray-breasted Wood-Wren, which is found at higher elevations. The songs of this talented songbird include a repertoire of complex warbling and three-note phrases.

In contrast to the House Wren and Rufous-naped Wren, which are closely associated with human habitations and cleared areas, the White-breasted Wood-Wren is found in the understory of mature lowland wet forests and older second-growth forests. It is particularly attracted to thick tangles of vines, leaf litter, and plant debris, where it hunts for insects, spiders, and other invertebrates.

White-breasted Wood-Wren sleeping quarters

This wren nests from February through May in globe-shaped nests on or near the ground. The nest is made from fine plant fibers, rootlets, moss, and liverworts, and there is an entrance hole on the side. Two eggs are incubated by the female for thirteen to fifteen days. Both parents care for the young, and the young may stay with the parents for an extended time after hatching. This species also uses dormitory nests, which are thin-walled globe-shaped nests attached to a sapling or vine two to ten feet above the ground. Individual birds or parents with young sleep in these nests outside the nesting season. The song is either a plaintive six-note whistle that starts with a sharp whistle, followed by a phrase that sounds like "o-wick-o-wick-o-way," or a series of ascending three-note phrases like "one-two-three."

The White-breasted Wood-Wren is found in the Caribbean lowlands, including the grounds of Tortuga Lodge, Tortuguero NP, La Selva (Stone Bridge, Arboretum, and Sendero Tres Ríos), at Rara Avis, lower and midlevels in and near Braulio Carrillo NP (Sendero Botarama, the Tapir Trail), and Rancho Naturalista. In the southern Pacific lowlands, it can be encountered at Los Cusingos and the Wilson Botanical Garden.

Henicorhina leucosticta
Costa Rican name: *Soterrey de selva pechiblanco.*
14/23 trips; 55 sightings.
Status: Permanent resident.
Length: 3.9–4.5 inches.
Weight: 0.6 ounce (16 grams).
Range: Central Mexico to northeastern Peru.
Elevational range: Sea level to 6,000 feet.

This bird can be extremely hard to see unless you call it out of thick undergrowth with a tape recording of the species' song, or tape its song and play it back. Playbacks should be limited to a few repetitions until the wren appears and then discontinued so the resident wren is not unduly distracted by the use of tapes.

White-breasted Wood-Wren adult

GRAY-BREASTED WOOD-WREN

The Gray-breasted Wood-Wren, found at middle and high elevations, has a gray breast, a striped throat, and a tail that is typically cocked upright. It lives in mountain forests, where it inhabits thick undergrowth and bamboo thickets. There it searches for small insects and other invertebrates. Timberline and Ochraceous Wrens are found in similar habitats; thus, it is worth reviewing tapes with the songs of these three wrens when birding in montane forests so you can distinguish them. The Gray-breasted Wood-Wren is a close relative of the White-breasted Wood-Wren, which is found in Costa Rica's lowland forests and foothills.

The song of this wren is a complex and beautiful expression of tumbling whistles and warbles. This bird is usually very responsive when a recording of its song is played. Tape recordings should be used briefly and with discretion to avoid disrupting the normal behavior of this bird.

On the Caribbean slope, the Gray-breasted Wood-Wren can be encountered at La Virgen del Socorro, Braulio Carrillo and Tapantí NPs, the Peace Waterfall (Catarata de la Paz), La Paz Waterfall Gardens, and Monteverde. On the Pacific slope, it occurs along the Pan American Highway in Cerro de la Muerte at kilometers 66, 80, and 96, at Savegre Mountain Lodge, and along the River Trail at the Wilson Botanical Garden.

Henicorhina leucophrys
Costa Rican name: *Soterrey de selva pechigrís.*
23/23 trips; 67 sightings.
Status: Permanent resident.
Length: 3.9–4.5 inches.
Weight: 0.6 ounce (16–18 grams).
Range: Central Mexico to northern Bolivia.
Elevational range: 2,600–10,000 feet.

Gray-breasted Wood-Wren adult

AMERICAN DIPPER

Cinclus mexicanus
Costa Rican name: *Mirlo acuático plomizo.*
16/23 trips; 22 sightings.
Status: Permanent resident.
Length: 5.5–7.9 inches.
Weight: 1.6 ounces (46 grams).
Range: Northern Alaska to western Panama.
Elevational range: 2,000–8,200 feet.

The American Dipper is a fascinating dark gray bird found in fast-flowing, boulder-strewn streams in Costa Rica's mountains and foothills. It has a small, rounded body, short tail, and relatively long legs. It is one of three birds to look for along boulder-strewn streams. The other two are the Torrent Tyrannulet and the Black Phoebe. The name dipper is derived from the bird's behavior of dipping up and down as it hops and flies from rock to rock.

The American Dipper will typically fly downstream and then hop, climb, and fly upstream from boulder to boulder while periodically submerging to capture larvae of mayflies, midges, mosquitoes, craneflies, dragonflies, beetles, and sometimes small fish.

From February through May, two to four eggs are laid in a well-camouflaged nest along the side of a stream. Look for the American Dipper from the bridge at La Virgen del Socorro, at the Peace Waterfall (Catarata de la Paz), at Bosque de Paz, at La Paz Waterfall Gardens, along the Río Savegre in the San Gerardo de Dota Valley, and from the bridges over the Río Grande de Orosi and its tributaries in Tapantí NP.

American Dipper adult

BLACK-FACED SOLITAIRE

One of the most magical sounds in Costa Rica's mountain forests is the ethereal, flutelike song of the Black-faced Solitaire. It fills the epiphyte-laden cloud forest with melodious one-, two-, and three-note phrases. This small slate-gray thrush has a black face highlighted by an orange bill, an orange eye-ring, and orange legs. Sexes are similar.

Habitats utilized by the endemic Black-faced Solitaire include mature cloud forest, montane forest, bamboo thickets, shrubby understory, brushy areas, and pastures. This solitaire forages for small fruits, berries, and a few insects.

The Black-faced Solitaire is found at middle and higher elevations of both Caribbean and Pacific slopes along the length of Costa Rica into western Panama. This thrush is heard more often than seen because its habitat is often very thick with epiphytes.

The Black-faced Solitaire can be seen—and heard—at the Monteverde Cloud Forest Reserve, La Virgen del Socorro, La Paz Waterfall Gardens, Bosque de Paz, and Rara Avis; at Braulio Carrillo, Poás Volcano, Tapantí, and Amistad NPs; and in the San Gerardo de Dota Valley along the road that descends from kilometer 80 on the Pan American Highway to Savegre Mountain Lodge.

Myadestes melanops
Costa Rican names: *Jiguero; solitario carinegro.*
21/23 trips; 56 sightings.
Status: Permanent resident.
Length: 6.3–7.3 inches.
Weight: 1.1–1.2 ounces (30–33 grams).
Range: Endemic to highlands of Costa Rica and western Panama.
Elevational range: 3,000–9,000 feet.

Black-faced Solitaire adult

BLACK-BILLED NIGHTINGALE-THRUSH

Catharus gracilirostris
Costa Rican name: *Zorzal piquinegro.*
20/23 trips; 50 sightings.
Status: Permanent resident.
Length: 5.7–6.3 inches.
Weight: 0.7 ounce (21 grams).
Range: Endemic to highlands of Costa Rica and western Panama.
Elevational range: 7,000–11,500 feet.

Five nightingale-thrushes occur in Costa Rica: the Black-billed, Black-headed, Slaty-backed, Ruddy-capped, and Orange-billed. Nightingale-thrushes look like miniature robins as they hop around on the ground in thick underbrush. Their fine features and beautiful flutelike songs make them memorable birds.

The Black-billed Nightingale-Thrush, the smallest of these species, is endemic to Costa Rica and western Panama; it is found at middle to high elevations in Costa Rica. It is the only nightingale-thrush with a black bill, and it has no eye-ring. It has a brown back, pale gray throat with a brown upper chest, and gray belly. The song includes one to three flutelike whistles, sometimes followed by a buzzy whistled trill.

The Black-billed Nightingale-Thrush occurs at higher-elevation montane oak forests, paramo, forest edges, roadsides, second growth, and gardens. It forages by hopping on the ground or along epiphyte-covered horizontal tree branches in search of insects and spiders.

Look for the Black-billed Nightingale-Thrush in Poás Volcano NP, Cerro de la Muerte at kilometers 66, 76 (the road to Providencia), 86 (Los Chespiritos 2), and 96 (Villa Mills), in the San Gerardo de Dota Valley along the road descending from the Pan American Highway at kilometer 80 to the Savegre Mountain Lodge, and the transmission tower site at kilometer 90.

Black-billed Nightingale-Thrush adult

ORANGE-BILLED NIGHTINGALE-THRUSH

The Orange-billed Nightingale-Thrush is distinguished by an orange bill, eye-rings, and legs. The wings and tail are brownish olive, and the head and breast are gray in the southern Pacific lowlands. In northwestern parts of its range, this bird has a grayish-olive head. The southern Pacific lowland gray-headed race of Orange-billed Nightingale-Thrush is considered by some taxonomists to be a separate species, *Catharus griseiceps*.

This nightingale-thrush is a second-growth species found in thick, shrubby habitats and the edges of forests, shade coffee plantations, and rural gardens. It forages for small insects, spiders, other invertebrates, small fruits, and berries. It frequently flips its wings upward and raises and lowers its tail in a manner similar to that of the Black-billed Nightingale-Thrush.

The Orange-billed Nightingale-Thrush is a middle-elevation species found in Caribbean forests at Tapantí NP and Rancho Naturalista. It is also found in Pacific premontane and lower montane forests, and in the Central Plateau east to Turrialba. It also occurs at higher elevations in hilly terrain of the Nicoya Peninsula. The best places to look for the Orange-billed Nightingale-Thrush are at the Wilson Botanical Garden, Monteverde, Savegre Mountain Lodge, Vista del Valle Restaurant, Talari Mountain Lodge, and Tapantí NP.

Catharus aurantiirostris
Costa Rican names: *Jiguerillo; inglesito; zorzal piquianaranja.*
7/23 trips; 19 sightings.
Status: Permanent resident.
Length: 6.25 inches.
Weight: 1 ounce (27 grams).
Range: Southern Mexico to Venezuela.
Elevational range: 2,000–7,500 feet.

Orange-billed Nightingale-Thrush adult

SLATY-BACKED NIGHTINGALE-THRUSH

Catharus fuscater
Costa Rican name: *Zorzal sombrío.*
8/23 trips; 12 sightings.
Status: Permanent resident.
Length: 6.7–7.5 inches.
Weight: 1.2–1.3 ounces (35–38 grams).
Range: Costa Rica to Bolivia.
Elevational range: 1,000–5,000 feet.

The Slaty-backed Nightingale-Thrush has a distinctive pale-whitish eye (iris). The body is grayish black with a light belly. The eye-ring, bill, and legs are bright orange. Its song, like those of other nightingale-thrushes, has a beautiful flutelike quality; the phrases of two or three notes are reminiscent of the song of the Black-faced Solitaire. The phrases often rise in pitch and then descend to a lower note.

This nightingale-thrush occurs in middle-elevation and lower montane forests of the Caribbean slope and at higher montane-level forests on the southern Pacific slope in the Talamanca Mountains. It is typically seen hopping along forest trails and pausing like an American robin as it searches for insects, spiders, and berries.

Look for this attractive nightingale-thrush at Monteverde, Bosque de Paz, and Tapantí NP. It is regularly seen at La Paz Waterfall Gardens.

Slaty-backed Nightingale-Thrush adult

RUDDY-CAPPED NIGHTINGALE-THRUSH

The Ruddy-capped Nightingale-Thrush is similar in size to the Orange-billed Nightingale-Thrush, but it has a rusty-colored cap, no eye-ring, brown feet, and a bicolored bill that is dark above and orange below. It is found in the shrubby undergrowth of montane forests, bamboo thickets, brushy ravines, and edges of forests and pastures. It usually feeds on the ground or in low shrubby cover. Foods include small invertebrates, fruits, and berries. The song is a delightful assortment of short whistles of two or three notes, flutelike phrases, trills, and warbles that are similar to the phrases of a Black-faced Solitaire.

Look for this bird at Monteverde, Bosque de Paz, Cerro de la Muerte along the Pan American Highway at kilometer 66, and in the San Gerardo de Dota Valley from kilometer 80 to the grounds of Savegre Mountain Lodge. It is also found in the Santa Elena Reserve and in Tapantí NP.

Catharus frantzii
Costa Rican name: *Zorzal gorrirojizo.*
15/23 trips; 31 sightings.
Status: Permanent resident.
Length: 6.1–7.1 inches.
Weight: 1.0–1.1 ounces (28–32 grams).
Range: Central Mexico to western Panama.
Elevational range: 4,500–8,200 feet.

Ruddy-capped Nightingale-Thrush adult

Wood Thrush adult

Hylocichla mustelina
Costa Rican name: *Zorzal del bosque.*
12/23 trips; 32 sightings.
Status: Northern migrant.
Length: 7.1–8.5 inches.
Weight: 1.4–2.5 ounces (40–72 grams).
Range: Southern Canada to eastern and central United States.
Elevational range: Sea level–5,600 feet.

WOOD THRUSH

The Wood Thrush has attracted considerable attention in recent years because of a long-term decline across North America. Some of its survival problems are apparently caused by loss of habitat and habitat fragmentation in the eastern United States and southern Canada. Nest parasitism by Brown-headed Cowbirds is another problem. Loss and degradation of wintering habitat is also a likely problem for this species.

The Wood Thrush looks like a small robin. It is distinguished by a cinnamon-brown back, rufous crown, white breast, and a belly highlighted by bold black spots. It is usually seen hopping on the ground in search of flies, beetles, ants, caterpillars, and spiders. Fruits and seeds are also eaten, including *Miconia, Clidemia, Henrietta,* and *Psychotria.*

Wintering habitat usually consists of older, more mature wet forests like those at La Selva and Tortuguero NP. The Wood Thrush can also be seen at Sueño Azul near La Selva, the lower levels of Braulio Carrillo NP (the Tapir Trail and Puesto Carrillo), Rancho Naturalista, and La Paz Waterfall Gardens. At higher elevations it has been encountered at Savegre Mountain Lodge, and on the Central Plateau it has been seen on the grounds of Hotel Bougainvillea. In the southwest, it has been recorded at Carara NP, Tiskita Jungle Lodge, and the Wilson Botanical Garden.

SOOTY THRUSH (SOOTY ROBIN)

The coal-black Sooty Thrush, the largest thrush in Costa Rica, is an endemic songbird found only at the highest elevations from central Costa Rica to western Panama. In 2008 the American Ornithologists' Union changed the name of Costa Rica's robins to "thrushes," so this is now the Sooty Thrush. Its black body is highlighted by an orange bill and eye-ring, orange legs, and pale bluish-gray irises. The iris is conspicuously lighter than that of the Mountain Thrush. The Slaty-backed Nightingale-Thrush is similar in plumage to the Sooty Thrush, but it is much smaller (only 6.75 inches long) and is found at lower elevations and in different habitats than the Sooty Thrush.

The Sooty Thrush is a bird of pastures, gardens, and open areas near the summit of volcanoes, paramo shrublands above the timberline, and parklands in montane forests. It eats fruits from the blueberry family (Ericaceae), blackberries (*Rubus*), melastome fruits, and small insects.

The Sooty Thrush should be looked for at upper elevations of Poás Volcano and Irazú Volcano NPs and in Cerro de la Muerte along the Pan American Highway at kilometers 66, 76 (the road to Providencia), 80 (the road to San Gerardo de Dota Valley), 86 (Los Chespiritos 2), 90 (the transmission tower site), and 96 (Villa Mills transmission tower site).

Turdus nigrescens
Costa Rican names: *Escarchado; escarchero; mirlo negruzco.*
21/23 trips; 62 sightings.
Status: Permanent resident.
Length: 9.4–10.0 inches.
Weight: 3.4 ounces (96 grams).
Range: Endemic to highlands of Costa Rica and western Panama.
Elevational range: 7,000–11,000 feet.

Sooty Thrush adult

Sooty Thrush with blackberry

MOUNTAIN THRUSH (MOUNTAIN ROBIN)

Turdus plebejus
Costa Rican names: *Mirlo*
  montañero; yigüirro de montaña.
23/23 trips; 93 sightings.
Status: Permanent resident.
Length: 9.1–10.0 inches.
Weight: 3 ounces (86 grams).
Range: Southern Mexico to
  western Panama.
Elevational range: 3,000–10,000
  feet (timberline).

The Mountain Thrush is a high-elevation thrush associated with montane forests. Darker than the Clay-colored Thrush, it is grayish brown, with an olive-green cast over the back, dark gray eyes, a black bill, and black legs. The male and female are identical and are similar in size to the Clay-colored Thrush. Its song is a long series of shrill chirps.

This thrush inhabits mountain forests and forest edges where there are fruit-bearing shrubs and trees covered with epiphytes and mosses. These produce fruits and harbor insects and other invertebrates that constitute its diet.

The Mountain Thrush ranges from southern Mexico to western Panama. It can be observed at the Monteverde Cloud Forest Reserve, San José de la Montaña, Poás Volcanoand Tapantí NPs, along the Pan American Highway in Cerro de la Muerte at kilometers 66, 80 (the road to the San Gerardo de Dota Valley including Savegre Mountain Lodge), 86 (Los Chesperitos 2), and 96 (Villa Mills transmission tower site).

Mountain Thrush adult

CLAY-COLORED THRUSH (CLAY-COLORED ROBIN), COSTA RICA'S NATIONAL BIRD

There are five thrushes that were formerly referred to as robins in Costa Rica: White-throated, Clay-colored, Pale-vented, Mountain, and Sooty. The Clay-colored Thrush is the most abundant and widely distributed. It also has the distinction of being Costa Rica's national bird. In a nation that has so many colorful and spectacular birds, it seems unusual that such a drab bird was selected as the national bird. The *yigüirro*, however, is an ever-present backyard bird with a varied musical repertoire that has won the hearts of Costa Ricans. It is their constant companion as they work in their yards and gardens.

Clay-colored Thrush adult

Turdus grayi
Costa Rican names: *Yigüirro; mirlo pardo.*
23/23 trips; 285 sightings.
Status: Permanent resident.
Length: 9.1–10.4 inches.
Weight: 2.3–3.0 ounces (65–86 grams).
Range: Southern Texas to northern Colombia.
Elevational range: Sea level to 8,000 feet.

The Clay-colored Thrush is largely silent until the start of the breeding season. Then it begins a rich and melodious serenade that coincides with the onset of the annual rainy season. It is therefore considered that this thrush "calls the rains" each year. This is the main thrush found at lowland elevations, but it also occurs up to the highlands, where it shares habitats with other thrushes.

The name "Clay-colored" describes this bird's markings. The bill is yellowish; the iris is reddish brown in adults and brown in first-year birds. The male and female are similar. The Pale-vented Thrush, on the Caribbean slope, is slightly darker brown, with a white belly and vent area. The White-throated Thrush, primarily on the Pacific slope, has a white throat patch with fine black striping above the throat patch and a conspicuous yellow eye-ring and bill.

The Clay-colored Thrush eats fruits, berries, worms, snails, lizards, and insects, and it visits bird feeders to eat bananas and papayas. This widespread bird is found in the yards and gardens of hotels, tourism lodges, ranches, farms, shade coffee plantations, and private homes throughout the country. It inhabits settled places in lowland areas ranging from the dry forests of Guanacaste to the wet forests of Tortuguero NP and high elevations in Cerro de la Muerte at 7,200 feet.

SILKY-FLYCATCHER FAMILY *(Ptilogonatidae)*

Long-tailed Silky-Flycatcher, close-up

Ptilogonys caudatus

Costa Rican names: *Timbre;*
pitorreal; capulinero colilargo.

19/23 trips; 61 sightings.

Status: Permanent resident.

Length: 7.8–9.6 inches.

Weight: 1.3 ounces (37 grams).

Range: Endemic to highlands of
Costa Rica and western Panama.

Elevational range: 4,000–10,000
feet.

LONG-TAILED SILKY-FLYCATCHER

The Long-tailed Silky-Flycatcher, a distinctive and beautiful songbird of Costa Rica's highlands, is an endemic bird found only from Poás volcano to western Panama. The plumage is elegant. The body and breast are medium gray highlighted by a yellow head, yellow throat, and crest. The belly and vent are yellow, and the wings and long tail are black. The female has a darker gray forehead, a more olive-green body, a whiter belly, and a shorter tail than the male. On the wing, they have a long-tailed profile and an undulating flight pattern.

This silky-flycatcher is typically encountered in small flocks in montane forests, along forest edges, and in solitary trees of mountain pastures. It feeds on small fruits and berries, including mistletoe (*Gaiadendron*), *Fuchsia,* and *Solanum.* From a perch at the top of a tree, it also sallies to capture insects on the wing.

The Long-tailed Silky-Flycatcher is found at Bosque de Paz, from Poás Volcano and Irazú Volcano NPs southeast to Tapantí NP, in the Talamanca Mountains, in Cerro de la Muerte, and at Amistad NP. Look for it along the Pan at American Highway, including kilometers 66, 80, and 96 (Villa Mills), and in the San Gerardo de Dota Valley.

Long-tailed Silky-Flycatcher adult

TENNESSEE WARBLER

The Tennessee Warbler is the second most commonly sighted migrant warbler in Costa Rica. The number of sightings is exceeded only by the Chestnut-sided Warbler. This bird has a straight, slender, pointed bill and an olive-gray body. The head is grayish on the male, with a subtle whitish line over the eye. On the female, the body is similar, but the head is olive gray and the stripe over the eye is yellowish. After arriving in Costa Rica in mid-September, the Tennessee Warbler remains until early May. It spends twice as many months on its wintering grounds as on its northern breeding grounds.

Tennessee Warbler adult

Vermivora peregrina
Costa Rican name: *Reinita verdilla.*
23/23 trips; 185 sightings.
Status: Northern migrant.
Length: 4.5 inches.
Weight: 0.3 ounce (8 grams).
Range: Alaska to northern United States; winters from southern United States to Colombia and Venezuela.
Elevational range: Sea level to 10,000 feet.

The Tennessee Warbler is adapted to dry, moist, and wet disturbed forests, early second growth, backyards, gardens, shade coffee plantations, and forest edges. During the breeding season, this warbler is insectivorous, but on the wintering grounds it eats insects and fruits. Often traveling in small flocks, these warblers search twigs, branches, and leaves for small insects, spiders, insect eggs, cocoons, and larvae. Small fruits eaten include *Didymopanax, Miconia, Xylopia, Hamelia, Trema, Urera,* mistletoe (*Gaiadendron*), and protein bodies on *Cecropia* trees. The Tennessee Warbler also drinks nectar at flowers of *Aphelandra sinclairiana, Inga, Calliandra,* banana (*Musa*), *Eucalyptus, Callistemon, Combretum,* poró (*Erythrina poeppigiana*), *Erythrina lanceolata* (a living fence-post species), and *Grevillea* (a shade tree in coffee plantations). This warbler regularly visits bird feeders to eat bananas and cooked rice.

Your birding skills may be put to the test in Guanacaste by Tennessee Warblers that have been feeding on *Combretum* flowers. The bright orange pollen creates a temporarily orange-faced warbler that you will not find in field guides.

On the Caribbean slope, the Tennessee Warbler may be encountered at La Selva, La Virgen del Socorro, Rancho Naturalista, and Cahuita NP. It is regularly encountered in the Central Plateau and throughout Guanacaste. In the highlands it occurs at Poás Volcano, Irazú Volcano, Tapantí, and Amistad NPs; San José de la Montaña; Monteverde; Cerro de la Muerte; and along the Pan American Highway at kilometers 66 and 80. It is common throughout the southern Pacific lowlands.

Flame-throated Warbler adult

Parula gutturalis
Costa Rican name: *Reinita garganta de fuego.*
19/23 trips; 50 sightings.
Status: Permanent resident.
Length: 4.7 inches.
Weight: 0.3 ounce (10 grams).
Range: Endemic to highlands of Costa Rica and western Panama.
Elevational range: 4,600–10,000 feet (timberline).

FLAME-THROATED WARBLER

The Flame-throated Warbler is one of the three "flaming" birds characteristic of Costa Rica's mountains. The other two are the Flame-colored Tanager and the Fiery-throated Hummingbird. The Flame-throated Warbler, with its bright orange-red throat, is readily spotted at a distance in the high mountain oak forests that are its favored habitat. Adults are similar, but the black mask is more pronounced on the male. This species has a gray back and a black triangular patch over the shoulders. Immatures resemble a pale Parula Warbler with a pale orange throat, but their ranges do not overlap.

The Flame-throated Warbler may be seen in small flocks or in mixed flocks that include Yellow-winged Vireos and bush-tanagers. It searches montane oak forests, forest edges, and forest openings in an acrobatic manner similar to that used by Black-and-white Warblers. It hangs upside down and sideways from twigs and branches to explore the leaves, mosses, lichens, bark, and branches for insects, caterpillars, and spiders. This warbler also eats small berries of plants like mistletoe.

Nesting occurs from March through May. The nest, a cup adorned with mosses and liverworts, is concealed in cut banks where it is protected from above by the overhanging bank or in trees where the nest is shielded from above by bromeliads or moss.

Among the best locations to look for this beautiful and distinctive warbler are Bosque de Paz, Poás Volcano NP, the San Gerardo de Dota Valley, Talamanca Mountains, and Cerro de la Muerte at kilometers 66, 76 (the road to Providencia), 86 (Los Chespiritos 2), 90 (transmission tower site), and 96 (Villa Mills).

YELLOW WARBLER

The Yellow Warbler is a bright yellow warbler that occurs as two different subspecies in Costa Rica. The migratory subspecies is characterized by chestnut streaking on the breast of the male. It nests from Alaska to Mexico, and it winters in Costa Rica from mid-August to May mainly at lower elevations. Wilson's Warbler is also bright yellow but is found mainly at higher elevations, and the male has a black cap. The Yellow Warbler usually is found in second-growth shrubby areas, gardens, mangrove forests, and second-growth forests.

Yellow Warbler, Mangrove race with chestnut head

Formerly considered a separate species, the Mangrove Warbler is found primarily in Pacific coastal mangrove forests. The male has a yellow body and chestnut streaking on the breast, and the head is entirely chestnut. The female has a chestnut tinge on top of the head. Both subspecies eat insects, which they capture while perched or by making short flights to capture their prey.

Migrant Yellow Warblers occur throughout most of Costa Rica, except at higher elevations. The resident mangrove race is limited mainly to mangrove lagoons of the Pacific coast. It can be encountered at mangrove forest estuaries at Río Tárcoles near Carara, Corcovado Lodge Tent Camp, Damas Island at Quepos, Tamarindo and Playa Grande NP vicinity, and the Río Abangares estuary at La Ensenada Lodge. A few may be encountered on the northern Caribbean coast.

Dendroica petechia
Costa Rican names: *Reinita amarilla; reinita de manglar.*
23/23 trips; 143 sightings.
Status: Permanent resident (Mangrove Warbler subspecies) and northern migrant (Yellow Warbler subspecies).
Length: 4.9 inches.
Weight: 0.3 ounce (9 grams).
Range: Mangrove Warbler subspecies, northwestern Mexico to Venezuela; Yellow Warbler subspecies, Alaska to central Mexico.
Elevational range: Mangrove Warbler, sea level; Yellow Warbler, sea level to 7,000 feet.

Yellow Warbler adult

Chestnut-sided Warbler, winter plumage

Dendroica pensylvanica

Costa Rican name: *Reinita de costillas castañas.*

23/23 trips; 203 sightings.

Status: Northern migrant.

Length: 4.5 inches.

Weight: 0.2–0.3 ounce (7–9 grams).

Range: Southern Canada to eastern United States; winters from southern Mexico to eastern Panama.

Elevational range: Sea level to 6,000 feet.

CHESTNUT-SIDED WARBLER

The Chestnut-sided Warbler is the most commonly observed Neotropical migrant warbler. Most Neotropical migrant warblers spend much of the winter in breeding plumage, but the Chestnut-sided Warbler lacks its familiar chestnut-sided markings until it molts into breeding plumage in late January to March. In winter plumage, it has a vireo-like appearance: the head and back are bright lime-green to olive-green. It has a white eye-ring, a white throat and belly, a gray tail, and grayish wings with two pale yellowish wing bars. A distinctive feature is its foraging posture of slightly drooped wings and the tail cocked in an upright posture like a wren or gnatwren.

Feeding occurs in second-growth forests, shrubby areas, forest edges, shade coffee plantations, and gardens. It feeds by gleaning insects, caterpillars, and spiders from the underside of leaves. A small percentage of the diet is made up of berries like *Miconia* and *Lindackeria*. This warbler maintains wintering territories of 2.4–4.0 acres. Individuals join mixed flocks of Golden-crowned Warblers and Checker-throated and Dot-winged Antwrens. Arriving in September, the Chestnut-sided Warbler winters in moist and wet forests throughout the Caribbean and southern Pacific lowlands and adjacent middle elevations. It returns north from mid-April to mid-May.

BLACK-AND-WHITE WARBLER

The Black-and-white Warbler is one
of the four most common Neotropical
migrant warblers in Costa Rica. The other
most common species are the Tennessee,
Chestnut-sided, and Wilson's Warblers. Of
fifty-two warblers in Costa Rica, forty are
migrants from northern latitudes. This warbler has longitudinal black and white stripes
that are unmistakable. It is the only member
of its genus, *Mniotilta*, which means "moss-
picking." This refers to its behavior of pecking into moss-covered bark to glean insects from trees.

Black-and-white Warbler adult

The Black-and-white Warbler arrives in late August
and is present through mid-April. It feeds much like a
nuthatch, climbing up and down tree trunks and branches
from ground level to the canopy while searching the
bark for small insects, insect eggs, caterpillars, and other
invertebrates. One of the most interesting features of its
wintering behavior is that it joins mixed foraging flocks
comprised of birds that are permanent residents—like
honeycreepers and tanagers.

Most sightings of this warbler are at middle- and
higher-elevation moist and wet mature forests, older sec-
ond growth, mature forest edges, and backyard gardens.
It can be seen at Monteverde, Vara Blanca, La Virgen del
Socorro, Bosque de Paz, Poás Volcano NP, Braulio Car-
rillo NP, and Tapanti NP, Rancho Naturalista, La Paz
Waterfall Gardens, Wilson Botanical Garden, Cerro de la
Muerte along the Pan American Highway at kilometers
66, 80, and 96 (Villa Mills), and the San Gerardo de Dota
Valley.

Mniotilta varia
Costa Rican name: *Reinita
trepadora.*
23/23 trips; 100 sightings.
Status: Neotropical migrant.
Length: 5 inches.
Weight: 0.4 ounce (11 grams).
Range: Canada to southeastern
United States; winters from
North Carolina to Venezuela,
Colombia, and the West Indies.
Elevational range: Sea level to
8,200 feet.

PROTHONOTARY WARBLER

Protonotaria citrea
Costa Rican name: *Reinita cabecidorada.*
13/23 trips; 30 sightings.
Status: Neotropical migrant.
Length: 5 inches.
Weight: 0.4 ounce (12 grams).
Range: Breeds in eastern Canada and eastern United States; winters from Mexico to Venezuela.
Elevational range: Sea level to 4,300 feet.

The Prothonotary Warbler is a swamp-dwelling warbler that migrates from eastern North America to Caribbean coastal areas of southern Mexico, Honduras, and Belize and to Pacific coastal areas from Nicaragua south to Colombia and Venezuela. It arrives in Costa Rica in August and winters there until March. This beautiful warbler is yellowish orange with distinctive bluish-gray wings and tail.

This warbler gleans flies, beetles, caterpillars, butterflies, and spiders from leaves as it hunts low in the canopy, usually below fifteen feet. Often it feeds at the water's edge. The diet may include seeds, fruit, and nectar in the wintering season.

Among typical wintering habitats of the Prothonotary Warbler are mangrove forests of the Pacific coast, including La Ensenada Lodge, Carara NP, Río Tárcoles estuary, and Damas Island near Quepos. In the Caribbean lowlands, the Prothonotary Warbler can be found in riparian forests at Caño Negro NWR, along canal edges of Tortuguero NP, and in Cahuita NP. Occasionally this warbler will stray inland to the Central Plateau, where it has been found on the grounds of Hotel Bougainvillea. The best way to see this warbler is to take a boat tour at any of the Pacific coastal mangrove lagoon sites mentioned above.

Prothonotary Warbler adult

GRAY-CROWNED YELLOWTHROAT

There are four yellowthroat warblers in Costa Rica: the Common, Olive-crowned, Masked, and Gray-crowned Yellowthroats. The Common Yellowthroat, a Neotropical migrant, is distinguished by a buffy-white belly. The male has a white border along the top edge of the facial mask. The Olive-crowned Yellowthroat is olive above with a yellow belly, and the male has a black mask that extends to the back of the head. There is no whitish edging above the black mask. It is found only in the Caribbean lowlands. The Masked Yellowthroat is found only in grassy areas adjacent to wetlands in extreme southwestern Costa Rica. Its black mask has gray edging above. It is regularly encountered at wetlands east of the airport at San Vito las Cruces.

Gray-crowned Yellowthroat adult

The male Gray-crowned Yellowthroat has a black mask that ends behind the eyes. Unlike other yellowthroats that have a black bill, the Gray-crowned Yellowthroat has a bicolored bill that is black above and yellow below. It has an eye-ring with a gap at the front and back edges of the eye.

The Gray-crowned Yellowthroat is found in pastures, sugarcane plantations, and cleared forest land in grassy stages of early succession. It gleans caterpillars, beetles, bugs, spiders, and other insects from low vegetation. Insects may be caught in flight. Some berries are also eaten.

This yellowthroat is found throughout the lowlands and lower middle elevations of both slopes, including dry, moist, and wet forests. This warbler may be seen at the Caño Negro NWR, Guapiles, El Gavilán Lodge, Puerto Viejo en Sarapiquí, Rara Avis, Bosque de Paz, Hotel Borinquen Mountain Resort, Palo Verde NP, La Pacífica, Talari Mountain Lodge, and Corcovado Lodge Tent Camp.

Geothlypis poliocephala
Costa Rican name: *Antifacito coronigrís.*
13/23 trips; 17 sightings.
Status: Permanent resident.
Length: 5.25 inches.
Weight: 0.5 ounce (16 grams).
Range: Northern Mexico to western Panama.
Elevational range: Sea level to 5,000 feet.

WILSON'S WARBLER

Wilsonia pusilla
Costa Rican name: *Reinita gorrinegra.*
23/23 trips; 141 sightings.
Status: Northern migrant.
Length: 4.25 inches.
Weight: 0.4 ounce (11 grams).
Range: Alaska to southwestern and northeastern United States; winters from southern United States to central Panama.
Elevational range: 3,000–12,000 feet.

One of the most easily identified Neotropical migrant warblers is Wilson's Warbler. The male has a yellow body and a black cap. On the female the cap is absent or gray instead of black. The Yellow Warbler resembles Wilson's Warbler but lacks the black cap, and frequently the breast shows longitudinal chestnut streaking. The Yellow Warbler also typically winters at lower elevations than Wilson's Warbler.

Wilson's Warbler inhabits moist and wet forests, second-growth forests, forest edges, shrubby fields, shade coffee plantations, and backyards. Most foraging occurs near the ground, consisting of gleaning insects, caterpillars, beetles, aphids, and wasps from the surface of leaves. This agile warbler may hover to pick insects from the undersurface of leaves and catch insects in flight. The diet includes some berries and protein bodies of *Cecropia*. Like the Chestnut-sided Warbler, Wilson's Warbler defends a winter territory for its feeding area. It may feed by itself or join mixed flocks or pairs of Rufous-capped Warblers. It is present in Costa Rica from mid-September to mid-May.

Wilson's Warbler is found primarily at middle and higher elevations in Poás Volcano, Braulio Carrillo, Tapantí, Amistad, and Irazú Volcano NPs and at Barva volcano, La Virgen del Socorro, Rara Avis, Rancho Naturalista, Savegre Mountain Lodge, Cerro de la Muerte along the Pan American Highway at kilometers 66, 76, 80, 86, 90, and 96, and the Wilson Botanical Garden. This warbler and the Black-cheeked Warbler are the only two warblers found in shrubs above the timberline. Smaller numbers winter in the Central Plateau and have been seen at Hotel Bougainvillea and the Xandari Plantation Resort.

Wilson's Warbler male

SLATE-THROATED REDSTART

The Slate-throated Redstart is the most widely distributed redstart in the Americas. The most notable characteristics of this bird are the white highlights on the sides of the tail that flash conspicuously as the bird forages. There are twelve subspecies between northern Mexico and Peru. The northernmost subspecies has a cherry-red breast, and the southernmost subspecies has a lemon-yellow breast. Two subspecies occur in Costa Rica: *Myioborus m. comptus* in northern and central Costa Rica (including Monteverde) and *Myioborus m. aurantiacus* in southeastern Costa Rica. Both have dark gray faces, throats, and backs; dark rufous caps; yellowish-orange breasts and bellies; and gray tails with white edging.

Slate-throated Redstart adult

The Slate-throated Redstart inhabits cloud forests, upper premontane forests, and lower montane forests throughout the length of the country. Ranging from the upper canopy to the understory, this inquisitive warbler explores vegetation and tree trunks while drooping its wings and flashing its tail open and closed. This behavior may help flush insects. This redstart also eats the protein bodies of *Cecropia* and may accompany mixed foraging flocks of other warblers and tanagers. Pairs remain together throughout the year. The call is a rapid high-pitched whistle "chee-chee-chee-chee chew-whee chee-chee-chee."

This warbler may be encountered at Catarata de la Paz (Peace Waterfall), Braulio Carrillo NP, Rancho Naturalista, Monteverde, Bosque de Paz, La Paz Waterfall Gardens, La Virgen del Socorro, and along the River Trail at the Wilson Botanical Garden.

Myioborus miniatus
Costa Rican name: *Candelita pechinegra.*
21/23 trips; 61 sightings.
Status: Permanent resident.
Length: 4.75 inches.
Weight: 0.3 ounce (10 grams).
Range: Northern Mexico to Peru.
Elevational range: 2,500–7,000 feet.

COLLARED REDSTART

Myioborus torquatus
Costa Rican names: *Amigo del hombre; candelita collareja.*
22/23 trips; 78 sightings.
Status: Permanent resident.
Length: 5 inches.
Weight: 0.4 ounce (11 grams).
Range: Endemic to highlands of Costa Rica and western Panama.
Elevational range: 5,000–10,000 feet.

One of the most delightful songbirds in Costa Rica is the spritely Collared Redstart. A nonmigratory highland warbler, this curious bird frequently comes out of the undergrowth to check out human visitors. It appears to be so friendly that it is locally referred to as *amigo del hombre,* or "friend of man." From only a few feet away it is possible to see its colorful markings: yellow face and throat, gray throat band, yellow breast, rufous crown, and gray back. The gray tail is edged with white.

The Collared Redstart lives in moist and wet montane forests, second growth, and brushy edges of forests and pastures, where it forages within ten to fifteen feet of the ground. It may catch flying insects by sallying from perches. This warbler will also join mixed flocks or follow cattle or horses in mountain pastures to catch insects flushed by livestock. Pairs remain together throughout the year.

The Collared Redstart is found in Costa Rica's mountains throughout the length of the country from the Tilarán Mountains in the north to the Panama border. It is regularly encountered at Monteverde, on volcanoes of the Central Cordillera, and in Bosque de Paz, Vara Blanca, and La Paz Waterfall Gardens, as well as in Braulio Carrillo, Tapantí, and Amistad NPs. It also occurs in the Talamanca Mountains and Cerro de la Muerte along the Pan American Highway at kilometers 66 and 80 and the San Gerardo de Dota Valley including Savegre Mountain Lodge.

Collared Redstart adult

BLACK-CHEEKED WARBLER

The Black-cheeked Warbler is a highly sought endemic species found only in the high-elevation montane forests from central Costa Rica to western Panama. It is nonmigratory and is distinguished by a rufous crown, a white stripe over the eye, and a black patch enclosing the eye and cheek. The back is olive and the breast is pale gray. Adults are identical. The call of this species is a single high-pitched "tsit" or a series of these calls in rapid succession (Stiles and Skutch 1989:403).

This warbler travels in pairs, in small groups, or in association with Sooty-capped Bush-Tanagers. It is an active species found at lower levels of the forest and especially in bamboo habitats. It can occur in paramo habitats. It will hang upside down or sideways to glean insects, spiders, beetles, crickets, caterpillars, and small berries from the foliage or bark. This warbler will also sally to capture prey.

Among good places to look for the Black-cheeked Warbler are Bosque de Paz, Tapantí NP, the Talamanca Mountains including Savegre Mountain Lodge and Chacón Mountain, and Cerro de la Muerte at kilometers 66 and 76 (the road to Providencia).

Basileuterus melanogenys
Costa Rican name: *Reinita carinegra.*
13/23 trips; 30 sightings.
Status: Permanent resident.
Length: 5.3 inches.
Weight: 0.4 ounce (12 grams).
Range: Endemic to highlands of Costa Rica and western Panama.
Elevational range: 5,300–11,000 feet.

Black-cheeked Warbler adult

THREE-STRIPED WARBLER

Basileuterus tristriatus

Costa Rican name: *Reinita cabecitalistada.*

12/23 sightings; 20 sightings.

Status: Permanent resident.

Length: 5.1 inches.

Weight: 0.4 ounce (13 grams).

Range: Costa Rica to northern Bolivia.

Elevational range: 3,300–7,200 feet.

A distinctive nonmigratory warbler of Costa Rica's middle elevations is the Three-striped Warbler. It has a pale head with three black stripes over the top of the head. One black stripe passes through each eye, and an additional stripe passes under the eyes and up through the ear coverts. The breast is pale yellow and the back is olive-gray. The song of this warbler is an assorted series of trills, twitters, warbles, and buzzes according to Stiles and Skutch (1989:402).

The Three-striped Warbler forages in family groups that include offspring from the previous breeding season. They search for food in lower levels and thick shrubby understory of mature premontane or lower montane forest canopy, second growth, and forest edges. This species frequently acts as a flock leader in mixed flocks that include antvireos, foliage-gleaners, and Spotted Barbtails. The warbler gleans insects from foliage and captures insects flushed by their mixed flock. The call is a faint, high-pitched, chittering whistle. When nesting occurs from April through May, it is believed that young from the previous year assist with rearing the young the following year.

Look for this warbler in the highlands at Monteverde, Bosque de Paz, La Virgen del Socorro, Peace Waterfall, La Paz Waterfall Gardens, and Cerro de la Muerte at kilometer 66. Birders may attract this bird for a closer look with "pishing" sounds (Curson, Quinn, and Beadle 1994:225).

Three-striped Warbler

BANANAQUIT

The Bananaquit, widespread throughout tropical America, is ever busy as it explores flowers in forests and gardens. Over thirty races are recognized throughout the American tropics. Distinguishing marks are a black cap, black eye mask, and white stripe above the eye. The throat is gray, and the breast and belly are yellow. The slender bill is slightly decurved. At higher elevations, the Bananaquit may be found in mixed flocks with tanagers and warblers.

Bananaquit adult

In lowland and middle-elevation moist and wet forests, the Bananaquit visits flowers of the forest canopy, understory, forest edges, clearings, plantations, hedges, parks, and gardens. It hangs from the stems of plants as it punctures the base of flowers to reach the nectar. On small flowers like *Stachytarpheta,* the Bananaquit apparently pollinates the flowers, but on larger flowers it steals the nectar without pollinating the plants. Among the flowers visited are *Erythrina, Symphonia, Hibiscus,* and *Allamanda.* It also eats the protein bodies on *Cecropia* trees, known as Müllerian bodies. Additional food items include fruit pulp, bananas, caterpillars, butterflies, beetles, wasps, and spiders.

This prolific little bird nests all year and may produce two or three broods annually. Throughout the year, male and female Bananaquits maintain separate sleeping quarters in globe-shaped nests similar to those used for nesting. The Bananaquit is common throughout lowland and middle elevations of the Caribbean slope up to Monteverde, La Paz Waterfall Gardens, and Rancho Naturalista and in the southern Pacific lowlands up to middle elevations, including Talari Mountain Lodge and the Wilson Botanical Garden at San Vito.

Coereba flaveola
Costa Rican names: *Pinchaflor, picaflor, cazadorcita; santa marta; reinita mielera.*
23/23 trips; 146 sightings.
Status: Permanent resident.
Length: 3.5 inches.
Weight: 0.3 ounce (10 grams).
Range: Southern Mexico to southern Brazil.
Elevational range: Sea level to 5,000 feet.

Bananaquit in nest

Common Bush-Tanager adult

Chlorospingus ophthalmicus
Costa Rican name: *Tangara de monte ojeruda.*
22/23 trips; 75 sightings.
Status: Permanent resident.
Length: 5.25 inches.
Weight: 0.7 ounce (20 grams).
Range: Central Mexico to northwestern Argentina.
Elevational range: 1,300–7,500 feet.

COMMON BUSH-TANAGER

The Common Bush-Tanager is a widely distributed bird of cloud forests and rainforests in middle elevations of Costa Rica's mountains. It is typically seen exploring epiphyte-covered branches of trees in search of flower nectar, small fruits, insects, and spiders. This tanager has a small, rounded body characterized by a grayish-brown head, a conspicuous white mark behind each eye, an olive back, yellowish sides, and a white belly.

The Common Bush-Tanager usually travels in mixed flocks of up to a dozen bush-tanagers, woodcreepers, tanagers, antwrens, and antvireos. The body shape and active, inquisitive foraging behavior resemble that of the Black-capped Chickadee of North America. The call consists of a high-pitched, descending series of notes best described as a twitter.

On the Caribbean slope, the Common Bush-Tanager frequents cloud forests and middle-elevation forests at Monteverde, La Virgen del Socorro, Peace Waterfall, Bosque de Paz, La Paz Waterfall Gardens, and Braulio Carrillo and Tapantí NPs. At the Hummingbird Gallery at Monteverde, this bird regularly visits the nectar feeders. On the Pacific slope, it can be found from Los Cusingos up to Savegre Mountain Lodge in San Gerardo de Dota, and it regularly visits the feeders at the Wilson Botanical Garden at San Vito to eat bananas.

SOOTY-CAPPED BUSH-TANAGER

The Sooty-capped Bush-Tanager is another high-elevation endemic that makes Costa Rica a special destination for birding. This tanager is characterized by a compact, rounded body that is yellowish on the upper chest and sides, olive above, white on the belly, and highlighted by a black head that has a wide white blaze extending from above the eyes to the back of the head. Like the Common Bush-Tanager, it travels in mixed flocks of over a dozen Sooty-capped Bush-Tanagers, warblers, and Ruddy Tree-runners. It is typically found at higher elevations than the Common Bush-Tanager.

This tanager inhabits montane forests, older second growth, and forest edges, where it searches thick, epiphytic vegetation for insects, spiders, and fruits. Preferred foods include small waxy berries of the blueberry family (Ericaceae), like *Cavendishia, Psammisia,* and *Satyria.* Other foods include blackberries (*Rubus*) and berries of *Miconia* and *Fuchsia.* The call is a series of faint high-pitched twittering notes.

Among the best places to look for the Sooty-capped Bush-Tanager are Monteverde; Poás Volcano NP; sites along the Pan American Highway in Cerro de la Muerte at kilometers 66, 76 (the road to Providencia), 80, 86 (Los Chespiritos 2), and 96 (Villa Mills); San Gerardo de Dota Valley; and Savegre Mountain Lodge.

Chlorospingus pileatus
Costa Rican name: *Tangara de monte cejiblanca.*
22/23 trips; 63 sightings.
Status: Permanent resident.
Length: 5.25 inches.
Weight: 0.7 ounce (20 grams).
Range: Endemic to mountains of Costa Rica and western Panama.
Elevational range: 6,500–10,000 feet.

Sooty-capped Bush-Tanager adult

DUSKY-FACED TANAGER

Mitrospingus cassinii
Costa Rican name: *Tangara
carinegruzca.*
4/23 trips; 8 sightings.
Status: Permanent resident.
Length: 7.25 inches.
Weight: 1.2–1.4 ounces (33–41
grams).
Range: Costa Rica to western
Ecuador.
Elevational range: Sea level to
3,200 feet.

One of the most unusual-looking and eagerly sought tanagers in Costa Rica is the Dusky-faced Tanager. Less common and more shy than other tanagers, it has an appearance more like a member of the blackbird family and the restless, active behavior of a jay. The bill is long, slender, and pointed like an oriole or blackbird bill. The eye is pale and has a caciquelike appearance. The face, forehead, and chin are dusky gray, the breast is dull brassy yellow, and there is a narrow brassy-yellow hood over the back of the head. The back, wings, and tail are dusky grayish olive.

The Dusky-faced Tanager is a skulking bird of the forest edge. It travels in small flocks of four to fifteen birds in low shrubs and brushy habitat along the edge of forests, along streams, and in second-growth forests, where it usually remains within thick cover. This species appears to forage in a regular circuit through its forest territory. It seeks out fruiting trees, where it eats small berries like *Hamelia* and fruits in the families Rubiaceae, Solanaceae, and Melastomaceae. Spiders, grasshoppers, caterpillars, and other insects are also eaten.

The social behavior of this tanager seems more like that of jays than tanagers, because small groups of these tanagers (perhaps parents and young from the previous year) feed young at a nest (Skutch 1987:217).

Found only in the Caribbean lowlands and foothills, the Dusky-faced Tanager can be seen at La Selva in the shrubbery near the Stone Bridge, where they come to feed on the ripe *Hamelia* fruits in January and February. It can also be seen at La Selva in the Arboretum and on the Sendero Tres Ríos trail. It also comes to the feeders at El Gavilán Lodge near La Selva and occurs at Rancho Naturalista.

Dusky-faced Tanager eating berry

Dusky-faced Tanager adult

GRAY-HEADED TANAGER

The Gray-headed Tanager is an ant-following bird; it follows swarms of army ants so it can catch insects that are flushed by the ants. It may travel singly or in small groups of three or four in the company of antbirds and antshrikes. It may also follow white-faced monkeys and coveys of wood quails to capture insects flushed by them.

This tanager is distinguished by a gray head, bright yellow breast and belly, and olive-green back. The head has a small and somewhat fluffy crest, and its call is usually a series of high-pitched "pseet" notes. It can give a loud wren-like song that sounds like "It's so great here—it's so great here—it's so great." It is worthwhile to learn the call of the Gray-headed Tanager because it may reveal the presence of other ant-following birds in the vicinity.

The habitat of the shy Gray-headed Tanager includes second growth and forest understory in moist lowlands. The preferred foods include insects like cockroaches and small fruits like *Miconia* berries.

The Gray-headed Tanager can be encountered in Caño Negro NWR south of Los Chiles and in tropical and premontane elevations of Pacific moist forests in the Cordillera of Guanacaste and the Nicoya Peninsula. It is not found in the Caribbean lowlands. It is primarily found from Carara NP south to the Panama border, including the Hotel Villa Lapas skywalk and forest vicinity, Manuel Antonio NP, Los Cusingos, Corcovado Lodge Tent Camp, Tiskita Jungle Lodge, and along the River Trail at the Wilson Botanical Garden near San Vito.

Gray-headed Tanager adult

Eucometis penicillata
Costa Rican name: *Tangara cabecigrís.*
14/23 trips; 21 sightings.
Status: Permanent resident.
Length: 6.3–6.7 inches.
Weight: 0.8–1.2 ounces (22–35 grams).
Range: Southern Mexico to eastern Brazil.
Elevational range: Sea level to 4,000 feet.

WHITE-LINED TANAGER

Tachyphonus rufus
Costa Rican names: *Fraile; tangara forriblanca.*
15/23 trips; 47 sightings.
Status: Permanent resident.
Length: 6.8 inches.
Weight: 0.9–1.4 ounces (26–40 grams).
Range: Costa Rica to southeastern Brazil; Trinidad.
Elevational range: Sea level to 4,600 feet.

In contrast to the stunning colors of most tanagers, the male White-lined Tanager is coal black. The name "White-lined" refers to inconspicuous white linings on the edge of the wings and white on the scapular feathers of the shoulder area. These white feathers are usually concealed when the bird is at rest. The bicolored bill is black above and white below, with a black tip. The similar White-shouldered Tanager is also black, but it is distinguished by a conspicuous white wing patch.

The female White-lined Tanager is a uniform rufous color and could be confused with the similar Cinnamon Becard, Rufous Mourner, or Rufous Piha. The female, however, is usually in the company of the black male and has a typical straight, thick tanager bill. The female White-shouldered Tanager is olive-colored above and yellowish below. The White-lined Tanager commonly visits feeders for bananas. The other rufous songbirds do not visit feeders and are associated with more mature forests.

The White-lined Tanager is an adaptable bird of forest second growth, forest edges, shrubby areas, hedges, gardens, and backyards. This bird travels in pairs throughout the year, and family groups can be observed together following the nesting season. Among fruits eaten are guavas (*Psidium guajava*), bananas (*Musa*), oranges, *Miconia* berries, *Cecropia,* and bromeliad fruits. Ants, beetles, bugs, flies, and spiders are captured in flight or caught while concealed on ground cover.

The White-lined Tanager is most abundant in Caribbean lowland and middle elevations. It can be seen in Tortuguero NP and the Cahuita area and inland to Guapiles, at La Selva, and at higher elevations like Rara Avis, Turrialba, and Rancho Naturalista. It regularly comes to the feeders at Rancho Naturalista for bananas. In the southern Pacific lowlands, it is less common but can sometimes be seen at Carara NP, Las Esquinas Rainforest Lodge, and the Wilson Botanical Garden.

White-lined Tanager female

White-lined Tanager male

RED-THROATED ANT-TANAGER*

The Red-throated Ant-Tanager and the Red-crowned Ant-Tanager are similar species with a common ancestor that have diverged into two separate species, one in the Caribbean lowlands and the other in the Pacific lowlands. This is similar to the relationship between Passerini's Tanager and Cherrie's Tanager. The Red-throated Ant-Tanager is a large tanager of the Caribbean lowlands. The Red-crowned Ant-Tanager is found in the Pacific lowlands. The ranges do not overlap, so they are referred to as allopatric species.

Red-throated Ant-Tanager female

Habia fuscicauda
Costa Rican name: *Tangara hormiguera georgiroja.*
12/23 trips; 23 sightings.
Status: Permanent resident.
Length: 7.1–7.8 inches.
Weight: 1.0–1.6 ounces (27–46 grams).
Range: Southeast Mexico to eastern Panama.
Elevational range: Sea level to 2,000 feet.

The Red-throated male is characterized by a dusky-red body and bright red throat patch. There is also a bright red crown patch but it is usually not visible. The female is brownish olive and has a yellowish throat patch and crown patch. Since this species usually occurs in groups of four to eight birds, it is often possible to identify the more distinctive males among the more nondescript females and immatures, which are more brownish than the females.

This tanager frequently occurs in mixed flocks accompanying army ant swarms. They are fairly noisy and conspicuous as they pursue insects flushed by the ants. The call includes short, squally chirps and clucks, like a wren, and the song is a robinlike phrase of three or four notes.

Its preferred habitat includes dense second-growth thickets, overgrown plantations, thick riparian forest edges, and river edges. Nesting occurs from April through June. The young hatched in the previous year may accompany the female and help her build the nest and feed the young.

One of the best places to see this ant-tanager is at Rancho Naturalista, where it comes to the insect light in the forest near the cabins to capture insects in the early morning. It can also be encountered at Lost Iguana Resort (Hanging Bridges site), Tortuga Lodge, Tortuguero NP, and La Selva (Sendero Tres Ríos and entry road).

*Birds of the genera *Habia* and *Piranga*, including this one, the Summer Tanager, and the Flame-colored Tanager, were recently reassigned by the AOU to the family Cardinalidae.

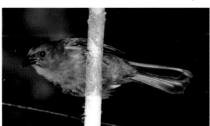

Red-throated Ant-Tanager male

Summer Tanager adult male

Piranga rubra
Costa Rican names: *Cardenal veranero; tangara veranera.*
23/23 trips; 193 sightings.
Status: Neotropical migrant.
Length: 6.7–7.1 inches.
Weight: 0.8–1.1 ounces (22–32 grams).
Range: Breeds in southern United States to northern Mexico; winters from central Mexico to central Brazil.
Elevational range: Sea level to 8,200 feet.

SUMMER TANAGER

The Summer Tanager is one of the most conspicuous and common migratory birds in Costa Rica. Males are bright red, and the bill is pale horn in color. The females are yellow-olive above and paler yellowish orange below. The Hepatic Tanager is also red but is very uncommon and can be distinguished by a black bill and darker eye mask. Young Summer Tanager males are yellowish like females but speckled with red feathers as they change to adult plumage while wintering in Costa Rica.

The Summer Tanager inhabits forest edges, second-growth forest, shade coffee plantations, scattered trees in forest openings and pastures, gardens, and backyards. Usually solitary, it occasionally joins mixed flocks of tanagers and warblers at fruiting trees and may follow army ants to catch escaping prey. Most tanagers predominantly eat fruits, but wasps and bees comprise a significant part of the wintering Summer Tanager's diet. Stingless bee and wasp larvae are eaten from their nests, and bees and other insects are caught in flight when the tanager sallies from perches. Preferred fruits include *Cecropia* catkins, *Ficus* (figs), *Miconia, Gaiadendron* (mistletoe berries), bananas, and oranges.

After arriving in mid-September, the Summer Tanager is common throughout lowland and middle elevations of Costa Rica on both the Caribbean and Pacific slopes and on the Central Plateau. A few are seen up to cloud forest and lower montane forest elevations. It returns north in mid-April.

Summer Tanager subadult male, showing red flecks; females are similar but show no red.

FLAME-COLORED TANAGER

The Flame-colored Tanager is a brightly colored endemic subspecies found in the mountains from the Central Highlands to western Panama. The male is bright orange-red on the head and breast. There is dark streaking on the back, and the dark wings have two conspicuous white wing bars. The female is yellowish olive with a streaked back and dark wings with two white wing bars. The call is a sharp two-note chirp with a second note that is higher. It sounds like a bird's version of a hiccup.

Flame-colored Tanager male

This tanager is frequently encountered in mixed open habitats like pasture edges, coffee plantations, gardens, and montane forests. Singly, in pairs, or in mixed flocks, they search foliage for insects and fruits. Foods include insects and berries like those of melastomes, figs, and members of the blueberry family (Ericaceae) like *Satyria*. They will also come to feeders stocked with bananas and to oriole nectar feeders.

Look for this tanager in Poás Volcano NP and in the Talamanca highlands, including the San Gerardo de Dota Valley, Savegre Mountain Lodge, Vista del Valle Restaurant, and Cerro de la Muerte at kilometer 66.

Piranga bidentata
Costa Rican name: *Tangara dorsirrayada.*
16/23 trips; 54 sightings.
Status: Permanent resident.
Length: 7.1–7.4 inches.
Weight: 1.1–1.4 ounces (32–40 grams).
Range: Northwestern Mexico to western Panama.
Elevational range: 4,000–10,000 feet.

Flame-colored Tanager female

CRIMSON-COLLARED TANAGER

*Ramphocelus sanguinolentus
(formerly Phlogothraupis
sanguinolentus)*

Costa Rican names: *Sangre de
toro; tangara capuchirroja.*

11/23 trips; 32 sightings.

Status: Permanent resident.

Length: 6.7–7.3 inches.

Weight: 1.2–1.7 ounces (35–48
grams).

Range: Southern Mexico to central
Panama.

Elevational range: Sea level to
3,500 feet.

Although not as common as Passerini's Tanager, the Crimson-collared Tanager is one of the most conspicuous and colorful tanagers in the Caribbean lowlands. Its brilliant red hood, shoulders, and upper breast, ivory-white bill, and red rump and vent are in dramatic contrast to the glistening black body. Sexes are similar.

This tanager occurs in the canopy of mature and second-growth moist and wet forests and is most frequently seen at forest edges, brushy edges of watercourses, pastures with scattered shrubs, gardens with hedges, and feeders stocked with bananas. It may join mixed flocks of other tanagers and saltators in search of figs (*Ficus*), berries, insects, and bananas.

The Crimson-collared Tanager can be seen in Caribbean lowland and middle-elevation sites like La Virgen del Socorro, La Selva, El Gavilán Lodge, Selva Verde Lodge, Lost Iguana Resort, Rancho Naturalista, La Paz Waterfall Gardens, and west to Kiri Lodge at the entrance to Tapantí NP. It comes to the feeders at Selva Verde Lodge, La Paz Waterfall Gardens, and Rancho Naturalista.

Crimson-collared Tanager male

PASSERINI'S TANAGER (SCARLET-RUMPED TANAGER)

Passerini's Tanager, a common resident of the Caribbean lowlands, was formerly known as the Scarlet-rumped Tanager until it was taxonomically split from Cherrie's Tanager. Males are identical to Cherrie's Tanager, but the females have a uniform dull-yellow breast and rump without the bright peach-colored upper chest and rump of the female Cherrie's Tanager. Other details of its description and natural history are similar to those of Cherrie's Tanager, given in the previous account.

Passerini's Tanager occurs throughout the Caribbean lowlands from Caño Negro NWR and Lodge to coastal areas and up to the elevations of Rara Avis, Turrialba, Rancho Naturalista, the Rainforest Aerial Tram, lower levels of Braulio Carrillo NP, and west to Kiri Lodge near the entrance to Tapantí NP.

Ramphocelus passerinii
Costa Rican names: *Tangara lomiescarlata; sargenta; sangre de toro.*
19/23 trips; 124 sightings.
Status: Permanent resident.
Length: 6.3 inches.
Weight: 0.9–1.3 ounces (25–37 grams).
Range: Southern Mexico to Panama.
Elevational range: Sea level to 4,500 feet.

Passerini's Tanager, male on left and female on right

CHERRIE'S TANAGER (SCARLET-RUMPED TANAGER)

Ramphocelus costaricensis
Costa Rican names: *Sargento;*
sangre de toro; tangara
Iomiescarlata.
18/23 trips; 127 sightings.
Status: Permanent resident.
Length: 6.3 inches.
Weight: 0.9–1.3 ounces (25–37
grams).
Range: Endemic from
southwestern Costa Rica to
western Panama.
Elevational range: Sea level to
5,500 feet.

Among the most distinctive, beautiful, and memorable tanagers in Costa Rica is the bird formerly known as the Scarlet-rumped Tanager. The Scarlet-rumped Tanager was found in both the Caribbean and southern Pacific lowlands, but it has been geographically separated for so long that the species became genetically different through natural selection. This bird has been split into Passerini's Tanager in the Caribbean lowlands and Cherrie's Tanager in the Pacific lowlands. The males on both slopes are identical: black with cherry-red rump patches and a bluish-gray bill.

The female Passerini's Tanager, in the Caribbean lowlands, has a dull-yellow breast. In the Pacific lowlands, females of Cherrie's Tanager have an upper breast and rump that are a bright peach color. Immature males look like females. When males molt into adult plumage they take on a dappled look, with black feathers throughout their female-looking plumage. Among the most common calls for Cherrie's Tanager is a burst of squeaky, irregular chirps.

Cherrie's Tanager is found in second-growth forests, forest edges, shrubby pastures, shade coffee plantations, gardens, backyards with fruiting shrubs, and at bird feeders stocked with bananas. It is often seen in open areas perched on fences, vines, or shrubs. Pairs and small flocks may join mixed flocks of tanagers, warblers, and saltators in search of *Cecropia* and *Piper* fruits, small berries, bananas (*Musa*), and insects.

Cherrie's Tanager can be seen throughout the southern Pacific lowlands and middle elevations, from Carara NP to the Panama border and inland to Talari Mountain Lodge, Vista del Valle Restaurant, and the Wilson Botanical Garden.

Cherrie's Tanager female

Cherrie's Tanager male

Cherrie's Tanager immature male with
black flecking

BLUE-GRAY TANAGER

The Blue-gray Tanager is one of the best known and most common songbirds in the country. It is known to Costa Ricans as *viuda,* meaning "widow," but the reason for that name is unclear, because this tanager occurs in pairs throughout the year. The Blue-gray Tanager has a gray body with bluish-turquoise wings and wing coverts. The tail is bluish, and the bill is relatively short and thick. Its calls are a series of bubbling, twittering squeaks.

This abundant tanager is common in parks, gardens, backyards, forest edges, hedges, shade coffee plantations, and second-growth forests. Occurring in small flocks or as pairs, the Blue-gray Tanager forages for fruits of figs (*Ficus*), *Miconia, Didymopanax, Cecropia, Piper,* bananas (*Musa*), and papayas. Other foods include nectar of balsa (*Ochroma lagopus*) and *Erythrina.* This is one of the only tanagers known to eat leaves and flowers. It regularly visits bird feeders to eat bananas. Insects are gleaned from leaves and twigs and are also caught in flight.

On the Caribbean slope, the Blue-gray Tanager inhabits lowlands from Nicaragua to Panama and inland to Puerto Viejo en Sarapiquí, La Selva, Turrialba, and Rancho Naturalista. It is uncommon in Guanacaste, but it is common throughout the southern Pacific lowlands, the Wilson Botanical Garden, and the Central Plateau. Some are found in the highlands at Monteverde, La Paz Waterfall Gardens, Bosque de Paz, Hotel El Pórtico on Barva volcano, and Savegre Mountain Lodge.

Thraupis episcopus
Costa Rican names: *Viuda; tangara azuleja.*
23/23 trips; 287 sightings.
Status: Permanent resident.
Length: 6 inches.
Weight: 1.0–1.6 ounces (27–45 grams).
Range: Central Mexico to central Brazil.
Elevational range: Sea level to 7,200 feet.

Blue-gray Tanager adult

Palm Tanager adult showing bluish and green iridescence

Thraupis palmarum
Costa Rican name: *Tangara palmera.*
22/23 trips; 176 sightings.
Status: Permanent resident.
Length: 6.2 inches.
Weight: 1.0–1.7 ounces (27–48 grams).
Range: Eastern Honduras to southern Brazil.
Elevational range: Sea level to 5,000 feet.

PALM TANAGER

The Palm Tanager is the most widespread tanager in Latin America. It is found from Honduras to southern Brazil. On a cloudy day, the plumage is plain and almost colorless, but in sunlight, the Palm Tanager's body may appear to glisten iridescent grayish olive or grayish blue. The head and face are greenish olive. True to its name, this tanager often perches and nests in the top of palms.

The Palm Tanager is the most common of three nondescript tanagers in Costa Rica. The others are the Plain-colored Tanager and Olive Tanager. The Plain-colored Tanager is medium gray with a lighter belly and bluish shoulder area. The Olive Tanager, found in the Caribbean lowlands, is more olive-green than the olive-gray Palm Tanager. The wings of the Olive Tanager are the same color as the back. The wings are blackish on the Palm Tanager.

This common tanager inhabits moist and wet tropical lowlands and is especially abundant in plantations of coconut, African oil palm, pejivalle palm, or ornamental palms. Common in backyards, gardens, and parks, it travels in pairs. Preferred foods include figs (*Ficus*), *Cecropia, Didymopanax, Miconia,* papaya, and banana (*Musa*). It gleans insects from palm and banana leaves in an acrobatic manner that frequently involves hanging upside down to catch its prey. The Palm Tanager will also sally to catch flying insects.

The Palm Tanager is found throughout the Caribbean lowlands from Nicaragua to the Panama border and inland to Puerto Viejo en Sarapiquí, La Selva, Rancho Naturalista, and Rara Avis. It is abundant at Tortuguero and Cahuita NPs. In the southern Pacific lowlands, its distribution extends along the coast from Puntarenas and Carara NP to Panama and inland to San Isidro del General and the Wilson Botanical Garden at San Vito.

Palm Tanager adult showing grayish iridescence in different light

GOLDEN-HOODED TANAGER

One of the most beautifully marked songbirds in Costa Rica is the Golden-hooded Tanager. Its Costa Rican name is *siete colores,* meaning "seven colors." A golden hood covers the head and is set off by a black face mask that has turquoise and blue highlights on the forehead and cheeks. The upper chest and back are black, the belly is white, and the sides and rump are turquoise. The black wing feathers are edged with gold. When viewed in good light, the Golden-hooded Tanager is one of the most memorable avian gems of the American tropics. In poor light, this species can be difficult to identify. Young have a greenish-yellow head, a grayish-black back, a pale grayish to olive breast, and a yellowish-green throat.

Golden-hooded Tanager adult

Tangara larvata
Costa Rican names: *Siete colores; mariposa; tangara capuchidorada.*
23/23 trips; 149 sightings.
Status: Permanent resident.
Length: 5 inches.
Weight: 0.6–0.8 ounce (17–24 grams).
Range: Southern Mexico to western Ecuador.
Elevational range: Sea level to 5,000 feet.

The Golden-hooded Tanager forages in the upper canopy of mature moist and wet forests in tropical lowlands and middle elevations. It occurs in secondary forests, shade coffee plantations, forest edges, forest openings, and backyards and gardens landscaped with fruiting trees and shrubs. This social species occurs in pairs, as groups of three or four, and occasionally in flocks of up to twenty-five or thirty individuals. Sometimes it occurs with other tanagers, warblers, and honeycreepers. It feeds on fruits of melastomes (*Miconia*), *Cecropia,* figs (*Ficus*), mistletoe, *Piper,* and bananas (*Musa*). Most fruits are eaten while perched, but fruits are sometimes plucked while hovering, and insects are frequently caught in flight as this agile tanager sallies from perches.

Two, and sometimes three, broods are produced during an extended nesting season from February through September. The young are fed by both parents and by tanagers in adult plumage that may be offspring from the previous year. Young from the first brood also help feed the second brood.

This attractive tanager may be encountered along the Caribbean coast from Caño Negro Lodge and the Río Frío region to Tortuguero NP, Limón, and Cahuita NP and inland to La Selva, Guapiles, Turrialba, and Rancho Naturalista. In southern Pacific lowland and middle elevations, the Golden-hooded Tanager can be observed at Carara, Manuel Antonio, and Corcovado NPs and at Vista del Valle Restaurant, San Isidro del General, Hotel del Sur, La Cusinga, Los Cusingos, Oro Verde BR, Las Esquinas Rainforest Lodge, Talari Mountain Lodge, Rancho Casa Grande, the Wilson Botanical Garden, Lapa Ríos, Corcovado Lodge Tent Camp, and Tiskita Jungle Lodge.

SPECKLED TANAGER

Tangara guttata

Costa Rican names: *Zebra; tangara moteada.*

18/23 trips; 47 sightings.

Status: Permanent resident.

Length: 5 inches.

Weight: 0.5–0.7 ounce (15–20 grams).

Range: Costa Rica to northern Brazil; Trinidad.

Elevational range: 1,000–4,600 feet.

Like the Silver-throated Tanager, the beautiful Speckled Tanager is a foothill species because it is found along the middle elevations of Costa Rica's mountains. The plumage has an intricate pattern of black feathers edged with lime-green over the back and wings. Black feathers over the head are edged with golden yellow, and black feathers on the throat and breast are edged with white. The belly is white and the flanks are lime-yellow. The overall speckled effect is unique among Costa Rican tanagers.

This tanager travels through the canopy of mature and second-growth forests in groups of three to six birds. It may sometimes join flocks of Silver-throated Tanagers, Golden-hooded Tanagers, and Green Honeycreepers. Forest-edge habitats, shrubby areas, forest openings, pastures, and shade coffee plantations are also visited. Foods include bananas and small fruits of *Miconia, Souroubea guianensis, Lantana,* and *Dipterodendron elegans.* Small insects, caterpillars, and spiders are gleaned from twigs and leaves.

The Speckled Tanager can be seen at La Virgen del Socorro, the Rainforest Aerial Tram, lower levels of Braulio Carrillo NP (Quebrada González Trail), and Rancho Naturalista. On the foothills of the Pacific slope, this attractive tanager may be seen at Los Cusingos, Talari Mountain Lodge, Vista del Valle Restaurant, and the Wilson Botanical Garden. It readily comes to bird feeders for bananas where they are offered.

Speckled Tanagers, two views showing detail of markings

SPANGLE-CHEEKED TANAGER

The Spangle-cheeked Tanager is a beautiful endemic inhabitant of high-elevation montane forests from north-western Costa Rica to western Panama. Both sexes have a bay-colored belly and a black bib with iridescent green scallops. The black head is highlighted with light-blue flecks on the crown and small golden-green spots on the cheeks and neck. The black back and tail are edged with iridescent blue, and the rump is pale green. The call is a single note or series of high-pitched notes described as "tsip" or "seek" by Stiles and Skutch (1989:425).

The preferred habitat of the Spangle-cheeked Tanager includes mature and second-growth montane forests characterized by mossy, epiphyte-laden foliage. Pairs or small groups of these tanagers acrobatically search the foliage, sometimes with bush-tanagers, to locate insects, spiders, and small berries of *Fuchsia*, *Satyria*, *Cavendishia*, and *Gaiadendron*.

This tanager can be encountered in Braulio Carrillo, Poás Volcano, Tapantí, Chirripó, and La Amistad NPs; at Monteverde and La Paz Waterfall Gardens; and in the Talamanca Mountains, including the San Gerardo de Dota Valley, and Cerro de la Muerte at kilometer 66.

Tangara dowii
Costa Rican name: *Tangara vientricastaña.*
13/23 trips; 19 sightings.
Status: Permanent resident.
Length: 4.7 inches.
Weight: 0.7 ounce (20 grams).
Range: Endemic to highlands of Costa Rica and western Panama.
Elevational range: 2,600–10,000 feet.

Spangle-cheeked Tanager adult

Bay-headed Tanager adult

Tangara gyrola

Costa Rican name: *Tangara cabecicastaña.*

19/23 trips; 60 sightings.

Status: Permanent resident.

Length: 5.25 inches.

Weight: 0.6–0.9 ounce (17.5–26.5 grams).

Range: Costa Rica to eastern Brazil and Trinidad.

Elevational range: 330–5,000 feet.

BAY-HEADED TANAGER

Another of Costa Rica's colorful tanagers is the Bay-headed Tanager. It is a foothill species on the Caribbean slope and a lowland and middle-elevation species on the southern Pacific slope. It has a bright reddish-chestnut (bay-colored) head. The back, wings, and tail are lime-green. The throat, chest, and rump are sky blue, the shoulders are golden yellow, and the thighs are tan. This tanager demonstrates interesting differences in plumage over its range in Central and South America. In Trinidad, northeastern Colombia, and northern Venezuela, the throat and chest are bright green instead of sky blue.

The Bay-headed Tanager inhabits mature moist and wet forests, second-growth forests, shade coffee plantations, clearings, and pastures with scattered tall trees. It travels as pairs or in family groups year-round, and it is frequently observed in the company of other tanagers and honeycreepers. Its preferred foods include fruits and berries of *Miconia*, figs (*Ficus*), *Lycianthes synanthera*, *Souroubea guianensis*, *Cecropia*, protein bodies on *Cecropia* leaves, and small insects.

On the Caribbean slope, the Bay-headed Tanager is found at elevations from 2,000 to 5,000 feet. It occurs at lower levels of Braulio Carrillo NP, the Rainforest Aerial Tram, and Rancho Naturalista. On the Pacific slope, this tanager occurs in Corcovado NP, Lapa Ríos, Corcovado Lodge Tent Camp, and Tiskita Jungle Lodge, and inland at Los Cusingos, Talari Mountain Lodge, and the Wilson Botanical Garden.

SILVER-THROATED TANAGER

Like the Speckled Tanager, the Silver-throated Tanager is another jewel of Costa Rica's foothills (middle-elevation forests). The bird's name is derived from the glistening, silvery-white throat. Viewed from the front, when the bird is all fluffed up, the throat appears to have a silver necklace against a background of golden yellow. The back and wings show similarities to the Speckled Tanager because the feathers are black with bright lime-yellow edgings.

Silver-throated Tanager adult

Tangara icterocephala
Costa Rican names: *Juanita;*
   tangara dorada.
22/23 trips; 83 sightings.
Status: Permanent resident.
Length: 5 inches.
Weight: 0.6–0.9 ounce (18–25
   grams).
Range: Costa Rica to western
   Ecuador.
Elevational range: Sea level to
   5,500 feet.

This tanager inhabits moist and wet forests of Costa Rica's foothills, including mature and second-growth forests and cloud forests where the vegetation is heavily laden with epiphytes, vines, and mossy growth. It also occurs along forest edges and in brushy second growth of forest openings and pastures. Foraging as pairs or in groups of up to a dozen individuals, the Silver-throated Tanager is often in the company of tanagers, warblers, and honeycreepers. Its preferred foods include fruits of *Miconia,* figs (*Ficus*), *Souroubea, Cecropia,* insects, caterpillars, and spiders. It searches for food by hopping along a branch, looking in all directions, and leaning diagonally or hanging down to view the underside of branches and leaves.

The Silver-throated Tanager can be seen at La Virgen del Socorro, Monteverde, Rara Avis, Tilajari Resort, Bosque de Paz, La Paz Waterfall Gardens, the Rainforest Aerial Tram, lower levels of Braulio Carrillo NP, Tapantí NP, Savegre Mountain Lodge, and Rancho Naturalista. The best places to see it are along the trails and at the feeders of the Wilson Botanical Garden at San Vito and at the Vista del Valle Restaurant feeders at kilometer 119 on the Pan American Highway. This bird can occasionally be seen at lower elevations during the postbreeding season at Corcovado Lodge Tent Camp in January and February.

Scarlet-thighed Dacnis adult

Dacnis venusta

Costa Rican name: *Mielero celeste y negro.*

7/23 trips; 11 sightings.

Status: Permanent resident.

Length: 4.75 inches.

Weight: 0.5–0.6 ounce (15–17 grams).

Range: Costa Rica to northwestern Ecuador.

Elevational range: 1,650–5,000 feet.

SCARLET-THIGHED DACNIS

The Scarlet-thighed Dacnis is another foothill species of the Caribbean and Pacific slopes. Its bold turquoise, black, and scarlet markings, as well as its intriguing name, command interest. The male has a turquoise hood featuring a black facial mask; the bill is sharp and warblerlike; the throat, breast, and wings are black; and the scapulars and rump are turquoise. The most notable features are the scarlet-red thighs. The female is greenish blue above with a buff-colored breast and cinnamon thighs. This species can sometimes be seen bathing in the water tanks of large bromeliad bracts.

This species inhabits the canopy of moist and wet lowland and middle-elevation forests. Its preferred habitat includes forest edges, shade coffee plantations, and isolated trees and shrubs in pastures and forest openings. It travels as pairs, in flocks of up to fifteen birds, or in mixed flocks containing warblers, honeycreepers, and other tanagers. Foods include small berries like *Miconia, Sapium, Cecropia* catkins, *Dendropanax,* bananas at bird feeders, arillate fruits of *Clusia* and *Zanthoxylum,* and some insects.

The Scarlet-thighed Dacnis occurs on the Caribbean slope at elevations from 1,650 to 4,000 feet, including Rancho Naturalista and lower levels of Braulio Carrillo NP. On the southern Pacific slope, it inhabits premontane forests from 3,000 to 5,000 feet, like those at the Wilson Botanical Garden. It descends to lower elevations after the breeding season, including La Selva and Sueño Azul on the Caribbean slope and Talari Mountain Lodge and Tiskita Jungle Lodge on the Pacific slope.

BLUE DACNIS

This attractive tanager is blue with a black back and wings. It has red eyes and a sharply pointed bill. The female has a lime-green body and bluish-green head. The agile Blue Dacnis is found in moist and wet tropical Caribbean and southern Pacific lowlands of Costa Rica. There it can be seen in pairs or in mixed flocks of tanagers, honeycreepers, and warblers as they acrobatically explore tree branches and leaves for fruits, flower nectar, and insects. They will hang upside down to look for insects hidden in dead curled-up leaves, and will also feed on ripe *Cecropia* catkins. Other fruits eaten include *Miconia* and *Clusia*. The Blue Dacnis will also come to feed on bananas at bird feeders.

Blue Dacnis female

Look for the Blue Dacnis in the Caribbean lowlands at La Selva, Sueño Azul, Tortuga Lodge, Tortuguero NP, Guacimo, and Cahuita NP. In the southern Pacific lowlands, it may be encountered at Carara and Manuel Antonio NPs, Rancho Casa Grande, Los Cusingos, Hotel Cristal Ballena, Las Esquinas Rainforest Lodge, and Tiskita Jungle Lodge.

Dacnis cayana
Costa Rican name: *Mielero azulejo.*
19/23 trips; 37 sightings.
Status: Permanent resident.
Length: 4.3–4.7 inches.
Weight: 0.4–0.5 ounce (10–16 grams).
Range: Northeastern Honduras to southern Brazil.
Elevational range: Sea level to 4,000 feet.

Blue Dacnis male

Green Honeycreeper female

Chlorophanes spiza
Costa Rican names: *Rey de trepadores; mielero verde.*
21/23 trips; 89 sightings.
Status: Permanent resident.
Length: 5 inches.
Weight: 0.7 ounce (19 grams).
Range: Southern Mexico to southeastern Brazil.
Elevational range: Sea level to 4,000 feet.

GREEN HONEYCREEPER

The name "Green Honeycreeper" applies best to the female of this tanager. It is lime-green above and lighter lime-green on the belly. The male has a bright yellow bill, which is black along the top edge, and there is a black hood over the front half of the head. The remainder of the male's body, however, is a beautiful turquoise hue.

The Green Honeycreeper inhabits lower and middle elevations of moist and wet mature forests, second growth, forest edges, scattered trees and shrubs in open areas, shade coffee plantations, and gardens. Usually traveling as pairs or in family groups, this honeycreeper often accompanies mixed flocks of tanagers, warblers, and other songbirds. Its preferred foods include fruits of *Miconia, Clusia,* bananas (*Musa*), *Cecropia,* and insects caught on the wing.

On the Caribbean slope, the Green Honeycreeper is found from Tortuguero NP through Limón to Cahuita NP and inland to La Selva, Sueño Azul, Tilajari Resort, and Rancho Naturalista. In the southern Pacific lowlands, it occurs at Manuel Antonio NP and inland to San Isidro del General, where it can be seen at the bird feeders eating bananas at Los Cusingos and Talari Mountain Lodge. Other locations include Corcovado Lodge Tent Camp, Tiskita Jungle Lodge, Lapa Ríos, and the Wilson Botanical Garden.

Green Honeycreeper male

SHINING HONEYCREEPER

The Shining Honeycreeper is one of those memorable Costa Rican rainforest birds that creates the lasting vision of a beautiful bird feeding among tropical flowers. The male is deep violet-blue with black wings, throat, lores, and tail. The black bill is slender and strongly decurved. The bright yellow legs differentiate it from the Red-legged Honeycreeper. The female is lime-green above and has a pale breast strongly streaked with blue. The female Red-legged Honeycreeper is similar, but the breast has pale green streaks.

This honeycreeper travels in pairs or small family groups in search of small insects, fruits of *Clusia* and *Spondias edulis*, and flower nectar. Insects and fruits are eaten while the birds acrobatically probe leaves and twigs. They also eat bananas at bird feeders. This honeycreeper's bill is so long and slender that it can insert it into the crack of *Clusia* fruit arils that are beginning to open, allowing the honeycreeper to eat the seeds before any other birds can get to them.

A resident of moist and wet Caribbean and southern Pacific lowlands, this beautiful honeycreeper can be encountered in the Caribbean lowlands at La Selva, Sueño Azul, and Tortuguero NP and south to Puerto Viejo near Cahuita and Rancho Naturalista. In the southern Pacific lowlands, it occurs from Carara NP south to Vista del Valle Restaurant, La Cusinga, Oro Verde BR, Las Esquinas Rainforest Reserve, Tiskita Jungle Lodge, and on the Osa Peninsula at sites like the Corcovado Lodge Tent Camp.

Cyanerpes lucidus
Costa Rican name: *Mielero luciente.*
12/23 trips; 24 sightings.
Status: Permanent resident.
Length: 4 inches.
Weight: 0.4 ounce (11 grams).
Range: Southern Mexico to northwestern Colombia.
Elevational range: Sea level to 4,000 feet.

Shining Honeycreeper male. Female is similar to female Red-legged Honeycreeper, but with more blue streaking on the breast.

Male Red-legged Honeycreeper with wing extended to show yellow highlights

Cyanerpes cyaneus
Costa Rican names: *Picudo; trepador; mielero patirrojo.*
22/23 trips; 79 sightings.
Status: Permanent resident.
Length: 4.5 inches.
Weight: 0.4–0.6 ounce (11–18 grams).
Range: Northern Mexico to eastern Brazil.
Elevational range: Sea level to 4,000 feet.

RED-LEGGED HONEYCREEPER

The Red-legged Honeycreeper is one of the most beautiful members of the tanager family. The male is richly patterned with royal blue and coal black over the back, and the breast is deep blue. It has a black mask, a slender decurved bill, and a pale iridescent turquoise forehead. The wings and tail are black, and the legs are bright red. The female is pale mint green and resembles the female Shining Honeycreeper, but the female of that species is brighter lime-green. Also, the female Red-legged Honeycreeper shows pale vertical green streaking on the breast. The female Shining Honeycreeper has conspicuous blue vertical streaking.

This stunning honeycreeper travels through the canopy of dry, moist, and wet mature forests of Costa Rica's lowlands. It is one of the few tanagers adapted to the tropical dry forests of the Guanacaste region. Pairs and small flocks of five to fifteen members inhabit shade coffee plantations, gallery forests in drier regions, savanna forests, and gardens in settled areas. It may join mixed flocks of other songbirds in search of flowering or fruiting trees.

Flower nectar is an important food of this honeycreeper, which explains why this bird adapts well in Guanacaste, where there are numerous flowering trees during the dry season. Nectar sources include *Inga, Calliandra, Erythrina,* and *Genipa.* While hovering or hanging upside down, this honeycreeper uses its long, slender bill to reach into the cracks of newly opening tropical fruit pods, called arils, for brightly colored seeds, like *Clusia,* before other tanagers can access them. Other foods are berries of *Miconia,* bananas, and the pulp of oranges. It also gleans small insects and spiders from foliage.

On the Caribbean slope, the Red-legged Honeycreeper occurs from Caño Negro Lodge in the Río Frío region south to Muelle and Tilajari Resort, La Selva, Sueño Azul and southeast to Cahuita NP. On the Pacific slope, this honeycreeper occurs in Guanacaste, Palo Verde, Santa Rosa, and Carara NPs, but it is most common in the moist lowlands from Carara NP southeast to the Panama border and inland to Talari Mountain Lodge and the Wilson Botanical Garden. It is also abundant on Isla del Caño.

Red-legged Honeycreeper male

Red-legged Honeycreeper female

BLUE-BLACK GRASSQUIT

There are several small black male seed-finches, seedeaters, and grassquits in open grassy and brushy areas of Costa Rica's lowlands: the Thick-billed and Nicaraguan Seed-Finches, the Variable Seedeater, and the Blue-Black Grass-quit. The seed-finches have short, thick, blunt bills; the bill of the Variable Seedeater (Caribbean race) is strongly curved downward along the top of the bill (culmen). The Blue-black Grassquit has a short, thinner, pointed bill and very glossy blue-black plumage. The brownish female has a streaked breast, whereas the other species mentioned have plain breasts. This species is often seen in the same habitats as the Gray-crowned Yellowthroat and Yellow-faced Grassquit. The call is a buzzy high-pitched "seez-zeet" that is repeated every few seconds.

The most distinctive and delightful feature of the Blue-black Grassquit is that it could be called Costa Rica's popcorn bird. Perched atop a fence, post, twig, or weed, the black male pops upward with a short fluttering flight to a height of one to three feet and then descends back to its original perch. At the peak of its jump, the tail is flared higher than the head and the wings are spread outward to display white shoulder markings, which are concealed while at rest.

Blue-black Grassquits are common and frequently seen in brushy pastures, roadsides, early second-growth clearings, along fencelines of the Caribbean lowlands and middle elevations, and in the southern Pacific slope lowlands from Carara NP to the Panama border. Some can also be encountered in Guanacaste and in pastures approaching the Central Plateau.

Volatinia jacarina
Costa Rican name: *Semillerito negro azulado.*
20/23 trips; 69 sightings.
Status: Permanent resident.
Length: 3.9 inches.
Weight: 0.3 ounce (10 grams).
Range: Northwestern Mexico to northern Argentina.
Elevational range: Sea level to 5,500 feet.

Blue-black Grassquit adult male

VARIABLE SEEDEATER

Sporophila americana (formerly Sporophila aurita)

Costa Rican names: *Espiguero variable; setillero de laguna.*

23/23 trips; 175 sightings.

Status: Permanent resident.

Length: 4 inches.

Weight: 0.4 ounce (10–12 grams).

Range: Southern Mexico to northwestern Peru.

Elevational range: Sea level to 5,000 feet.

The Variable Seedeater is the most common of six seed-eaters in Costa Rica. A lowland bird of grassy areas, this seedeater occurs in two color phases. The male of the Caribbean slope race (*S. a. corvina*) is black with a white spot (not a wing bar) on the primaries. The male in the Pacific lowlands race (*S. a. aurita*) has a white rump, a white lower breast and belly, a white wing spot, a narrow and incomplete neck collar, and a black throat.

The White-collared Seedeater differs from the Pacific race of the Variable Seedeater by having two white wing bars, a white throat, and a complete white collar around the neck. The females of both races are dark olive above and paler below. The Pacific race female has more yellow-ish white on the belly. The similar Blue-black Grassquit is all black with no white wing spots and has a more pointed bill than the Variable Seedeater.

The Variable Seedeater inhabits forest edges, roadsides, grassy fields, pastures, gardens, and small patches of forest. It lives in pairs and travels in small, single-species flocks or with seedeaters, seed-finches, and grassquits. Preferred foods include seeds, berries, and insects. The Variable Seedeater is found in grassy habitats throughout the lowlands of both the Caribbean and Pacific slopes.

Variable Seedeater adult male, Caribbean race

Variable Seedeater adult male, Pacific race

NICARAGUAN SEED-FINCH (PINK-BILLED SEED-FINCH)

The largest and most distinctive of Costa Rica's black male seed-finches, grassquits, and seedeaters is the Nicaraguan Seed-Finch. Nearly six inches long, it has an enormous pink bill that is unmistakable. The Thick-billed Seed-Finch is found in some of the same habitats as the Nicaraguan Seed-Finch, but it has a smaller black bill that is short, thick, and straight along the top (culmen). The female of the Nicaraguan Seed-Finch is brownish and similar to the Thick-billed Seed-Finch, but the bill is also much larger. This species is endemic in the Caribbean lowlands from Nicaragua to northwestern Panama.

The Nicaraguan Seed-Finch is usually seen in wet, grassy lowlands near ponds or marshes. It occurs in pairs or in small groups that perch atop tall grasses where they eat grass seeds. The song is an extended, rich series of chirps and whistles.

Among the best places to see this species is along grassy roadside wetlands from Los Chiles en route to Caño Negro NWR and in the Selva Verde Lodge vicinity.

Oryzoborus nuttingi
Costa Rican name: *Semillero piquirosado.*
2/23 trips; 2 sightings.
Status: Permanent resident.
Length: 5.7 inches.
Weight: 0.8 ounce (24 grams).
Range: Endemic from eastern Nicaragua to northwestern Panama.
Elevational range: Sea level to 3,000 feet.

Nicaraguan Seed-Finch, showing bill detail

Nicaraguan Seed-Finch adult male

YELLOW-FACED GRASSQUIT

Tiaris olivacea
Costa Rican names: *Gallito;*
  semillerito cariamarillo.
23/23 trips; 95 sightings.
Status: Permanent resident.
Length: 4 inches.
Weight: 0.4 ounce (10 grams).
Range: Central Mexico to
  northwestern Venezuela;
  Greater Antilles.
Elevational range: Sea level to
  7,200 feet.

One of the most easily identified birds of grassy habitats is the Yellow-faced Grassquit. When viewed from the front, the male appears to have a bright yellow X across its black face. The head, face, and upper chest are black; the back is yellowish olive; and the belly is grayish olive. The female is paler olive-green, and the X pattern on the face is pale yellow.

The Yellow-faced Grassquit is common in open grassy habitats and shrubby edges. Traveling in small flocks or as singles or pairs, it strips seeds from grass or eats it from the ground. Small berries are plucked from trees and shrubs, and insects are gleaned from foliage. It may occur with Variable or White-collared Seedeaters.

In the Caribbean lowlands, the Yellow-faced Grassquit occurs from Puerto Viejo en Sarapiquí and Guapiles to Cahuita and inland to La Selva and at middle elevations at Turrialba and Rancho Naturalista. In the highlands, it occurs at Vara Blanca, Monteverde, and Savegre Mountain Lodge. In the southern Pacific zone, it occurs at Quepos, San Isidro del General, Rancho Casa Grande, Talari Mountain Lodge, Los Cusingos, Lapa Ríos, Corcovado Lodge Tent Camp, Tiskita Jungle Lodge, and the Wilson Botanical Garden.

Yellow-faced Grassquit adult male

PEG-BILLED FINCH

Like the Volcano Junco and Large-footed
Finch, the Peg-billed Finch is a high-
elevation endemic bird found only in the
mountains from central Costa Rica to western Panama. This mysterious and rare species depends on the fruiting of bamboo species that may undergo massive fruiting only
every twenty to thirty years. When the bamboo seeds become abundant, the Peg-billed
Finch becomes extremely abundant. Then
it seems to disappear until the next bamboo
fruiting event. The nest of this rare species

Peg-billed Finch adult male

was not described until the bamboo bloomed in the Talamanca Mountains in 1990. In that same year, the author
recorded the call of this species for the first time and
donated the historic tape recording to the Sound Library
at the Cornell Laboratory of Ornithology for its archives.
Sporadic sightings have been made in the ensuing years in
the upper elevations of Cerro de la Muerte and in the San
Gerardo de Dota Valley.

The Peg-billed Finch has a long, pointed, slightly
upturned bill. The male is dark gray above and lighter gray
on the breast and belly. The Slaty Flowerpiercer is super-
ficially similar, but the male is bluish gray and the upper
mandible has a distinctly hooked tip, like the end of a can
opener. The female Peg-billed Finch is more olive-brown,
with a paler breast, a long-pointed bill like the male, and
two wing bars. The song of this finch is a quick series of
three to four quick buzzy notes.

The Peg-billed Finch inhabits bamboo thickets at 8,000
to 11,000 feet, including paramo habitats, but this species
will occasionally descend to lower elevations. It may also
travel in mixed flocks with bush-tanagers and warblers in
search of insects, berries, or flower nectar.

The Peg-billed Finch can be seen in the San Gerardo
de Dota Valley, including the Savegre Mountain Lodge
courtyard, and Cerro de la Muerte at kilometers 86 (along
the road across from Los Chespiritos 2) and 90 (along the
access road from the Pan American Highway to the transmission towers).

Acanthidops bairdii
Costa Rican name: *Fringilo
piquigudo.*
7/23 trips; 12 sightings.
Status: Permanent resident.
Length: 5.3 inches.
Weight: 0.6 ounce (16 grams).
Range: Endemic to highlands of
Costa Rica and western Panama.
Elevational range: 5,000–11,000
feet.

Slaty Flowerpiercer adult female

Diglossa plumbea
Costa Rican name: *Pinchaflor
plomizo.*
21/23 trips; 74 sightings.
Status: Permanent resident.
Length: 4 inches.
Weight: 0.3 ounce (9 grams).
Range: Endemic to highlands of
Costa Rica and western Panama.
Elevational range: 4,000–10,000
feet.

SLATY FLOWERPIERCER

One of the most fascinating birds in Costa Rica's highlands is the Slaty Flowerpiercer. Both the slate-gray male and the tan-colored female have sharp-pointed bills with a distinctive kink near the tip, like the end of a can opener. This unique tip facilitates puncturing the base of flowers so that it is possible to take the nectar without pollinating the flowers. Bananaquits do the same thing with flowers in the lowlands. The Slaty Flowerpiercer is a member of the flowerpiercer genus *Diglossa,* which includes at least eighteen species in mountainous areas from southern Mexico through the Andes of South America.

The Slaty Flowerpiercer frequents highland meadows, roadsides, forest edges, shrubby clearings, backyard gardens, and montane forests. Small insects are also caught in flight. This highland endemic can be observed visiting flowers at Monteverde, Bosque de Paz, and La Paz Waterfall Gardens; on Poás, Barva, and Irazú volcanoes; at Tapantí NP and Savegre Mountain Lodge (visiting flowers and hummingbird feeders in the courtyard); and along the Pan American Highway in Cerro de la Muerte at kilometers 66, 76, 80, 86, and 96.

Slaty Flowerpiercer adult male

YELLOW-THIGHED FINCH

The Yellow-thighed Finch is a large, dark gray, highland-endemic finch with a black head and bright yellow thighs. Traveling as mated pairs or in small family groups, this finch ranges through montane forests and is especially common in forest edges, thickets, brushy ravines, bamboo clumps, and thick shrubby areas near pastures. Sometimes it joins mixed flocks of tanagers and warblers in search of berries, nectar, insects, and spiders.

Look for this highland bird in Poás Volcano and Tapantí NPs, Bosque de Paz, La Paz Waterfall Gardens, Savegre Mountain Lodge, and along the Pan American Highway in Cerro de la Muerte at kilometers 66, 76 (the road to Providencia), 86 (Los Chespiritos 2), and 96 (Villa Mills).

Pselliophorus tibialis
Costa Rican name: *Saltón de muslos amarillos.*
22/23 trips; 59 sightings.
Status: Permanent resident.
Length: 7.25 inches.
Weight: 1.1 ounces (31 grams).
Range: Endemic to highlands of Costa Rica and western Panama.
Elevational range: 4,000–10,000 feet.

Yellow-thighed Finch adult

LARGE-FOOTED FINCH

Pezopetes capitalis
Costa Rican name: *Saltón patigrande.*
16/23 trips; 28 sightings.
Status: Permanent resident.
Length: 7.8 inches.
Weight: 2 ounces (56 grams).
Range: Endemic to highlands of Costa Rica and western Panama.
Elevational range: 7,000–11,000 feet.

Another of Costa Rica's highland specialty birds is the Large-footed Finch. It is endemic in montane and paramo habitats from central Costa Rica to western Panama. The markings are dark gray to black, the colors of many high-elevation birds, like the Yellow-thighed, Slaty, and Peg-billed Finches, the Slaty Flowerpiercer, and the Black Guan. It has a chunky dark gray body and head with black stripes over the top of the head and a yellowish-olive belly.

The Large-footed Finch forages on the ground in the manner of a towhee. It uses forward and backward jumps to scratch and throw ground cover aside to expose seeds and insects. Its preferred habitats include mature highland oak forests, second growth and forest edges, and paramo bamboo thickets. The memorable song of this finch includes a sharp series of loud whistled notes that rapidly cascades downward in pitch.

Among the best places to look for the Large-footed Finch are Poás Volcano and Tapantí NPs, San Gerardo de Dota Valley including Savegre Mountain Lodge, and Cerro de la Muerte at kilometers 66, 86 (the road across from Los Chespiritos 2), 90 (the transmission tower site), and 96 (Villa Mills).

Large-footed Finch adult

ORANGE-BILLED SPARROW

The Orange-billed Sparrow is a lowland rain-forest bird whose name describes its most conspicuous feature, an orange bill. This brightly marked sparrow has a black facial mask and contrasting white throat, a narrow black band across the upper chest, yellow shoulders, and a white lower chest and belly. The crown is black, and there is a slender grayish-white line above each eye. Sexes are identical. The song—a thin, high-pitched whistled twittering phrase—is usually given while perched in thick underbrush. The bill of the immature is black, not orange.

Orange-billed Sparrow adult

An inhabitant of mature wet forest and older second-growth forest, this sparrow lives in thick understory vegetation. Occurring as pairs or in family groups, this sparrow forages on the ground and in low shrubs in search of small fruits, berries, and insects. It will sometimes attend army ant swarms to capture escaping insects.

The subspecies of Orange-billed Sparrow found in the Caribbean lowlands (*A. a. ruficorsalis*) can be encountered along the loop trail at Tortuga Lodge, in the Arboretum and along Sendero Tres Ríos at La Selva, and on the grounds of Rancho Naturalista. The Pacific slope subspecies (*A. a. aurantiirostris*) can be seen from Carara NP southeast to Manuel Antonio and Corcovado NPs; at Hotel Villa Lapas, Rancho Casa Grande, Las Esquinas Rainforest Lodge, Lapa Ríos, Drake Bay Wilderness Resort, and Tiskita Jungle Lodge; and along the River Trail at the Wilson Botanical Garden.

Arremon aurantiirostris
Costa Rican name: *Pinzón piquinaranja.*
17/23 trips; 43 sightings.
Status: Permanent resident.
Length: 6 inches.
Weight: 1.2 ounces (35 grams).
Range: Southern Mexico to northwestern Ecuador.
Elevational range: Sea level to 4,000 feet.

SOOTY-FACED FINCH

Arremon crassirostris
Costa Rican name: *Pinzón barranquero.*
3/23 trips; 3 sightings.
Status: Permanent resident.
Length: 6.3 inches.
Weight: 1.2 ounces (33 grams).
Range: Endemic to Costa Rica and western Panama.
Elevational range: 2,000–6,000 feet.

The Sooty-faced Finch is an elusive and highly sought-after endemic bird of Costa Rica's middle-elevation forests on the Caribbean slope and upper locations of the Talamanca Mountains on the Pacific slope. This distinctive finch has a chestnut cap, black face and throat, yellow belly, and white malar stripe that extends from the back edge of the bill. The back, wings, and upper breast are dark olive-green.

This is a skulking bird of thick underbrush. It can sometimes be called out for viewing with a tape recording of its call, which is described as a high-pitched two-note "Pseé-seé" by Slud (1964:384). Please remember to limit calling to a few minutes. Usually occurring in pairs, small groups, or mixed flocks, the Sooty-faced Finch forages for invertebrates, berries, and fallen seeds on the ground. It may occasionally follow swarms of army ants to catch insects flushed by the ants. Its preferred habitat includes moist or wet upper premontane or lower montane forest. It usually is encountered along trails on hillsides and in ravines near mountain streams.

The best place to look for the Sooty-faced Finch is along the hillside nature trails of La Paz Waterfall Gardens.

Sooty-faced Finch adult

CHESTNUT-CAPPED BRUSH-FINCH

Most of Costa Rica's ground-sparrows, finches, and brush-finches are reclusive dark birds found on the ground in thick understory habitats. One of the most distinctively marked of those species is the Chestnut-capped Brush-Finch. It has a chestnut crown, a black mask through the forehead and eye, an olive-green body, and a conspicuous white throat. There is a small white spot in front of each eye.

The Chestnut-capped Brush-Finch is found in pairs or in family groups in mature or second-growth forests at middle elevations of both the Caribbean and Pacific slopes. This species will travel in mixed flocks that include Gray-breasted Wood-Wrens, Three-striped and Black-cheeked Warblers, and Yellow-throated Brush-Finches. The bill is used to move forest litter in search of insects, spiders, and centipedes. Berries are also eaten. The song of this brush-finch is a series of prolonged high-pitched whistles and assorted high notes.

The Chestnut-capped Brush-Finch can be encountered on the Caribbean slope at Monteverde, around the garden edges of Bosque de Paz, La Paz Waterfall Gardens, and Rancho Naturalista, and on the grounds of Hotel Bougainvillea. On the Pacific slope, it can be seen in the Talamanca Mountains at San Gerardo de Dota, including Savegre Mountain Lodge, Vista de Valle Restaurant, and the Wilson Botanical Garden.

Arremon brunneinucha (formerly Atlapetes brunneinucha)
Costa Rican name: *Saltón cabecicastaño.*
9/23 trips; 18 sightings.
Status: Permanent resident.
Length: 7.3 inches.
Weight: 1.5 ounces (42 grams).
Range: Central Mexico to southeastern Peru.
Elevational range: 3,000–8,200 feet.

Chestnut-capped Brush-Finch adult

Black-striped Sparrow adult

Arremonops conirostris
Costa Rican name: *Pinzón cabecilistado.*
21/23 trips; 113 sightings.
Status: Permanent resident.
Length: 6.5 inches.
Weight: 1.3 ounces (38 grams).
Range: Northern Honduras to northern Brazil.
Elevational range: Sea level to 5,000 feet.

BLACK-STRIPED SPARROW

Though not brightly marked like the Orange-billed Sparrow, the Black-striped Sparrow adds a special touch to lowland and middle-elevation forests with its distinctive song—an accelerating series of about two dozen chirps that start slowly and continue with increasing frequency to a trill at the end. It gives the impression of a bird trying to start its motor. This sparrow has a gray head with two black stripes on top of the head, a black stripe through each eye, a black bill, and olive-yellow back, tail, and wings. The sides are light gray fading to white on the belly, and there are yellow highlights on the outer edges of the primary wing feathers. Sexes are identical.

The Black-striped Sparrow lives in moist and wet forest edges, thickets, young second growth, weed patches, gardens, shade coffee plantations, and banana plantations. Living as pairs or in family groups, this sparrow explores short trees, shrubs, and ground cover for insects, small frogs, lizards, bananas, corn, berries, and small seeds.

On the Caribbean slope, this sparrow can be seen and heard from Caño Negro Lodge in the Río Frío region to Tortuguero and Cahuita NPs, Tortuga Lodge, El Pizote Lodge, La Selva, Selva Verde Lodge, Lost Iguana Resort, Sueño Azul, El Gavilán Lodge, Rara Avis, and Rancho Naturalista. On the Pacific slope, the Black-striped Sparrow inhabits Carara, Manuel Antonio, and Corcovado NPs and forested sites at San Isidro del General, Los Cusingos, Hotel Villa Lapas, Las Esquinas Rainforest Lodge, Rancho Casa Grande, Talari Mountain Lodge, Lapa Ríos, Corcovado Lodge Tent Camp, Tiskita Jungle Lodge, and the Wilson Botanical Garden, where it visits the feeders for bananas.

STRIPE-HEADED SPARROW

The Stripe-headed Sparrow is a distinctive sparrow of the Guanacaste dry forest. Its black mask through the eye and paired black stripes over the top of the head make it easy to distinguish. It inhabits brushy forest edges, roadsides, and fencerows and can be seen in gardens of ranches, farms, and backyards throughout Guanacaste. The range extends south at least to Carara NP.

In a towheelike manner, this sparrow forages in groups and hops along the ground in search of small seeds and occasional invertebrates. The Stripe-headed Sparrow sleeps in communal groups in trees, and when raising young a group of sparrows attends the offspring.

The Stripe-headed Sparrow may be seen along roadsides and at ranches and lodges throughout most of Guanacaste and south to Carara NP and Hotel Villa Lapas. They occur east to Rincón de la Vieja NP and along the road to Monteverde, and sightings have been reported along the Pacific coast south to Dominical.

Aimophila ruficauda
Costa Rican name: *Sabanero cabecilistado.*
12/23 trips; 35 sightings.
Status: Permanent resident.
Length: 7 inches.
Weight: 1.2 ounces (35 grams).
Range: North-central Mexico to northwestern Costa Rica.
Elevational range: Sea level to 2,600 feet.

Stripe-headed Sparrow adult

RUFOUS-COLLARED SPARROW

Zonotrichia capensis
Costa Rican names: *Come maíz; pirrís; chingolo.*
23/23 trips; 209 sightings.
Status: Permanent resident.
Length: 5.25 inches.
Weight: 0.7 ounce (20 grams).
Range: Southeastern Mexico to Tierra del Fuego; Hispaniola.
Elevational range: 2,000–10,000 feet.

Well known throughout Costa Rica, the Rufous-collared Sparrow has a broad distribution that ranges from middle elevations to 10,000 feet. Known as *come maíz* to Ticos, the nickname means "corn eater." This attractive sparrow has a short black crest and a gray face. Two black stripes extend from the back corner of each eye and the lower mandible. The chin and throat are white. Black spots on each side of the throat create a bow-tie look. The most conspicuous marking is the rufous collar over the back of the neck. The back and wings have a streaked pattern of brown, rufous, and black. Sexes are similar. Young birds have a streaked breast, indistinct collar, and no bow tie. The distinctive song is a three-note slurred whistle with a thin, high tone, a lower tone, and a third note that slurs from a higher to lower note. Described as a "drink-your-tea" phrase, it is reminiscent of the whistled song of an Eastern Meadowlark.

Mated pairs remain together on their territory all year and nest throughout the year. Their territories include backyards, gardens, shade coffee plantations, croplands, pastures, and shrubby forest edges. This abundant sparrow hops on the ground in search of fallen weed seeds and insects. It will come to feeders for cooked rice.

The adaptable Rufous-collared Sparrow is a common backyard bird that can be found at middle and high elevations throughout the length of Costa Rica, including the Central Plateau and downtown San José. The male's tendency to sing from high perches makes this bird easy to see.

Rufous-collared Sparrow adult and young

VOLCANO JUNCO

One of Costa Rica's most highly sought endemic birds is the Volcano Junco. Its distribution extends only from the Turrialba volcano to western Panama. It is found at or above the treeline (about 10,000 feet), in shrubby, bamboo-dominated paramo atop the Irazú and Turrialba volcanoes, in Cerro de la Muerte, and at high elevations of the Talamanca Mountains to the Panama border. The Volcano Junco has a large sparrowlike body, brownish above and grayish below, with black streaking over the back. Its unique features are its yellow eyes, pink bill, and flesh-colored legs. The yellow eyes are surrounded by black shading that gives this bird a sinister look.

As is characteristic of juncos, this species hops and runs along the ground, amid bamboo thickets, in search of insects, spiders, fallen seeds, and berries. It is often encountered as pairs or in family groups.

The best place to look for the Volcano Junco is along the access road leading from the Pan American Highway at kilometer 90 up to the transmission towers in Cerro de la Muerte (elevation 11,450 feet).

Junco vulcani
Costa Rican name: *Junco paramero.*
10/23 trips; 14 sightings.
Status: Permanent resident.
Length: 6.3 inches.
Weight: 1 ounce (28 grams).
Range: Endemic to highlands from Costa Rica to western Panama.
Elevational range: 8,500–12,000 feet.

Volcano Junco adult, showing yellow eyes and pink legs

STREAKED SALTATOR

*Saltator striatipectus (formerly
    Saltator albicollis)*
Costa Rican name: *Saltator listado.*
10/23 trips; 26 sightings.
Status: Permanent resident.
Length: 7.25 inches.
Weight: 1.4 ounces (40 grams).
Range: Costa Rica to Peru; Lesser
    Antilles.
Elevational range: Sea level to
    6,000 feet.

Costa Rica has four saltators: Black-headed, Buff-throated, Grayish, and Streaked. The Streaked Saltator is the only saltator in Costa Rica with a streaked pattern of brownish stripes on a white breast. The bill has a typical saltator profile—with an extremely thick base. The back is yellowish olive, the tail is grayish, and the gray head has a white stripe above each eye. Sexes are identical.

Inhabitants of forest edges, shrubby thickets, second growth, brushy pastures, and backyard gardens, Streaked Saltators live as pairs. Foods include fruits, flower petals, young leaf buds, ants, beetles, and slow-moving insects.

The Streaked Saltator is found only in the southern Pacific lowlands. It can be seen at Vista del Valle Restaurant, Los Cusingos, Talari Mountain Lodge, brushy woodlots and hedges near San Isidro del General, Lapa Ríos, Corcovado NP, Corcovado Lodge Tent Camp, and Tiskita Jungle Lodge. It is regularly encountered at the Wilson Botanical Garden at San Vito.

Streaked Saltator adult

GRAYISH SALTATOR

Like other saltators, the Grayish Saltator has an oversized bill that is long, straight, and very thick at the base. The body is uniformly gray, with buffy areas near the flanks. There is a white line above the eye, a small white spot under the lower eyelid, and a small white throat patch edged by a short black stripe on each side. The throat patch does not have the bib appearance of the Buff-throated and Black-headed Saltators. Sexes are identical.

This saltator inhabits forest edges, brushy fields, second growth, shade coffee plantations, and backyard gardens with hedges—even in San José. Pairs stay together throughout the year and search for fruits, flowers, leaf buds and new leaves, vine tendrils, and insects. It will visit feeders for bananas.

Grayish Saltator adult

This saltator has an unusual distribution that includes the Central Plateau (Hotel Bougainvillea and Xandari Plantation Resort), Sarchí, San José, and brushy pastures and second growth on middle elevation slopes of Barva, Poás, and probably Irazú volcanoes up to about 6,000 feet. It is also found at Caño Negro Lodge and NWR, Tilajari Resort, and Muelle and eastward from the Central Plateau to La Selva, Sueño Azul, Turrialba, Rancho Naturalista, and the Wilson Botanical Garden at San Vito.

Saltator coerulescens
Costa Rican names: *Sensontle; sinsonte; saltator grisáceo.*
16/23 trips; 35 sightings.
Status: Permanent resident.
Length: 8 inches.
Weight: 1.8 ounces (52 grams).
Range: Northwestern Mexico to eastern Brazil.
Elevational range: Sea level to 6,000 feet.

BUFF-THROATED SALTATOR

Saltator maximus
Costa Rican names: *Sinsonte verde; saltator gorgianteado.*
23/23 trips; 151 sightings.
Status: Permanent resident.
Length: 8 inches.
Weight: 1.8 ounces (50 grams).
Range: Southeastern Mexico to southeastern Brazil.
Elevational range: Sea level to 5,000 feet.

The Buff-throated Saltator is the most common saltator in Costa Rica. It has a small white chin patch with a conspicuous bib that is buffy and edged with black. The head is gray with a slender white line above each eye. The back is olive-green, and the breast and belly are light grayish brown. This large, heavy-bodied songbird has a long, thick bill, which is characteristic of saltators. Sexes are identical. The song is a series of chirps and warbles reminiscent of a thrush.

The Buff-throated Saltator inhabits forest edges, shade coffee plantations, second growth, and gardens. It seeks out fruits, insects, and soft plant materials like flowers and buds. Traveling in pairs, this bird sometimes accompanies Cherrie's or Passerini's Tanagers. It will follow army ants to catch escaping insects and visits backyard bird feeders to eat bananas.

This saltator lives in moist and wet lowland and middle-elevation habitats. Along the Caribbean slope, it occurs from Tortuguero NP to Cahuita NP and inland to Guapiles, Puerto Viejo en Sarapiquí, and Turrialba. It is common at La Selva, Selva Verde Lodge, El Gavilán Lodge, Rancho Naturalista, and Tilajari Resort. It is common throughout the southern Pacific lowlands.

Buff-throated Saltator adult

BLACK-HEADED SALTATOR

The Black-headed Saltator is the largest saltator in Costa Rica. The back and tail are yellowish olive, the top of the head is black, and the sides of the face and head are gray. There is a white line above each eye. The large bib marking on the upper chest is white edged with black on the sides. The bill is long and extremely thick at the base. The habitat preferences and foods are similar to those of the Buff-throated Saltator, but the Black-headed Saltator has a stronger affinity for locations near water. It travels in family groups but often is difficult to see. A vocal species, its repertoire includes loud chirps, a unique smacking note, and a wrenlike bubbling phrase ("I-thought-it-sounded-like-this").

This distinctive saltator, which ranges from central Mexico to eastern Panama, is a bird of Caribbean lowland and middle elevations to about 4,000 feet. It occurs from Limón to Cahuita and El Pizote Lodge and inland to La Selva, Turrialba, Rancho Naturalista, Sueño Azul, Lost Iguana Resort, and Tilajari Resort, where it comes to the feeders for bananas and papayas.

Saltator atriceps
Costa Rican name: *Saltator cabecinegro.*
14/23 trips; 53 sightings.
Status: Permanent resident.
Length: 9.4 inches.
Weight: 3 ounces (85 grams).
Range: Central Mexico to eastern Panama.
Elevational range: Sea level to 4,300 feet.

Black-headed Saltator adult

Black-faced Grosbeak adult

Caryothraustes poliogaster
Costa Rican name: *Picogrueso carinegro.*
8/23 trips; 16 sightings.
Status: Permanent resident.
Length: 6.5 inches.
Weight: 1.3 ounces (36 grams).
Range: Southeastern Mexico to central Panama.
Elevational range: Sea level to 3,000 feet.

BLACK-FACED GROSBEAK

There are six species of grosbeaks in Costa Rica. The Rose-breasted Grosbeak and the accidental Black-headed Grosbeak are migratory species. The other four are permanent residents, including the Black-thighed Grosbeak of the mountains, the Blue-black Grosbeak of the Caribbean and Pacific lowlands, and two species found only in the Caribbean lowlands, the Slate-colored Grosbeak and the Black-faced Grosbeak. The Slate-colored Grosbeak is all gray with a white throat patch and bright red bill. The Black-faced Grosbeak is a small species with a yellow head and breast, olive-green body, pale gray belly, and distinctive black face and chin.

This social species travels in vocal and conspicuous groups of up to thirty birds, which may include other forest birds like tanagers and honeycreepers. With buzzing notes and whistles, they search for insects, caterpillars, berries, nectar, and ripe fruits like guavas. The song is usually a sweet whistled phrase that matches the expression "One-two-three-cherry-two."

This attractive grosbeak may be seen at La Selva, lower levels of Braulio Carrillo NP (the Tapir Trail), and Rara Avis. One of the most dependable sites is along the entry road to Sueño Azul Resort south of La Selva. Fruiting trees along the road provide a dependable food source for the grosbeaks.

BLACK-THIGHED GROSBEAK

Among Costa Rica's distinctive and easily identified highland songbirds is the endemic Black-thighed Grosbeak. This nonmigratory species has the short, thick bill characteristic of grosbeaks. The body is straw-yellow with black wings, back, and tail. A small black mask highlights the face, and there is a small white spot at the base of the primary wing feathers. This species gets its name from the black thighs that contrast with the yellow underparts. It is closely related to the Yellow Grosbeak of Mexico and Guatemala and the Golden-bellied Grosbeak of South America. The beautiful song consists of about seven to eight slurred, whistled notes that alternately rise and fall, ending with a slow trill. The phrases within the song approximately match the expression "Look at me, you can't catch me—find me," followed by the trill.

An inhabitant of highland forests, the Black-thighed Grosbeak occurs in mature cloud forests and montane oak forests through the length of the country. It is associated with mature forests, older second growth, forest edges, and mountain pastures with scattered mature trees. Single birds or pairs usually forage in the forest canopy for fruits, seeds, and insects. They sometimes descend to shrubs to feed on berries.

Although found from the Cordillera of Tilarán to western Panama, this beautiful grosbeak is most abundant in the Talamanca Mountains. Look for the Black-thighed Grosbeak along the road at La Virgen del Socorro, at upper levels of Braulio Carrillo and Tapantí NPs, in the San Gerardo de Dota Valley including Savegre Mountain Lodge, and along the Pan American Highway in Cerro de la Muerte at kilometer 66.

Pheucticus tibialis
Costa Rican name: *Picogrueso vientriamarillo.*
13/23 trips; 18 sightings.
Status: Permanent resident.
Length: 8 inches.
Weight: 2.5 ounces (70 grams).
Range: Endemic to highlands of Costa Rica and western Panama.
Elevational range: 3,300–8,500 feet.

Black-thighed Grosbeak adult

ROSE-BREASTED GROSBEAK

Pheuticus ludovicianus
Costa Rican name: *Picogrueso pechirosado.*
20/23 trips; 69 sightings.
Status: Northern migrant.
Length: 7–8 inches.
Weight: 1.6 ounces (45 grams).
Range: Breeds from Canada to eastern and central United States; winters from central Mexico to Peru.
Elevational range: Sea level to 5,000 feet.

The Rose-breasted Grosbeak is a common and regular migrant throughout much of the country from September through May. The male is unmistakable, with its cherry-red breast, black head, and thick pale bill. The chunky female is streaked brownish over the back, with two white wing bars, a pale bill, and a brown head with a white stripe over the eye. The white breast is heavily streaked.

An inhabitant of forest edges, plantations, gardens, and pastures with scattered trees, small groups of Rose-breasted Grosbeaks are conspicuous as they travel in small flocks. This species forages for insects, palm fruits, and berries. It also visits bird feeders to eat ripe bananas and papayas. In the past, live-trapping of Rose-breasted Grosbeaks for use as caged songbirds has been a problem.

Among the locations where Rose-breasted Grosbeaks can be seen in the Caribbean lowlands are the Lake Arenal area, La Selva, and Guapiles. In Guanacaste, it has been observed at the Hotel Borinquen Mountain Resort and Hacienda Solimar. At middle and higher elevations of the Caribbean lowlands, it has been encountered at Monteverde, La Virgen del Socorro, La Paz Waterfall Gardens, Rancho Naturalista, and the grounds of Hotel Bougainvillea in Santo Domingo de Heredia. In the southern Pacific lowlands and middle elevations, it has been seen in the San Gerardo de Dota Valley, Savegre Mountain Lodge, Talari Mountain Lodge, Vista del Valle Restaurant, Hotel del Sur at San Isidro del General, and the Wilson Botanical Garden.

Rose-breasted Grosbeak adult male

Rose-breasted Grosbeak adult female

EASTERN MEADOWLARK

Several migratory birds in North America have evolved in Costa Rica into nonmigratory permanent residents, including Red-tailed Hawks, Red-winged Blackbirds, and Eastern Meadowlarks. Eastern Meadowlarks have become more abundant as tropical forests have been cleared and converted to pastures that provide grassland habitats for them. There are no Western Meadowlarks in Costa Rica.

Eastern Meadowlarks are similar to those found in the eastern United States. They have a streaked brownish back, bright yellow breast and belly, and a black chevron on the breast. The species is conspicuous as it perches on roadside fence posts and forages in grassy areas, airport properties, and pastures from lowlands to highlands. Foods include insects, caterpillars, invertebrates, fruits, and berries.

This adaptable species may be encountered in the Caribbean lowlands at Muelle, Los Chiles, El Gavilán Lodge, and Guapiles. It is most abundant in Guanacaste and has been seen at La Ensenada Lodge, Hotel Borinquen Mountain Resort, Palo Verde NP, La Pacífica, and Hacienda Solimar. At higher elevations it occurs at Cartago, Pavas, and Monteverde. In the southern Pacific lowlands, the Eastern Meadowlark and a close relative, the Red-breasted Blackbird, have been seen in pastures between the Pan American Highway and Las Esquinas Rainforest Lodge.

Sturnella magna
Costa Rican name: *Zacatero común.*
18/23 trips; 51 sightings.
Status: Permanent resident (not a migrant).
Length: 7.8 inches.
Weight: 3 ounces (86 grams).
Range: Southeastern Canada to Brazil.
Elevational range: Sea level to 8,200 feet.

Eastern Meadowlark adult

GREAT-TAILED GRACKLE

Quiscalus mexicanus
Costa Rican names: *Sanate;*
zanate; zanate grande.
23/23 trips; 269 sightings.
Status: Permanent resident.
Length: 17 inches.
Weight: 4.4–8.1 ounces (125–230
grams).
Range: Southwestern United
States to northwestern Peru.
Elevational range: Sea level to
5,000 feet.

Like grackles everywhere, the Great-tailed Grackle is widely distributed and little appreciated. It is common around farms, towns, and cities, where it adapts to all the nesting sites and food sources that humans inadvertently provide them. In bright sunlight, the black male grackle has purple, greenish, and blue iridescent highlights. It is nearly twice the size of the female, which has more subdued brown to grayish-black plumage. This grackle makes its presence known by a wide variety of assorted chirps, clucks, squeaks, and metallic toots and whistles.

Grackles occur in open, cleared, and settled areas in lowland and middle elevations of both slopes. Early in the twentieth century it was found only along the Pacific coast, but it had spread to the Caribbean slope by the 1960s and into the Central Plateau by the 1970s. It is usually regarded as a pest, because it eats the eggs and young of songbirds as well as fruits, berries, and grain on farms and plantations. This omnivorous bird eats lizards, dragonflies, millipedes, snails, mice, toads, grasshoppers, carrion, food scraps, small fish, spiders, crayfish, salamanders, frogs, and snakes.

The Great-tailed Grackle nests from January through July in loose aggregations or colonies. Both males and females are promiscuous. The young stay with the female for up to ten weeks after fledging. Large groups frequently become a nuisance when they roost together at night in yards, parks, or gardens. This abundant bird is found throughout most settled areas of Costa Rica and is scarce only in large areas of unbroken forest and at montane levels.

Great-tailed Grackle adult male

Great-tailed Grackle adult female

YELLOW-TAILED ORIOLE

Of the seven orioles in Costa Rica, three are migrants and four are residents. The migrants include Baltimore, Bullock's, and Orchard Orioles. The four residents are the Yellow-tailed, Black-cowled, Spot-breasted, and Streak-backed Orioles. Black-cowled and Yellow-tailed Orioles are found in the Caribbean lowlands. Streak-backed and Spot-breasted Orioles inhabit the Guanacaste dry forest. The Yellow-tailed Oriole is bright yellow with a black face and bib, black shoulders and wings, and a tail with yellow outer feathers and black central feathers. Sexes are similar.

Yellow-tailed Oriole adult

The Yellow-tailed Oriole inhabits moist and wet lowland second-growth forests, forest edges, roadsides, low wet areas, and thick vegetation near water. These birds are usually observed in pairs as they glean invertebrates from the surface of vegetation. Ripe fruits are also eaten.

This oriole's musical, wrenlike song was described by Dr. Alexander Skutch: "In the mellowest of voices, he would repeat over and over, with hardly a pause, a verse of five, six, or rarely more notes, then choose a wholly different phrase, of which he had great variety, and reiterate it in the same delightful manner" (1996:187). This beautiful song has been the species' undoing. It has become extremely rare because people trap it to keep it as a cage bird.

The Yellow-tailed Oriole may be seen on the grounds of Tortuga Lodge and at La Selva.

Icterus mesomelas
Costa Rican names: *Chiltote;*
   chiltotle; bolsero coliamarillo.
3/23 trips; 7 sightings.
Status: Permanent resident.
Length: 9 inches.
Weight: 2.5 ounces (70 grams).
Range: Southern Mexico to
   western Peru.
Elevational range: Sea level to
   1,000 feet.

Spot-breasted Oriole adult

Icterus pectoralis
Costa Rican name: *Bolsero
pechimanchado.*
3/23 trips; 9 sightings.
Status: Permanent resident.
Length: 8.2 inches.
Weight: 1.7 ounces (50 grams).
Range: Central Mexico to Costa
Rica; introduced to Florida and
Cocos Island.
Elevational range: Sea level to
1,650 feet.

SPOT-BREASTED ORIOLE

Five different orioles may be seen in the Guana-caste region. The Orchard, Bullock's, and Balti-more Orioles are northern migrants. The other two are resident orioles characteristic of tropical dry forests: the Streak-backed and Spot-breasted Orioles. In each case, the name provides the key to species identification. Both resident orioles are yellowish orange with a black face and bib and a black tail. The Streak-backed Oriole, how-ever, has orange and black streaking on the back, and the Spot-breasted Oriole has black spots on the front and sides of the upper breast. Sexes are similar.

The Spot-breasted Oriole inhabits groves of trees at farms and ranches as well as woodlands along rivers and in backyard gardens of towns and cities. The diet includes insects found by exploring foliage. Nectar is also taken at flowering trees, including species of *Caesalpinia, Eryth-rina, Inga, Calliandra,* and *Gliricidia,* and from the orange flowers of *Combretum* vines. Dr. Alexander Skutch had a very high regard for the beautiful song of the Spot-breasted Oriole. In his book *Orioles, Blackbirds, and Their Kin,* he ranked it as "the finest oriole's song that I know, a little better even than the song of the Yellow-backed Oriole, to which it is very similar. . . . the song blended a series of the clearest, most mellifluous whistles into a con-tinuous liquid stream of melody." The song has about nine notes and sounds like "It cheers and cheers, and it gives you cheer" (188).

The Spot-breasted Oriole has been observed in Guana-caste at La Ensenada Lodge, Palo Verde NP, and Hacienda Solimar.

BALTIMORE ORIOLE (NORTHERN ORIOLE)

One of the most common Neotropical migrants in Costa Rica is the Baltimore Oriole. Formerly known as the Northern Oriole, it has a black head and shoulders with a bright orange breast, belly, and rump. The wings are black with single white wing bars and white edging on the primaries. The female is yellowish orange with black wings and single white wing bars.

The Baltimore Oriole inhabits the canopy of dry, moist, and wet forests and is abundant in farm woodlots, among trees of living fencerows, and in shade coffee plantations, orchards, and backyard gardens. This songbird has benefited from the extensive use of *Inga, Erythrina, Calliandra,* bananas (*Musa*), and citrus trees by humans. It eats flowers, nectar, and fruits from those plants. Other foods include nectar of *Combretum* vines, balsa (*Ochroma*), *Ceiba*, and *Norantea* flowers.

One of the most delightful birding experiences in Costa Rica is watching an *Erythrina* or *Inga* tree in full bloom, alive with a feeding frenzy of Baltimore Orioles, Tennessee Warblers, Rufous-tailed Hummingbirds, Clay-colored Thrushes, Hoffmann's Woodpeckers, and Palm and Blue-gray Tanagers. Additional foods taken by Baltimore Orioles include insects and spiders.

This migratory oriole is present from early September to early May. It winters on both slopes at lowland and middle elevations and sporadically at higher elevations. The greatest abundance is in Guanacaste, the Río Frío region, Caribbean lowlands, and the Central Plateau.

Icterus galbula
Costa Rican names: *Cacicón; cacique veranero; bolsero norteño.*
23/23 trips; 258 sightings.
Status: Northern migrant.
Length: 7 inches.
Weight: 1.2 ounces (34 grams).
Range: Southeastern Canada to eastern United States; winters from central Mexico to northern South America.
Elevational range: Sea level to 7,200 feet.

Baltimore Oriole adult male

Scarlet-rumped Cacique adult displaying

Cacicus uropygialis
Costa Rican names: *Plío; cacique lomiescarlata.*
21/23 trips; 65 sightings.
Status: Permanent resident.
Length: 9 inches.
Weight: 2.4 ounces (68 grams).
Range: Northeastern Honduras to northeastern Peru.
Elevational range: Sea level to 3,600 feet.

Scarlet-rumped Caciques sometimes place their nest by a wasp nest to help protect their nest from predators.

SCARLET-RUMPED CACIQUE

At first glance, the Scarlet-rumped Cacique is easily mistaken for a Passerini's or Cherrie's Tanager. All are black with a bright red rump patch. The cacique, however, has a slender, pointed bill that is pale ivory, and the eyes are blue. The tanagers have shorter, thicker bills that are silvery white with a black tip, and their eyes are chestnut-brown.

An inhabitant of moist and wet forest regions, the Scarlet-rumped Cacique is found in both Caribbean and southern Pacific lowlands. In groups of four to ten birds, it forages through the forest canopy searching for caterpillars, insects, spiders, small lizards, berries, seeds, and nectar. It also explores foliage in second growth, edges of forest openings, and scattered trees in cleared areas. It feeds on insects by gleaning them from nooks and crannies of twigs, branches, dead curled leaves, and palm fronds. This species is often encountered in mixed flocks that include oropendolas, flycatchers, nunbirds, trogons, and Black-faced Grosbeaks.

The Scarlet-rumped Cacique is monogamous and nests from February through June. The female builds a solitary pendulous nest, about two feet long, from fine black plant fibers that are gathered from epiphtyes. The nest is often placed over water at the tip of a branch near a wasp nest. Wasps attack any potential predators that may approach the cacique nest. The call is a rapid series of high-pitched whistled notes, "Pieu-pieu-pieu-pieu-pieu-pieu." The pitch may change during the calling.

This cacique is regularly observed in the Caribbean lowlands at Tortuguero and Cahuita NPs, Tortuga Lodge, Puerto Viejo, La Selva, Selva Verde Lodge, Sueño Azul, El Gavilán Lodge, and Rancho Naturalista. In the southern Pacific lowlands, it occurs at La Cusinga, Las Esquinas Rainforest Lodge, Corcovado NP, Sirena Biological Station, Corcovado Lodge Tent Camp, and Tiskita Jungle Lodge.

Scarlet-rumped Cacique at nest

CRESTED OROPENDOLA

Several species of birds have expanded their range from Panama to southern Costa Rica in the past ten to fifteen years, including the Pearl Kite, Southern Lapwing, and Crested Oropendola. Each is now nesting in Costa Rica. There are two species of oropendola in southern Costa Rica near the Panama border, the Chestnut-headed and the Crested Oropendolas. The Chestnut-headed Oropendola has a chestnut head and a bone-white bill. The Crested Oropendola has a black head with a bone-white bill.

Like other oropendolas, this species lives in colonies at the top of tall trees where their long, pendulous nests are safe from most predators. Its habitat includes mixed forest and pasture where there is a variety of food, including fruits (mango, *Cordia lutea*), seeds (*Inga*), nectar, invertebrates, and small vertebrates.

The current range of the Crested Oropendola is only in extreme southern Costa Rica near San Vito las Cruces. A colony can be seen along the road from San Vito en route to Paso Canoas near Villa Neily. Inquire at the Wilson Botanical Garden about the location of other colonies in the area.

Psarocolius decumanus
Costa Rican name: *Oropéndola crestada.*
1/23 trips; 1 sighting.
Status: Permanent resident.
Length: 13–17 inches.
Weight: 4.4–11.8 ounces (124–335 grams).
Range: Expanded to Costa Rica from Panama in 1999.
Elevational range: 300–4,500 feet.

Crested Oropendola nesting colony

Crested Oropendola adult

Chestnut-headed Oropendola adult

Psarocolius wagleri
Costa Rican name: *Oropéndola cabecicastaña.*
15/23 trips; 43 sightings.
Status: Permanent resident.
Length: 10.6–13.8 inches.
Weight: 3.9–7.5 ounces (110–212 grams).
Range: Southern Mexico to northwestern Ecuador.
Elevational range: Sea level to 5,500 feet.

CHESTNUT-HEADED OROPENDOLA

The Chestnut-headed Oropendola is a crow-sized member of the blackbird family, with a black body, a chestnut-colored head, a black tail with yellow edges, pale blue eyes, and a huge yellowish-ivory bill. The upper bill extends to the top of the head in a bizarre casque configuration that may give extra resonance to its unusual call, which sounds like several drops of water loudly falling into a pool. Males are twice as large as females.

The Chestnut-headed Oropendola lives in lowland and middle-elevation forests of the Caribbean slope and in the southern Pacific region near the Panama border. It inhabits mature forests, forest edges, and clearings where tall, solitary trees provide secure nesting sites for their colonies. A colony usually includes thirty to forty pairs. Flocks of oropendolas roam the forest searching for ripe fruits, bananas, *Cecropia* catkins, nectar, and invertebrates.

At the onset of the nesting season (April), the female weaves an intricate pendulous nest at the end of a tree branch. Each female lays two or three eggs. Some nesting colonies are built in the presence of wasp nests or stingless bee colonies (*Trigona*). These insects attack and kill parasitic botfly larvae (*Philornis*) that infest the skin of newly hatched oropendolas. In colonies not protected by bees or wasps, oropendolas tolerate visits by Giant Cowbirds, which lay eggs in their nests. Baby cowbirds pluck botfly larvae off oropendola chicks and eat the larvae, which helps oropendolas survive. This long-lived species may live and reproduce for more than twenty-six years.

Look for Chestnut-headed Oropendolas on the Caribbean slope near Cahuita, El Pizote Lodge, and La Selva and in the Guapiles lowlands at the lower levels of Braulio Carrillo NP. They visit the feeders at Rancho Naturalista to eat bananas and are common at Tapantí NP. In the southern Pacific lowlands, they occur at the Wilson Botanical Garden.

MONTEZUMA OROPENDOLA

The imposing—and noisy—Montezuma Oropendola is twice as large as the Chestnut-headed Oropendola. Its colorful facial markings include pale blue fleshy areas on its cheeks, pinkish to orange fleshy wattles under the cheeks, and a black bill tipped with reddish orange. The body is chestnut brown with a black head and chest. The central two tail feathers are black, and the remainder of the tail is yellow.

Montezuma Oropendola adult male

The calls of the Montezuma Oropendola are among the most impressive sounds of the rainforest. Perched on a horizontal branch, the male gives its distinctive call, a resonant gurgling, bubbling series of ascending notes, as it tips upside down and flops out its wings. The call resembles the sound of bubbles rising in a water cooler, but the tones are more metallic. This impressive display attracts females in the promiscuous colony, where the females outnumber males by three to one.

This oropendola inhabits lowland and middle elevations of the Caribbean slope and eastern portions of Guanacaste. It occurs in forested and semiforested habitats where tall, solitary trees provide ideal sites for nesting colonies. These colonies may contain thirty to sixty pendulous nests, hanging from the end of slender branches that are too small to support the weight of approaching predators. Flocks range through moist and wet forests in search of ripe fruits, bananas, *Cecropia* catkins, nectar of banana (*Musa*) and balsa (*Ochroma*) flowers, small vertebrates, and invertebrates.

Nesting behavior is similar to that of the Chestnut-headed Oropendola. The female does all the nest building, incubation, and care of the young. The finely woven pendulous nests are slightly longer than Chestnut-headed Oropendola nests—from three to six feet long. The male oropendola could be considered something of a male chauvinist. He watches the female build the nest, and if he does not like her handiwork, he will tear it apart and make her start over. Actually, this behavior helps to ensure that the final nest will be durable enough to

Psarocolius montezuma
Costa Rican name: *Oropéndola de Montezuma.*
21/23 trips; 180 sightings.
Status: Permanent resident.
Length: 15–20 inches.
Weight: 8.1–18.3 ounces (230–520 grams).
Range: Southern Mexico to central Panama.
Elevational range: Sea level to 5,000 feet.

Montezuma Oropendola adult male displaying. Photo taken with permission at the Milwaukee Public Museum.

withstand use and weather through the nesting period.

The Montezuma Oropendola is common throughout the Caribbean lowlands. It can be seen at Rancho Naturalista near Turrialba and is found in the Central Plateau at Hotel Bougainvillea, Casa de Finca, Cachí Reservoir, Curridabat, and Tapantí NP. In Guanacaste it can be found at Cañas, Tilarán Mountains, Río Lagarto, La Ensenada Lodge, Hacienda Solimar, Palo Verde NP, and Hotel Borinquen Mountain Resort and along the road from the Pan American Highway to Monteverde.

LESSER GOLDFINCH

The Lesser Goldfinch is a well-known bird of the western and southwestern United States, but like the Acorn Woodpecker and Magnificent Hummingbird, its range extends through Central America at higher elevations. In the United States, the Lesser Goldfinch occurs in two color phases; in one the male has an iridescent blue-black back, and in the other the male has a greenish back. Males of the Costa Rican variety have a blue-black back. The population in Costa Rica extends from the Central Plateau southward in premontane and lower montane forests, mainly at an elevation of 3,900 to 7,200 feet, along the Pacific slope of the Talamanca Mountains to Panama. This population is geographically isolated from Lesser Goldfinches found farther north in the United States, Mexico, and Central America and from the same species in Venezuela, Ecuador, Colombia, and Peru.

The Lesser Goldfinch differs from another finch of the highlands in southern Costa Rica, the Yellow-bellied Siskin. The siskin is also black with a yellow belly, but it has a black bib and a yellow wing patch.

The Lesser Goldfinch has adapted well to disturbed habitats, roadsides, fields, pastures, and plantations, where it seeks out seeds of composite flowers, thistles, berries, flower petals, flower buds, and a few small insects. This great variety of foods undoubtedly has helped the Lesser Goldfinch adapt to many habitats in North, Central, and South America.

Look for the Lesser Goldfinch in the San Gerardo de Dota Valley, in Cerro de la Muerte, and also in the vicinity of San Vito las Cruces, including the Wilson Botanical Garden.

Spinus psaltria*
Costa Rican name: *Jilguero minor.*
7/23 trips; 12 sightings.
Status: Permanent resident.
Length: 4 inches.
Weight: 0.35 ounce (10 grams).
Range: Northwestern United States to Peru.
Elevational range: 2,800–9,000 feet.

Lesser Goldfinch adult male

*This species was recently reassigned by the AOU to the family Mohoidae.

Thick-billed Euphonia adult male

Thick-billed Euphonia adult female

Thick-billed Euphonia subadult male plumage

Euphonia laniirostris
Costa Rican names: *Agüío; eufonia piquigruesa.*
16/23 trips; 45 sightings.
Status: Permanent resident.
Length: 4.25 inches.
Weight: 0.5 ounce (15 grams).
Range: Costa Rica to eastern Brazil.
Elevational range: Sea level to 4,000 feet.

THICK-BILLED EUPHONIA

Euphonias have recently undergone a dramatic change in identity. Previously, they were considered tanagers, but DNA studies have shown that they are actually in the family Fringillidae, along with goldfinches and siskins. Short, chunky birds with small bills, they have a green or gunmetal-blue back and yellow belly, with varying patterns of yellow, powder blue, or rufous on the forehead, crown, and throat. There are nine euphonias in Costa Rica: the Yellow-crowned, Yellow-throated, Spot-crowned, Tawny-capped, Elegant, Olive-backed, Scrub, White-vented, and Thick-billed. Look at the pattern of yellow on the forehead and throat to distinguish them.

The Thick-billed Euphonia is yellow on the forehead and crown. The throat is yellow. The Yellow-throated Euphonia is similar but has yellow only on the forehead (not on the crown), and the vent is white, whereas the vent is yellow on the Thick-billed Euphonia. The female Thick-billed Euphonia is greenish olive above and yellowish olive below. A subadult male is similar to the female but has a yellow forehead and black face mask that extends from the bill to the eye and upper cheek area.

The Thick-billed Euphonia forages in small groups in second growth, forest edges, gardens, and pastures where shrubs provide fruits and small berries from melastomes and mistletoes. They also come to feeders for bananas. Sometimes this euphonia forages with mixed flocks of tanagers and honeycreepers.

This monogamous bird nests from March through September. Two or three broods may be raised each season. This is the only euphonia whose young of the previous year apparently help the parents care for the young hatched the following year.

The Thick-billed Euphonia is found only in southern Pacific lowland and middle-elevation forests from Carara NP southeast to Villa Caletas, La Cusinga, Las Esquinas Rainforest Lodge, Rancho Casa Grande, Manuel Antonio and Corcovado NPs, Corcovado Lodge Tent Camp, and Tiskita Jungle Lodge. The best place to see it is at the Wilson Botanical Garden at San Vito, where it regularly visits the bird feeders to eat bananas.

YELLOW-THROATED EUPHONIA

Among the nine euphonias found in Costa Rica, only two have yellow on the throat. The others have a black throat. The Thick-billed Euphonia, found only in the southern Pacific region, has a yellow throat and yellow on top of its head that extends from the bill to behind the eyes. The Yellow-throated Euphonia has a yellow throat, but the yellow on the forehead extends only to above the eye, not behind the eye. The female Yellow-throated Euphonia has a body similar to the female Thick-billed Euphonia, with olive above and a yellowish breast. The belly, however, is white on the Yellow-throated and yellow on the Thick-billed Euphonia.

The Yellow-throated Euphonia is found mainly in the humid forests of Guanacaste and rarely in the southern Pacific lowlands where the Thick-billed Euphonia occurs. This species travels in pairs and in small groups as it searches for small fruits and insects. Its preferred habitat includes forest edges, plantations, gallery forests, and second-growth forests. The call is an assortment of high-pitched chirps and slurred warbles.

Look for this uncommon euphonia in the Río Frío region, Caño Negro NWR, Caño Negro Lodge and village, La Ensenada Lodge, Hotel Borinquen Mountain Resort, and Carara NP.

Euphonia hirundinacea
Costa Rican name: *Eufonia gorgiamarilla.*
3/23 trips; 5 sightings.
Status: Permanent resident.
Length: 4 inches.
Weight: 0.4–0.6 ounce (12–18 grams).
Range: Northeastern Mexico to western Panama.
Elevational range: Sea level to 4,600 feet.

Yellow-throated Euphonia adult male

ELEGANT EUPHONIA (BLUE-HOODED EUPHONIA)

Euphonia elegantissima
Costa Rican name: *Eufonia capuchiceleste.*
6/23 trips; 6 sightings.
Status: Permanent resident.
Length: 4 inches.
Weight: 0.5–0.6 ounce (13–17 grams).
Range: Northwestern Mexico to western Panama (subspecies, northwestern Costa Rica to western Panama).
Elevational range: 2,500–6,600 feet.

The Elegant Euphonia lives up to the name "Elegant." Its markings include a powder-blue hood, rufous forehead, gunmetal-blue back, and bay-colored breast. The female is olive-green over the back and yellowish olive on the breast, but it also has a pale blue hood and rufous forehead like the male. It is an endemic subspecies found mainly at middle and lower montane elevations of Costa Rica's mountains, from the Cordillera of Tilarán to western Panama.

The species occurs at middle and upper levels of moist to wet forests and forest edges where epiphytes provide abundant fruits like mistletoe berries. The Elegant Euphonia ventures as pairs and small groups into openings and gardens, where they might be noticed by their trills, whistles, and chirps.

This beautiful euphonia may be encountered from the Tilarán Mountains to the Talamanca Mountains, San Gerardo de Dota Valley, grounds of Savegre Mountain Lodge, Bosque de Paz, La Virgen del Socorro, Talari Mountain Lodge, and the Wilson Botanical Garden.

Elegant Euphonia adult male

SPOT-CROWNED EUPHONIA

The Spot-crowned Euphonia is an endemic bird found only in Costa Rica's southern Pacific lowlands and middle elevations and adjacent areas of Panama. This euphonia has a dark blue throat and yellow on the forehead and crown that covers the top front of the head. Speckles of dark blue in the yellow crown are barely visible but give this euphonia its name. The female is distinctive because the forehead and breast are rufous.

An inhabitant of moist and wet forests at lowland and middle elevations, the Spot-crowned Euphonia usually forages singly or as pairs for ripe fruits and small berries. It visits forest edges and scattered trees and shrubs in open areas to eat guavas (*Psidium guajava*), melastome berries, epiphytes, and the upright fruiting stalks of *Piper* plants. Some insects and caterpillars are also eaten.

This euphonia occurs only in the southern Pacific lowlands. It is rarely seen as far north as Carara NP, but it is commonly encountered from Rancho Casa Grande near Quepos southeast to Corcovado NP, Corcovado Lodge Tent Camp, Lapa Ríos, and Tiskita Jungle Lodge. The best place to see it is at the Wilson Botanical Garden along the River Trail and at the bird feeders there where it eats bananas.

Euphonia imitans
Costa Rican names: *Agüío barranquillo; eufonia vientrirrojiza.*
8/23 trips; 27 sightings.
Status: Permanent resident.
Length: 4 inches.
Weight: 0.5 ounce (14 grams).
Range: Endemic from southwestern Costa Rica to western Panama.
Elevational range: Sea level to 4,500 feet.

Spot-crowned Euphonia adult male   Spot-crowned Euphonia adult female

Olive-backed Euphonia adult male with a yellow forehead. The female has a rufous forehead.

Euphonia gouldi
Costa Rican name: *Eufonia olivácea.*
12/23 trips; 47 sightings.
Status: Permanent resident.
Length: 3.5–3.9 inches.
Weight: 0.4–0.6 ounce (11–16 grams).
Range: Southern Mexico to western Panama.
Elevational range: Sea level to 3,300 feet.

OLIVE-BACKED EUPHONIA

The Olive-backed Euphonia is a common euphonia of the Caribbean lowlands from the Nicaragua border to Panama. It is not as boldly marked as most euphonias. The male is olive-green over the back with a yellow forehead and rufous belly. The female is olive-green with a rufous forehead and rufous belly. The female is similar to the Spot-crowned Euphonia, but that species is found only in the southern Pacific lowlands, so their ranges do not overlap.

This rainforest species travels through the forest in pairs, in small family groups, and in mixed flocks with tanagers, honeycreepers, warblers, and other birds in search of small fruits in the middle to upper canopy. They are typically seen acrobatically feeding on the catkins of *Cecropia* trees at forest openings and in second growth. They also eat the fruits of *Miconia, Urera, Anthurium,* mistletoe, and melastomes. The call is usually a short buzzy whistle that descends from a higher note to a lower note followed by a middle-tone note.

This euphonia can be seen at Caño Negro NWR and vicinity, La Selva (the entry road and Sendero Tres Ríos), Sueño Azul grounds and pastures, Selva Verde Lodge, Tortuga Lodge courtyard and cabin area, Tortuguero NP, Cahuita, El Pizote Lodge, and Rancho Naturalista.

TAWNY-CAPPED EUPHONIA

The Tawny-capped Euphonia, a distinctive euphonia of the Caribbean foothills, is endemic from northwestern Costa Rica to northwestern Colombia. The back and throat of the male are blue-black, like many other euphonias, but the crown is a bright cinnamon-orange. The breast is yellow. The female has an olive-green back with a grayish breast and rufous forehead.

This euphonia inhabits mature montane forests characterized by lots of epiphytes, second growth, and forest clearings. It travels in pairs, family groups, and mixed flocks with other species. Its diet of small fruits includes mistletoe, figs, *Miconia*, *Anthurium*, melastomes, and fruits in the Ericaceae family. The call is usually a high-pitched, double-note whistle, "peeee—peee."

The best place to look for this euphonia is at the bird feeding station at La Paz Waterfall Gardens, where it eats bananas and papayas. It can also be seen at Braulio Carrillo NP (the Tapir Trail and Sendero Botarama), La Virgen del Socorro, and Rancho Naturalista (the forest loop trail and hummingbird meadow).

Euphonia anneae
Costa Rican name: *Eufonia gorricanela.*
11/23 trips; 21 sightings.
Status: Permanent resident.
Length: 4 inches.
Weight: 0.5 ounce (15 grams).
Range: Regional endemic from Costa Rica to northwestern Colombia.
Elevational range: 1,000–6,600 feet.

Tawny-capped Euphonia adult male

Golden-browed Chlorophonia adult male

Chlorophonia callophrys
Costa Rican names: *Ruadlo;*
clorofonia cejidorada.
18/23 trips; 24 sightings.
Status: Permanent resident.
Length: 5.1 inches.
Weight: 0.8 ounce (23–24 grams).
Range: Endemic to highlands of
Costa Rica and western Panama.
Elevational range: 3,000–10,000
feet.

GOLDEN-BROWED CHLOROPHONIA

The Golden-browed Chlorophonia is a tropical beauty that will provide lifetime memories for a birder. Chunky in profile, this bird is endowed with a vivid green body, powder-blue nape and crown, yellow eyebrow marking, and yellow belly. The female is green overall and lacks the yellow eyebrow marking.

The Golden-browed Chlorophonia inhabits moist and wet high-elevation forests among mossy, epiphyte-laden branches that provide food and nesting sites. The preferred habitat includes mature forest, forest edges, shrubby areas adjacent to forest openings, and pastures where sunshine stimulates greater fruiting. Outside the breeding season, flocks of ten to twelve chlorophonias forage for small fruits and berries of mistletoes (*Gaiadendron* and *Psittacanthus*), melastomes, fruits of the blueberry family (*Satyria* and *Psammisia*), and figs. They also glean foliage and twigs for small insects and spiders. The call is an extended series of loud, even-toned clucks given at a rate of about two per second.

The Golden-browed Chlorophonia can be observed at Monteverde, Catarata de la Paz (Peace Waterfall), Rancho Naturalista, Turrialba, Tapantí NP, Cerro de la Muerte along the Pan American Highway at kilometers 66 and 80, and San Gerardo de Dota Valley including Savegre Mountain Lodge.

Golden-browed Chlorophonia adult female

GLOSSARY

Accidental species: A species of bird that occasionally wanders far beyond its normal range and is sighted in new regions or countries.

Altricial: Helpless at hatching, requiring extensive parental care before fledging.

Arboreal: Adapted to living in trees (e.g., squirrels and monkeys are arboreal).

Aril, arillate fruit: Fruit, often brightly colored, that is typically contained in a fleshy outer covering that opens to expose the aril when it is ripe.

Arthropod: A member of the phylum Arthropoda, including segmented invertebrates like insects, spiders, and crustaceans.

Avifauna: A broad term for birdlife.

Bird of prey: A bird that eats other birds and animals and typically has strong claws and a sharp beak for catching and killing or tearing open food species. Examples are kites, hawks, falcons, vultures, and owls.

BR: Biological Reserve.

Brood: A family of newly hatched young birds from the same nest.

Cache (v.): The activity of storing food for later use, as practiced by species like Acorn Woodpeckers, which store acorns in holes in trees for later meals. (n.): The supply of food, such as acorns, that has been stored for later use.

Canopy: A layer within the overall structure of a forest. *Lower canopy* refers to the shrub layer and short trees; *midcanopy* refers to middle levels of foliage and structure among trees; *upper canopy* refers to the foliage and vegetative structure in the tops of the trees; and *supercanopy* refers to trees like *Ceiba* that project above the upper canopy.

Caribbean slope: The northern and eastern portion of Costa Rica from the continental divide in the mountains eastward to the lowlands that drain toward the Caribbean.

Caruncle: An enlarged cere (fleshy growth above the bill) on birds such as Muscovy Ducks.

Casque: A helmetlike structure on the head of a bird; for example, the enlarged posterior area of the maxilla on a Chestnut-headed Oropendola.

Cere: A fleshy feature on the head of some birds located between the upper bill and the feathered portion of the face.

Clutch: The eggs laid in a single bird's nest, usually by a single female. (After hatching, the young are collectively referred to as a brood.)

Color morph: A color variety within a species that deviates from the normal coloration. For example, there are dark or black morphs among some birds of prey and blue or yellow color morphs among parrots and parakeets.

Crepuscular: A species of wildlife that is active at dawn and dusk.

Crop: The enlarged portion of the gullet at the base of a bird's throat. It is used for temporary storage of food prior to entering the gizzard.

Crustacean: A type of arthropod that typically has a hard shell covering the body; includes lobsters, shrimp, and crabs.

Cryptic: A type of coloration that makes a creature difficult to see because it blends in with the background.

Culmen: The dorsal ridge on a bird's bill.

Cut bank: An exposed vertical bank of dirt, usually along a road or river. Birds like motmots, kingfishers, and jacamars excavate nesting burrows in such sites.

Decurved: Curving downward, like the bills of some hummingbirds.

Dewlap: A fold of fleshy skin that hangs down from the chin and throat area, as on a Crested Guan.

Diurnal: Being active during daylight hours; opposite of nocturnal.

Dry forest: A forest in which the range of total annual rainfall is 40–80 inches per year. The dry forest in Costa Rica is found primarily in

Guanacaste Province and is a tropical deciduous forest with distinct wet and dry seasons.

Dry season: That portion of the year in which less rainfall occurs. In Costa Rica, the dry season occurs from December through March.

Endemic: Occurring only within a limited geographic area and nowhere else in the world, such as species found only in the mountains of Costa Rica and western Panama, only in the lowlands of southeastern Costa Rica and adjacent Panama, or only on Cocos Island.

Epiphyte: A plant that grows above the ground on the surface of another plant and depends on that plant for physical support. Examples include some bromeliads and orchids.

Eye-ring: A contrasting ring of flesh or feathers that encircles the eye. The ring may be complete or open at the front and back.

Fledge: To leave the nest (on the part of young birds).

Fledging period: The time between the hatching of a bird and its departure from the nest.

Foothills: Hilly terrain at the base of mountains with elevations of about 1,500–4,500 feet (approximately the same as the premontane or subtropical zone). The distribution of some species is limited to foothills and not to either lowlands or highlands.

Gallery forest: A forest adjacent to a stream or river; also referred to as riparian forest.

Gestation period: The time from breeding to the birth of young.

Gorget: The iridescent area on a hummingbird's throat.

Highlands: For the purposes of this book, regions at 5,000–11,000 feet in elevation, including moist, wet, and rainforests. They are characterized by 40–200 inches of rainfall per year. Such areas can have large numbers of epiphytes on the trees, and the area's diversity is lower than at lower elevations. It includes 15 percent of Costa Rica's land area.

Incubation period: For birds, the time between when a bird begins to sit on its eggs and when the eggs hatch.

Lek, or singing assembly: A gathering of courting male hummingbirds or manakins, or the place where they gather to sing and display to attract females for mating.

Lores: The area on each side of a bird's face, between the eye and the upper bill.

Lowlands: Relatively flat terrain between foothills and the coast, in the elevation range from sea level to about 2,000 feet. It includes dry, moist, and wet forests and accounts for 57 percent of Costa Rica's land area.

Malar stripe: A marking on a bird's cheek that extends back from the posterior edge of the lower bill and gives the impression of a mustache.

Mandible: Lower bill of a bird.

Maxilla: Upper bill of a bird.

Melanistic: Having excess pigmentation, as in a color phase in which an individual creature is very dark or black.

Middle elevation: Elevations known as subtropical or premontane, including elevations of about 2,000 feet–4,500 feet; also referred to as foothills. This may include moist, wet, and rainforest habitats. The Central Plateau and San José are at middle elevations. This zone includes 28 percent of Costa Rica's land area.

Moist forest: A forest in tropical lowlands that receives 80–160 inches of rainfall per year. This type of forest covers 24 percent of Costa Rica's land area. At premontane and lower montane levels, moist forest receives 40–80 inches of rainfall and includes about 5 percent of Costa Rica's land area.

Mollusks: Invertebrates including snails, clams, squids, and octopus. They have one or two external shells that protect all or part of the body.

Monogamy: A reproductive strategy by which a single male and female create a pair bond with each other and do not have multiple mates.

Montane forest: A highland wet forest (40–80 inches of rainfall per year) or rainforest (80–160 inches of rainfall per year) at 8,200–10,500 feet in elevation.

Nape: The back of the neck.

Nocturnal: Active at night; the opposite of diurnal.

NP: National Park.

NWR: National Wildlife Refuge.

Pacific slope: That portion of the Costa Rican landscape that drains from the mountains west and south to the Pacific Ocean.

Paramo: A highland elevational zone above the montane zone, ranging from about 10,500 feet to the peaks of Costa Rica's mountains.

The zone is above tree line and is characterized by stunted shrubs, bamboo, and many composites. It includes 0.2 percent of the country's land area.

Polyandry: A reproductive strategy of birds (e.g., the Great Tinamou and Northern Jacana) in which the female defends a territory and mates with multiple males and the males incubate the eggs and raise the young.

Postocular stripe: A stripe that extends from behind a bird's eye toward the back of the head.

Precocial: Active from hatching and needing little parental care; for example, newly hatched birds that are so well developed that they can leave the nest within a day or two of hatching.

Premontane: The elevational zone between approximately 2,000 and 4,900 feet; also referred to as foothills, subtropical, or middle elevations. The zone includes moist forests, wet forests, and rainforests at those elevations.

Primary feathers: The outermost nine or ten flight feathers of a bird's wing. These feathers are attached to the "hand bones" of the wing and provide forward thrust on the downstroke of the wing.

Primary forest: A mature forest that has not been cut in recent times.

Race: A geographically or morphologically distinct grouping within a species; may be differentiated by plumage, range, song, or behavior.

Rainforest: A forest that receives more than 320 inches of rainfall per year. The term may also be used more generally to describe moist or wet forests.

Rainy season: That portion of the year in which most rain falls. In Costa Rica, this is the period from April to December.

Raptor: A bird of prey, such as a kite, hawk, falcon, owl, or vulture.

Riparian forest: A forest along a stream or river; also referred to as gallery forest.

Sally (v.): To fly out from a perch to catch an insect or to pick fruit on the wing.

Savanna: An arid habitat of northwestern Costa Rica, near the Nicaragua border, characterized by open grassy ground cover and scattered stunted trees like *Byrsonima* and *Curatella*. It is an arid extreme of tropical dry forest maintained by fire.

Scapular feathers: Feathers that lie along the contour of the back of a bird and cover the upper portions of the folded wing, including the tertial feathers.

Secondary feathers: The inner medium-length flight feathers that trail on the back portion of a bird's wing. They are attached to the ulna bone and generate lift in flight.

Secondary forest: A forest that has grown back after a previous disturbance like burning or cutting.

Subspecies: A distinctive grouping of a population within a species; may be distinguished by its range, plumage, song, or behavior.

Superciliary line: A line above the eye of a bird.

Taxonomist: A person who specializes in the classification and naming of species.

Termitary: A nest of termites, usually located on a tree or fence post. Some birds like trogons and parakeets excavate their nest within a termitary.

Terrestrial: Living on the ground.

Tertial feathers: The feathers on the wing of a bird, closest to the body, that lie over the contour of the back and cover the upper portion of the wing when it is closed.

Tico: A person from Costa Rica.

Traplining: A behavior in which a hummingbird repeatedly visits the same flowers within its defended territory.

Understory: Smaller trees, shrubs, and other vegetation that are generally less than 25 feet in height within a taller forest.

Undertail coverts: Those feathers that are underneath the base of the tail.

Wading bird: A bird with long legs that wades in shallow water in order to locate its food, such as small fish. Examples include herons and egrets.

Wet forest: A tropical forest that receives 160–320 inches of rainfall per year.

Wet season: The season when most rainfall occurs in an area. Same as rainy season. In Costa Rica, this generally includes the period from April to December. In some areas like the northeastern Caribbean lowlands, the wet season extends through most of the year.

BIBLIOGRAPHY

Amadon, Dean. 1983. Great Curassow (*Crax rubra*). In *Costa Rican Natural History,* ed. Daniel H. Janzen, 569–570. Chicago: Univ. of Chicago Press. 816 pp.

Ammon, Elizabeth M., and William M. Gilbert. 1999. Wilson's Warbler (*Wilsonia pusilla*). In *The Birds of North America,* no. 478, ed. Alan Poole and Frank Gill. Philadelphia, Pa.: Academy of Natural Sciences; Washington, D.C.: American Ornithologists' Union. 28 pp.

Arnold, Keith A. 1983. Great-tailed Grackle (*Quiscalus mexicanus*). In *Costa Rican Natural History,* ed. Daniel H. Janzen, 601–603. Chicago: Univ. of Chicago Press. 816 pp.

Banks, Richard C., R. Terry Chesser, Carla Cicero, Jon L. Dunn, Andrew W. Kratter, Irby J. Lovette, Pamela Rasmussen, J. V. Remsen, Jr., James D. Rising, Douglas F. Stotz, and Kevin Winker. 2008. Forty-ninth Supplement to the American Ornithologists' Union Check-list of North American Birds. *Auk* 125(3):758–768.

Bednarz, James C. 1995. Harris' Hawk (*Parabuteo unicinctus*). In *The Birds of North America,* no. 146, ed. Alan Poole and Frank Gill. Philadelphia, Pa.: Academy of Natural Sciences; Washington, D.C.: American Ornithologists' Union. 24 pp.

Bibles, Brent D., Richard L. Glinski, and R. Roy Johnson. 2002. Gray Hawk (*Astruina nitida*). In *The Birds of North America,* no. 652, ed. Alan Poole and Frank Gill. Philadelphia, Pa.: Academy of Natural Sciences; Washington, D.C.: American Ornithologists' Union. 16 pp.

Bowen, Bonnie S. 2002. Groove-billed Ani (*Crotophaga sulcirostris*). In *The Birds of North America,* no. 612, ed. Alan Poole and Frank Gill. Philadelphia, Pa.: Academy of Natural Sciences; Washington, D.C.: American Ornithologists' Union. 16 pp.

Brown, Leslie, and Dean Amadon. 1989. *Eagles, Hawks, and Falcons of the World.* Vols. 1 and 2. Secaucus, N.J.: Wellfleet Press. 945 pp.

Brush, Timothy, and John W. Fitzpatrick. 2002. Great Kiskadee (*Pitangus sulphuratus*). In *The Birds of North America,* no. 622, ed. Alan Poole and Frank Gill. Philadelphia, Pa.: Academy of Natural Sciences; Washington, D.C.: American Ornithologists' Union. 20 pp.

Buckley, Neil J. 1999. Black Vulture (*Coragyps atratus*). In *The Birds of North America,* no. 411, ed. Alan Poole and Frank Gill. Philadelphia, Pa.: Academy of Natural Sciences; Washington, D.C.: American Ornithologists' Union. 24 pp.

Buckley, P. A., and Francine G. Buckley. 2002. Royal Tern (*Sterna maxima*). In *The Birds of North America,* no. 700, ed. Alan Poole and Frank Gill. Philadelphia, Pa.: Academy of Natural Sciences; Washington, D.C.: American Ornithologists' Union. 28 pp.

Burger, Joanna. 1996. Laughing Gull (*Larus atricilla*). In *The Birds of North America,* no. 225, ed. Alan Poole and Frank Gill. Philadelphia, Pa.: Academy of Natural Sciences; Washington, D.C.: American Ornithologists' Union. 28 pp.

Burton, John A., ed. 1973. *Owls of the World.* New York: E. P. Dutton. 216 pp.

Butler, Robert W. 1992. Great Blue Heron (*Ardea herodias*). In *The Birds of North America,* no. 25, ed. Alan Poole and Frank Gill. Philadelphia, Pa.: Academy of Natural Sciences; Washington, D.C.: American Ornithologists' Union. 20 pp.

Byers, Clive, Jon Curson, and Urban Olsson. 1995. *Sparrows and Buntings: A Guide to the Sparrows and Buntings of North America and the World.* Boston, Mass.: Houghton Mifflin. 334 pp.

Corbat, Carol A., and Peter W. Bergstrom. 2000. Wilson's Plover (*Charadrius wilsonia*). In *The Birds of North America,* no. 516, ed. Alan Poole and Frank Gill. Philadelphia, Pa.:

Academy of Natural Sciences; Washington, D.C.: American Ornithologists' Union. 16 pp.

Coulter, Malcolm C., James A. Rodgers, John C. Odgen, and F. Chris Depkin. 1999. Wood Stork (*Mycteria americana*). In *The Birds of North America*, no. 409, ed. Alan Poole and Frank Gill. Philadelphia, Pa.: Academy of Natural Sciences; Washington, D.C.: American Ornithologists' Union. 28 pp.

Curson, Jon, David Quinn, and David Beadle. 1994. *Warblers of the Americas*. Boston, Mass.: Houghton Mifflin. 252 pp.

Davis. William E., Jr., and James A. Kushlan. 1994. Green Heron (*Butorides virescens*). In *The Birds of North America*, no. 129, ed. Alan Poole and Frank Gill. Philadelphia, Pa.: Academy of Natural Sciences; Washington, D.C.: American Ornithologists' Union. 24 pp.

Diamond, Antony W., and Elizabeth A. Schreiber. 2002. Magnificent Frigatebird (*Fregata magnificens*). In *The Birds of North America*, no. 601, ed. Alan Poole and Frank Gill. Philadelphia, Pa.: Academy of Natural Sciences; Washington, D.C.: American Ornithologists' Union. 24 pp.

Dumas, Jeannette V. 2000. Roseate Spoonbill (*Ajaia ajaja*). In *The Birds of North America*, no. 490, ed. Alan Poole and Frank Gill. Philadelphia, Pa.: Academy of Natural Sciences; Washington, D.C.: American Ornithologists' Union. 32 pp.

Farquhar, C. Craig. 1992. White-tailed Hawk (*Buteo albicaudatus*). In *The Birds of North America*, no. 30, ed. Alan Poole and Frank Gill. Philadelphia, Pa.: Academy of Natural Sciences; Washington, D.C.: American Ornithologists' Union. 20 pp.

Ffrench, Richard. 1991. *A Guide to the Birds of Trinidad and Tobago*. New York: Cornell Univ. Press. 426 pp.

Fitzpatrick, John W. 1983. Tropical Kingbird (*Tyrannus melancholicus*). In *Costa Rican Natural History*, ed. Daniel H. Janzen, 611–613. Chicago: Univ. of Chicago Press. 816 pp.

Foster, Mercedes S. 1983. Long-tailed Manakin (*Chiroxiphia linearis*). In *Costa Rican Natural History*, ed. Daniel H. Janzen, 563–564. Chicago: Univ. of Chicago Press. 816 pp.

Frederick, Peter C. 1997. Tricolored Heron (*Egretta tricolor*). In *The Birds of North America*, no. 306, ed. Alan Poole and Frank Gill. Philadelphia, Pa.: Academy of Natural Sciences; Washington, D.C.: American Ornithologists' Union. 28 pp.

Frederick, Peter C., and Douglas Siegal-Causey. 2000. Anhinga (*Anhinga anhinga*). In *The Birds of North America*, no. 522, ed. Alan Poole and Frank Gill. Philadelphia, Pa.: Academy of Natural Sciences; Washington, D.C.: American Ornithologists' Union. 24 pp.

Garrigues, Richard, and Robert Dean. 2007. *The Birds of Costa Rica*. New York: Cornell Univ. Press. 387 pp.

Gill, Robert E., Brian J. McCaffery, and Pavel S. Tomkovich. 2002. Wandering Tattler (*Heteroscelus incanus*). In *The Birds of North America*, no. 642, ed. Alan Poole and Frank Gill. Philadelphia, Pa.: Academy of Natural Sciences; Washington, D.C.: American Ornithologists' Union. 32 pp.

Gladstone, Douglas E. 1983. Cattle Egret (*Bubulcus ibis*). In *Costa Rican Natural History*, ed. Daniel H. Janzen, 550–551. Chicago: Univ. of Chicago Press. 816 pp.

Goochfeld, Michael, and Joanna Burger. 1994. Black Skimmer (*Rynchops niger*). In *The Birds of North America*, no. 108, ed. Alan Poole and Frank Gill. Philadelphia, Pa.: Academy of Natural Sciences; Washington, D.C.: American Ornithologists' Union. 28 pp.

Goodrich, Laurie J., Scott C. Crocoll, and Stanley E. Senner. 1996. Broad-winged Hawk (*Buteo platypterus*). In *The Birds of North America*, no. 218, ed. Alan Poole and Frank Gill. Philadelphia, Pa.: Academy of Natural Sciences; Washington, D.C.: American Ornithologists' Union. 28 pp.

Hogan, Kelly M. 1999. White-tipped Dove (*Leptotila verreauxi*). In *The Birds of North America*, no. 436, ed. Alan Poole and Frank Gill. Philadelphia, Pa.: Academy of Natural Sciences; Washington, D.C.: American Ornithologists' Union. 16 pp.

Howe, Hank F. 1983. Chestnut-mandibled Toucan (*Ramphastos swainsonii*). In *Costa Rican Natural History*, ed. Daniel H. Janzen, 603–604. Chicago: Univ. of Chicago Press. 816 pp.

Howell, Steven N. G., and Sophie Webb. 1995. *The Birds of Mexico and Northern Central America*. New York: Oxford Univ. Press. 851 pp.

Hoyo, Josep del, Andrew Elliott, and Jordi Sargatal. 1992. *Handbook of the Birds of the*

World. Vols. 1–10. Barcelona, Spain: Lynx Edicions.

Hughes, Janice M. 1997. Mangrove cuckoo (*Coccyzus minor*). In *The Birds of North America,* no. 299, ed. Alan Poole and Frank Gill. Philadelphia, Pa.: Academy of Natural Sciences; Washington, D.C.: American Ornithologists' Union. 20 pp.

Isler, Morton, and Phyllis Isler. 1999. *The Tanagers: Natural History, Distribution, and Identification.* Washington, D.C.: Smithsonian Institution Press. 406 pp.

Janzen, Daniel H. 1983a. *Costa Rican Natural History.* Chicago: Univ. of Chicago Press. 816 pp.

———. 1983b. Scarlet Macaw (*Ara macao*). In *Costa Rican Natural History,* ed. Daniel H. Janzen, 547–548. Chicago: Univ. of Chicago Press. 816 pp.

———. 1983c. Orange-chinned Parakeet (*Brotogeris jugularis*). In *Costa Rican Natural History,* ed. Daniel H. Janzen, 548–550. Chicago: Univ. of Chicago Press. 816 pp.

Jenni, Donald A. 1983. Northern Jacana (*Jacana spinosa*). In *Costa Rican Natural History,* ed. Daniel H. Janzen, 584–586. Chicago: Univ. of Chicago Press. 816 pp.

Jenni, Donald A., and Terrence R. Mace. 1999. Northern Jacana (*Jacana spinosa*). In *The Birds of North America,* no. 467, ed. Alan Poole and Frank Gill. Philadelphia, Pa.: Academy of Natural Sciences; Washington, D.C.: American Ornithologists' Union. 20 pp.

Johnsgard, Paul A. 2000. *Trogons and Quetzals of the World.* Washington, D.C.: Smithsonian Institution Press. 223 pp.

Johnson, L. Scott. 1998. House Wren (*Troglodytes aedon*). In *The Birds of North America,* no. 380, ed. Alan Poole and Frank Gill. Philadelphia, Pa.: Academy of Natural Sciences; Washington, D.C.: American Ornithologists' Union. 32 pp.

Kaufmann, Ken. 1996. *Lives of North American Birds.* Boston, Mass.: Houghton Mifflin. 675 pp.

Keppie, Daniel M., and Clait E. Braun. Bandtailed Pigeon (*Columba fasciata*). In *The Birds of North America,* no. 530, ed. Alan Poole and Frank Gill. Philadelphia, Pa.: Academy of Natural Sciences; Washington, D.C.: American Ornithologists' Union. 28 pp.

Kingery, Hugh E. 1966. American Dipper

(*Cinclus mexicanus*). In *The Birds of North America,* no. 229, ed. Alan Poole and Frank Gill. Philadelphia, Pa.: Academy of Natural Sciences; Washington, D.C.: American Ornithologists' Union. 28 pp.

Kirk, David A., and Michael J. Mossman. 1998. Turkey Vulture. In *The Birds of North America,* no. 339, ed. Alan Poole and Frank Gill. Philadelphia, Pa.: Academy of Natural Sciences; Washington, D.C.: American Ornithologists' Union. 32 pp.

Koenig, Walter D., Peter B. Stacey, Mark T. Stanback, and Ronald L. Mumme. 1995. Acorn Woodpecker (*Melanerpes formicivorus*). In *The Birds of North America,* no. 194, ed. Alan Poole and Frank Gill. Philadelphia, Pa.: Academy of Natural Sciences; Washington, D.C.: American Ornithologists' Union. 24 pp.

Kricher, John C. 1995. Black-and-white Warbler (*Mniotilta varia*). In *The Birds of North America,* no. 158, ed. Alan Poole and Frank Gill. Philadelphia, Pa.: Academy of Natural Sciences; Washington, D.C.: American Ornithologists' Union. 20 pp.

Kushlan, James A., and Keith L. Bildstein. 1992. White Ibis (*Eudocimus albus*). In *The Birds of North America,* no. 9, ed. A. Poole, P. Stettenheim, and F. Gill. Philadelphia, Pa.: Academy of Natural Sciences; Washington, D.C.: American Ornithologists' Union. 20 pp.

La Bastille, Anne. 1983. Resplendent Quetzal (*Pharomachrus mocinno*). In *Costa Rican Natural History,* ed. Daniel H. Janzen, 599–601. Chicago: Univ. of Chicago Press. 816 pp.

Latta, Steven C., and Michael E. Baltz. 1997. Lesser Nighthawk (*Chordeiles acutipennis*). In *The Birds of North America,* no. 314, ed. Alan Poole and Frank Gill. Philadelphia, Pa.: Academy of Natural Sciences; Washington, D.C.: American Ornithologists' Union. 20 pp.

Latta, Steven C., and Christine A. Howell. 1999. Common Pauraque (*Nyctidromus albicollis*). In *The Birds of North America,* no. 429, ed. Alan Poole and Frank Gill. Philadelphia, Pa.: Academy of Natural Sciences; Washington, D.C.: American Ornithologists' Union. 16 pp.

Lawton, Marcy F. 1983. Brown Jay (*Cyanocorax morio*). In *Costa Rican Natural History,* ed. Daniel H. Janzen, 573–574. Chicago: Univ. of Chicago Press. 816 pp.

Leck, Charles F. 1983. Bananaquit (*Coereba*

flaveola). In *Costa Rican Natural History,* ed. Daniel H. Janzen, 567–568. Chicago: Univ. of Chicago Press. 816 pp.

Lowther, Peter E. 2002. Red-billed Pigeon (*Columba flavirostris*). In *The Birds of North America,* no. 644, ed. Alan Poole and Frank Gill. Philadelphia, Pa.: Academy of Natural Sciences; Washington, D.C.: American Ornithologists' Union. 12 pp.

McDonald, David B., and Wayne K. Potts. 1994. Cooperative Display and Relatedness among Males in a Lek-Mating Bird. *Science* 266: 1030–1032.

Preston, C. R., and R. D. Beane. 1993. Red-tailed Hawk (*Buteo jamaicensis*). In *The Birds of North America,* no. 52, ed. Alan Poole and Frank Gill. Philadelphia, Pa.: Academy of Natural Sciences; Washington, D.C.: American Ornithologists' Union. 24 pp.

Meyer, Kenneth D. 1995. Swallow-tailed Kite (*Elanoides forficatus*). In *The Birds of North America,* no. 138, ed. Alan Poole and Frank Gill. Philadelphia, Pa.: Academy of Natural Sciences; Washington, D.C.: American Ornithologists' Union. 24 pp.

Meyer de Schauensee, Rodolphe, and William H. Phelps, Jr. 1978. *A Guide to the Birds of Venezuela.* Princeton, N.J.: Princeton University Press. 424 pp.

Miller, Karl E., and Kenneth D. Meyer. 2002. Short-tailed Hawk (*Buteo brachyurus*). In *The Birds of North America,* no. 674, ed. Alan Poole and Frank Gill. Philadelphia, Pa.: Academy of Natural Sciences; Washington, D.C.: American Ornithologists' Union. 16 pp.

Mock, Douglas W. 1983. Boat-billed Heron (*Cochlearius cochlearius*). In *Costa Rican Natural History,* ed. Daniel H. Janzen, 565–567. Chicago: Univ. of Chicago Press. 816 pp.

Morrison, Joan L. 1996. Crested Caracara (*Caracara plancus*). In *The Birds of North America,* no. 249, ed. Alan Poole and Frank Gill. Philadelphia, Pa.: Academy of Natural Sciences; Washington, D.C.: American Ornithologists' Union. 28 pp.

Morton, Ed S. 1983. Clay-colored Thrush (*Turdus grayi*). In *Costa Rican Natural History,* ed. Daniel H. Janzen, 610–611. Chicago: Univ. of Chicago Press. 816 pp.

Moskoff, William. 2002. Green Kingfisher (*Chloroceryle americana*). In *The Birds of*

North America, no. 621, ed. Alan Poole and Frank Gill. Philadelphia, Pa.: Academy of Natural Sciences; Washington, D.C.: American Ornithologists' Union. 12 pp.

Mueller, Allan J. 1992. Inca Dove (*Columbina inca*). In *The Birds of North America,* no. 28, ed. Alan Poole and Frank Gill. Philadelphia, Pa.: Academy of Natural Sciences; Washington, D.C.: American Ornithologists' Union. 12 pp.

Nettleship, David N. 2000. Ruddy Turnstone (*Arenaria interpres*). *The Birds of North America,* no. 537, ed. Alan Poole and Frank Gill. Philadelphia, Pa.: Academy of Natural Sciences; Washington, D.C.: American Ornithologists' Union. 32 pp.

Nol, Erica, and Michele S. Blanken. 1999. Semipalmated Plover (*Charadrius semipalmatus*). In *The Birds of North America,* no. 444, ed. Alan Poole and Frank Gill. Philadelphia, Pa.: Academy of Natural Sciences; Washington, D.C.: American Ornithologists' Union. 24 pp.

Nol, Erica, and Robert C. Murphy. 1994. American Oystercatcher (*Haematopus palliatus*). In *The Birds of North America,* no. 82, ed. Alan Poole and Frank Gill. Philadelphia, Pa.: Academy of Natural Sciences; Washington, D.C.: American Ornithologists' Union. 24 pp.

Oring, Lewis W., Elizabeth M. Gray, and J. Michael Reed. 1997. Spotted Sandpiper (*Actitis macularia*). In *The Birds of North America,* no. 289, ed. Alan Poole and Frank Gill. Philadelphia, Pa.: Academy of Natural Sciences; Washington, D.C.: American Ornithologists' Union. 32 pp.

Parsons, Katharine C., and Terry L. Master. 2000. Snowy Egret (*Egretta thula*). *The Birds of North America,* no. 489, ed. Alan Poole and Frank Gill. Philadelphia, Pa.: Academy of Natural Sciences; Washington, D.C.: American Ornithologists' Union. 24 pp.

Pérez, Óliver. 2008. Biólogos encuentran más nidos de jabirú en Guanacaste. *La Nación* February 3, p. 23A.

Poole, Alan F., Rob O. Bierregaard, and Mark S. Martell. 2002. Osprey (*Pandion haliaetus*). In *The Birds of North America,* no. 683, ed. Alan Poole and Frank Gill. Philadelphia, Pa.: Academy of Natural Sciences; Washington, D.C.: American Ornithologists' Union. 44 pp.

Powers, Donald R. 1996. Magnificent

Hummingbird (*Eugenes fulgens*). In *The Birds of North America,* no. 221, ed. Alan Poole and Frank Gill. Philadelphia, Pa.: Academy of Natural Sciences; Washington, D.C.: American Ornithologists' Union. 20 pp.

Proudfoot, Glenn A., and Roy Johnson. 2000. Ferruginous Pygmy-Owl (*Glaucidium brasilianum*). In *The Birds of North America,* no. 498, ed. Alan Poole and Frank Gill. Philadelphia, Pa.: Academy of Natural Sciences; Washington, D.C.: American Ornithologists' Union. 20 pp.

Quinn, James S., and Jennifer M. Startek-Foote. 2000. Smooth-billed Ani (*Crotophaga ani*). *The Birds of North America,* no. 539, ed. Alan Poole and Frank Gill. Philadelphia, Pa.: Academy of Natural Sciences; Washington, D.C.: American Ornithologists' Union. 16 pp.

Remsen, J. Van, Jr. 1983. Green Kingfisher (*Chloroceryle americana*). In *Costa Rican Natural History,* ed. Daniel H. Janzen, 564–565. Chicago: Univ. of Chicago Press. 816 pp.

Richardson, Michael, and Daniel W. Brauning. 1995. Chestnut-sided Warbler (*Dendroica pensylvanica*). In *The Birds of North America,* no. 190, ed. Alan Poole and Frank Gill. Philadelphia, Pa.: Academy of Natural Sciences; Washington, D.C.: American Ornithologists' Union. 20 pp.

Rimmer, Christopher C., and Kent P. McFarland. 1998. Tennessee Warbler (*Vermivora peregrina*). In *The Birds of North America,* no. 350, ed. Alan Poole and Frank Gill. Philadelphia, Pa.: Academy of Natural Sciences; Washington, D.C.: American Ornithologists' Union. 24 pp.

Rising, James D., and Nancy J. Flood. 1998. Baltimore Oriole (*Icterus galbula*). In *The Birds of North America,* no. 384, ed. Alan Poole and Frank Gill. Philadelphia, Pa.: Academy of Natural Sciences; Washington, D.C.: American Ornithologists' Union. 32 pp.

Robinson, Julie A., J. Michael Reed, Joseph P. Skorupa, and Lewis W. Oring. 1999. Black-necked Stilt (*Himantopus mexicanus*). *The Birds of North America,* no. 449, ed. Alan Poole and Frank Gill. Philadelphia, Pa.: Academy of Natural Sciences; Washington, D.C.: American Ornithologists' Union. 32 pp.

Robinson, W. Douglas. 1996. Summer Tanager (*Piranga rubra*). In *The Birds of North America,* no. 248, ed. Alan Poole and Frank Gill. Philadelphia, Pa.: Academy of Natural Sciences; Washington, D.C.: American Ornithologists' Union. 24 pp.

Rodgers, James A., Jr., and Henry T. Smith. 1995. Little Blue Heron (*Egretta caerulea*). In *The Birds of North America,* no. 145, ed. Alan Poole and Frank Gill. Philadelphia, Pa.: Academy of Natural Sciences; Washington, D.C.: American Ornithologists' Union. 32 pp.

Ross, David L. Jr. 1999. *Costa Rican Bird Songs Sampler.* Ithaca: Cornell Laboratory of Ornithology. Audiotape.

———. 2001. *Costa Rican Bird Songs.* Ithaca: Cornell Laboratory of Ornithology. Compact disk.

Ross, David Jr., and Bret M. Whitney. 1995. *Voices of Costa Rican Birds: Caribbean Slope.* Ithaca: Cornell Laboratory of Ornithology, American Birding Association. Two audiotapes.

Roth, R. R., M. S. Johnson, and T. J. Underwood. 1996. Wood Thrush (*Hylocichla mustelina*). In *The Birds of North America,* no. 246, ed. Alan Poole and Frank Gill. Philadelphia, Pa.: Academy of Natural Sciences; Washington, D.C.: American Ornithologists' Union. 28 pp.

Scharf, William C. 1996. Orchard Oriole (*Icterus spurius*). In *The Birds of North America,* no. 255, ed. Alan Poole and Frank Gill. Philadelphia, Pa.: Academy of Natural Sciences; Washington, D.C.: American Ornithologists' Union. 24 pp.

Schnell, Jay H. 1994. Common Black-Hawk (*Buteogallus anthracinus*). In *The Birds of North America,* no. 122, ed. Alan Poole and Frank Gill. Philadelphia, Pa.: Academy of Natural Sciences; Washington, D.C.: American Ornithologists' Union. 20 pp.

Schreiber, E. A., and R. L. Norton. 2002. Brown Booby (*Sula leucogaster*). In *The Birds of North America,* no. 649, ed. Alan Poole and Frank Gill. Philadelphia, Pa.: Academy of Natural Sciences; Washington, D.C.: American Ornithologists' Union. 28 pp.

Schreiber, Ralph W. 1983. Magnificent Frigatebird (*Fregata magnificens*). In *Costa Rican Natural History,* ed. Daniel H. Janzen, 577–579. Chicago: Univ. of Chicago Press. 816 pp.

Schreiber, Ralph W., and Michael B. McCoy.

1983. Brown Pelican (*Pelecanus occidentalis*). In *Costa Rican Natural History*, ed. Daniel H. Janzen, 594–597. Chicago: Univ. of Chicago Press. 816 pp.

Schwertner, T. W., H. A. Mathewson, J. A. Roberson, M. Small, and G. L. Waggerman. 2002. White-winged Dove (*Zenaida asiatica*). In *The Birds of North America*, no. 710, ed. Alan Poole and Frank Gill. Philadelphia, Pa.: Academy of Natural Sciences; Washington, D.C.: American Ornithologists' Union. 28 pp.

Shealer, David. 1999. Sandwich Tern (*Sterna sandvicensis*). In *The Birds of North America*, no. 405, ed. Alan Poole and Frank Gill. Philadelphia, Pa.: Academy of Natural Sciences; Washington, D.C.: American Ornithologists' Union. 28 pp.

Sherry, Tom W. 1983a. Rufous-tailed Jacamar (*Galbula ruficauda*). In *Costa Rican Natural History*, ed. Daniel H. Janzen, 579–581. Chicago: Univ. of Chicago Press. 816 pp.

———. 1983b. Ochre-bellied Flycatcher (*Mionectes oleaginea*). In *Costa Rican Natural History*, ed. Daniel H. Janzen, 586–587. Chicago: Univ. of Chicago Press. 816 pp.

———. 1983c. Common Tody-Flycatcher (*Todirostrum cinereum*). In *Costa Rican Natural History*, ed. Daniel H. Janzen, 608–610. Chicago: Univ. of Chicago Press. 816 pp.

Shields, Mark. 2002. Brown Pelican (*Pelecanus occidentalis*). In *The Birds of North America*, no. 609, ed. Alan Poole and Frank Gill. Philadelphia, Pa.: Academy of Natural Sciences; Washington, D.C.: American Ornithologists' Union. 36 pp.

Skeel, Margaret A., and Elizabeth P. Mallory. 1996. Whimbrel (*Numenius phaeopus*). In *The Birds of North America*, no. 219, ed. Alan Poole and Frank Gill. Philadelphia, Pa.: Academy of Natural Sciences; Washington, D.C.: American Ornithologists' Union. 28 pp.

Skutch, Alexander F. 1977. *Aves de Costa Rica*. San José, Costa Rica: Editorial Costa Rica. 148 pp.

———. 1983a. *Birds of Tropical America*. Austin: Univ. of Texas Press. 305 pp.

———. 1983b. Ruddy Ground-Dove (*Columbina talpacoti*). In *Costa Rican Natural History*, ed. Daniel H. Janzen, 568–569. Chicago: Univ. of Chicago Press. 816 pp.

———. 1983c. Laughing Falcon (*Herpetotheres*

cachinnans). In *Costa Rican Natural History*, ed. Daniel H. Janzen, 582–583. Chicago: Univ. of Chicago Press. 816 pp.

———. 1987. *Helpers at Birds' Nests: A Worldwide Survey of Cooperative Breeding and Related Behavior*. Iowa City: Univ. of Iowa Press. 298 pp.

———. 1996. *Orioles, Blackbirds and Their Kin: A Natural History*. Tucson: Univ. of Arizona Press. 291 pp.

———. 1997. *Life of the Flycatcher*. Norman: Univ. of Oklahoma Press. 162 pp.

Slud, Paul. 1964. *The Birds of Costa Rica: Distribution and Ecology*. Vol. 128. New York: Bulletin of the American Museum of Natural History. 430 pp.

Smith, Susan M. 1983a. Turquoise-browed Motmot (*Eumomota superciliosa*). In *Costa Rican Natural History*, ed. Daniel H. Janzen, 577. Chicago: Univ. of Chicago Press. 816 pp.

———. 1983b. Tropical Screech-Owl (*Otus choliba*). In *Costa Rican Natural History*, ed. Daniel H. Janzen, 592. Chicago: Univ. of Chicago Press. 816 pp.

———. 1983c. Rufous-collared Sparrow (*Zonotrichia capensis*). In *Costa Rican Natural History*, ed. Daniel H. Janzen, 618. Chicago: Univ. of Chicago Press. 816 pp.

Stiles, F. Gary. 1983a. Green Heron (*Butorides virescens*). In *Costa Rican Natural History*, ed. Daniel H. Janzen, 552–554. Chicago: Univ. of Chicago Press. 816 pp.

———. 1983b. Long-tailed Hermit (*Phaethornis superciliosus*). In *Costa Rican Natural History*, ed. Daniel H. Janzen, 597–599. Chicago: Univ. of Chicago Press. 816 pp.

———. 1983c. Variable Seedeater (*Sporophila aurita*). In *Costa Rican Natural History*, ed. Daniel H. Janzen, 604–605. Chicago: Univ. of Chicago Press. 816 pp.

———. 1983d. Tennessee Warbler (*Vermivora peregrina*). In *Costa Rican Natural History*, ed. Daniel H. Janzen, 613–614. Chicago: Univ. of Chicago Press. 816 pp.

Stiles, F. Gary, and Daniel H. Janzen. 1983a. Turkey Vulture (*Cathartes aura*). In *Costa Rican Natural History*, ed. Daniel H. Janzen, 560–562. Chicago: Univ. of Chicago Press. 816 pp.

———. 1983b. Roadside Hawk (*Buteo magnirostris*). In *Costa Rican Natural History*, ed.

Daniel H. Janzen, 551–552. Chicago: Univ. of Chicago Press. 816 pp.

Stiles, F. Gary, and Alexander F. Skutch. 1989. *A Guide to the Birds of Costa Rica*. Ithaca, N.Y.: Cornell Univ. Press. 511 pp.

Stouffer, Philip C., and R. Terry Chesser. 1998. Tropical Kingbird (*Tyrannus melancholicus*). In *The Birds of North America*, no. 358, ed. Alan Poole and Frank Gill. Philadelphia, Pa.: Academy of Natural Sciences; Washington, D.C.: American Ornithologists' Union. 20 pp.

Strauch, Joe G., Jr. 1983. Spotted Sandpiper (*Actitis macularia*). In *Costa Rican Natural History*, ed. Daniel H. Janzen, 544. Chicago: Univ. of Chicago Press. 816 pp.

Sykes, P. W., Jr., J. A. Rodgers, Jr., and R. E. Bennetts. 1995. Snail Kite (*Rostrhamus sociabilis*). In *The Birds of North America*, no. 171, ed. Alan Poole and Frank Gill. Philadelphia, Pa.: Academy of Natural Sciences; Washington, D.C.: American Ornithologists' Union. 32 pp.

Telfair, Raymond C. II. 1994. Cattle Egret (*Bubulcus ibis*). In *The Birds of North America*, no. 113, ed. Alan Poole and Frank Gill. Philadelphia, Pa.: Academy of Natural Sciences; Washington, D.C.: American Ornithologists' Union. 32 pp.

Telfair, Raymond C. II, and Michael L. Morrison. 1995. Neotropic Cormorant (*Phalacrocorax brasilianus*). In *The Birds of North America*, no. 137, ed. Alan Poole and Frank Gill. Philadelphia, Pa.: Academy of Natural

Sciences; Washington, D.C.: American Ornithologists' Union. 24 pp.

Watts, Bryan D. 1995. Yellow-crowned Night-Heron (*Nyctanassa violacea*). In *The Birds of North America*, no. 161, ed. Alan Poole and Frank Gill. Philadelphia, Pa.: Academy of Natural Sciences; Washington, D.C.: American Ornithologists' Union. 24 pp.

West, Richard L., and Gene K. Hess. 2002. Purple Gallinule (*Porphyrula martinica*). In *The Birds of North America*, no. 626, ed. Alan Poole and Frank Gill. Philadelphia, Pa.: Academy of Natural Sciences; Washington, D.C.: American Ornithologists' Union. 28 pp.

Wiley, R. Haven. 1983. Rufous-naped Wren (*Campylorhynchus rufinucha*). In *Costa Rican Natural History*, ed. Daniel H. Janzen, 558–560. Chicago: Univ. of Chicago Press. 816 pp.

Wolf, Blair O. 1997. Black Phoebe (*Sayornis nigricans*). In *The Birds of North America*, no. 268, ed. Alan Poole and Frank Gill. Philadelphia, Pa.: Academy of Natural Sciences; Washington, D.C.: American Ornithologists' Union. 20 pp.

Wyatt, Valerie E., and Charles M. Francis. 2002. Rose-breasted Grosbeak (*Pheucticus ludovicianus*). In *The Birds of North America*, no. 692, ed. Alan Poole and Frank Gill. Philadelphia, Pa.: Academy of Natural Sciences; Washington, D.C.: American Ornithologists' Union. 24 pp.

APPENDICES

APPENDIX A: COSTA RICAN CONSERVATION ORGANIZATIONS, RESEARCH STATIONS, BIRDING GROUPS, AND BIRD INFORMATION SOURCES

Asociación Ornitológica de Costa Rica: Apdo. 2289-1002, San José, Costa Rica. E-mail: chidalgo@una.ac.cr or drivera@una.ac.cr. Newsletter: *Zeledonia*. Office address: Avenida 6, Calles 21 Y 25, Casa 2194. Telephone: 506-2256-9587.

Association for the Conservation of Nature (ASCONA): Apartado 83790-1000, San José, Costa Rica. Telephone: 506-2233-3188.

Birding Club of Costa Rica: Web newsletter *Tico Tweeter* reports on recent and upcoming birding trips and birding discoveries at various sites and lodges. www.ticotours.home.att.net/Tweeter.

Caribbean Conservation Corporation: Gainesville, Florida. Telephone: 1-800-678-7853. www.cccturtle.org.

Corcovado Foundation: A nonprofit organization dedicated to protection of the rainforest and wildlife in Corcovado National Park, where there have been recent problems with poaching of endangered wildlife species. www.corcovadofoundation.org.

Costa Rica Birding Trail: A new effort in the northern region of Costa Rica to promote birding along a trail of lodges and protected areas that provide a stimulating variety of habitats. www.costaricanbirdroute.

Gone Birding: Web newsletter about birding and birding activities in Costa Rica, authored by expert birder Richard Garrigues. www.angelfire.com/bc/gonebirding.

Great Green Macaw Research and Conservation Project: Cooperative project headed by the Tropical Science Center and dedicated to the protection and restoration of the Great Green Macaw in the Caribbean lowlands of Costa Rica. www.lapaverde.or.cr/lapa.

Henderson Birding: www.hendersonbirding.com. The author's Web site, where updates, new information, and corrections to the *Field Guide to the Wildlife of Costa Rica* will be posted. Includes Costa Rica birding information, trip tips, preparation checklist, and itineraries for future birding trips.

La Selva Biological Field Station, OTS: Apartado 53-3069, Puerto Viejo en Sarapiquí, Heredia, Costa Rica. Telephone: 506-2766-6565; e-mail: laselva@sloth.ots.ac.cr.

Las Cruces Biological Station and Wilson Botanical Garden, OTS: Apartado 73, 8257 San Vito, Coto Brus, Costa Rica. Telephone: 506-2773-4004; e-mail: lcruces@hortus.ots.ac.cr.

Los Cusingos Neotropical Bird Sanctuary: The former home of Dr. Alexander Skutch, now managed by the Tropical Science Center. P.O. Box 8-3870-1000, San José, Costa Rica. Telephone: 506-2253-3276; e-mail: cecitrop@sol.racsa.co.cr.

Monteverde Conservation League: Apartado 10165-1000, San José, Costa Rica. Manages the Children's Eternal Rainforest. Telephone: 506-2645-5003; e-mail: acmmcl@sol.racsa.co.cr. www.acmcr.org; also www.monteverdeinfo.com.

National Biodiversity Institute (INBIO): Apdo. 22-3100, Santo Domingo, Heredia, Costa Rica. National organization dedicated to the creation of a comprehensive inventory of all of Costa Rica's plant and wildlife species; with biological collections now exceeding 3.5 million specimens and many excellent publications. Telephone: 506-2507-8100. www.inbio.ac.cr.

National Parks Foundation (Fundación de Parques Nacionales): Apartado 236-1002, San José, Costa Rica. Telephone: 506-2222-4921 or 506-2223-8437.

Organization for Tropical Studies, Inc.: North American Headquarters, Box 90630, Durham, NC 27708-0630. www.ots.duke.edu; also www.ots.ac.cr. Costa Rican office: Apartado 676, 2050 San Pedro de Montes de Oca, San José, Costa Rica. Telephone: 506-2240-6696; e-mail: oet@cro.ots.ac.cr.

Rainforest Action Network: 221 Pine Street, Suite 500, San Francisco, CA 94104. Telephone: 415-398-4404. www.ran.org.

Rincón Rainforest: A protected

tropical forest of 13,838 acres in northern Costa Rica. Donations to the Guanacaste Dry Forest Conservation Fund help to save Costa Rica's biodiversity; tax-deductible donations can be matched from conservation foundations and will be used 100 percent for land acquisition (no overhead or administrative

charges). Contact Dr. Daniel H. Janzen for further details; djanzen@sas.upenn.edu. Donations made out to the Guanacaste Dry Forest Conservation Fund can be sent to Prof. Daniel H. Janzen, Dept. of Biology, 415 South University Ave., University of Pennsylvania, Philadelphia, PA 19104. http://janzen.sas

.upenn.edu/RR/rincon_rainfor est.htm.

Tirimbina Rainforest Center: A tropical science research and tourism center initiated by the Milwaukee Public Museum. Telephone: 506-2761-1579 or 506-2761-0055; e-mail: info@ tirimbina.org. www.envirolink .org.

APPENDIX B: WILDLIFE TOURISM SITES AND FIELD STATIONS REFERRED TO IN THE DISTRIBUTION MAPS

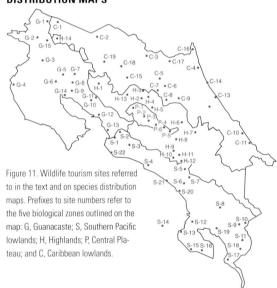

Figure 11. Wildlife tourism sites referred to in the text and on species distribution maps. Prefixes to site numbers refer to the five biological zones outlined on the map: G, Guanacaste; S, Southern Pacific lowlands; H, Highlands; P, Central Plateau; and C, Caribbean lowlands.

Each dot on the distribution maps represents one or more sightings for a species in that area by Henderson Birding Tour groups from 1987 through 2008. Sightings for La Laguna del Lagarto Lodge include species reported as "common" or "abundant" by lodge owner Vinzenz Schmack. In the following key, the site code from Figure 11 is followed by the name of the site, its biological zone and elevation, its coordinates, a brief description, and contact information. Abbreviations: BR, Biological Reserve. NP, National Park. NWR, National Wildlife Refuge.

OTS, Organization for Tropical Studies. PAH, Pan American Highway.

GUANACASTE REGION

G-1: Los Inocentes Ranch: Tropical moist forest. Elev. 750'. Lat. 11°02.50'N, long. 85°30.00'W. Address: P.O. Box 228-3000, Heredia, Costa Rica. This lodge is now closed to tourism.

G-2: Santa Rosa NP: Tropical dry forest/premontane moist forest. Elev. 1350'. Lat. 10°51.50'N, long. 85°36.50'W. This park contains 181,186 acres and is an excellent

example of tropical dry forest and premontane moist forest, as well as gallery forests. The Pacific ridley turtle nesting beaches of Nancite are within this park. Telephone: Santa Rosa NP, 506-2666-5051; Guanacaste Conservation Area, 506-2666-4740.

G-3: Liberia, road to Tamarindo: Tropical dry forest. Elev. 100'. From lat. 10°37.50'N, long. 85°27.00'W, to lat. 10°18.60'N, long. 85°55.00'W. Many species of the tropical dry forest can be spotted along this road en route to see the leatherback turtles at Tamarindo.

G-4: Tamarindo, Playa Grande, Las Baulas NP, and Sugar Beach: Tropical dry forest. Elev. Sea level. Lat. 10°18.60'N, long. 85°55.00'W. Las Baulas NP, which covers 1,364 acres, protects the nesting beaches of the leatherback turtles at Playa Grande. Mangrove lagoons and beaches in the vicinity are important wintering sites for shorebirds, wading birds, and local wildlife. Tropical dry forests of the area provide opportunities for viewing howler monkeys and other upland wildlife. Tamarindo NWR and Las Baulas National Marine Park, telephone: 506-2653-0470. Turtle tours available October through March at El Mundo de las Tortugas, 506-2653-0471, at Playa Grande. Telephone: Hotel Bula Bula, 506-2653-0975, www.hotelbulabula.com; Hotel Las Tortugas, 506-2653-0423, www.cool.co.cr/usr/turtles; Hotel Villa Baula, 506-2653-0644; www.hotelvillabaula.com.

G-5: Lomas Barbudal BR: Tropical dry forest. Elev. 100'. Lat. 10°26.20'N, long. 85°16.00'W. Lomas Barbudal is a reserve of 5,631 acres that provides an excellent example of riparian forest within the Guanacaste region. Elegant Trogons, Scrub Euphonias, and Long-tailed Manakins are among the featured wildlife there.

G-6: Palo Verde NP: Tropical dry forest. Elev. 30'. Lat. 10°22.21'N, long. 85°11.84'W. Palo Verde NP is one of the best examples of both dry forest and tropical wetlands. This park includes the area that was formerly designated as the Dr. Rafael Lucas Rodríguez Caballero NWR, with 45,511 acres of tropical dry forest, riparian forest, and marshes. It is an important wintering site for migratory waterfowl and local Black-bellied Whistling-Ducks and Muscovy Ducks; also home to Jabiru storks, Scarlet Macaws, and Snail Kites. This is an important research and education site for the OTS and for the National Biodiversity Institute. Palo Verde OTS Biological Station, telephone: 506-2524-0607; www.threepaths.co.cr. Reservations: edu.travel@ots.ac.cr.

G-7: La Pacífica (Hotel Hacienda La Pacífica) and Cañas: Tropical dry forest. Elev. 150'. Lat. 10°27.21'N, long. 85°07.68'W. This lodge, on a 6,548-acre ranch and private forest reserve formerly known as Finca La Pacífica, is an excellent place to stay when visiting locations like Guanacaste, Santa Rosa, and Palo Verde NPs and Lomas Barbudal BR. Address: Apartado 8, 5700 Cañas, Guanacaste, Costa Rica; www.pacificacr.com. Telephone: 506-2669-

6050; e-mail: pacifica@racsa.co.cr. On the east boundary of this property is Las Pumas, a wild cat rescue and rehabilitation center. All six of Costa Rica's wild cats can be observed there. Telephone: 506-2669-6044. Donations are appreciated.

G-8: Estancia Jiminez Nuñez and lagoons: Tropical dry forest. Elev. 250'. Lat. 10°20.55'N, long. 85°08.69'W. Private ranch with large man-made lagoons with many waterbirds; good raptor viewing on the road from the PAH west to this ranch. Get permission from the guard at the entrance to see the lagoons.

G-9: Hacienda Solimar: Tropical dry forest. Elev. 100'. Lat. 10°15.58'N, long. 85°09.40'W. Excellent dry forest and riparian forest, with exceptional wetland wildlife, including Roseate Spoonbills, Snail Kites, nesting Jabiru storks, Boat-billed Herons, Bare-throated Tiger-Herons, and crocodiles. Owners have made significant improvements to this 5,000-acre ranch to accommodate wildlife tourism. Telephone, at ranch: 506-2669-0281; e-mail: solimar@racsa.co.cr.

G-10: Río Lagarto bridge and farm lagoon: Premontane moist forest. Elev. 140'. Lat. 10°09.76'N, 84°54.93'W. This is a farm pond just off the PAH north of the bridge over the Río Lagarto. It is at Ganadería Avancari. Black-bellied Whistling-Ducks, Least Grebes, Purple Gallinules, and Northern Jacanas are regularly observed along the road in the marsh.

G-11: Pulperia La Pita and lowlands to Monteverde: Tropical moist forest. Elev. 700'. From lat. 10°10.09'N, long. 84°54.38'W to lat. 10°18.00'N, long. 84°49.20'W. This is the road from the turnoff from the PAH by Río Lagarto, past a small store known as Pulperia La Pita and through mixed

pasture and woodland en route to Monteverde. Wildlife includes species of the Guanacaste dry forest, like White-throated Magpie-Jays, Rufous-naped Wrens, and Long-tailed Manakins.

G-12: Puntarenas, Hotel Tioga, and Playa Doña Ana: Premontane wet forest. Elev. Sea level. Lat. 9°58.46'N, long. 84°50.34'W. The lagoons and beaches of Puntarenas and Playa Doña Ana provide excellent areas to observe waterbirds. Lodging—Hotel Tioga. Address: P.O. Box 96-5400, Puntarenas, Costa Rica; www.hoteltioga.com. Telephone: in San José, 506-2255-3115; in Puntarenas, 506-2661-0271.

G-13: Bajamar: Tropical dry forest. Elev. Sea level. Lat. 9°50.50'N, long. 84°40.50'W. This area of tropical dry forest and mangrove lagoons near the coast represents the southern range limit for dry forest birds.

G-14: La Ensenada Lodge: Tropical dry forest. Elev. Sea level to 250'. Lat. 10°08.304'N, long. 85°02.394'W. A privately owned national wildlife reserve, this 939-acre ranch is a wildlife mecca at the head of the Gulf of Nicoya. It contains tropical dry forest, pastures, mangrove lagoons, shoreline habitat, wetlands, and commercial salt ponds that attract great varieties of shorebirds. This ranch is used by Three-wattled Bellbirds from roughly December through February, as well as Turquoise-browed Motmots and White-throated Magpie-Jays. Boat tours in nearby mangrove lagoons provide the chance to see the Mangrove Vireo, Mangrove Hummingbird, Mangrove Cuckoo, and Mangrove race of the Yellow Warbler. This is one of the only places in Costa Rica where the Northern Potoo can be encountered at night. www.laensenada.net. Telephone: 506-

2289-6655 or 506-2289-7443; e-mail:la_ensenada@yahoo.com.

G-15: Hotel Borinquen Mountain Resort and Thermal Spa: Tropical moist forest/premontane moist forest transition. Elev. 2,500'. Lat. 10°48.704'N, long. 84°04.965'W. This resort and spa features thermal springs and also provides good birding opportunities on the grounds and vicinity, including access to nearby Rincón de la Vieja NP. Wildlife is typical of the tropical dry forest but also features some species of the Caribbean slope. There are Turquoise-browed Motmots, Crested Caracaras, Red-lored Parrots, White-fronted Parrots, Keel-billed Toucans, White-throated Magpie-Jays, Double-striped Thick-knees, and Plain-capped Starthroats. www.borinquenresort.com. Telephone: 506-2690-1900; e-mail: borinque@racsa.co.cr.

SOUTHERN PACIFIC LOWLANDS

S-1: Carara NP, Río Tárcoles estuary, Tárcol Lodge, Villa Caletas, Crocodile Jungle Safari, and Villa Lapas: Carara NP: Premontane moist forest. Elev. Sea level–100'. Lat. 9°47.72'N, long. 84°36.16'W. Carara NP is an excellent reserve, covering 12,953 acres, that has wildlife of both the Guanacaste tropical dry forest and tropical wet forests of the southern Pacific lowlands. It is one of the best places to observe Scarlet Macaws and crocodiles in the country. www.costaricagateway.com. Telephone: Carara NP, 506-2383-9953; in Costa Rica, 506-2433-8278; toll-free in USA: 1-888-246-8513; e-mail: crgateway@rracsa.co.cr. Tárcol Lodge is at the mouth of the Río Tárcoles, where a great variety of waterbirds, raptors, and tropical songbirds can be viewed from the veranda and surrounding roads and trails. Villa Caletas: Tropical moist forest. Elev. Sea

level–150'. Lat. 9°41.207'N, long. 84°39.597'W. Villa Caletas is an excellent seaside resort that provides easy access to Carara NP and boat tours in the Río Tárcoles mangrove lagoons. Many notable wildlife species can be seen right on the grounds, including Zone-tailed Hawks, parrots, chachalacas, and hummingbirds. Address: P.O. Box 12358-1000, San José, Costa Rica; www.villacaletas .com. Telephone: Reservations, 506-2637-0606; Hotel, 506-2637-0505; e-mail: reservations@vil lacaletas.com. Crocodile Jungle Safari Tour: Tropical dry forest. Elev. Sea level. Lat. 9°46.930'N, long. 84°38.187'W. Crocodile Jungle Safari offers outstanding boat tours in the mangrove lagoons and estuaries of the Río Tárcoles near Carara NP. The guides are exceptional at bird identification and are successful in locating a variety of birds and providing great photo opportunities. This tour company provides good opportunities for viewing the crocodiles. They are recommended because they do not feed or habituate the crocodiles to their presence like some tour operators. Address: P.O. Box 1542, San Pedro, Costa Rica; www.cos taricanaturetour.com. Telephone: 506-2637-0338; e-mail: croco dile@costaricanaturetour.com. Hotel Villa Lapas: Tropical moist forest. Elev. approx. 150'. Lat. 9°45.368'N, long. 84°36.573'W. The grounds of this resort offer some outstanding birding and easy access to nearby Carara NP and the Río Tárcoles mangrove lagoons. Trogons, owls, tiger-herons, and even Scarlet Macaws can be observed on the property. The skywalk facility in the adjacent forest provides outstanding opportunities to see wildlife of the moist and dry forest, including Long-tailed Manakins, hummingbirds, parrots, tanagers,

and trogons. Address: P.O. Box 419-4005, Heredia, Costa Rica; www.villalapas.com. Telephone: 506-2637-0232; e-mail: info@ villalapas.com. Hotel Xandari by the Beach: South of Carara; www.hotelxandari.com. Telephone: 506-2778-7070.

S-2: Orotina, road to lowlands approaching Carara: Tropical moist forest. Elev. 500'. Lat. 9°51.80'N, long. 84°34.00'W. This route includes the famous city park in Orotina where a pair of Black-and-white Owls and an introduced Two-toed Sloth have lived for many years.

S-3: Parrita, road to Puriscal: Tropical moist forest. Site 1: Elev. 1,600'. Lat. 9°42.46'N, long. 84°24.22'W. Site 2: Elev. 2,000'. Lat. 9°43.90'N, long. 84.23.64'W.

S-4: Manuel Antonio NP, Rancho Casa Grande, Damas Island mangrove tours, and Quepos: Tropical wet forest. Elev. Sea level. Lat. 9°22.94'N, long. 84°08.62'W. Manuel Antonio NP covers 4,015 acres of land and 135,905 acres of ocean. It provides excellent opportunities to see squirrel monkeys, agoutis, white-faced monkeys, ctenosaurs, butterflies, and many species of the southern Pacific lowlands. Telephone: 506-2777-3130, 506-2777-1646; toll-free reservations, 1-888-790-5264; e-mail: osrap@minae.go.cr. Foresta Resort Rancho Casa Grande: Premontane wet forest. Elev. approx. 100–250'. Lat. 9°26.414'N, long. 84°08.185'W. Rancho Casa Grande is an excellent lodge to stay at while exploring the Quepos area, including Manuel Antonio NP and the nearby mangrove lagoons. There are some outstanding trails for birding on the 180 acres. It is a good place to see endangered squirrel monkeys, tityras, Streaked Flycatchers, and other wildlife of the southern Pacific lowlands. Address: P.O. Box

618-2010 Zapote, San José, Costa Rica; www.ranchocasagrande.com. Telephone: 506-2777-3130, 506-2777-1646; e-mail: hotelrc@sol.racsa.co.cr. Damas Island mangrove lagoons: Iguana Tours (Jorge's Mangrove Tours) in Quepos can arrange boating tours to see the wildlife of the mangrove lagoons near Damas Island. It is one of the best places to look for the rare Silky Anteater, Mangrove Hummingbird, Mangrove Vireo, and the Mangrove subspecies of the Yellow Warbler. www.iguanatours.com. Telephone: 506-2777-1262; e-mail: iguana@racsa.co.cr.

S-5: Talari Mountain Lodge near San Isidro del General: Premontane wet forest. Elev. 2,800'. Lat. 9°24.14'N, long. 83°40.12'W. This rustic lodge near San Isidro has great wildlife viewing opportunities on the grounds. It is easy to observe seventy species in a morning of birding there. This is an excellent place to see the Slaty Spinetail, Pearl Kite, and Redlegged Honeycreeper. Many birds come to the feeders. Address: Talari Albergue de Montaña, Rivas, San Isidro del General, Apdo 517-8000, Pérez Zeledón, Costa Rica; www.talari.co.cr. Telephone and fax: 506-2771-0341; e-mail: talaricostarica@gmail.com. This is a good place to stay if visiting Los Cusingos, the former home of famous ornithologist Alexander Skutch, now managed by the Tropical Science Center in San José (see details for site S-7).

S-6: La Junta de Pacuares resort on Río General: Tropical moist forest. Elev. 2,200'. Lat. 9°16.51'N, long. 83°38.33'W. A variety of wildlife can be seen along the river at this site, including Gray-headed Chachalacas.

S-7: Los Cusingos, San Isidro del General, City Lagoons, and Hotel del Sur: Tropical moist forest. San Isidro del General: Elev. 2,200'. Lat. 9°20.40'N, long. 83°28.00'W.; City sewage lagoons: Elev. 2,000'. Lat. 9°22.25'N, long. 83°41.80'W.; Los Cusingos: Elev. 2,500'. Lat. 9°19.10'N, long. 83°36.75'W. Los Cusingos Neotropical Bird Sanctuary is the former homestead of the late Dr. Alexander and Pamela Skutch. It is now managed by the Tropical Science Center. Los Cusingos is an excellent remnant forest reserve where it is possible to make a day trip to see Bayheaded Tanagers, Gray-headed Chachalacas, Speckled Tanagers, White-breasted Wood-Wrens, and other wildlife of the southern Pacific moist forest. Make arrangements for visits with the Tropical Science Center, Apartado 8-3870-1000, San José, Costa Rica; www.cct.or.cr (Refugio Los Cusingos). Telephone: 506-2253-3267; e-mail: cct@cct.oor.cr. Hotel del Sur in San Isidro del General and Talari Mountain Lodge (site S-5) provide convenient places to stay. Address: Hotel del Sur, P.O. Box 4-8000, San Isidro del General, Costa Rica; Google "Hotel del Sur, Costa Rica." Telephone: 506-2771-3033; e-mail: reservas@hoteldelsur.com.

S-8: Río Térraba bridge crossing: Tropical moist forest. Elev. 200'. Bridge over Río Térraba: Lat. 9°00.20'N, long. 83°13.20'W. This bridge crossing is well known for the huge crocodiles that can be seen near the sewage, as well as herons and egrets.

S-9: Wilson Botanical Garden at San Vito–OTS Las Cruces Biological Field Station: Premontane rainforest. Elev. 3,900'. Wilson Botanical Garden, lat. 8°49.61'N, long. 82°57.80'W. This OTS field station has cabins for tourists and an excellent trail system. There are regionally endemic birds on the property, and many birds come to the feeders there. Address: Apartado 73-8257, San Vito, Costa Rica; main OTS address: Apartado 676-2050 San Pedro de Montes Oca, Costa Rica; www.threepaths.com. Telephone: in USA, 1-919-684-5774; in San José, 506-2524-0607; reservations in San José, 506-2524-0628; e-mail: edu.travel@ots.ac.cr. Wetland birds can be observed nearby at the lagoons by the airport (for a fee; this is on private property) and at Los Contaros, a private nature park and wetland with a gift shop owned by Gail Hewson. It has indigenous crafts of the Guaymi community and is on the outskirts of San Vito, near the Wilson Botanical Garden.

S-10: Sabalito, road from San Vito: Premontane wet forest. Elev. 2,200'. From lat. 8°49.61'N, long. 82°57.80'W, to lat. 8°49.80'N, long. 82°53.80'W. When exploring the San Vito area, along this road is a good place to look for southern specialties like the Bran-colored Flycatcher, Pearl Kite, Masked (Chiriquí) Yellowthroat, and Crested Oropendola.

S-11: Paso Canoas: Premontane wet forest. Elev. 300'. From lat. 8°32.00'N, long. 82°50.30'W, to lat. 8°49.61'N, long. 82°57.80'W. Paso Canoas is the town in southern Costa Rica where the PAH enters Panama. Wildlife of the area is typical of the southern Pacific lowlands.

S-12: Sierpe, on the Río Térraba, to Drake Bay: Premontane wet forest. Elev. Sea level. From Sierpe at lat. 8°51.50'N, long. 83°28.20'W, to the Río Sierpe estuary at lat. 8°46.50'N, long. 83°38.00'W. Local lodging includes Río Sierpe Lodge, where boat trips are available to Corcovado NP and Caño Island. Telephone: 506-2283-5573; e-mail: vsftrip@racsa.co.cr.

S-13: Drake Bay Wilderness Resort, northwest end of Corcovado NP: Tropical wet forest. Elev.

Sea level. Lat. 8°41.80'N, long. 83°41.00'W. www.drakebay.com. Telephone: 506-2770-8012 (also fax), 506-2384-4107; in San José, 506-2256-7394; at resort, 506-2371-3437; e-mail: hdrake@sol.racsa.co.cr. **S-14: Caño Island:** Tropical wet forest. Elev. Sea level. Lat. 8°43.000'N, long. 83°53.000'W. This island includes 741 acres and is six miles from the Osa Peninsula. It is possible to see humpback whales while en route between the mainland and the island. Arrange for visits with local lodges like Río Sierpe Lodge, Drake Bay Wilderness Resort, Aguila de Osa Inn, La Paloma Lodge, or Marenco Lodge.

S-15: Sirena Biological Station, Corcovado NP: Tropical wet forest. Elev. Sea level. Lat. 8°78.740'N, long. 35.810'W. This biological station is one of the best examples of remote, wild rainforest in Costa Rica. There are significant populations of Scarlet Macaws, tapirs, White-lipped Peccaries, Great Curassows, Jaguars, Cougars, and other species characteristic of tropical wet forests. Accessible by air or on foot by hiking along the beach from La Leona or San Pedrillo.

S-16: Corcovado Lodge Tent Camp, Carate, and southeast end of Corcovado NP: Tropical wet forest. Elev. Sea level. Lat. 8°26.880'N, long. 83°28.970'W. This excellent tent camp lodge provides great access for wildlife viewing on the beachfront property, along trails in the rainforest behind the lodge, and in nearby Corcovado NP. A wildlife tower allows viewing of wildlife in the forest canopy. Wildlife includes Scarlet Macaws, parrots, King Vultures, and many raptors. Address: Costa Rica Expeditions, P.O. Box 6941-1000, San José, Costa Rica; www.costaricaexpeditions.com. Telephone: 506-2257-0766, 506-2222-0333; e-mail:

costaric@expeditions.co.cr. Similar wildlife can be observed at Marenco Beach and Rainforest Lodge (506-2770-8002; www.marencolodge.com), Bosque del Cabo (506-2735-5206; www.bosquedelcabo.com), Luna Lodge (506-2380-5036; www.lunalodge.com), La Paloma Lodge (506-2239-2801; www.lapalomalodge.com), and Lapa Ríos (506-2735-513; www.laparios.com).

S-17: Tiskita Jungle Lodge: Tropical wet forest. Elev. Sea level to 200'. Lat. 8°21.480'N, long. 83°8.050'W. A 400-acre private forest reserve and tropical fruit experimental field station, this is one of the best places in Costa Rica to see squirrel monkeys and White Hawks. Many tanagers and honeycreepers are present because of the variety of fruiting trees on the grounds. Address: Costa Rica Sun Tours, P.O. Box 13411-1000, San José, Costa Rica; www.tiskita.com. Telephone: 506-2296-8125.

S-18: Road from San Vito to Paso Canoas: Premontane moist forest. Elev. 900'. Lat. 8°44.500'N, long. 82°56.900'W. The highway from San Vito de Java to Paso Canoas provides a good opportunity for viewing wildlife of the southern Pacific lowlands, including Blue-headed Parrots, squirrel monkeys, and relatively new arrivals in Costa Rica like the Pearl Kite and Crested Oropendola. There is a colony of Crested Oropendolas nesting along the highway near Villa Neily.

S-19: Las Esquinas Rainforest Lodge: Tropical wet forest. Elev. 800'. Lat. 9°33.131'N, long. 83°48.624'W. This is an excellent ecolodge at the head of the Osa Peninsula near the town of Gamba and Piedras Blancas NP. It has a great variety of wildlife of the southern Pacific lowlands, ranging from Spectacled Owls to antbirds, hummingbirds,

Baird's Trogons, and the endemic Black-cheeked Ant-Tanager. www.esquinaslodge.com. Telephone: 506-2741-8001.

S-20: La Cusinga, Oro Verde, Cristal Ballena, Ballena Marine NP: La Cusinga Lodge: Tropical wet forest. Elev. Sea level–400'. Lat. 9°8.500'N, long. 83°42.900'W. This outstanding ecolodge, an ecologically sustainable facility that is sensitive to environmental protection, provides a rustic and attractive setting overlooking the Pacific Ocean. It is possible to see a great variety of rainforest wildlife, including Great Tinamous, Spectacled Owls, manakins, toucans, and oropendolas in the vicinity of the cabins, along the beach, and along the trails. The owners of this property, John Tressemer and his son, Geiner Guzman, were instrumental in the establishment of the Ballena Marine NP. Address: La Cusinga, S.A., Apdo. 41-8000, San Isidro del General, Costa Rica; www.lacusingalodge.com. Telephone: 506-2770-2549. While staying at La Cusinga, it is possible to take a whale- and dolphin-watching excursion to see the migrant humpback whales, false killer whales, dolphins, and marine birds of the offshore areas in Ballena Marine NP. This national park was created in 1991 by President Oscar Arias after photos taken by the author on a Henderson Birding Tour in 1990 documented the winter calving grounds of humpback whales offshore from Caño Island and Punta Uvita. The park includes 425 acres of oceanfront land and 12,750 acres of ocean. For a boat tour to see the whales and dolphins, contact Delfin Tours (506-2743-8169), Ballena Tours (506-2831-1617), or Pelican Tours (506-2743-8047; cabinaslarr@hotmail.com). Other resorts in this vicinity include Hotel Cristal

Ballena: Lat. 9°7.441'N, long. 83°41.855'W. www.cristal-ballena .com. Telephone: 506-2786-5354. Whales and Dolphins: A four-star hotel. www.whalesanddolphins .net. Telephone: in USA (toll-free), 1-866-429-3958; in Costa Rica, 506-2743-8150; e-mail: sales@whalesanddolphins.net. Oro Verde Tropical Rainforest Reserve: Tropical wet forest. Lat. 9°12.400'N, long. 83°45.600'W. Elev. 1,000'–2,200'. This private rainforest reserve is about two miles northwest of the village of Uvita along the coast road and two miles east. It does not have lodging available but is a good destination for a day trip to explore the rainforest. It has good trails and an observation tower. Distinctive birds of this site are the Black-crested Coquette, Blue-throated Goldentail, Brown-hooded Parrot, Chestnut-mandibled Toucan, Blue-crowned Motmot, and Crested Owl. www .costarica-birding-oroverde.com. Telephone: 506-2743-8072, 506-2843-8833, 506-2827-3325.

S-21: Hacienda Barú Natural Reserve: Tropical wet forest. Elev. Sea level. Lat. 9°15.984'N, long. 83°53.028'W. Playa Dominical and Hacienda Barú Natural Reserve are beach areas with migrant shorebirds, like Willets and Whimbrels, and adjacent forest with abundant birdlife. Hacienda Barú Resort; www.haciendabaru .com. Telephone: 506-2787-0003.

S-22: Playa Hermosa: Tropical wet forest. Elev. Sea level. Lat. 9°34.495'N, 84°36.673'W. Playa Hermosa and adjacent pastures are noted for wetland birds, many wintering Barn Swallows, and recent records of Southern Lapwings.

CENTRAL PLATEAU

P-1: Sarchí vicinity: Premontane wet forest. Elev. 3,100'. Lat.

10°5.10'N, long. 84°20.80'W. Birds of this urban area include the Blue-gray Tanager, Summer Tanager, Baltimore Oriole, Grayish Saltator, Rufous-tailed Hummingbird, Yellow Warbler, and Clay-colored Thrush.

P-2: Xandari Plantation Resort, Juan Santamaría International Airport–Pavas vicinity, Hotel Alta, and Tobias Bolaños Airport: Premontane moist forest. Elev. 3,200'. Lat. 9°59.60'N, long. 84°08.40'W. The Xandari Plantation Resort has beautifully landscaped grounds with many ornamental flowers and birds. Blue-crowned Motmots, Ferruginous Pygmy-Owls, Tropical Screech-Owls, and even Long-tailed Manakins can be encountered there. The shade coffee plantation on the grounds is one of the only places in Costa Rica to find the Buffy-crowned Wood-Partridge. Address: Xandari Plantation, Apdo 1485-4050, Alajuela, Costa Rica; www.xan dari.com. Telephone: 506-2443-2020; e-mail: hotel@xandari.com. Telephone: 506-2443-2020. Hotel Alta has beautifully landscaped grounds and is an excellent hotel near the airport. www .thealtahotel.com. Telephone: 506-2282-4160; e-mail: info@ hotelalta.com. Hotel Aeropuerto: www.hotelaeropuerto-cr.com; telephone: 506-2433-7333.

P-3: San José vicinity and downtown: Premontane moist forest (urban). Elev. 3,700'. Lat. 9°56.96'N, longitude 84°04.05'W.

P-4: Tres Ríos, Curridibat: Premontane moist forest. Elev. 3,900'. Lat. 9°54.14'N, long. 84°00.37'W.

P-5: Cartago vicinity, Lankester Gardens, and Las Concavas marsh: Premontane moist forest. Elev. 4,700'. Lat. 9°50.20'N, long. 83°53.55'W. The Parque de Expression in Cartago has ponds with waterbirds like Northern Jacanas. The private Las Conca-vas marsh and adjacent pastures

can be viewed with permission; look for wintering Blue-winged Teal, Killdeer, Eastern Meadow-larks, and Least Grebes.

P-6: Hotel Bougainvillea: Premontane moist forest. Elev. 3,910'. Lat. 9°58.244'N, long. 84°04.965'W. Hotel Bougainvillea in Santo Domingo de Heredia is an excellent hotel for beginning or ending a stay in Costa Rica. The eight acres of gardens are beautifully landscaped and attract a great variety of birds, including Blue-crowned Motmots, Grayish Saltators, Ferruginous Pygmy-Owls, and rare White-eared and Prevost's Ground-Sparrows, which regularly visit the compost pile on the east side of the garden. Mailing address: P.O. Box 69-2120, San José, Costa Rica; www.hb.co.cr. Telephone: in USA (toll-free), 1-866-880-5441; in Costa Rica, 506-2244-1414; e-mail: info@hb.co.cr. Motel staff can arrange for rides to the nearby INBIO Parque, the biodiversity park and interpretive center of the National Institute of Biodiversity in Santo Domingo de Heredia. www.inbio.ac.cr; www.inbioparque.com; Telephone: INBIO, 506-2507-8100 or 506-2507-8107; INBIO Parque, 506-2507-8107.

CARIBBEAN LOWLANDS

C-1: Inocentes–Río Frío region; road from Los Inocentes Ranch east to lowlands by Santa Cecilia: Tropical moist forest. From lat. 11°02.70'N, long. 85°30.00'W. at Los Inocentes Ranch (now closed to tourism) to lat. 11°03.70'N, long. 85°24.40'W. at Santa Cecilia. This region has wildlife species of the Caribbean lowlands. Owls and Common and Great Potoos can be seen along the road at night with the aid of spotlights.

C-2: Caño Negro NWR and Natural Caño Negro Lodge: Tropical moist forest. Elev. 175'. Lat. 10°54.50'N, long. 84°47.70'W. An exceptional refuge of 24,483 acres, providing habitat for wetland wildlife of the Caribbean lowlands, including waterfowl, wading birds, and rare species like the Nicaraguan Seed-Finch, Nicaraguan Grackle, Agami Heron, and Green Ibis. There is a recent record of nesting by Jabiru storks. The Caño Negro wetlands have been designated one of the most important wetlands in the world. Lodging, boat trips, and tarpon fishing in the nearby lake and channels of the Río Frío can be arranged at Caño Negro Lodge; www .canonegrolodge.com. Telephone: central office, 506-2265-1204, 506-2265-3302, 506-2265-1298; hotel, 506-2471-1000, 506-2471-1426; e-mail: info@ canonegrolodge.com.

C-3: Laguna del Lagarto and Ara Ambigua Lodges: Tropical wet forest. Elev. 200'. Lat. 10°41.20'N, long. 84°11.20'W. The area of Laguna del Lagarto Lodge has wildlife species of the Caribbean lowland rainforest and many wetland species. Address: P.O. Box 995-1007 Centro Colón, San José, Costa Rica; www.lagarto-lodge-costa-rica.com. Telephone: 506-2289-8163; e-mail: info@ lagarto-lodge-costa-rica.com. Ara Ambigua, a rainforest lodge, is north of Puerto Viejo en Sarapiquí; it has a frog garden and opportunities for viewing wildlife along the Río Sarapiquí and forest trails. www.hotelaraambigua .com. Telephone: 506-2766-7101, 506-2766-6401; e-mail: info@ hotelaraambigua.com.

C-4: Tortuga Lodge and Tortuguero NP: Tropical wet forest. Elev. Sea level. Lat. 10°34.36'N, long. 83°31.04'W. An exceptional area of lowland wet forest with great opportunities to view macaws, monkeys, toucans, bats, crocodiles, hummingbirds, and

butterflies along the canals and foot trails behind Tortuga Lodge. Address: Costa Rica Expeditions, Apartado 6941-1000, San José, Costa Rica, or Dept. 235, Box 025216, Miami, FL 33102-5216; www.costaricaexpeditions .com. Telephone: 506-2222-0333, 506-2257-0766; e-mail: costaric@ expeditions.co.cr.

C-5: La Selva, Selva Verde Lodge, Sueño Azul, Puerto Viejo, and El Gavilán Lodge: Tropical wet forest. Elev. 200'. Lat. 10°25.89'N, long. 84°00.27'W. La Selva Biological Field Station is a biological research station operated by OTS. The author first studied tropical ecology in a course at La Selva in 1969. It is a great destination for observing wildlife of the Caribbean lowlands along well-maintained trails and boardwalks through the forest. There is an excellent opportunity to see owls, motmots, hummingbirds, trogons, antbirds, tinamous, collared peccaries, and other rainforest species. Address: Organization for Tropical Studies, Apartado 676-2050, San Pedro de Montes de Oca, San José, Costa Rica; www.threepaths.co.cr. Telephone: in USA, 1-919-684-5774; in Costa Rica, 506-2524-0607; e-mail: edu.travel@ots.ac.cr. Selva Verde Lodge, Sueño Azul Resort, and El Gavilán Lodge are all excellent places to stay while visiting La Selva. It is also possible to stay in cabins at the La Selva OTS facility by contacting the OTS for reservations. Selva Verde Lodge address: Chilamate, Sarapiquí, Costa Rica; www .selevaverde.com. Telephone: in USA (toll-free), 1-800-2451-7111; in Costa Rica, 506-2766-6800; e-mail: selvaver@racsa.co.cr. El Gavilán Lodge, www.gavilan lodge.com. Telephone: 506-2766-6743, 506-2234-9507; e-mail: gavilan@racsa.co.cr. Sueño Azul Resort is an outstanding lodge

a few miles south of La Selva. The grounds and adjacent pastures and river provide excellent birding for such specialties as Fasciated Tiger-Herons, trogons, motmots, guans, Scaled Pigeons, Black-faced Grosbeaks, and Sunbitterns. www.suenoazulresort .com. Telephone: in San José, 506-2253-2020; hotel, 506-2764-1000, 506-2764-1048, 506-2764-1049; e-mail: info@suenoazulresort.com.

C-6: Guacimo, road from La Selva to Guacimo lowland turnoff: Tropical wet forest. Elev. 200'. From lat. 10°25.89'N, long. 84°00.27'W, to lat. 10°13.00'N, long. 83°56.00'W. This is an area of cleared pastureland and scrub, small ponds, and some rivers—good for herons, egrets, anis, and an occasional King Vulture. La Tirimbina Biological Reserve; www.tirimbina .org. Telephone: 506-2761-1579; e-mail: info@tirimbina.org.

C-7: Rara Avis: Premontane rainforest. Elev. 2,000'. Lat. 10°17.30'N, long. 84°02.47'W. This 1,500-acre reserve is an excellent place to observe wildlife of the Caribbean lowlands and foothills, including the rare Snowcap Hummingbird. Address: Apartado 8105-1000, San José, Costa Rica; www.rara-avis.com. Telephone: 506-2764-1111; e-mail: info@rara-avis.com.

C-8: Rainforest Aerial Tram, Tapir Trail, and Braulio Carrillo NP: Tropical wet forest. Elev. 2,000'. Lat. 10°10.80'N, long. 83°56.60'W. The tram and trails on the property provide excellent places to observe wildlife of middle elevations. Address: Apdo Postal 1959-1002, San José, Costa Rica; www.rfat.com. Telephone: 506-2257-5961; e-mail: info@rfat.com. At Tapir Trail, a private reserve along the highway east of Braulio Carrillo NP, it is possible to see Black-crested Coquettes and Snowcaps.

C-9: Guapiles and Guacimo lowlands: Tropical wet forest. Elev. 900'. Lat. 10°12.85'N, long. 83°47.35'W. The highway from Guapiles east to Limón is excellent for spotting sloths along the highway. Rare Fasciated Tiger-Herons can sometimes be seen on rocks near the Río Roca bridge. East of Guapiles is the famous EARTH University, a tropical sustainable research station for agriculture that also provides rooms for tourists and excellent birding opportunities on a forest reserve of more than 1,000 acres. www.earth.ac.cr. Telephone: 506-2713-0000.

C-10: Road from Limón to Cahuita: Tropical moist forest. Elev. Sea level. From lat. 9°59.20'N, long. 83°02.00'W, to lat. 9°45.00'N, long. 82°50.20'W. Along this coastal highway it is possible to see Collared Aracaris, Blue-headed Parrots, and many shorebirds and wading birds in the estuaries that flow into the Caribbean. See safety warning for Cahuita, site C-11.

C-11: Cahuita NP, El Pizote Lodge: Tropical moist forest. Elev. Sea level. Lat. 9°45.00'N long. 82°50.20'W. This national park, encompassing 2,637 acres, was designated for protection of the coral reef there. It is the best example of coral reef in the country, but it has suffered in recent times from chemical pollution and siltation from banana plantations. This is one of the best places in the country to observe sloths, and there are many shorebirds, tangers, and other wildlife species that can be seen. In late October the Cahuita and Puerto Viejo area is a major passage site for raptors migrating from North America to Panama and South America. Over a million raptors were counted passing through this area during late October 2000 (Jennifer

McNicoll, personal communication). Warning: Violence associated with the local drug culture can make this area unsafe for careless tourists who visit local bars and stray from major hotels and public beaches. El Pizote Lodge is a good lodge there. www.pizotelodge.com. Telephone: 506-2750-0088; e-mail: pizotelg@hotmail.com. Another good lodging facility is Punta Cocles. www.hotelpuntacocles .com. Telephone: 1-888-790-5264; reservations: booking@hotel puntacocles.com.

C-12: Valle Escondido: Tropical wet forest. Elev. 1,700'. Lat. 10°16.500'N, long. 84°31.800'W. Valle Escondido Lodge is a rainforest resort at the town of San Lorenzo, north of San Ramón. It provides opportunities for birding on 150 acres of primary rainforest and adjacent mixed forest pastures. Birds are characteristic of the Caribbean lowlands, including Keel-billed Toucans, Red-billed Pigeons, Red-lored Parrots, and White-crowned Parrots. Address: Apdo. 452, 1150 La Uruca, Costa Rica; www.cos taricareisen.com (go to "hotels"). Telephone: 506-2231-0906.

C-13: Siquirres: Premontane wet forest. Elev. 500'. Lat. 10°6.000'N, 83°30.000'W. This site includes downtown Siquirres, where Tropical Mockingbirds can be seen in the church courtyard. In pasturelands to the northeast it is possible to see Red-breasted Blackbirds. The Costa Rican Amphibian Research Center, eight miles south of Siquirres, has the highest documented diversity of amphibians in Costa Rica. It is also regularly visited by flocks of Great Green Macaws. www .cramphibian.com.

C-14: Río Parismina: Tropical wet forest. Elev: Sea level. Lat. 10°18.388'N, long. 83°21.302'W. The canal from Tortuguero NP

to Moin north of Limón provides an excellent opportunity for watching wildlife from a boat. The mouth of the Río Parismina is particularly rich in aquatic birdlife, including Black-necked Stilts, Greater Yellowlegs, Snowy Egrets, Tricolored Herons, Royal Terns, and Willets.

C-15: Jalova: Tropical wet forest. Elev: Sea level. Lat. 10°20.642'N, long. 83°23.935'W. The Jalova ("four corners") field office of Tortuguero NP is along the canal that leads from Tortuguero NP to Moin. Boating along the canal and in the courtyard at the office provides opportunities to see crocodiles, Blue-winged Teal, Golden-hooded Tanagers, Green Honeycreepers, Plumbeous Kites, American Pygmy Kingfishers, and Mangrove Swallows. Even the rare manatee has been seen along the canal between this site and Tortuguero NP.

C-16: Río San Juan: Tropical wet forest. Elev: Sea level. Lat. 10°53.765'N, long. 83°40.826'W. This site is along the Río San Juan near its mouth at the Caribbean, in far northeastern Costa Rica. It is near Río Indio Lodge, which is north across the river in Nicaragua. Wildlife of the area includes the Common Black-Hawk, Mantled Howler Monkey, Collared Forest-Falcon, crocodile, Three-toed Sloth, Bare-throated Tiger-Heron, Purple-throated Fruitcrow, Strawberry Poison Dart Frogs, and the rare White-flanked Antwren. Río Indio Lodge, www.rioindiolodge .com. Telephone: in USA, 1-800-2593-3176; lodge, 506-2296-3338, 506-2296-0095; e-mail: info@ rioindiolodge.com.

C-17: Río Sarapiquí: Tropical wet forest. Elev: Sea level. Lat. 10°42.918'N, long. 83°56.314'W. This site is near the mouth of the Río Sarapiquí, where it enters the Río San Juan on the Nicaragua border. Wildlife that can be seen by boat include crocodiles, Green and Amazon Kingfishers, King Vultures, Green Iguanas, Brazilian Long-nosed Bats, and Mantled Howler Monkeys.

C-18: Tilajari Resort: Tropical moist forest. Elev: 350'. Lat. 10°28.308'N, long. 84°28.099'W. The Tilajari Resort is an excellent resort that provides good access to the surrounding Arenal volcano area and to the Caño Negro NWR. The grounds provide good birding on forty acres along the Río San Carlos. The lodge also provides access for birding on a 600-acre cattle ranch and a 1,000-acre rainforest reserve. Address: Muelle, San Carlos, Costa Rica; www.tilajari.com. Telephone: 506-2462-1212; e-mail: info@tilajari.com.

C-19: Lost Iguana, Hanging Bridges, Arenal: Tropical wet forest. Elev. 1,600'. Lat. 10°29.128'N long. 84°45.316'W. Lost Iguana Resort is a delightful rainforest lodge that provides a spectacular view of the Arenal volcano and excellent birding on the 100 acres of habitat on the grounds. Early morning excursions by the lodge can offer sightings of Great Antshrikes, Barred Antshrikes, Dusky Antbirds, Purple-crowned Fairies, and Crested Guans. www.lostiguanaresort.com. Telephone: 506-2479-1555; e-mail: maritzalostiguana@mac.com. Arenal volcano is the third most active volcano in the world and is part of the 30,000-acre Arenal Volcano NP. Lost Iguana Resort and Spa is close to the 250-acre Arenal Hanging Bridges rainforest. The trails and suspended bridges there provide access to great birding in a rainforest setting. www.hangingbridges.com. Telephone: 506-2479-9686. Another excellent lodge in the vicinity is the Arenal Observatory Lodge,

owned and operated by one of Costa Rica's most prominent tourism companies, Costa Rica Sun Tours. Address: Apdo. 13411-1000, San José, Costa Rica; www.arenalobservatorylodge.com. Telephone: 506-2692-2070, 506-2290-7011. Another birding location is B&B The Birdhouse. It features tropical gardens, bird feeders, orchids, and trails. Telephone: 506-2694-4428.

HIGHLANDS

H-1: Monteverde Cloud Forest Reserve: Lower montane rainforest. Elev. 4,500'. Lat. 10°19.00'N, long. 84°49.19'W. Monteverde Cloud Forest Reserve (Tropical Science Center) is an excellent example of cloud forest, with Resplendent Quetzals, Three-wattled Bellbirds, Black Guans, and many hummingbirds, including the endemic Coppery-headed Emerald. Telephone: 506-2645-5122; e-mail: montever@sol.racsa.co.cr. Santa Elena Cloud Forest Reserve; www.monteverdeinfo.com; telephone: 506-2645-5390. There are many excellent hotels in the vicinity, including: Monteverde Lodge: address: Apartado 6941-1000, San José, Costa Rica; www.costaricaexpeditions.com; telephone: 506-2645-5057, 506-2257-0766; e-mail: costaric@expeditions.co.cr. Hummingbird Gallery: www.fondavela.com; telephone: 506-2645-5030. Hotel Fonda Vela: address: Apartado 70060-1000, San José, Costa Rica; telephone: 506-2645-5125; e-mail: info@fondavela.com. Hotel Belmar: address: Apartado 17-5655, Monteverde, Costa Rica; www.centralamerica.com; telephone: 506-2645-5201; e-mail: belmar@racsa.co.cr.

H-2: Poás Volcano NP and Poás Volcano Lodge: Montane rainforest. Elev. 8,200'. Lat. 10°11.45'N, long.

84°13.95'W. Excellent example of montane forest, includes 16,076 acres. It is a good place to see Sooty Thrushes, Yellow-thighed Finches, Large-footed Finches, Magnificent and Volcano Hummingbirds, Slaty Flowerpiercers, and Bare-shanked Screech-Owls. An easy day trip while staying in San José. Poás Volcano Lodge: Lower montane wet forest. Elev. 6,342'. Lat. 10°09.746'N, long. 84°09.816'W. This facility provides convenient lodging near Vara Blanca while visiting Poás Volcano NP. Wildlife can be enjoyed in the excellent gardens on the grounds of the lodge, including Black Guans, Violet Sabrewings, Purple-throated Mountain-gems, Ruddy-capped Nightingale-Thrushes, and Bare-shanked Screech-Owls. Address: Apartado 1935-3000, Heredia, Costa Rica; www.poasvolcanolodge.com. Telephone: 506-2482-2194; e-mail: info@poasvolcanolodge.com.

H-3: La Virgen del Socorro: Premontane wet forest. Elev. 2,600', road descending to 2,200'. Lat. 10°15.68'N, long. 84°10.47'W. This road has long been a popular birding trail in the Caribbean foothills. Birds that can be seen in the forest along this road include the White Hawk, Violet-headed Hummingbird, and Black-crested Coquette. From the bridge at the lower end of the road it is possible to see Torrent Tyrannulets and dippers.

H-4: La Paz Waterfall Gardens and Peace Waterfall: Lower montane rainforest. Elev. 4,760'. Lat. 10°12.260'N, long. 84°9.695'W. This outstanding site on the east slope of Poás volcano has 3.5 kilometers of trails and seventy acres of rainforest, with excellent trails for viewing wildlife of higher elevations, including rare species like the Sooty-faced Finch, dipper, and Azure-hooded

Jay. At feeders it is possible to see Crimson-collared Tanagers and Prong-billed Barbets. A hummingbird feeder area hosts local specialties like the Green Thorntail, Brown Violet-ear, White-bellied Mountain-gem, Black-bellied Emerald, and endemic Coppery-headed Emerald. There is also a serpentarium, butterfly observatory, and large aviary. Restaurant and cabins are available. www.waterfallgardens .com. Telephone: 506-2482-2720, ext. 573; 506-2482-2721; e-mail: wgardens@racsa.co.cr. Peace Waterfall (Catarata de la Paz): Lower montane rainforest. Elev. 4,500′. Lat. 10°15.60′N, long. 84°10.70′W. This site can be good for viewing tanagers, hummingbirds, Torrent Tyrannulets, and dippers.

H-5: Hotel El Pórtico, San José de la Montaña: Lower montane rainforest. Elev. 5,800′. Lat. 10°05.00′N, long. 84°07.00′W. An excellent location for higher elevation tanagers, hummingbirds, migrant warblers, and raptors.

H-6: La Ponderosa farm near Turrialba: Premontane wet forest. Elev. 3,760′. Lat. 9°57.31′N, long. 83°42.42′W. Private land. Not accessible for tourism purposes.

H-7: Rancho Naturalista Mountain Lodge: Premontane wet forest. Elev. 3,200′. Lat. 9°49.92′N, long. 83°33.85′W. This is an exceptional site in the Caribbean foothills that has species of both lowlands and higher elevations. It is one of the best places in the country to see many hummingbirds, including the rare Snowcap. It is the only place where the rare Tawny-chested Flycatcher can be regularly seen. Many birds come to the feeders in the courtyard, and the viewing of hummingbirds at the hummingbird pools in the forest is unique in the country. Excellent naturalist guides and

trails. Address: 3428 Hwy 465. Sheridan, AR 72150; www.costa ricagateway.com. Telephone: in the USA (toll-free), 1-888-246-8513; reservations, 506-2433-8278; e-mail: crgateway@racsa.co.cr.

H-8: Tapantí NP and Kiri Lodge: Premontane wet forest. Entrance elev. 4,300′. Lat. 9°45.620′N, long. 83°47.038′W. Bridge over the Río Grande de Orosi elev. 5,000′. Lat. 9°42.21′N, long. 83°46.93′W. This national park covers 12,577 acres and is a great place to see wildlife of montane forests, like Collared Trogons, Costa Rican Pygmy-Owls, Red-headed and Prong-billed Barbets, Spangle-cheeked Tanagers, dippers, and Azure-hooded Jays. Kiri Lodge telephone: 506-2533-2272. Google "Kiri Lodge, Costa Rica."

H-9: Cerro de la Muerte, San Gerardo de Dota region: Montane rainforest. Four popular birding sites, on the PAH. Kilometer 66 elev., road descending from 8,300′N to 7,700′W. Lat. 9°40.24′N, long. 83°51.92′W. This site, Finca El Jaular, is a private road on the west side of the PAH that is closed by a large gate. The road can be birded on foot—by permission only—by making arrangements to pay an entrance fee ahead of time (call Savegre Mountain Lodge at the telephone number listed for site H-10). Vehicles must be left at the main highway. The land is owned by the Vindas family, who live in the valley at the end of the road. The road descends through excellent primary montane rainforest and is a good place to see quetzals and other highland wildlife. Kilometer 76 elev., 9,400′. Lat. 9°35.68′N, long. 83°48.59′W. Near Los Chespiritos Restaurant 1 is a turnoff to Providencia. Along this road it is possible to see Silvery-throated Jays, Slaty Flowerpiercers, Yellow-thighed

Finches, Fiery-throated Hummingbirds, and Black-billed Nightingale-Thrushes. The road is twelve kilometers long, but some of the best birding is in the first two kilometers from the PAH. Kilometer 86 elev. 9,100′. Lat. 9°36.88′N, long. 83°49.07′W. This site is a trail on the west side of the PAH, across the road and a couple hundred feet south of Los Chespiritos Restaurant 2. It is an excellent place to encounter the Timberline Wren, Peg-billed Finch, and high-elevation wildflowers. Kilometer 96 elev. 9,300′. Lat. 9°33.46′N, long. 83°42.67′W. This is west across the PAH from La Georgina Restaurant and Villa Mills, at the site of an old highway construction camp where there is shrubby cover that is excellent for Volcano and Scintillant Hummingbirds and Timberline Wrens.

H-10: Savegre: Lower montane rainforest. Elev. 9,400′–7,200′. Lat. 9°32.92′N, long. 83°48.64′W. The turnoff from the PAH at kilometer 80 (at 9,400′ elevation) descends for 5.5 kilometers into the valley of San Gerardo de Dota to Savegre Mountain Lodge (Albergue de Montaña Savegre, Cabinas Chacón) along the Río Savegre. This is an excellent area to see Black Guans, Resplendent Quetzals, Long-tailed Silky-Flycatchers, Black-faced Solitaires, Acorn Woodpeckers, Collared Trogons, and resident Red-tailed Hawks. Savegre Mountain Hotel, www.savegre .co.cr. Telephone: 506-2740-1028, 506-2740-1029; in USA (toll-free), 1-800-593-3305.

H-11: Transmission tower site, Cerro de la Muerte: Subalpine rain paramo. Elev. 10,800′. Lat. 9°33.25′N, long. 83°45.16′W. The gravel road leading to the transmission towers from the PAH is approximately at kilometer 90. It is an excellent place to see Volcano Juncos, Peg-billed Finches, resident Red-tailed Hawks, and high-elevation wildflowers. **H-12: Vista del Valle:** Elev. 5,650'. Lat. 9°27.78'N, long. 83°42.12'W. Vista del Valle is an excellent spot with both a restaurant and cabins (Cabins Mirador Vista del Valle) that provide birding along the PAH, at kilometer 119 as the highway begins its descent from Cerro de la Muerte to San Isidro del General. In late January and early February, this is an excellent location to watch Swallow-tailed Kites migrating north from South America. There are hummingbird feeders that feature the Violet Sabrewing, Red-headed Barbet, Cherrie's Tanager, Flame-colored Tanager, Bay-headed Tanager, and rare

White-tailed Emerald. www .vistadelvallecr.com. Telephone: 506-2384-4685. **H-13: Bosque de Paz Ecolodge:** Lower montane rainforest. Elev. 4,580'–8,000'. Lat. 10°12.272'N, 84°19.032'W. Bosque de Paz is an outstanding lodge on 1,800 acres of montane rainforest on the slope of Poás volcano. Birds of the area include the Resplendent Quetzal, Golden-browed Chlorophonia, Long-tailed Silky-Flycatcher, Purple-throated Mountain-gem, Chestnut-capped Brush-Finch, and American Dipper. Black Guans come to the feeders in the courtyard by day, and tepescuintles, coatis, and agoutis come to the feeders in the evening. Address: P.O. Box 130-1000, San José, Costa Rica; www .bosquedepaz.com. Telephone:

506-2234-6676; e-mail: info@ bosquedepaz.com. **H-14: Rincón de la Vieja NP:** Premontane wet forest. Elev. 2,400'. Lat. 10°46.363'N, long. 85°20.002'W. This national park covers 34,992 acres, with a good system of trails and an interesting mix of wildlife characteristic of both rainforest and dry forest, including Great Curassows, Crested Guans, Long-tailed Manakins, woodcreepers, white-faced capuchin monkeys, and boa constrictors. There are also some unusual features like hot springs and bubbling mud pits. Telephone: Los Pailas administration office, 506-2661-8139; Guanacaste Conservation Area, 506-2666-5051; e-mail: acg@ acguanacaste.ac.cr.

APPENDIX C: COSTA RICAN TRIP PREPARATION CHECKLIST

This trip preparation checklist has been prepared by Carrol and Ethelle Henderson and is based on their experience leading twenty-four birding tours to Costa Rica. The clothing and equipment listed are suggested for a two-week birding or natural history type of tour.

LUGGAGE

One or two pieces of soft, durable, canvas-type bags. Tagged and closed with small padlocks during air travel and storage at hotels. Think light! The less you bring, the easier your travel will be.

CLOTHING

Bring lightweight wash-and-wear clothes you can wash out yourself. Bring detergent double-bagged in self-sealing bags if laundry service is not available.

3–4 sets of field clothes: shirts/ blouses; pants, shorts, or jeans; and one long-sleeved shirt.
Socks (4–5 pairs)
Underwear (4–5 pairs)
Handkerchiefs or tissues
Belt
Sweatshirt/sweater/light jacket
Towel (optional)
Hat or cap
Sleepwear
One pair walking shoes; one pair tennis or hiking shoes
Rain poncho or raincoat (lightweight)
Swimsuit and beach thongs
Wash cloth

TOILETRY ITEMS

Pack of Wet Ones or similar towelettes
Deodorant
Shaving cream
Toothbrush
Toothpaste/dental floss

Shampoo, without citronella base
Comb/hairbrush
Razor/shaver (electric current is 110 ac, but some outlets don't take wide prong; bring adapter plug)

PHOTO AND OPTIC EQUIPMENT

Camera with flash unit or video camera
Binoculars
Camera bag
Extra batteries for camera and flash unit and/or battery recharger
Lenses and filters
Lens tissue
Memory chips/film: 2 gigs/6 rolls—average interest in photos; 4 gigs/12 rolls—moderate interest; 8 gigs/24 rolls—enthusiastic. (Bring more than you think you will need. Film and memory chips can be hard to find and very expensive to buy on the road.)

OTHER EQUIPMENT

Fingernail clippers
Sunglasses
Suntan lotion or sunscreen (at least SPF 30)
Chapstick
Insect repellent (up to 30 percent DEET)
Aspirin
Imodium or Lomotil
Q-Tips
Notebook and pens
Small flashlight
Field guides
Knapsack/daypack/fannypack
Spending money, at least $400 in clean, undamaged bills (U.S. currency and credit cards are accepted in most hotels and larger stores. You can change some currency to Costa Rican colones at most hotels. Use colones in small towns.)
Prescriptions for personal medication, including original containers.
Travel alarm
Passport, plus photocopy packed separately from passport
Tip for naturalist guide (about $8–$12 per day)
Tip for driver (about $6–$8 per day)
Earplugs for sleeping near noisy highways or near loud surf
Umbrella (compact)

OTHER OPTIONAL ITEMS

Hunting or fishing vest for gear
Spare camera
Mending kit

Water bottle
20' cord for indoor clothesline

MAP

There is one exceptional map for Costa Rica that shows topographical features in great detail. Called a "tactical pilotage map," it is published by the U.S. Department of Defense. These maps are available for all regions of Latin America in a scale of 1:500,000. The map for Costa Rica is TPC K-25C. It can be ordered from the Latitudes Map and Travel Store in Minneapolis, Minnesota (www.latitudesmapstore.net), or from the NOAA Distribution Branch (N/CG33, National Ocean Service, Riverdale, MD 20737).

APPENDIX D: TRAVEL TIPS FOR A SUCCESSFUL WILDLIFE VIEWING TRIP IN COSTA RICA

1. Begin trip planning at least six months prior to your trip. The best lodges fill early during their high season from January to March. This is the dry season, which is typically the best time to visit Costa Rica. The first half of July can also be a good time to go.

2. Decide if you wish to travel independently or participate in a birding tour. A well-organized birding tour with a good guide and outfitter company will take care of logistics, driving, lodging arrangements, meals, and safety considerations. You will typically see two to four times more birds on a guided tour than if you travel by yourself.

3. Be aware that there are several levels of intensity for birding tour groups. Some groups are determined to see the maximum number of birds in the time available, around 400-plus species in two weeks. The pace is intense and is focused only on birds. Other birding groups are moderately paced. You may see about 300–350 bird species in two weeks with a group that is still focused primarily on birds but takes time to enjoy a broader spectrum of the flora and fauna, like butterflies, flowers, and culture. General natural history groups are more passive, walk less, and are broadly interested in nature; you will see perhaps 100–125 species in two weeks. Get references and contact former clients to make sure you sign up for a group that matches your expectations, interests, and preferred level of physical activity.

4. Traveling by yourself can be cheaper, but you need to deal with lodging, meals, travel arrangements, and the Spanish language. If traveling by yourself, visit lodges that have naturalist birding guides, or lodges where you can hire local birding guides for day trips. Otherwise, hire a birding guide to accompany you on your entire trip.

5. When you finish eating at a restaurant, always check your tables and chair backs for binoculars, cameras, sunglasses, daypacks, and other items for yourself and for other members of your party.

6. While birding in Costa Rica, share the experience. After you have spotted a bird, help others in the group find it if they can't see it. If you encounter other birders or Costa Rican families while birding, let them take a peek through your spotting scope or binoculars if they have no optics.

7. When traveling in a bus, sit in a different seat every day to give everyone equal access to the best seats.

8. When birding along a narrow

trail, switch positions with others every fifteen to twenty minutes to avoid dominating the best positions behind the guide.

9. When organizing your itinerary, try to include at least three of Costa Rica's biological zones (for example, Guanacaste, highlands, and Caribbean slope).

10. Bring any trip problems or complaints about your tour to the attention of your guide or tour leader in a discreet manner if you feel there is a problem in protocol, behavior, or group etiquette that needs to be addressed. Do not wait until after the trip to complain.

APPENDIX E: ECO-MISCONCEPTIONS ABOUT BIRD FEEDING, FLASH PHOTOGRAPHY, AND SOUND RECORDINGS

During the past several years I have become aware of some well-intentioned but sorely misguided misconceptions about tropical bird feeding, flash photography, and use of sound recordings by some guides, tour companies, rainforest advocacy groups, and even avid birders that are inaccurate and without basis in scientific fact.

BIRD FEEDING: Some companies and rainforest organizations that are creating new ecotourism criteria for sustainability certification of ecolodges have decided that it is not ethical to provide bird feeders because "if the feeders go empty, the birds will die." This is total fallacy. Birds of the rainforest as well as in temperate regions of North America generally have a nomadic tendency; they constantly move through their habitat in search of trees and shrubs bearing fruit, seeds, or hatches of insects. Once a food source, like a tree filled with fruit, has been cleaned out, the birds move on. The same applies at feeders. If the feeders are emptied, the birds move on to other sources of food. They do not sit by the feeder and die. North American studies have shown that even birds that are common visitors at feeders, like Black-capped Chickadees, derive only about 20 percent of their food from feeders. The rest is derived from natural sources in their habitats.

The presence of feeders at rainforest lodges greatly enhances the opportunity to observe the beauty of tropical birds that are often seen only at a distance in the forest canopy. This is an advantage for visitors with walking disabilities and for children who can observe wildlife that they might otherwise miss while visiting in Costa Rica.

The best rainforest lodges in Costa Rica have discovered that an array of feeders offering fruit and hummingbird nectar is a great attraction and a source of enjoyment for their guests, and it provides wonderful photographic opportunities as well.

Feeders can be a problem where resident coatis or monkeys come and steal the food. In that case, providing feeders can be a greater challenge. Of course, it is important for the staff at the lodges to keep the feeders filled on a regular basis and to clean the feeders as necessary.

One significant feature of feeders of note to rainforest lodge managers is that Costa Rican visitors with a strong interest in birds tend to return to those lodges where feeders enhance the opportunity to see the birdlife of the area. Repeat business is an important consideration in the world of nature tourism in Costa Rica.

FLASH PHOTOGRAPHY: Costa Rica is a wonderful destination to enjoy photography of landscapes, birds, monkeys, butterflies, and flowers. The use of flash photography needs to be addressed in some special situations. On sea turtle nesting beaches like Playa Grande NP or Tortuguero NP, use of flash is prohibited because it could discourage a turtle from approaching the beach or from beginning to lay eggs.

Flash is acceptable and generally useful, however, in the dimly lit rainforest, where not enough light reaches the understory to allow good photos of butterflies, flowers, and birds. Some well-meaning hard-core birdwatchers are severely critical of birders and photographers who photograph birds with flash. They assert that flash will blind the birds, it will chase them away from their feeding areas, and it will disrupt their natural behavior. None of these accusations is based on fact or scientific research. This is another piece of misguided folklore. The brief flash of light from a camera is generally similar to the brief flicker of sunlight that may occur in a sun-dappled forest, and the birds are so accustomed to such incidents that they tend to ignore the flash. It is far more important for birders to be quiet and unobtrusive, whether they are taking photos or not. It is also important for them to remember not to make quick movements and start pointing at birds when they sight something wonderful. The birds won't go blind from the flash. They will typically keep right on feeding, and they won't be driven from their habitat. In fact, at most tourism lodges, the birds are very accustomed to the presence of tourists and not deterred by the presence of people, whether they are taking photos with flash or not. I find that it is often beneficial to take some photos with flash and some without flash in order to see which photos create the best image.

SOUND RECORDINGS: There have been incidents in heavily birded areas of the United States, like Ramsey Canyon in Arizona, where the excessive use of sound recordings of bird calls in the breeding season has been disruptive to rare birds like the Elegant Trogon. This concern can be valid in heavily birded areas and in regard to rare bird species, whose breeding behavior could be affected by misuse of tape recordings.

In Costa Rica, however, I have not observed problems with the use of bird call recordings because the number of guides who use them is small and because the frequency of tape use in many remote areas is low. The use of recordings of bird

calls to attract birds in Costa Rica falls into three categories. Prerecorded bird calls or playbacks of birds heard nearby may be used to attract a specific bird from heavy forest cover, like antbirds, wood-quail, or wrens. Without the use of the calls, you will likely never see those species. This can often provide a short viewing opportunity to see these tropical birds. These opportunities are often in remote areas that see little use of recordings by other tourists. In nature, such a bird call or song serves to challenge the resident bird within its territory to defend its territory. If birders discontinue the use of calling after calling a bird out of cover, the resident bird resumes its normal activity and believes it has chased off the intruder. This is a routine activity within a bird's home territory, so it should not be too disruptive—especially since most birding, and potential use of tapes, takes place in January and February before the main breeding season begins for most birds in March and April.

Another type of bird-call use is to play the call of a Ferruginous Pygmy-Owl, which is a diurnal predator of songbirds. This call can attract a wide variety of local songbirds and hummingbirds that come to drive off their potential predator. This does not disrupt the territorial instincts of

the individual bird involved and is again a normal response in a tropical forest to the presence of this owl. Some guides use a call to imitate the "toot-toot" calls of the pygmy-owl, and others are able to whistle the call. It can be very effective in attracting many different songbirds.

A third type of calling is use of owl calls at night in suitable habitat. A series of three or four calls of different species can be played sequentially to see if there is a response to any of those calls by local owls. When successful, an owl will fly to the sound and perch momentarily in a tree nearby to check and see if its territory has been entered by another owl of the same species. The calling is done in the dark. Once the owl has been attracted, a flashlight can be used to observe the owl. Once the owl has been viewed, the calling can be discontinued, and the resident owl will believe that it has successfully chased off the interloper.

If calling is limited to a short duration, and if calling is discontinued after a bird is viewed, use of bird calls is not believed to be detrimental. The use of calls and tapes, done responsibly, can result in seeing some of the elusive and beautiful birds of the tropical forest that may otherwise never be observed while visiting Costa Rica.

About the Author

Carrol L. Henderson, a native of Zearing, Iowa, received a bachelor of science degree in zoology from Iowa State University in 1968 and a master of forest resources degree in ecology from the University of Georgia in 1970. He did his graduate studies on the fish and wildlife of Costa Rica through the Organization for Tropical Studies and the University of Costa Rica.

Henderson joined the Minnesota Department of Natural Resources (DNR) in 1974 as assistant manager of the Lac qui Parle Wildlife Management Area near Milan. In 1977 he became supervisor of the DNR's newly created Nongame Wildlife Program, and he continues in that role to the present. During the past thirty-three years, Henderson developed a statewide program for the conservation of Minnesota's nongame wildlife and has planned and developed projects to help bring back bluebirds, Bald Eagles, Peregrine Falcons, River Otters, and Trumpeter Swans.

Henderson received the national Chevron Conservation Award in 1990, the 1992 Chuck Yeager Conservation Award from the National Fish and Wildlife Foundation, the 1993 Minnesota Award from the Minnesota Chapter of The Wildlife Society, and the 1994 Thomas Sadler Roberts Memorial Award from the Minnesota Ornithologists' Union.

His writings include *Woodworking for Wildlife*, *Landscaping for Wildlife*, *Wild about Birds: The DNR Bird Feeding Guide*, and co-authorship of *The Traveler's Guide to Wildlife in Minnesota* and *Lakescaping for Wildlife and Water Quality*. He also wrote the first edition of the *Field Guide to the Wildlife of Costa Rica* in 2002, *Oology and Ralph's Talking Eggs* in 2007, and *Birds in Flight: The Art and Science of How Birds Fly* in 2008. He is a regular

The author with his wife, Ethelle, in Costa Rica, 2005.

contributor of feature stories in *Birder's World* and *Seasons* magazines.

An avid wildlife photographer, Henderson has taken most of the photos in his books and was the primary photographer for the 1995 book *Galápagos Islands: Wonders of the World*. His bird photography has been featured in the *New York Times*, *World Book Encyclopedia of Science*, *Audubon* magazine, and Discovery Online. He received seven national bird photography awards from *Wild Bird* magazine between 1995 and 1998.

Henderson and his wife, Ethelle, developed their expertise in tropical wildlife by leading forty-four birding tours to Latin America since 1987. This includes twenty-five trips to Costa Rica and additional trips to Panama, Belize, Nicaragua, Trinidad, Tobago, Venezuela, Bolivia, Chile, Ecuador, Brazil, Argentina, Peru, and the Galápagos Islands.

INDEX

Spanish names for birds are set in **boldface text.**